Also by David Sears

At War with the Wind

The Last Epic Naval Battle

Such Men as These

Pacific Air

DUEL IN THE DEEP

THE HUNTERS, THE HUNTED, AND A HIGH SEAS FIGHT TO THE FINISH

DAVID SEARS

Naval Institute Press
Annapolis, Maryland

Naval Institute Press
291 Wood Road
Annapolis, MD 21402

Library of Congress Cataloging-in-Publication Data

Names: Sears, David, author.

Title: Duel in the deep : the hunters, the hunted, and a high seas fight to the finish / David Sears.

Description: Annapolis, MD : Naval Institute Press, 2023. | Includes bibliographical references and index.

Identifiers: LCCN 2023006303 (print) | LCCN 2023006304 (ebook) | ISBN 9781682475607 (hardcover) | ISBN 9781682475614 (ebook)

Subjects: LCSH: World War, 1939–1945—Campaigns—Atlantic Ocean. | Borie (Destroyer : DD215) | U-405 (Submarine) | World War, 1939–1945—Naval operations—Submarine. | World War, 1939–1945—Naval operations.

Classification: LCC D772.B65 S4377 2023 (print) | LCC D772.B65 (ebook) | DDC 940.54/293—dc23/eng/20230228

LC record available at https://lccn.loc.gov/2023006303

LC ebook record available at https://lccn.loc.gov/2023006304

♾ Print editions meet the requirements of ANSI/NISO z39.48–1992 (Permanence of Paper).

Printed in the United States of America.

31 30 29 28 27 26 25 24 23 9 8 7 6 5 4 3 2 1

First printing

CONTENTS

ACKNOWLEDGMENTS AND SOURCES

IN A 1986 LETTER to former *Borie* officer Lawrence S. Quinn, James E. Wise Jr. outlined plans for "a book on the ship and its men." Rather than "doing a straight narrative," Wise (a retired U.S. Navy captain and maritime historian who died in 2013) aimed to capture "the words, thoughts and emotions of those who served aboard the *BORIE* during the moments of battle."

Wise reached Quinn through Robert A. Maher, who led the ship's veterans' association before his passing in 2013. While Captain Wise didn't produce the book originally envisioned, he and Maher collaborated on two *Borie*-themed projects. First, in 1993, they cowrote "Stand by for a Ram!," a two-part *Naval History* magazine feature detailing the Halloween battle between *Borie* and *U-405*. Five years later, the pair wrote *Sailors' Journey into War*, a wartime memoir that recounts the decisive battle while also covering Maher's and his buddies' experiences in the Caribbean and South Atlantic. I first learned of the battle from a December 1943 *Life* magazine feature, "U.S.S. *Borie's* Last Battle," written by John Hersey.

"Mid-Atlantic Brawl," which I wrote for the Spring 2014 edition of *Military History Quarterly*, offers a U.S. Navy perspective on the Battle of the Atlantic. Though I sourced Hersey, Wise, and Maher, I relied as well on archived documents retrieved by E. Andrew Wilde Jr., a former junior naval officer with a "true passion" (according to his 2018 obituary) for "researching destroyers sunk during World War II." His *Borie* compilation, self-published in 2001, contains oral histories, deck log excerpts, war diaries, crew rosters, photos, official action reports, personnel reports, damage reports, and award citations.

Nearly eight decades have passed since the events and actions portrayed here. Still, in choosing *Borie*'s exploits as the primary thread of a broader narrative, I strove to incorporate "the words, thoughts and emotions" of both principal and peripheral characters. To do so, I drew on a range of sources.

The Hersey account, for example, contains contemporaneous quotes and reconstructed dialogue, as does "Destroyer Captain," Charles Hutchins' rendition (as told to Ray Mackland) in the December 1943 edition of *Shipmate* magazine. Useful but less reliable magazine sources for *Borie* include ghost-written "first person" accounts in tabloids such as *Men True Adventure* ("Captain Hutchins and His U-BOAT Killers," by Stan Smith, February 1944) and *True* ("The *Borie's* Last Fight," by Kenneth Reynolds, Gunner's Mate 1/c, March 1944). Quotes and perspectives for VC-9 aviators, meanwhile, come from "U-boat Meets Its Master" in the September 18 and 25, 1945, editions of the *Saturday Evening Post.*

Scouring newspaper accounts yielded quotes from veterans and their loved ones as well as government officials, military leaders, politicians, pundits, and private citizens. Hometown newspapers documented social events, personal milestones, and nuggets of human interest, some included here.

Next-generation family members shared veterans' correspondence, diaries, scrapbooks, photographs, mementoes, and personal recollections. For these I thank: Dianne Kropp, daughter of *Borie* sailor James Allegri; Deborah A. Anderson, daughter of Joseph Desch of the National Cash Register Company (NCR); Morrison R. "Sunny" Brown, daughter of *Borie* officer Morrison R. Brown; Sunny's cousins Alexander "Sandy" Creighton, Mary Felder, Carol Hadley, and Martha Levering; Dr. Michael N. Brown, MD, son of *Borie* officer Philip Bosche Brown; Dr. Judith Dietz Win and John Dietz, daughter and brother of *Borie* officer Walter H. Dietz Jr.; Donald B. Fennessey, son of Donald F. Fennessey, a cadet midshipman on board the Liberty ship *James Smith*; Dr. Kenneth A. Knowles Jr., son of Capt. Kenneth A. Knowles; and Beth Quinn Barnard, Martha Hussain, Chip Quinn, and Jeff Quinn, the sons and daughters of *Borie* officer Lawrence C. Quinn. Many of these family members were also kind enough to review and comment on selected portions of early drafts depicting their loved ones.

This narrative emphasizes America's experience in the Battle of the Atlantic. To convey the backdrop of the broader conflict, I referred frequently to volumes I and X of Samuel Eliot Morison's *History of United States Naval Operations in World War II.* For Britain's counterbalancing perspective, I relied on volumes I, II, IV, and V of Winston S. Churchill's six-volume *The Second World War* and volumes I and II of Capt. S. W. Roskill's *The War at Sea 1939–1945.*

Even many decades after publication, these masterful works lay a solid foundation. However, to capture more recent findings and perspectives, I turned to more contemporary works: Patrick Abbazia's *Mr. Roosevelt's Navy*; Jim DeBrosse and Colin Burke's *The Secret in Building 26*; Jonathan Dimbleby's *The Battle of the Atlantic*; Nigel Hamilton's *FDR at War*; Max Hastings's *The Secret War*; David Kohnen's *Commanders Winn and Knowles*; and Craig Symonds's *World War II at Sea.*

For German U-boat operations and terminology, I relied on Timothy P. Mulligan's *Neither Sharks nor Wolves*; Clay Blair's encyclopedic two-volume *Hitler's U-Boat War*; and Guðmundur Helgason's internet site Uboat.net. For merchant convoys, I relied on Richard Woodman's book *The Real Cruel Sea*; and for escort carriers, William T. Y'Blood's *Hunter-Killer.*

In addition to E. Andrew Wilde Jr.'s *Borie* compendium, three other unpublished works guided me: Midn. Brian F. Hussey Jr.'s U.S. Naval Academy Trident Scholar Project Report "The U.S. Navy, the Neutrality Patrol, and Atlantic Fleet Escort Operations, 1939–1941";* retired U.S. Navy admiral Francis S. Low's "A Personal Narrative of My Associations with Fleet Admiral Ernest J. King, U.S. Navy"; and M. J. Spear's (editor) "Wildcats and Avengers: The History of Composite Squadron Nine."

I was fortunate to have respected authors agree to review portions of the manuscript-in-progress. For example, Colin Burke and David Kohnen (both

*Hussey, a 1991 graduate and later a Marine captain, tragically died in an aviation training accident on August 23, 1996.

cited above) reviewed matters related to Enigma and cryptographic technology. Tom Cutler, author of *A Sailor's History of the U.S. Navy*, cross-checked my understanding of bluejacket norms, customs, and vernacular. Timothy Mulligan (also cited above) cross-checked matters for Germany's Kriegsmarine. Aviation historian Barrett Tillman scanned my depictions of carrier aviation. At the Naval Institute's behest, naval historians Vincent P. O'Hara and Paul Stillwell made insightful recommendations for and corrections to my preliminary manuscript. Masterful copy editing by Pelham Boyer rounded it into final shape

Of course, any shortcomings, gaps, or inaccuracies on these—and other—matters in this book are wholly attributable to me.

I thank the editors of Naval Institute Press for their enthusiasm for this project. Particular thanks go to Senior Acquisitions Editor Susan Brook and Senior Production Editor Ashley Baird for their patience and assistance in navigating the publication process.

This book is dedicated to the memory of Ed Cochrane.
We miss you, "Bucco."

MAP 1. Eastern United States *Created by author*

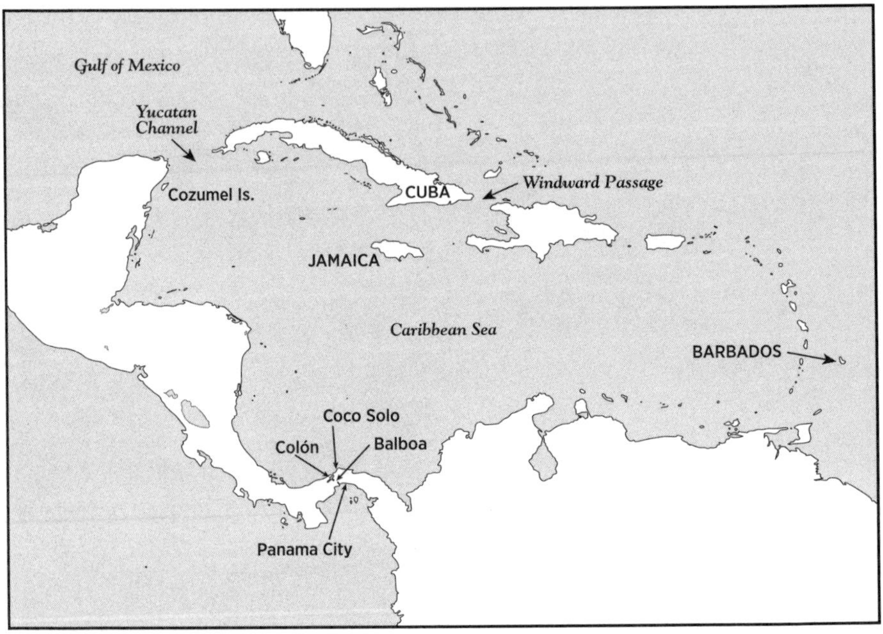

MAP 2. **Central America** *Created by author*

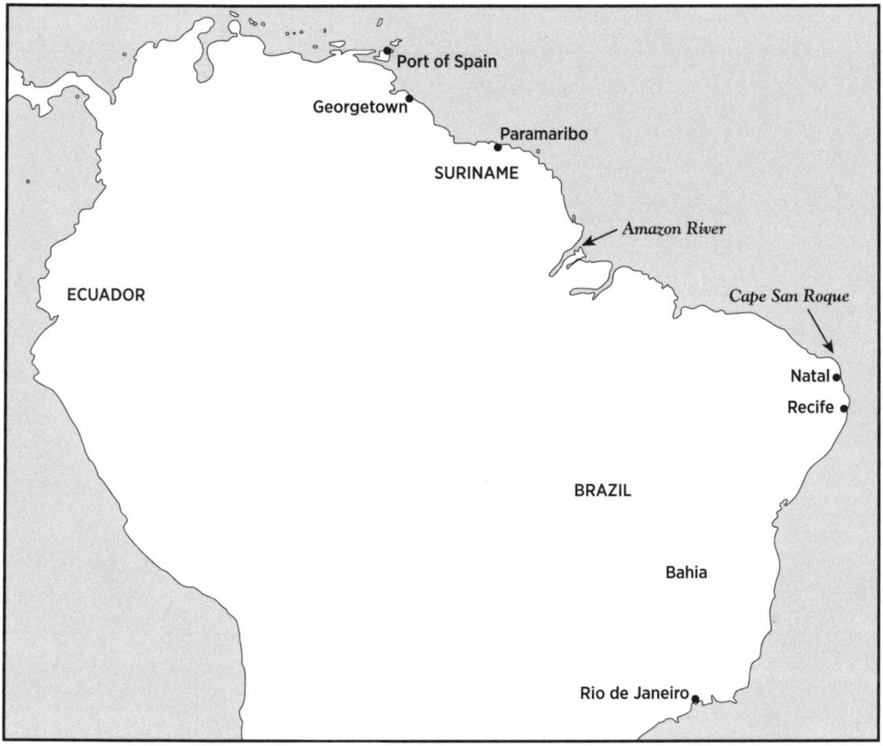

MAP 3. **South America** *Created by author*

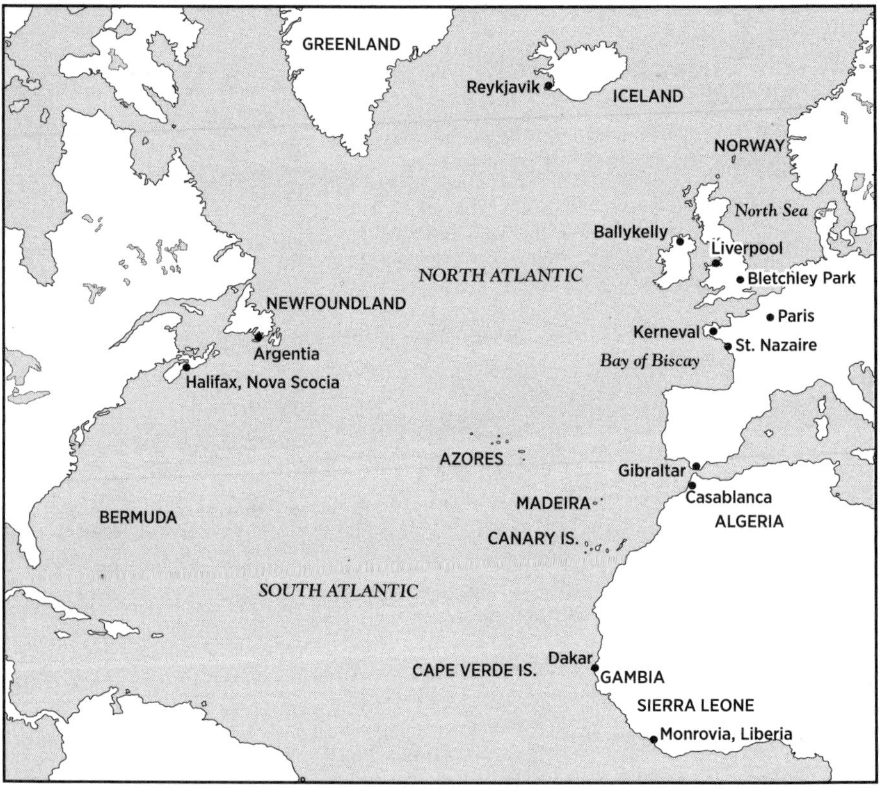

MAP 4. **Atlantic perimeter** *Created by author*

INTRODUCTION

HARD, WIDESPREAD, AND BITTER

IN DECEMBER 1940, a year before America went to war, dozens of recruits from the Naval Reserve's Seventh Battalion's 24th Division, stepped onto a Portsmouth, Virginia, pier carrying orders to report to USS *Borie*, an aging U.S. Navy destroyer.[1] Most were Depression-era New Jersey "street kids" who had enlisted to avoid the prewar draft. Many had only just been issued uniforms; relatively few had received any military training.

Six months before, Congress had passed a Naval Expansion Act authorizing the construction of hundreds of new warships. During the chaotic transition that followed, ships in the fleet seemed either "too old" or "too new." The "too old" included outmoded destroyers such as *Borie*—one of a type called "four-stackers" because of their distinctive appearance.

The Naval Expansion Act entailed "bleeding the fleet": shifting experienced sailors from old ships (like *Borie*) to new. It also witnessed an influx of "90-Day Wonders": novice reserve officers tasked with somehow leading the raw replacements.

Critics complained that such wholesale shuffling compromised effectiveness. Ship captains "accustomed to skilled work of veteran professionals . . . had to condition themselves to tolerate adequate performances and acceptable solutions." Still, most savvy commanders judged the young officers and sailors to be "damn fine men" who quickly "developed enough confidence and judgment to know what they *did not* know and could call for help."[2]

As war began, *Borie* patrolled the backwaters of the Caribbean. Bereft of home and consigned to tedium, the crew longed to prove its mettle—most likely against Nazi Germany's U-boats in the Battle of the Atlantic.

Britain's Winston Churchill portrayed this prolonged campaign as "hard, widespread and bitter, a war of groping and drowning, a war of ambuscade and stratagem, a war of science and seamanship."[3] To his mind, "everything happening elsewhere . . . depended ultimately on its outcome."[4] President Franklin D. Roosevelt—FDR—likewise believed that World War II's outcome "is going to be decided in the Atlantic."[5]

Advantage in the Battle of the Atlantic swung wildly. Early on, Britain's Royal Navy (RN) took the lead for the Allies. When advantage swung towards Germany, the RN bore the brunt. When the Allies gained the upper hand, British breakthroughs in tactics, weaponry, and technology made the difference.

Anglo-American cooperation, meanwhile, was tenuous and fractious. Each navy saw the other as too grasping and assertive. Even as U-boats ravaged America's Eastern Seaboard, Ernest J. King, America's topmost admiral, resisted making the U.S. Navy subordinate to the Royal Navy.

During the Battle of the Atlantic's darkest days, *Borie* mattered little in the big picture. But on Halloween 1943, the confluence of "ambuscade and stratagem, science and seamanship" propelled *Borie* and its crew towards an epic high-seas duel.

1 | SHOVE OFF

IN THE SUMMER OF 1940, life hadn't changed all that much for Robert Maher. Three years since graduating high school, he still lived with his parents and followed their rules, careful not to embarrass the family name. Maher worked now, and out of his eighty-dollar monthly salary he paid room and board and train fare from his home in Kearny, New Jersey, to a job in New York City. What was left went to seeing movies with a friend and, afterwards, to beers at a local bar.

Kearny (pronounced "CAR-knee"), a suburb of Newark, New Jersey's largest city, had been a shipbuilding town since the Great War. Federal Shipbuilding and Drydock Company, a subsidiary of U.S. Steel, occupied Kearny Point, waterfront bordering the Hackensack River and Newark Bay. After the wartime shipping boom faded, Federal had still built commercial ships, tankers, and barges, somehow staying solvent through the Depression.

But hard times for shipbuilding were over. With war—potentially a repeat of the Great War—raging in Western Europe, President Franklin Roosevelt had endorsed the Two-Ocean Navy Act, a bill expanding naval warship tonnage 70 percent.* According to local newspapers, Federal was ramping up for unprecedented business. "New Jersey shipyards have enough orders on hand to keep them going full blast for the next 13 years," proclaimed one

---

*Also called the Naval Expansion Act.

story. "Federal Shipbuilding and Drydock Company here has contracts to build 43 men-o'-war and merchantmen for the government."[1]

Bob Maher and his friends were unlikely to pay much attention to news of impending war or its impact on business. Instead, their interests and summer lives revolved around weekend trips to Belmar, a New Jersey–shore town about sixty miles south. Rain or shine, the friends left right after work on Friday and returned Sunday night, late. If the weather was good—at least not raining—they rose early from their beds in rows of communal two-dollar-a-night cabins and went to the beach. They belly-rode the waves or played stickball, using a tennis ball and a broom handle for a bat. Saturday nights they walked the boardwalk, eating their hearts out at the sight of pretty girls dancing (most with each other) at a local pavilion.

Shrimpy Graham, one of Maher's best friends, owned a Model A Ford, a coupe with two doors, two seats, and missing passenger-side window. Maher and Graham often cruised shore-town streets, conspicuously passing groups of girls, usually without results. As far as Maher knew, only one guy in his circle had actual sexual experience. That guy also happened to own a car and sometimes left Belmar on Saturday afternoon to drive to a bordello in Scranton, Pennsylvania, four hours away.

Maher had worked at the Mutual Insurance Company ever since graduation. At first he hated it. After all, he had placed in the top ten of his class and excelled in the school's academic college program. But these were still Depression times, with money tight and few scholarships to be had. Fortunately, Maher's dad had a friend at Mutual. With time, Maher grew to consider himself lucky, not least because Mutual provided a free full lunch. And the food was pretty good.

During the week, Maher sat at a desk in a large workspace along with about a hundred other employees. The setting was pretty congenial. People were free to walk around and chat, provided their work got done by day's end. Maher's coworkers ranged in age from eighteen to sixty-four, though most were over thirty.

Occasionally after work, money and train schedules permitting, Maher visited New York attractions like Radio City Music Hall. Sometime in early

1940, a coworker even introduced him to burlesque. Its comedy skits, elaborate dance routines, and beautiful, bare-breasted chorines might have proved addictive were it not for the cost and late hours.

One hot August night, Bob Maher and five friends drove to Jersey City. Having heard about the Burke-Wadsworth Bill, legislation calling for compulsory military training and service, they decided to join the Naval Reserve. Burke-Wadsworth would require American men between the ages of eighteen and sixty-four (a population of some 42,000,000) to register for twelve months' training in the Army and National Guard.

Under Burke-Wadsworth, as many as 1,500,000 men might be drafted during the first year—more if needed. And most would be summoned from the 11.5 million cohort of those between ages twenty-one and thirty. Twenty-one (soon to be twenty-two)—this caught Maher's attention. Fortunately, eligible men could volunteer before being called. Draft registration was almost imminent, so there was little time to waste if Maher hoped to exert some control over his destiny.

The six boys' Jersey City destination was USS *Newton*, a 1919-vintage vessel used as a training ship by the U.S. Naval Reserve's Seventh Battalion. They arrived to find *Newton* crowded with young men, all with the same idea.

Ordered to strip, the applicants formed two lines, side by side. Doctors moved down between the lines, cursorily questioning, peering, inspecting, and probing. Those passing this rudimentary physical went next before a recruiting chief petty officer for swearing in.

When his turn came, Maher volunteered for a year of active duty. It excused him from the draft. For reasons Maher never learned, he was the only one of the six to make the cut.*

Maher went on with his life that fall, hearing nothing further from the Navy. Then, in the afternoon of November 19, his boss at Mutual unexpectedly

---

*All eventually served. "Shrimpy" Graham, for example, became a mountain-troop mule skinner who fought in the Italian Alps. Another became a South Pacific fighter pilot. A third became a combat corpsman who landed in North Africa, Sicily, Anzio, and Normandy.

asked to see him. Maher worried he might be in trouble, but he wasn't. His mother had called. A telegram had arrived ordering him to active duty. Somebody in the office scrounged up a pen-and-pencil set as a going-away present. Maher took a train home.

Maher's orders were to report to *Newton* on November 21—Thanksgiving Day. It made little sense, but orders were orders. Bob's brother Ed drove him to Jersey City early on Thanksgiving morning. Hundreds had been ordered to report the same day; and even more relatives and loved ones were there to see them off. As Bob and Ed waited, a muscular man in uniform walked up to say hello. His name was Dick Wenz, a football trainer who knew Ed well. Wenz told them he'd be joining the same ship as Bob. He'd be sure to look out for him.

That encouraged Bob. But once the recruits were ordered aboard *Newton*, no one seemed to know what to do next. Finally, they were told to go home and return early next morning.

Things seemed more organized on Friday. Family and friends said their good-byes at Exchange Place, Jersey City's commuter hub.

The reservists—officially members of the Naval Reserve's Seventh Battalion's 24th Division—boarded a train that departed Exchange Place at 9:55 a.m., headed south. En route, Maher made friends and shared speculation about just where they were going—and why. Many fellow passengers had been in the Reserve longer than Maher—long enough anyway to receive uniforms. Yet some, including Bob, had gotten no military training at all.[2]

Detraining seven hours later at Cape Charles, Virginia, the reservists rode a ferry across Chesapeake Bay then boarded buses to Norfolk Naval Operating Base. At last, they bedded down in brand-new, Spartan-clean barracks—part of a building boom then transforming Tidewater Virginia into a sprawling armed camp. As one local newspaper summarized it: "War abroad and this nation's preparations against it at home made 1940 a billion-dollar [18 billion in 2022 dollars] defense year for Virginia."[3]

After an early breakfast, those still without them received uniforms. Maher, who weighed just 130 pounds, found himself loaded down not just with clothing but with mattress, mattress covers, blankets, and hammock, gear he carried wherever he went next. The barracks contained revelations. Raised in a spacious suburban New Jersey home with his own bedroom, for example, he'd never seen two-tier bunk beds. A bigger surprise, and quite a shock, were barracks toilets, none equipped with doors.

On Monday afternoon, it was "Pack your gear and get ready to shove off." A huge, flat, high-sided, open barge awaited them at one of the Operating Base's docks. Men stood shoulder to shoulder, barely able to see where they were going. With a tugboat towing, they began a slow, cold, and windy trip down Hampton Roads into the Elizabeth River. Four hours later they reached the Norfolk Navy Yard at Portsmouth, Virginia. Before them stretched a long pier. It was crisscrossed with hoses, power lines, and thick ropes—connected like leashes or umbilical cords to ships of all sizes and types.

After sorting out their gear, the men, lined up by rate and length of service, went to find their ships. Maher discovered that destroyer *Borie*, his ship, was small, certainly compared to others nearby. It was about 2 a.m. when Maher's contingent climbed on board and were divided into two groups: deckhands and "black gang" (engineers, who generally worked below decks). Maher, joining the deckhands, walked towards *Borie*'s bow then descended two near-vertical ladders.

The compartment they entered was about twenty-five feet long, tapered at the bow and maybe thirty feet wide aft. Compared to the barracks Maher had left—and certainly compared to his mother's housekeeping standards—the compartment was filthy.

It contained thirty-six bunks arranged in tiers of three, not two. These bunks folded up against the walls—what these "boots" (slang for recruits in training) learned to call "bulkheads." Below the bunks was an equal number of ("deck"-level) lockers, their tops doubling as seats. Two dining ("mess") tables extended the compartment's length.

None of the new arrivals had eaten since leaving the Norfolk barracks, so someone rousted a ship's cook and several mess men from their bunks. Loaves of bread and a large tureen of chili eventually arrived. Afterwards, all were assigned bunks and lockers and divided into three watch sections: slices of *Borie*'s around-the-clock routines.[4]

2 | FOUR-STACKERS

THE NEW CREWMEN asleep on board *Borie* that night in November 1940 were about the same age as their ship, launched in 1919 and first commissioned by the U.S. Navy in 1920. Between 1917 and 1922, American shipyards had turned out 267 destroyers like *Borie*, known colloquially as "four-stackers" or "four-pipers" because of their distinctive quartets of exhaust funnels, lined up single file.

Though built in two distinct classes—*Wickes* and *Clemson* (names of the lead ship in each class; *Borie* was a *Clemson*)—they were very similar. They were light (1,200 tons), long (314 feet stem to stern), slender (30 feet at the beam), and swift (up to 35 knots). Armaments varied, but most four-stackers were equipped with twelve torpedo tubes, four 4-inch guns, a 3-inch antiair gun, and racks for depth charges—what sailors called "ashcans" because of their resemblance to refuse bins. Some carried what were called "Y-guns" or "fork throwers," devices to catapult ashcans.

They were "flush-deckers"—another colloquialism—meaning they were built with a single unbroken main deck extending stem to stern. The ships' major framing—their foundations of strength—extended athwartships, not fore and aft.

A quirky design feature common to both *Wickes* and *Clemson* destroyers was a tapered stern (or "fantail") resembling a second prow (some said a canoe.) Because the propellers extended outboard of the fantail, sturdy cage-like "propeller guards" jutted from either side. At high speeds the stern tended to squat and drag. The result was a large turning radius—not great for acceleration and maneuvering. When "backing" (going astern), the fantail (and spaces below) tended to flood.

All the *Wickes* and *Clemson* destroyers were built within five years of each other. Naval experts predicted a reckoning for producing so many such "war babies." Warships built too deep into one crisis and too far ahead of the next become obsolete—perhaps useless. The U.S. Navy might be stuck with a glut of outmoded destroyers (effective service was supposedly sixteen years) as other nations—friend and potential foe—launched bigger, better destroyers. Ships with, as military affairs journalist Hanson Baldwin put it, "longer legs and bigger fists."[1]

Postwar events seemed to confirm this. Between 1922 and 1924 many of both classes were mothballed, some "low-mileage" models having steamed less than six hundred miles. Others were scrapped as a result of the 1930 London Naval Arms Limitation Conference. Altogether, 102 of the original 267 were either scrapped or accidently wrecked.*

Now, a decade later, experts reconsidered, arguing that "scrapping a ship with the turn of the calendar" was simply ridiculous. "If a ship's hull is sound, her guns effective and her speed adequate for her duty, she is not obsolete."[2] Other countries' interest may have sparked this volte-face. Suitors included Norway and several Latin American republics, but it was Great Britain, host nation for the Naval Arms Limitation Conference, that most ardently coveted them.

Since September 3, 1939, America's longtime ally had been locked in an air, sea, and land struggle with Germany. To combat the ravages of German submarines (what Winston Churchill, now prime minister, decreed be called "U-boats") the Britain's Royal Navy had organized convoys protected by armed escorts.

---

*On the evening of September 8, 1923, seven *Clemson*-class destroyers traveling in heavy fog ran aground and were lost off the California coast near Santa Barbara. Twenty-three sailors died in what was the largest peacetime loss of U.S. Navy ships.

Escorted merchant ship convoys had amply proven their worth in the Great War, though not until late in the fighting and not before Great Britain had suffered enormous maritime losses. During the first three months of 1917, for example, 1,300,000 tons of British and neutral ships were sunk, with many lives lost.

Naval strategists had at first objected to convoying. Merchant ships were too slow and unruly. Merchant ship masters couldn't—or wouldn't—keep formation. Convoy loading and unloading jammed port facilities. And, not least, there simply weren't enough armed convoy escorts available.

This last objection was answered in 1917 when U.S. Navy vice admiral William S. Sims, a convoy proponent, dispatched thirty-five American destroyers to Great Britain. Operating out of Queenstown, Ireland, the Yanks joined a mixed British-American force commanded by Royal Navy admiral Sir Lewis Bayly. Bayly's mandate was to keep the Atlantic sea-lanes near Britain—the so-called Western Approaches—safe from U-boat attacks. By one estimate, during their twenty months of wartime service American destroyers rode shotgun for nearly four hundred inbound convoys.

Ironically, identical objections to convoys resurfaced in 1939. Indeed, while escorted convoys were initiated more promptly this time, they were not the sole long-term U-boat counterstrategy considered. One alluring alternative was to assemble U-boat-chasing "hunter-killer" groups. This concept honored a tradition of taking the fight to the enemy. Not surprisingly, Winston Churchill fancied pitting that tradition against the U-boats. In a 1940 note to First Sea Lord Dudley Pound, he wrote that "nothing can be more important to the anti-submarine war than to try to obtain an independent flotilla which could work like a cavalry division . . . [which] could search large areas over a wide front . . . [making] these areas . . . untenable to U-boats."[3]

Even with anti-U-boat strategy settled, Britain still lacked adequate escorts. Some convoys were guarded by just one or two.

One Royal Navy escort mainstay was the Flower-class corvette. Bearing quaint names like *Azalea*, *Begonia*, *Bluebell*, and *Buttercup*, the corvettes were so small (just 940 tons) and lightly armed (a single 4-inch gun on the foredeck and twin .50-caliber machine guns) that they were originally limited to inshore escort. With a sixteen-knot top speed, a Flower was slower than a surfaced U-boat and could barely outpace fast merchant ships. Indeed, if a corvette dallied to hunt a U-boat or rescue survivors, it might take hours to rejoin the convoy.

Despite such shortcomings, corvettes (adapted from designs for commercial whalers) were rugged and seaworthy. Churchill touted them as his "Cheap and Nasties." Certainly "Cheap" to build, they also boasted such vital antisubmarine gear as depth charges and ASDIC (an antisubmarine underwater sound-detection system and precursor of American sonar, "sound navigation and ranging"). Intended as "Nasties" to the Germans, corvettes were likewise "Nasties" to their crews: upwards of fifty men crammed into a two-hundred-foot hull that North Atlantic seas heaved about—as one corvette veteran recalled—"like a terrier shaking a bit of rag."[4]

When World War II began, Flower-class escorts were just coming into service. To fill the gap, the Royal Navy considered all expediencies. "Any type of ship," wrote British naval historian Stephen Roskill, "with a turn of speed, with even rudimentary anti-submarine equipment and obsolete guns, was most welcome."[5] Many such "make-do" escorts, however, couldn't extend protection very far, leaving outbound convoys to continue unprotected.

Under such constraints, convoying stumbled out of the gate. Between September and December 1939, 221 merchants went to the bottom, half dispatched by U-boats. Many sank off the northwest corner of Ireland, now called Bloody Foreland.

Old as the mothballed American flush-deckers were and as desperately in need of refit, Winston Churchill all but begged Roosevelt—FDR—in May 1940 to gift them to Britain. Though America's prospects depended on Britain's survival, Roosevelt warned Churchill that doing so was a political impossibility.

Lord Lothian, Britain's ambassador to Washington, pled Churchill's case through the summer. Lothian reminded Secretary of the Navy Frank Knox of a British idea to lease base sites in Bermuda, Newfoundland, and Trinidad. Why not do that in return for the destroyers? Knox and FDR thought an outright trade better, but Churchill was loath to part with pieces of Britain's Sovereign Empire.

Subsequent horse-trading, some of it conducted via a scratchy transatlantic telephone connection, proved tense. Once, Churchill purportedly complained, "Empires just don't bargain!" Came the retort from across the Atlantic: "Well, Republics do!"[6]

In late August, a presidential executive order finally consummated the "Destroyers-for-Bases" deal. On September 3, in exchange for ninety-nine-year leases on naval, air, and military base sites, most in the Caribbean, America would transfer fifty *Wickes*- and *Clemson*-class destroyers to Britain.

There were critics on both sides. Adm. James O. Richardson, Commander in Chief United States Fleet (CinCUS), complained that "these destroyers . . . were essential if there was to be any submarine protection of our coastal merchant shipping."[7] For their part, British critics thought it too steep a price to pay. But, as a grateful Churchill wrote Roosevelt, "Every destroyer you can spare us is measured in rubies."[8]

British crews took over the first four-pipers that month. After refit—some critics of the tradition-bound Royal Navy called the process "de-modernizing"—most were to be recommissioned as Town-class destroyers, named for municipalities that existed both in the United States and the British Commonwealth.

One reporter, seizing the opportunity to ride on board one of the "U.S. Navy's fifty tokens of esteem" as it left for Britain, wrote his impressions. He slept in a junior officers' cabin that contained "American steel furniture, including twin desks, chairs, safes, chests of drawers, clothes closet, wash basin, radiator . . . air duct . . . and upper and lower berths. . . . Spread over the bed, made up in the lower, the blue counterpane bore the pleasing design of an anchor encircled by the words UNITED STATES NAVY."

The captain's cabin was "nothing ornate." But at sea, he reminded his readers, "the captain's time is spent almost continuously on the bridge, day and night."

The reporter mentioned "the extra comfort of the sleeping berths for the crew." In fact, "a yielding mattress on springs does seem luxurious to British navy men, but some of the older hands after one night of lively rolling were heard to remark that there is much to be said for a well slung hammock."*

What most captured the reporter's attention were the ship's "highly efficient propelling engines." There were no "whirling crankshafts . . . no sliding crossheads . . . no eccentrics, no connecting rods. . . . Turbine engines operated under high pressure with superheated steam are as completely encased . . . as the motor of a modern car."[9]

Ultimately, the British were to learn just how much work, modification, and upgrade their "rubies" required. (One U.S. Navy four-stacker veteran predicted that "the British Government will probably go bankrupt trying to keep those boats in oil.")[10] It took four months for most to reach England, months more before they became operational. But back in the States, as one newspaper editorial put it, "if these old four-stackers are valuable to Britain they are valuable to us, with our chances of having to protect both coastlines of the entire Western Hemisphere."[11]

Four-stacker *Borie*, named for Adolph R. Borie, a post–Civil War Secretary of the Navy, had neither endured the indignity nor enjoyed the respite of mothballing. In continuous service since commissioning, *Borie* was, without question, "high mileage."

After shakedown and a year operating in Turkish waters, it had served four years with the Asiatic Fleet and, in September 1923, was one of the first ships succoring victims of a Japanese earthquake. Afterwards, *Borie* joined what was then the Atlantic Squadron for deployments in Europe and the Caribbean. Beginning in 1929, it went west for a decade, first in the Asiatic Fleet and then off America's West Coast.

Altogether, it added up to a strenuous twenty-year career. Despite intervening maintenance, repairs, and overhauls, this vessel, conceived as a thoroughbred, now showed its age. *Borie*'s weaponry, communications, and electrical gear were outmoded. Though equipped with sonar, *Borie* lacked radar. The once "highly efficient propelling engines" now behaved temperamentally, even reluctantly.

*At least one British sailor compared it to "lying on a bloody sack of jelly."

Borie's thin hull and deck plates explained why destroyers were jokingly reviled as "tin cans." Fashioned from rolled steel just three-eighths inches thick, in service at sea the plates were pounded, buckled, and worn down to the point of no return. As lore had it, the engineering officer of a four-piper once hammered the hull's interior only to have seawater, mixed with flecks of "red lead" paint used to coat the exterior, gush up into his face.[12]

In September 1939, *Borie*'s long list of incapacities and infirmities notwithstanding, the four-piper joined U.S. Navy operations "short of war." To emphasize the U.S. Navy's readiness to defend the Western Hemisphere, Roosevelt had organized a Neutrality Patrol. Its ostensible purpose: report and track any belligerent air, surface, or underwater naval force approaching U.S. or Caribbean coasts.

In October, the Act of Panama, affirmed by North and Latin American foreign ministers, warned potential belligerents against "warlike operations" inside a perimeter drawn roughly three hundred miles offshore. Because no Latin American power boasted more than a handful of warships capable of enforcing such a patrol, the U.S. Navy organized patrol units comprising cruisers and destroyers.

At the time, *Borie* served as flagship of Destroyer Squadron (DesRon) 36, a Galveston, Texas–based baker's dozen of four-stackers. All save *Borie* were "low mileage," having just been recommissioned. Of the thirteen, only *Borie* had been even modestly modernized. Distant from the rest of the Atlantic Squadron and sustained by Galveston's local economy, DesRon 36 sailors called themselves the "Texas Navy."

In March 1940, DesRon 36 took over the West Gulf of Mexico Neutrality Patrol, a low-priority zone west of a line running south from New Orleans. As needed, DesRon 36 ships also patrolled out of Key West. All this changed with September's Destroyers-for-Bases deal. DesRon 36's least-upgraded, lowest-mileage four-stackers were easy choices for the swap. All except *Borie* promptly left Galveston bound for Halifax, Nova Scotia.[13]

Now, with the Texas Navy dissolved, *Borie* was assigned to "inshore patrol" of the "Panama Sea Frontier." As a first step, it set sail for Norfolk, Virginia, to fill out its crew with green recruits.

For Bob Maher and his fellow "boots," new to the U.S. Navy, *Borie* and life at sea, a December voyage south from Portsmouth, Virginia, into the Caribbean, was a revelation. "You have to realize," Maher would write years later, "that most of us were street kids from middle class to poor families. We hadn't been anywhere. . . . That first week was wonderful, exciting. . . . We started to learn to be sailors and to accept military discipline."[14]

3 | WIZARD WAR

ON AUGUST 16, 1940, as the Destroyers-for-Bases deal neared fruition, another wartime exchange took shape. Its harbinger, a four-engine flying boat, emerged from the mid-August haze over Quebec Province, dropped onto the smooth waters of the St. Lawrence River, then taxied to the Shell Oil dock in Boucherville.

Clare, operated by British Overseas Airways Corporation (BOAC), had once been a familiar sight in Boucherville, a riverbank town twenty miles from Montreal. Several years before *Clare* and two siblings—*Clyde* and *Caledonia*—had made special flights to Boucherville, each time drawing large crowds. But now, instead of its signature gray paint job *Clare* was camouflaged a drab olive with streaks of blue.

Boucherville was a stopover for weekly flights between the United States and England. After layover, *Clare* would next fly to the Marine Air Terminal at New York's LaGuardia Field. From LaGuardia it was back to Boucherville before flying east to complete the circuit. Each transoceanic leg took twenty-two hours, punctuated by a refueling stop in Newfoundland.

Clare carried diplomatic mail, but perhaps its most anticipated deliveries were English newspapers giving blow-by-blow accounts of the Battle of Britain, under way since July. Except for five seats in the rear, *Clare*'s passenger accommodations had been stripped. Thus, *Clare*'s human cargo was strictly VIP.

Headlining August 16's manifest was Capt. H. H. Balfour, a Great War flying ace and now Britain's undersecretary for air. "Yes," Balfour answered smilingly when asked how the Royal Air Force (RAF) fared against the Luftwaffe, "the RAF is on the top line and our people in the United Kingdom have their tails up." Pleading that he was "in an awful rush," Balfour and two aides left to board another flying boat, bound for Ottawa.

Only then did reporters turn attention to *Clare*'s two remaining passengers. One, a short, muscular man with grizzled red hair, a close-cropped moustache, and a pince-nez, was Sir Henry T. Tizard, chairman of the British Aeronautical Research Committee. Sir Henry explained that he was in Canada for meetings with officials to discuss aircraft manufacturing. Afterwards, however, he and his assistant, an RAF group captain named Frederick L. Pearce, would "make a visit on 'important matters' to Washington, traveling there by motor car."[1]

Though an afterthought that day, Sir Henry soon demonstrated that he was—by far—*Clare*'s most consequential VIP. He was to deliver what an American scientist later described as "the most valuable cargoes ever brought to our shores."[2]

Anglo-American technical exchanges—knowledge transfer, in today's argot—offered President Roosevelt another way to help Great Britain while keeping America neutral. Unfortunately, the British Admiralty and the U.S. Navy viewed each other less as allies than as rivals. The sharing of technical secrets was strictly "quid pro quo."

As things stood, Britain held the better hand regarding secret war tactics and technology. Indeed, when Rear Adm. John H. Godfrey, RN, the director of the Royal Naval Intelligence Division (NID), assessed prospects for technical exchange with his American "cousins," he hesitated. The Americans, he noted, were "technically behind and ashamed of the bareness of [their] cupboard." Why trade gold for dross? Worse, the Yanks were "very sticky" with their own information and possessed inferior "security arrangements."

Still, Godfrey conceded, important benefits might flow. America's industrial capacity was essential to scaling up promising prototypes. Moreover, technical exchanges would cement "common interests" while "ensuring that the U.S. Navy would be equipped . . . to work in British waters should America enter the war."[3]

The Admiralty took a tentative step in October 1939, when it proposed exchanging naval liaison officers. The Navy Department, for its part, though eager to learn about ASDIC, was also skittish. Even after liaison officers were in place, exchange discussions sputtered out.

Even as he pleaded for U.S. Navy (USN) destroyers and hoped to draw America into the war, Winston Churchill resisted technology reciprocity. Not until June 1940, when Britain finally stood alone against Hitler's Germany, would he consider releasing the "most cherished" of Britain's military secrets.[4]

A turning point for the U.S. Navy arrived on August 5, when Chief of Naval Operations (CNO) Harold R. "Betty" Stark agreed to release a trove of U.S. Navy technical information to the Admiralty. By month's end, Navy Department officers had compiled 349 pouches of secret material and were partnering with British counterparts to produce code books, ciphers, and instructions for joint communications between U.S. and British ships.[5]

In Britain, meanwhile, as Sir Henry and Pearce prepared for their trans-oceanic flight, Tizard's associates assembled and crated samples for separate transport by sea.

Henry Tizard, then in his midfifties, was the son of a noted RN hydrographer. When poor vision (the result of a boyhood accident) thwarted his seagoing ambitions, Henry pivoted to science, acquiring a reputation as a rising Oxford-educated physical chemist. Until war intervened, Tizard seemed destined for a successful—if not quite "first-rank"—academic career.

By 1915, poor vision notwithstanding, Henry was in the Royal Flying Corps (RFC) doing aerial experiments that produced the RFC's first practical bomb-sight. Such accomplishments earned Tizard respect, accolades, and rank as a lieutenant colonel in what became the RAF.

After the war, Tizard turned to industrial research. His experiments in fuel volatility established what became known as "octane" ratings. In 1934, sensing war ahead, Tizard joined Britain's Air Ministry as its first—and only—civilian member. Tizard could be "mischievous, provocative," even "disconcertingly outspoken." Offered reactivation and military rank, for example, he adamantly refused to "wear a busby."*[6]

As chair of the Air Ministry's Committee for the Scientific Study of Air Defense, Tizard quickly discovered Britain's vulnerabilities. Once, when a runaway barrage balloon wandered over London streets, RAF pilots scrambled aloft but couldn't find the rogue balloon, much less shoot it down.[7]

In January 1935, Tizard and fellow committee members received a startling memorandum from Robert Watson-Watt, director of the Air Ministry's Radio Research Station. During the 1920s Watson-Watt had pioneered the use of radio waves to detect thunderstorms. Now Watson reported that a young colleague had determined radio direction finding (RDF) might also be used to detect incoming aircraft.

RDF could establish direction (the bearing of thunderstorms or aircraft) but not distance (range). However, the success of a top-secret test that same February pointed to the prospect of a RADAR (radio direction and ranging) air-defense system. Conceptually at least, Tizard's committee soon concluded, radar "might possibly . . . work in real war." Otherwise, "nothing else possibly could."[8]

By 1937, funding in hand, Watson-Watt had constructed and equipped the towers of a prototype station capable of spotting aircraft at altitudes of ten thousand feet as far away as eighty miles. As "Chain Home"—or CH, a network of early-warning stations—sprouted along England's east and south coasts, Tizard (who was knighted that year) devised a means for nontechnical RAF personnel to track and intercept enemy "bandits."

Two years later, Winston Churchill accompanied Sir Henry in a "rather disreputable aeroplane" to obtain a personal "glimpse of where we are in the Radar field." Churchill (who then held no government leadership role) became convinced that radar could also "be of high consequence to the Navy," indeed, "one of the biggest things that had happened in a long time."[9] When Prime

---

*A reference to a tall fur hat worn by British cavalry.

Minister Churchill finally agreed to share Britain's utmost secrets, Sir Henry became his emissary.

With Churchill's sign-off, what became the Tizard Mission moved fast. In mid-August, as Tizard and his assistant flew to Boucherville then drove to Washington, the balance of the mission's seven-man team—an Army brigadier, a Navy captain, a research professor, a radar specialist, and a mission secretary—gathered, documented, and packed an unprecedented assortment of technological wares.

In late August, this contingent sailed for America on board the liner *Duchess of Richmond.* Because the ship was infamously unstable in heavy seas, weaponry hardware stowed in the holds of the "Drunken Duchess" had to be tightly secured and closely guarded. The gear, by one account, included a 450-pound depth charge, a Rolls Royce aircraft engine, a Swedish-built antiaircraft cannon, and a power-driven bomber gun turret.[10]

However, the Tizard Mission's bigger cargo—by import, not size—was secured in the stateroom of Edward G. Bowen, the mission's young radar expert. Deposited in what "Taffy" Bowen later described as a "black deed box, of the kind found in solicitor's offices," were manuals, circuit diagrams, blueprints, films—all the factual documentation backing up the Anglo-American exchange.[11] Also packed in the box—tiny, fragile, and therefore wrapped with utmost care—were three fully functional examples of a device soon to revolutionize radar technology.

Because of its low generating frequency, the long-radio-wave (meter-length) system employed by Chain Home was perhaps closer to RDF than to radar. And, as soon became clear to Bowen, America already possessed something comparable, though its systems, unlike Chain Home, "existed only in ones and twos . . . [without] . . . much operational use."[12]

Shorter (centimeter-length) radio waves—so called microwaves or centimetric waves—held the key to dramatically more compact, powerful, fast, precise, and versatile radar devices. And what made microwave technology possible—what were so painstakingly wrapped inside the black deed box—were three cavity magnetrons.

Essentially a high-powered, microwave-generating vacuum tube, the cavity magnetron* had been invented in February 1940 by British researchers.[13] At first, only laboratory models were available. But a just-completed production run of twelve self-contained cavity magnetrons demonstrated spectacular performance—delivering high-powered 9.1-centimeter microwaves. Now "the most valuable cargoes ever to arrive upon the shores of America" were westbound on board the *Drunken Duchess*.

During a two-month stay in America, the Tizard Mission stayed at Washington's Shoreham Hotel, near the British embassy. A British security official later described the accommodations as "so stuffed with blueprints, scientific data, models, and working plans that you could barely maneuver."[14]

After Sir Henry established contacts and made initial arrangements with the U.S. Army, Navy, and the National Defense Research Council, formal meetings began at the Wardman Park Hotel. It was there, on September 19, that Taffy Bowen revealed the cavity magnetron. Within a few days American scientists tested the device—the vital heart of radar—and learned that it gave a thousand times the power previously available. Soon after, the Massachusetts Institute of Technology's (MIT) Radiation Laboratory was founded, in no small part to adapt and reproduce the cavity magnetron for use in ships, planes, and gunfire-control systems—anything that sharpened detection of enemy craft or added accuracy in destroying them.

If there was a singular juncture that defined the transfer of Anglo-American knowledge for defeating the Axis, it came in these Autumn 1940 meetings. More than exchanging documents and technology samples, it initiated a stream of interchanges that mobilized military personnel, research labs,

*Easy in concept but hard to execute, the cavity magnetron uses a magnetic field to "herd" electrons within a precisely hollowed-out piece of copper. Think of it like a whistle—a loose, hard (spherical) object inside a cavity. When you blow a whistle the hard object bounces, creating *sound* waves. In a cavity magnetron, when a magnetic field is applied to electric current flowing through the copper, electrons bounce in the cavity, emitting *electromagnetic* waves. If the hollowed-out cavity is small, the waves are small—but powerful.

academics, and industrialists in what Churchill termed a secret "Wizard War." Its achievements might be "unintelligible to ordinary folk. . . . Yet if we had not mastered its profound meaning and used its mysteries" all other efforts "would have been in vain."[15]

Unfortunately, Churchill soon mustered Sir Henry out of the Wizard War. In 1934, shortly after Tizard took the chair of Committee for the Scientific Study of Air Defense, Frederick A. Lindemann, an Oxford professor of physics, joined the committee. Though Tizard and Lindemann had been close friends in student days, they were now mortal enemies. After Lindemann joined, a close observer recalled, the meetings "did not know half an hour's harmony or work undisturbed."[16]

Lindemann, who also happened to be a scientific advisor and friend to Winston Churchill, not yet in power, was soon ousted. But once Churchill ascended, tables turned. During one cabinet meeting, Tizard blundered by dismissing Lindemann's theory that the Germans used radio beams to guide their bombers. Lindemann proved right, Tizard wrong—and Churchill never forgot. Upon his return from America Tizard was banished to academia for the duration.

4 | RITES OF PASSAGE

IT WAS MID-DECEMBER 1940 when *Borie*, its new recruits on board, reached Panama's Coco Solo. The wonder and excitement of the first days at sea had given way to the gut-wrenching ordeal of transiting the Windward Passage, the straits between Cuba and Haiti. The ocean turned rough.

Borie constantly pitched and rolled, forcing sailors to grasp "lizards," old-fashioned hand straps (like those on a street trolley) hanging above the main deck.[1] Even asleep, they clutched bunk stanchions to avoid being thrown to the deck.* During this stretch Maher first stood lookout with another sailor in the crow's nest—a barrel-shaped enclosure atop the ship's fifty-foot mainmast. *Borie* lacked any radar, so crow's nest lookouts were best positioned to see what lay all around.

Bob wasn't there long before his stomach churned. Cautioned to avoid the voice tube if he felt queasy, Bob grabbed for his sailor's hat. Too late. Instead of filling the hat, wind-whipped vomit splattered men atop *Borie*'s after deckhouse. Succumbing to the contagion, the other lookout threw up

---

*Rhymed couplets capture the sea-tossed sailor's mood:

Pitch, pitch, goddamn your soul
The more you pitch the less you roll.
Roll, roll you mean old bitch
The more you roll, the less you pitch.

too. Both men wobbled as they descended the mast ladder. Bob reached the deck okay, but the other sailor froze and had to be rescued. Neither was of much use for the rest of the voyage.[2]

Built in 1918 on the Atlantic side of the Panama Canal Zone, Coco Solo was principally a U.S. submarine base. For most of the recruits, it was their first experience in the tropics. At first, they loved it. Soon, though, the isthmus' blazing sun, relentless heat, sweltering humidity, and torrential downpours wore them down. Conditions on board *Borie* made life no easier. Interior spaces were cramped, and none were air-conditioned. Enlisted men shared two shower heads and washed their own clothes in buckets of water. The after deckhouse, far from the forward berthing compartment, contained the only enlisted toilet ("head"). When nature called urgently, frantic sailors racing the distance didn't always reach the finish line in time.

⌖

The U.S. Navy then had—and still has—an apprentice system for enlisted sailors, a way to join specialty professions (called "ratings") and climb the petty officer rates. Lowly seamen recruits first advanced to become seamen second class ("seamen deuces" for short.) Eventually, as seamen first class, they joined a ship's division—gunnery, for example, or engineering or communications—to become "strikers" (apprentices). They learned their crafts and, when ready, took qualifying exams to become rated petty officers.

It was a good system if you had interest and aptitude for the rating you pursued. Like all too many others, though, Bob Maher got no choice. He was simply told he would strike for commissaryman. Becoming a commissaryman striker, what was called a "jack of the dust," held little appeal, but Bob saw no way out. Then, a few weeks after reaching Coco Solo, *Borie*'s gunnery officer approached Bob about becoming a fire controlman.

At first Bob thought this meant joining the engineering black gang—working in fire and engine rooms, where heat was especially brutal. The officer laughed, assuring him he wouldn't be an engineering division *fireman* but a gunnery division *fire controlman*, working on the gear used to aim and shoot the ship's weaponry. Grasping the difference, Bob warmed to the idea and was flattered to learn he was one of the few *Borie* sailors with the math skills—especially trigonometry—needed for the job.[3]

This began Bob Maher's oddball apprenticeship with a fire controlman second class named Walter A. "Smitty" Smith. Smitty, Bob quickly realized, never studied to keep up with the new equipment arriving. In fact, Smitty never read anything but comic books. Worse, Smitty was always in trouble, invariably returning drunk from liberty and being disciplined.

At first, Smitty was always on Maher's back, screaming "Maaar!" whenever Bob questioned unclear instructions. Bit by bit, however, the worm turned.

All Bob knew about the ship and the sea was what he'd learned since coming on board. But it didn't take long to realize that learning your way around was not anyone else's responsibility. Dick Wenz, Ed's friend from football, was just being a good guy when he promised to look out for Bob. Wenz, though, just like everyone else on board, had his own job and problems to tend to.

Fortunately, Maher—unlike Smitty—was eager to pore through instruction manuals. And he possessed the aptitude, intellect, and curiosity to figure out how the fire-control gear actually worked. The more Bob studied the more proficient he became and the more Smitty left his striker unmolested.

Meanwhile, Smitty's drinking finally caught up with him. He went on unauthorized absence (UA)—or seemed to—just as *Borie* got under way. Once the ship was at sea, however, someone noticed a big lump in a rolled-up section of deck awning. Trapped inside was Smitty—passed out, soaked in sweat, and seriously dehydrated. Hauled to his bunk to recover, Smitty was eventually court-martialed and thrown in the brig ashore. Once out, Smitty would receive a dishonorable discharge.

Bob was glad to be rid of the guy but also felt sorry for him. Smitty, after all, was just three months shy of a pension. His Navy career, maybe even his life, was ruined.

When Bob visited Smitty in the brig, the forlorn and haggard sailor asked a personal favor: bring him a bucket, towel, soap, and shaving gear so he could at least clean himself up. "Hey kid," Smitty added as Bob was about to leave, "do you have any Bay Rum?" *Borie* had been to Jamaica where Bay Rum aftershave was so cheap that Bob had bought plenty. He promised to bring a bottle.

Bob returned the next day with what Smitty had requested. As soon as the guard left the two of them, though, Smitty immediately gulped down the bottle of Bay Rum. This was the last Maher ever saw or heard of Walter A. Smith.[4]

Maher continued to learn a lot: fire-control electronics, optics, gyro principles, instrument repair, and more mathematics—all the knowledge and skills needed to align *Borie*'s guns so that rounds would hit where aimed. After passing the qualifying test, Bob became a petty officer third class. Jim Allegri, already a close friend, got assigned to Bob as a striker. Allegri's family owned a fuel and ice business in Nutley, New Jersey, just five miles from Kearny. Jim had left high school at fifteen to join Allegri Ice and Coal, but what he lacked in schooling Jim made up for in practical know-how and a strong work ethic.

Borie went out to sea more—and for longer stretches. There were constant drills. Men were either at work, on watch, or racing to battle stations (at General Quarters, or "GQ"), damage-control stations, Sea and Anchor Detail stations, or abandon-ship stations. They drilled until they could do things eyes closed, then drilled some more.

Gunnery practice, the peacetime apex of all the gunnery and fire-control teams' work, was the most exciting. But because of the constant patrolling, it was too often neglected. Under Smitty's regime *Borie*'s fire-control gear had languished. Because the big guns were seldom fired, much sloppy handiwork went undetected. Now, though, with all the talk of war, that was bound to change. Much of fire control's electrical and optical gear was topside, exposed to wind and saltwater. Maher and Allegri worked overtime, ensuring telescopes were clear, dry, and aligned, firing circuitry in good shape.

At GQ, Bob operated the gun director, the heavy pedestal-mounted electrical-mechanical gear used to aim and fire the big guns remotely. Now, whenever the director "locked on" to a target, *Borie*'s main-battery 4-inchers—one forward, two amidships, one aft—were sure to move (train side to side and elevate) in smooth synchronization. And whenever Bob pulled the director's fire-control key—its remote trigger—one or more of the guns barked, projectiles zooming exactly where aimed.

A rare gunnery competition against two other squadron ships offered proof of Bob's and Jim's work. Firing at a towed target five miles distant and moving at fifteen knots, *Borie*'s guns scored twenty bull's-eyes to win the contest.[5]

Bob Maher's life with his parents in Kearny and Jersey Shore weekends with his friends suddenly seemed far away and long ago. Now, Bob liked to think, he did what he wanted and went where he wanted, never worrying about parental approval. In truth, of course, Bob was accountable to the U.S. Navy, which could be as harsh and demanding a parent as ever imposed discipline.

Borie was its own separate community, with a common purpose. All its roughly 120 officers, petty officers, deckhands, and firemen were shipmates, and Bob, in some fashion, knew just about everyone.

There were, for example, all the New Jersey boys of 7th Battalion who came on board at the same time. And there were also the boys from Maryland. Their organization, called the Old Baltimore Battalion, had actually been mobilized before the 7th, sent first by train to New York, then shipped down to Panama by transport.[6] Among its ranks were Jim Aikenhead, a small, wiry signalman striker, and Tommy Morris, an electrician's mate striker.

Smitty aside, there was also a core of proficient petty officers. One was James F. "Pete" Clubb, a twenty-two-year-old radioman from Port Huron, Michigan.[7] Another, Ken O'Kelly, a twenty-five-year-old water tender from Cedar Rapids, Iowa, had served on *Borie* since 1937.[8]

Not surprisingly, Bob became closest with New Jersey boys like Jim Allegri and Eddie "Meat" Johnson—also from gunnery. It was Eddie, a close pal and workmate at Allegri Ice and Coal, who had persuaded Jim to enlist. Bob first crossed paths with the pair when *Borie* sat dockside in Norfolk.

"Hey Maaahhhhr, give us a hand!" Bob heard someone shout as he was about to dump a dishpan of dirty water over the side. Poking his head over the lifeline, Bob saw Jim and Eddie below him, both dressed in new uniforms, peacoats, and white hats, standing on a scaffold suspended at either end by block and tackle. They wanted Bob's help lowering the scaffold a little at a time, first one end, then the other.

They shouldn't have asked a former insurance clerk. One pull on the line spilled Jim and Eddie into the water.[9]

Maher, Allegri, Johnson, and Signalman Third Class Ed Malaney became a companionable quartet whose liberty time in Panama followed a familiar routine: dinner, then drinks at a bar or cocktail lounge.

Women didn't dominate the picture, at least not the type you'd bring home to meet your parents.* More than once a sailor based at Coco Solo "shacked up" with a Panamanian woman, only to learn she also cohabited with another—sometimes a shipmate.

Once, in Cuba, Mahar, who spoke some Spanish, was recruited to join two *Borie* veterans for some all-night partying with three gorgeous Latinas in a posh Santiago suburb. By comparison, shore leave in Panama City, on the isthmus' Pacific side, and Colón, on the Atlantic side, was generally tame.

Colón was perhaps better for shopping and sightseeing, but Panama City boasted a district called "the Limits," where bars featured live bands and "B-girls" who kept patrons' company in exchange for buying them diluted drinks. The Limits' dives seemed right out of Hollywood casting: beaded rope curtains, bands playing Latin music, dark smoky rooms, and short-skirted Latinas pleading, "Buy me a drink, sailor?"

The quartet's favorite nightspot was called the Milwaukee, which sold beer actually brewed in Milwaukee. Its main bar was large and brightly lit, with white marble floors. There you could get hamburgers and sit around talking, uninterrupted by B-girls. On the other side of the beaded curtain, however, enterprising Latinas swarmed. To Maher, buying a B-girl drinks was a chance to practice his high school Spanish with someone attractive. After the Spanish lesson, it was time to go back to the ship.[10]

By Maher's reckoning, *Borie* passed through the Panama Canal dozens of times. Negotiating the "Ditch's" twelve locks was no sightseeing adventure.

---

*An invitation for *Borie* sailors to a party hosted by "Lt. Commander and Mrs. William H. Vanderbilt" (heirs to the Vanderbilt fortune) made clear the character of female companions eligible to attend: "Transportation and ladies will be furnished." (U.S. *Borie* memo dated October 24, 1941)

Far from the postcard images of white concrete walls, colorful "donkeys" (the small locomotives that pulled ships through the locks), and swaying palm trees, all he saw were stained walls, rusted engines, and contaminated water.

The forty-four-mile trip took six to ten hours. After exiting on either the Pacific or Atlantic side, *Borie*'s main job was to prevent merchant vessels from straying into minefields protecting canal entrances. For a week or so at a time, the ship patrolled the minefield fringes until relieved by another ship. The crew saw many Japanese ships, the ones heading west often laden with American scrap metal.

Late in August 1941, patrolling on the Pacific side, this time bound for the equator, *Borie* entered the Humboldt Current, a wide, northbound, cold ocean stream, counterpart to the Atlantic's warm Gulf Stream. Water and air temperatures dipped going south.

At times, as *Borie* paralleled South America's coast, the Andes Mountains came into view. What looked to be snow-capped ridges were instead covered with guano—bird droppings prized for fertilizer. *Borie* got its own guano splatters from huge condors with wingspans so wide they appeared to be dive-bombers.

Borie eventually turned west from the coast of Ecuador, heading for the Galapagos Islands. There were more sights en route—huge sea turtles and pods of playful, high-speed porpoises. When *Borie* anchored close to one island, a few lucky sailors went ashore to inspect the antic penguins—and be inspected in turn—up close.

On September 4, 1941, *Borie* crossed the equator. For "polliwogs," sailors who like Maher, Allegri, Johnson, Malaney, Aikenhead, Morris and many others had not yet crossed the equator, it was time for initiation into the "Solemn Mysteries of the Ancient Order of the Deep" by "shellbacks," sailors like Ken O'Kelly and Pete Clubb, who had.

Hazing by "King Neptune" and his Shellback Court flirted with torture and respected no rank. The highest-ranking polliwog could be fair game for the lowest-ranking shellback—and often was. While infantile, debasing, and often perverse, "Crossing the Line" was also an important rite of passage, transforming street kids into sailors.[11]

5 | SHOT FROM THE BUSHES

IN JULY 1941, despite a burst of shipbuilding, America's navy was still stretched thin. As President Franklin Roosevelt lamented to his cabinet, "I simply have not got enough Navy to go around!"[1] Yet, in a May 27 broadcast declaring a state of "unlimited national emergency," FDR advised the American public that the Neutrality Patrol would expand. "The war," he warned, "is coming very close to home. . . . The Battle of the Atlantic [a term recently coined by Winston Churchill] now extends from . . . the North Pole to . . . the Antarctic. . . . We have, accordingly, extended our patrol. . . . We are steadily adding more ships and planes."[2]

By now, most Americans—71 percent, according to one poll—supported aiding Britain.[3] Suggesting that extending aid to Allies was like loaning a garden hose to a neighbor whose house was on fire, FDR induced Congress to approve—narrowly—a "Lend-Lease" program vastly expanding military production and shipping it (free of charge for the duration) to Britain and other "friendly belligerents."

The threat now, however, wasn't limited to the Western Hemisphere. FDR realized that Japan's aggression in the Far East boded a two-ocean war. There was every reason to avoid overextension. But with Hitler pointing his blitzkrieg eastward to invade the Soviet Union, the president judged the time right to commit the U.S. Navy to Atlantic convoy escort duties.

In mid-July (according to Robert E. Sherwood, a Pulitzer Prize–winning playwright and Roosevelt speechwriter), Roosevelt was sitting in the White House with Harry Hopkins, another close aide, when he tore a map of the Atlantic Ocean from the pages of *National Geographic* magazine. Spreading the excised sheet before him, Roosevelt, a self-proclaimed "map man," took a pencil and traced a north–south line from a point two hundred miles west of Iceland down to the Azores, a rough approximation of the 26th meridian. FDR told Hopkins, his regular emissary to Churchill, to inform the prime minister that the U.S. Navy would assume responsibility for convoy security west of this line.[4]

Sherwood suggests an impromptu decision. But it followed months of debate, planning, preparation—and mind-changing. On March 27, 1941, following two months of secret meetings, American and British military staffs had produced the "ABC-1 Staff Agreements." ABC-1 (the acronym stood for "American British Conversations") delineated the concept of "Germany first"—the strategy to defeat Germany before Japan in a global war.

The staffs had been duly cautioned not to overcommit. Roosevelt insisted the sides be referred to as "associates," not allies. No diplomatic representatives got involved, and "agreements" would be subject to future events and policy decisions.

Going into the ABC meetings, worried about British assertiveness, the U.S. side avoided subordinating America's future to Britain's. "Germany first," in fact, originated with "Plan Dog," Chief of Naval Operations Betty Stark's effort to corral FDR's "improvisations" into a strategy framework. Stark submitted four alphabetized plan options. On the eve of ABC, FDR and his advisors chose Plan D (for "Dog"), specifying an Atlantic Ocean offense balanced by a Pacific Ocean defense.*

---

*Plan A: Hemispheric defense avoiding a European war. Plan B: Offense against Japan, defense in the Atlantic. Plan C: Assist Britain in both oceans. Stark's underlying logic for Plan Dog: "If Britain wins decisively against Germany, we could win anywhere." But if Britain loses, "while we [America] might not lose everywhere, we might possibly not win anywhere." (Abbazia, *Mr. Roosevelt's Navy*, 120–21)

One ABC-1 arrangement called for the U.S. Navy to take control of protecting Allied shipping in the Atlantic. In other words, once ready, its Atlantic Fleet (the former Atlantic Squadron upgraded to fleet status and commanded by a tall, lean, and acerbic sixty-two-year-old admiral named Ernest J. King) would protect transatlantic merchant convoys all the way from North America to Great Britain.

This meant organizing and training a convoy escort force plus building bases on both shores. The "Atlantic Fleet Support Group," drawn mostly from the Neutrality Patrol, was to consist of five U.S. Navy destroyer divisions plus five flying-boat squadrons. Ships, planes, and crews, along with a security force of 15,000 U.S. Army troops, would be based in Northern Ireland.

In all, it was an unprecedented, ambitious, and far-reaching concept. So much so, in fact, that ardor for it soon cooled. For one thing, overseas bases could not be ready before 1942.[5] For another, eastbound convoys might carry Canadian troops—a risk Roosevelt shied from. For yet another, the Destroyers-for-Bases deal was in the process of stripping King's Atlantic Fleet of fifty destroyers. And finally, neither the USN nor the RN could sort out the logistic and command complexities.

This mutual rethinking ultimately led to FDR's penciling-in of a demarcation line on the *National Geographic* map. Even then, not until August, when Roosevelt and Churchill rendezvoused secretly in Newfoundland, did an actual Anglo-American convoy protection plan get finalized.

Beginning August 9, off Argentia, the two leaders and their staffs traded visits between U.S. Navy cruiser *Augusta* and Royal Navy battleship *Prince of Wales*. Political deliberations for this Atlantic Conference—code name Riviera—produced the Atlantic Charter, an eight-point statement of visionary postwar principles.

During naval staff discussions, meanwhile, CNO Stark and Sir Dudley Pound, Britain's arthritic, dark-browed, and single-minded First Sea Lord, hashed out the terms of "Western Hemisphere Defence Plan Number 4," WPL-51 for short. In simplest terms, under WPL-51 (to take effect September 16) Canadian warships would escort convoys eastward to Newfoundland. From there, U.S. Navy escorts (based in Newfoundland and Iceland) would take charge as far as a "Mid-Ocean Meeting Point" (MOMP), where Royal Navy escorts would take over. (Conversely U.S. Navy escorts would escort convoys westward from the MOMP.) "From the British point of view," wrote Stephen Roskill, "the changes . . . brought an immediate sense of relief and a conviction . . . the Battle of the Atlantic would finally be won."[6]

Meanwhile, using the Atlantic Charter as cover, Roosevelt and Churchill got down to brass tacks on the coming war. According to one British delegate, while FDR said he would not declare war, he would wage it if necessary. The mere presence of U.S. escort vessels in U-boat waters was bound to provoke incidents. "If the Germans did not like it, they could attack American forces."[7]

⌖

Riviera ended on August 12. As WPL-51's implementation date neared, American destroyers practiced antisubmarine tactics against American submarines off Argentia. Meanwhile, Roosevelt awaited the "incident" that would justify escorting convoys in the Western Atlantic. It came on September 4.

Back in June, at Churchill's urging, Roosevelt had decided to occupy Iceland, a geographic bottleneck to German naval operations in the North Sea. Four thousand Marines landed there on July 8. To protect supply convoys bound for Iceland, FDR ordered CNO Stark to authorize U.S. Navy ships to attack any U-boats "actually within sight or sound contact."[8]

At 8:40 a.m. on September 4, destroyer *Greer*, a *Wickes*-class four-stacker carrying mail and passengers to Reykjavik, was 125 miles southwest of its destination when an emergency buzzer sounded. *Greer*'s officer of the deck (OOD) alerted its skipper, Laurence H. "Jack" Frost. Lieutenant Commander Frost, then thirty-nine, had been on board *Greer* little more than a month in what was his first seagoing command.

A British twin-engine bomber had just overflown *Greer*, Frost learned, signaling a German U-boat nearby. He called his crew to GQ, intending to track the U-boat and transmit position reports but not attack. Frost ordered speed reduced to ten knots and commenced a zigzagging patrol using sonar.

Five minutes later, *Greer*'s soundman reported a contact at 2,100 yards, straight ahead. The contact tried to evade, but *Greer* held on.

At 10:30 a.m., after asking *Greer*'s intentions—Skipper Frost still declined to attack—the British pilot swooped low, dropped four depth charges, and then, low on fuel, left the scene.

Two hours later, *Greer*'s soundman called out changes in the contact's bearing, and lookouts saw "something in the water" pass about a thousand yards to starboard. At 12:48 p.m., sonar warned of a torpedo firing. Frost ordered flank speed and hard left rudder. Lookouts spotted the torpedo pass astern as *Greer* barreled in for a counterattack.

A pattern of eight depth charges sent shock waves that rattled *Greer*—and surely the U-boat too. But any damage sustained didn't deter the sub's skipper. Less than two minutes later a second torpedo passed three hundred yards to port.

Afterwards, rough seas interrupted sonar. The skipper of a British destroyer reaching the scene asked Frost to join a coordinated attack, but the American declined. Two hours later, sonar contact reestablished, *Greer* dropped eleven more depth charges, then continued to Iceland.[9]

The attack on *Greer* afforded FDR the perfect opportunity to advance what was already in the works. The next day, according to newspaper accounts, "President Roosevelt indicated his conviction that the submarine attack . . . was deliberate and . . . that American naval forces are trying . . . to 'eliminate' the attacker."

Roosevelt emphasized that the incident "definitely occurred on the American side of the Atlantic." When asked whether the attack might nonetheless have "been in the blockade zone proclaimed by Adolf Hitler," FDR replied that "the United States recognized no such zone."

The president then offered another homespun analogy. "It reminded him," he told reporters, "of an incident in which school children on their way to classes were fired upon one day by a marauder who shot at them from some bushes. The father of the children . . . took the position there was nothing to do about it—not even search the bushes—because the children were not hit by the gunfire."

Roosevelt grimly insisted, "That is not the position of this government in the attack upon its destroyer. The bushes are being searched." He rejected "the position of the allegorical father." It might be said that "the schoolteacher of the allegory is the one conducting the search."

When the president identified himself as the schoolteacher, one reporter asked, "What should be done if we find the marauder?"

"Eliminate it," Roosevelt replied. "'Eliminate' is a very good word."[10]

As Roosevelt prepared a September 11 radio address, reporters fanned out to obtain firsthand details. There were few to get. *Greer* remained at sea, with neither the skipper nor crew available for interviews.

Reporters did, however, supply comments from those closest to Frost. "They couldn't have a better person in a better place right then," his wife said when contacted at their home in Washington, DC. "I know how Jack would react. He's very cool."[11] Reached in Los Angeles, Mary Sue English, Frost's eighteen-year-old niece, enthused: "If there's anyone in the United States Navy, who can keep a destroyer off the bottom, it's my Uncle Larry." Martha Anne, Mary Sue's thirteen-year-old sister, chimed in: "Uncle Larry is a real sailor[;] . . . he knows what to do when his ship is attacked by a submarine."[12]

During his September 11 radio address the president described an unprovoked German attack, conveniently omitting *Greer*'s prolonged counterattacks. Henceforth, Atlantic Fleet ships would "shoot on sight" when they encountered U-boats. Furthermore, U.S. Navy ships would commence convoy escort operations. The United States, after all, had every right to protect its trade.

During WPL-51's inaugural convoy run, no U-boats threatened a fifty-ship eastbound convoy shepherded by five U.S. destroyers. That was fortunate. Nearly every day of the run from Newfoundland to MOMP was plagued by breakdowns, miscues, and near collisions. After one merchant ship caught fire and had to be abandoned, a nighttime rescue amidst heavy winds and high seas saved sixty-three lives. U-boats actually missed their best opportunity at the MOMP. As the convoy awaited storm-delayed British escorts, merchant ships milled around like sitting ducks.

"At first," escort group commander U.S. Navy captain Morton L. Deyo said of his warship sailors, "the great difficulty was to keep people alert. Then, when they actually found themselves escorting a convoy . . . they became 'jumpy' and saw a submarine or heard one in every wave. Now, after dropping a depth charge on nothing and getting a shell stuck in a gun . . . they are beginning to steady down and become more businesslike. This will teach them fast."[13]

6 | BROWNIE AND GULLY

ONE DAY THAT FALL, as *Borie* docked in Balboa, admiring gazes fell on a young woman awaiting the ship's return. Clearly an American, scarcely older than a teenager, she was slender and fresh-faced, with long blonde hair. Amidst the waterfront's bustle and profanity, she looked out of place.

Frances Gullion Brown, however, was better prepared for this unruly setting than many of *Borie*'s ogling sailors. She'd come here on her own, flying from Miami via Colombia.[1] She'd even wrangled an office job in Balboa with the U.S. Army. The daughter of a colonel and niece of a famous general, Frances was an "Army brat," long accustomed to navigating new destinations, sizing up new situations, and fitting right in.

Walter, her father, was a 1914 West Point graduate. In August 1934, while stationed at Hawaii's Schofield Barracks, Major Gullion was interviewed by the *Honolulu Star-Bulletin*'s military editor.

Before Schofield, Gullion's overseas tours had included three years in China. Gullion and his wife Martha, both bluegrass Kentuckians, had been married while Walter was on graduation leave from West Point. Frances Mary, the couple's only child, was born in Washington, and she and her mother shared the nomadic life of "dependents" of a career Army officer. Aged fifteen at the time of the *Star-Bulletin* profile, Frances Mary, Gullion told Nash, was best known as "Gully" to classmates at Wahiawa's Leilehua High School.[2]

In the months leading up to war, Gully doubled her military allegiances by marrying twenty-two-year-old Morrison Ropes "Brownie" Brown, a reserve ensign serving as *Borie*'s new assistant engineer and stores officer.

Brownie (called "Son" by his parents and "Morie" by other relations) was a 1939 Duke University engineering graduate, collegiate footballer, and automotive enthusiast. Though raised in Swampscott, Massachusetts, his maternal lineage stretched to colonial Salem, where the Ropes family, natives of England, first settled in the mid-seventeenth century.

Carroll Ropes Brown, Brownie's dad, had suffered a heart attack while still young. Fortunately, Carroll had had a windfall inheritance from his own father Jonathan, owner of shoe manufacturer J. Brown & Sons. Carroll could also rely on the generosity of older sister Alice, heiress by marriage to the F. W. Woolworth fortune. Heeding doctors' orders to avoid stress, Carroll, his wife Marion, and their two children (Son and older sister Mary) relocated to Miami Beach. They rented an apartment just blocks from where the children's Aunt Alice—then widowed and likewise ailing—maintained a winter estate.[3]

Brownie (his daughter "Sunny" recalled) met Gully in Miami Beach. "She and my grandmother saw him working on a car and Grandmother said: 'Why don't you go down and meet that handsome man and say hi.' My mother did, and they hit it off."[4]

In time, the details of their engagement caught the attention of Miami Beach society scribes. "Silver Hearts Reveal Engagement" proclaimed the headline of a July 19, 1941, *Miami News* society page item. "Two silver hearts marked 'Gully' and 'Morie' tied to streamers dangling from tiny old-fashioned nosegays revealed the engagement. . . . The wedding will take place early in September."

"Miss Gullion," the article mentioned, "lived several years in China and Honolulu when her father was in active service." Meanwhile, "Ensign Brown, who is now stationed at Jacksonville[,] recently graduated from the United States naval reserve midshipman's school in New York City."[5]

Brownie was a product of training ship *Prairie State*, site of the Naval Reserve Midshipmen's School, or V-7 Program. In 1940, battleship *Illinois*, long docked at New York City's 136th Street for use by naval militia, became the locus for a new crash training program destined to produce tens of thousands of naval reserve officers. The program graduated its first class of 264 in November 1940.

In March 1941, with *Illinois* renamed *Prairie State*, a second class of 441 graduated.[6] The new reserve ensigns, ranging in age from nineteen to twenty-six, came from more than two hundred American colleges and universities. On June 7, 1941, *Prairie State*'s next crop—406 "middies" (Brownie among them) clad in high-collared "dress whites"—convened for an address by Vice Adm. Adolphus "Dolly" Andrews, the somewhat pompous commandant of the North Atlantic Naval Coastal Frontier.[7]

"In the navy," Andrews told the middies, "we have ships, guns and men; but the greatest of these is men." Dolly urged them to gird themselves for more strenuous training and warned, "One officer, one man, on board ship who is not alert and does not know his job, may either wreck the ship or have it fail at a critical time in battle."

"Your job," Dolly concluded, "will require a steady hand and cool nerve. You must use your brains to think ahead and to be ready for the next emergency."[8]

Graduates of this V-7 class were, for the first time, designated either deck officers or engineer officers. Morrison Brown, who'd earned an engineering degree and been elected to Duke's Physics Honor Society, was one of 206 with the engineer designation.

After commissioning, Brownie reported first to Section Base No. 1 Inshore Patrol, in Jacksonville, Florida, on June 14. In a letter to "Mother + Dad" dated June 22, he described the enthusiasm he felt. "Yesterday, I was appointed *assistant engineering officer to the Captain*—a capacity in which I will really begin to learn what motors are. . . . [A]ny ships that come in for repairs from sea it is my duty to find out just what they need. So, you can see that I will come in contact with about every type of engine."[9]

Though immersed in his new milieu, Brownie also attended to details of his upcoming wedding. One day he'd visited Jacksonville's naval aviation facility and learned that about twenty Duke classmates were stationed there as flight cadets. "So maybe," Brownie conjectured, "Gully's dream about a naval wedding isn't as far-fetched as it seemed." Son also had a request for his dad: "Will you be my best man[?] I don't know of anybody I would rather have."[10]

In the countdown to Gully and Brownie's Saturday, September 6, wedding, society pages previewed the bride's festivities. "The final whirl of prenuptial entertainment," gushed the Wednesday, September 3, *Miami News*, "promises to keep her busy every one of these last few days."[11]

"Ensign Brown, the bridegroom-to-be," scheduled to arrive from Jacksonville late Thursday, would join a Friday soiree where decorations featured, according to a September 5 *Miami News* recap, "a miniature bride and bridegroom in bathing suits of red, white and blue." Following the buffet supper, "many of the guests went swimming in the moonlight."

The *Miami News* article also noted the Friday afternoon arrival of Maj. Gen. Allen W. Gullion. Tragedy had befallen Gully and her mom in April 1940, when Lt. Col. Walter Gullion, then retired and just fifty-one, suffered a fatal heart attack.[12] His untimely death prompted Gully to cut short studies at the College of William and Mary, return home, and begin working in real estate. Uncle Allen, Walter's older brother, would now stand up for his niece at her wedding.

"Gold Braid of Both Army and Navy Add Glamor," announced a society news headline in the September 7 *Miami Herald*. There would be no sword-wielding arch of Navy ensigns. Instead, "The bride . . . was given in marriage by her uncle, Maj. Gen. Allen W. Gullion, U.S.A. of Washington, D.C."[13]

Allen W. Gullion's presence certainly added prestige. A 1905 West Point graduate who had served under famed Gen. John J. Pershing, Gullion had earned a law degree and gone on to become judge advocate general, the Army's top legal officer. At the time of the wedding, he was on the verge of being appointed provost marshal.[14]*

Brownie embarked for Panama from Norfolk on Tuesday, September 24, on board *Solace*, a newly commissioned U.S. Navy hospital ship. He alerted Gully

*In that capacity, Gullion would press for the wartime internment of Americans of Japanese ancestry.

by letter on Sunday, and, as he wrote his parents a day before departure, "I am going to make the best of it. . . . As you say, thank goodness I'm not going to Iceland. Hardly believe I could take the very cold weather."[15]

Solace's ultimate destination was Pearl Harbor.* By Brownie's estimate, fifteen other ensigns accompanied him on the converted passenger vessel, all bound for assignments in either Cuba or the Canal Zone. "I just thank my lucky stars," Brownie wrote his parents on September 25, "that I'm not getting off in Guan. [Guantánamo, Cuba]"[16]

If Panama's allure had faded for *Borie*'s enlisted veterans, not so for Morrison Brown. "Gully arrived yesterday, as beautiful as ever," Morrison advised his parents in a letter dated October 24, 1941. "Don't believe I was ever so glad to see anyone in my life."

Brownie had been on board *Borie* out at sea when Gully was scheduled to arrive in Colón. Learning this, Lt. Cdr. Harry F. "Pete" Miller, *Borie*'s skipper, arranged for Brownie to board a sister destroyer heading back to Balboa. "I came in about 7 [a.m.]. Caught the train with plenty of time to spare. The plane came in right on the dot at 5:15. Now that my dear wife is here, we have to find a place to 'hang our hat.'"[17]

*During the December 7 attack on Pearl Harbor, *Solace* was moored less than a half-mile from battleship *Arizona*. After Solace moved to a safer spot, boat crews steered launches through flaming waters to rescue survivors. Back on *Solace*, ships' doctors, Public Health Service physicians, and civilian nurses treated wounded and dying. (Robert J. Cressman, "Historic Fleets," *Naval History* [December 2011])

7 | THE SHOOTING HAS STARTED

THAT SAME OCTOBER, as American escort ships and crews learned to detect (and, if able, kill) U-boat aggressors, a Canadian troop convoy, two merchant convoys bound for Halifax, and an eastbound merchant convoy designated SC-48 crowded the North Atlantic.

Because of its pace, the *SC* in SC-48 might have meant "slow convoy." SC-48's fifty merchants averaged between five and seven knots, well below the nine-knot minimum required to join a "fast convoy." But *SC* referred to the convoy's assembly/departure point: Sydney (*S*) on Cape Breton (*C*), Nova Scotia.[1] (*HX*-designated "fast convoys" originated in Halifax, two hundred miles down the coast.) On October 15, SC-48 (covered on its first leg by four Canadian escorts) was ten days out from Sydney when it crossed paths with *Korvettenkapitän* (Lieutenant Commander) Karl Thurmann's *U-553*.[2]

U-553 was eight days out from St. Nazaire, one of the Atlantic ports converted for U-boat use after Germany overran France. Though smaller and more limited in range than other U-boat models, the Type VIICs were nonetheless considered U-boat workhorses. They were fast and highly maneuverable on the surface, easily handled and elusive below. They presented low silhouettes for night surface attacks and were relatively quick (about thirty seconds) to dive.[3]

Adm. Karl Dönitz, the austere, reedy-voiced fifty-two-year-old commander of Kriegsmarine submarines (Befehlshaber der Unterseeboote, BdU for short), considered the Type VIICs ideal for *Rudeltaktik*—"pack tactics." Described by author Jonathan Dimbleby as a man of "clear views but narrow horizons," Dönitz saw pack tactics as the answer to escorted convoys.[4] "A U-boat attacking a convoy on the surface and under cover of darkness," he concluded, "stood very good prospects for success. . . . The greater the number of U-boats . . . the more favourable . . . the opportunities."[5]

Dönitz had experimented with *Rudeltaktik* during manuevers in 1936 and briefly in combat during the first month of the war, but it was well into 1940 before enough U-boats were available to make *Rudeltaktik* practicable. Dönitz once considered delegating pack control to on-scene "command submarines." But realizing that their skippers would "only get caught up in the action," BdU chose instead to coordinate *Rudeltaktik* from headquarters in Lorient, France.

Centralized this way, *Rudeltaktik* depended on fast and reliable long-range, wireless radio and message transmissions that were concise, actionable, and safe from prying ears. To meet these needs, experts from B-Dienst, the Kriegsmarine cryptographic service, had supplied BdU with an ingenious cipher system. Its foundation was the Enigma, a portable, electric-powered typewriter-like machine.

Enigma machines encoded messages by scrambling keystrokes to produce text that seemed random. Three parallel rotors—narrow wheels or disks with letters stamped along their rims—inserted into Enigma could generate billions of possible letter combinations. Each time a keyboard letter was pressed, a rotor turned incrementally ("stepped") and an electrical current would illuminate a different letter on a lamp board. Once a rotor rotated fully, the adjacent rotor would begin stepping. This arrangement produced unpredictable sequences of letters. Only identically configured Enigma machines could unscramble the result.

A built-in switchboard—called a "*stecker*"—added further complications. The stecker used connecting wires to substitute one letter for another. (The letter *A* might be set to produce *G*, and so forth.)

Each day, Enigma operators used printed "key lists" specifying which rotors to use, how to arrange them inside the machine (left, center, or right), and how to cross-connect the stecker wires. With key-list instructions followed precisely, Enigmas were ready to send and receive that day's message traffic.

While all German military branches used Enigma, Kriegsmarine messaging was considerably more complex and secure. For example, the Kriegsmarine employed different codes (lexicons substituting coded words, letter groups, or numbers for plain text), depending on the types of vessels and where they operated. Each day, while operators in other branches chose three rotors from a collection of five, Kriegsmarine operators chose three from a possible eight. Kriegsmarine rotor setting variations were virtually infinite.[6]

For its part, B-Dienst also exploited lapses in Allied code security. In fact, its ability to crack Allied convoy codes not only gave Dönitz an advantage but heightened his confidence in Enigma security. After all, if Enigma wasn't secure, the British would have learned about their own security lapses and responded accordingly.[7]

⌖

A *Rudeltaktik* operation began when U-boats established a patrol line athwart anticipated convoy routes. Dönitz used a grid of "attack squares" assigned to individual U-boats.[8] Once a U-boat skipper sighted a convoy (as *U-553*'s Thurmann sighted SC-48 in the early hours of October 15, 1941), he would radio its size, composition, speed, and direction.

In rare instances, and only with Dönitz's explicit permission, the spotting U-boat might attack immediately. Most often, her skipper would instead shadow the quarry while a "pack" gathered. Once it assembled, tactical control passed from BdU to individual U-boat commanders. They were then free to pounce—usually at night, on the surface, and from all points of the compass.

Thurmann was on his third war cruise. His crew was a tightly interdependent fifty-man team of seamen, technicians, and weapons specialists. By and large they were young volunteers, many from Germany's coastal regions or industrial centers. Most had received eight years' primary education supplemented by apprenticeships and technical schooling.[9]

BdU's younger deputy, Hans-Georg von Friedeburg, selected, trained, and organized U-boat sailors. But it was Dönitz—"*Der Löwe*" (the Lion)—who stamped the U-boat arm with an enduring sense of comradeship. Despite his limitations, the Lion was a good leader with a special affinity for dealing with young officers. He conceived of each U-boat as a community bound by fate, in which even one man's failure risked the lives of everyone.[10] This sense of "all for one, one for all" inspired them, he believed, to endure, even celebrate a U-boat's confinement, privation, stultifying routines, and terrifying ordeals under fire.

Yet while Dönitz considered crew members of every rank—officer, noncommissioned officer, and seaman—as essential, he believed the U-boat's soul was her commanding officer (*kommandant*). He was the vessel's master of seamanship, battle tactics, marksmanship, split-second decision-making, and leadership. He was always visible, expected to master any situation, obliged to calm all his crew's fears while suppressing his own.

At age thirty-two, Thurmann, as a naval officer, represented a prized, carefully groomed cohort. Each year, from the 1920s through the mid-1930s, the German navy (the Reichsmarine until 1935, thereafter the Kriegsmarine) screened potential officer cadets. In 1926, for example, six thousand prospects competed for just 124 slots. To earn a spot, cadets passed grueling intellectual, physical, and psychological tests. One "test of courage" was to hold an iron bar aloft as a painful electric current coursed through it.[11]

Once accepted, cadets joined a class (later denoted a "Crew") designated by the year selected. Thurmann, for example, was part of Crew 28. Crew membership forged indelible bonds, replete with shared experiences and embarrassments, values, special nicknames, caricatures, and inside jokes.

Cadet preparation was intense and varied, lasting about four and a half years, much of it at sea. Until the mid-1930s, however, exposure to submarines was scant. In 1937, for example, of Crew 35's 325 graduates, none were yet in the submarine branch, while half were detailed to naval aviation.[12]

After Hitler's rise to power and the rapid expansion of all service branches, officer selection accelerated, while its rigors evolved. In that sense, Thurmann's Crew 28 represented a fading ideal. As war progressed and the U-boat fleet expanded, qualifying for command became less about painstaking training and education and more about bottom-up, hands-on experience—intense, but often brief. Dönitz's preference for "older," seasoned *kommandanten* would phase out, replaced by more reliance on youth.[13]

⊕

With BdU's permission, Thurmann maneuvered *U-553* to attack SC-48. Thurmann's first torpedo shots missed, but he eventually sank two ships and possibly a third. Then he withdrew, surfaced, transmitted a position report, and began shadowing. Meanwhile, Dönitz ordered nine other U-boats to home in on 553's radio beacon.

Several pack members reached SC-48 that night. One was *Kapitänleutnant* Lt. Joachim Preuss' *U-568*, another Type VIIC from St. Nazaire. Before being driven off by a Flower-class corvette, Preuss, a twenty-seven-year-old from Crew 33, managed to sink a six-thousand-ton British merchant steamer.

With SC-48 clearly in the grip of a wolf pack, Allied help came in the form of escorts from Reykjavik plus several from other convoys not yet endangered. Reinforcements arrived before sunset on October 16. First on-scene were four U.S. Navy destroyers. British and Free French destroyers and corvettes brought the total to eighteen escorts, perhaps the strongest protection yet afforded a North Atlantic convoy—though not the most effective.

As senior officer escorts (SOE), U.S. Navy captain Leo H. Thebaud assumed tactical command. Thebaud, stationed on board *Gleaves*-class destroyer *Plunkett*, was a fifty-one-year-old destroyer veteran with Great War convoy escort experience. But these circumstances were new to him. America was not officially at war. What if he sank a U-boat and picked up survivors? Would they become POWs or merely seamen in distress?

Thebaud also had concerns about his American destroyers and skippers. Only one of the destroyers had ever fired her big guns, others not even their machine guns. Some skippers had considerable seniority but little destroyer experience. Their ship handling, Thebaud wrote later, was "far from an inspiration." The skippers of these "beautiful ships" were pitting their "ignorance and lack of skill against enemy submarines experienced from two years of war."[14]

The Canadian escorts—and the British and French escorts en route—would bolster Thebaud's capabilities but also add confusion. They used different tactics, signals, and, sometimes, languages.

To keep U-boats from slipping in amidst the merchants, Thebaud kept escorts close to the convoy's perimeter. But this involved trade-offs, particularly at night. U-boats could lurk outside sonar range, firing torpedoes with impunity while getting a head start if they had to flee escorts. Most of Thebaud's units lacked even rudimentary radar, relying instead on illumination projectiles—star shells—to locate threats. Illumination often benefitted the U-boats more than the convoy.

Just after 10 p.m. on October 16, Thurmann moved in again. Approaching on the surface, he launched a three-torpedo spread that sank a Norwegian freighter. Other merchants responded with red flares, while escorts shot star shells into what one sailor called "as black a night as I've ever seen." Convinced the attacker lay off to port, Thebaud ordered American destroyer *Kearny* to respond.[15]

Kearny was a member of the modern 1,630-ton *Gleaves* class built by Federal Shipbuilding in Kearny, New Jersey (Robert Maher's hometown). Her skipper, short, stocky, forty-two-year-old Lt. Cdr. Anthony L. Danis, ran a well-drilled ship. Having survived two U.S. Navy dirigible mishaps early in his career, Danis was no stranger to peril.[16] But he worried that Thebaud kept escorts in too close. Flares and star shells blinded lookouts and helped U-boats find targets.[17]

Responding to the SOE's order, Danis turned *Kearny* to port, ranged out into the darkness, and dropped a single "nuisance" depth charge. After Danis brought his ship back to station, the night went still, and SC-48 plodded on.

But not for long.

Within a half-hour, a tanker erupted in flames three hundred feet high. And just two minutes later, a second merchant nearby exploded with a deep, leaden thud. Lookouts on *Plunkett* spotted a vessel low in the water about a mile off. The destroyer's torpedo tubes swung out, but the suspect turned out to be one of the corvettes.

Another short respite followed. Escorts quit scurrying. The sky went black. Crews secured from GQ. Even Danis retreated to his cabin but soon, unable to relax, returned to the bridge. Just then, two more ships exploded off *Kearny*'s starboard quarter. Called back to GQ, sailors, fumbling with helmets and life jackets, stumbled across lurching decks as *Kearny* swung off to port.

Eyes scanned the darkness but found nothing.

The night's biggest cataclysm—the torpedoing of another Norwegian tanker loaded with aviation gasoline—erupted at midnight. As described by the *kommandant* who fired the single torpedo: "A colossal flame leapt from the convoy . . . accompanied by a roaring . . . like an express train. The great column of fire . . . seemed almost to reach the cloud base. The whole convoy was lit up by its brilliance."[18]

Certain the attacking U-boat lay off his port quarter, Anthony Danis once more swung *Kearny* to port, dropped a depth charge, then looped back to station. As he did, however, a Canadian corvette came steaming down the convoy's port side, its skipper intent on rescuing tanker survivors. Spotting this hazard from the port bridge wing, Danis reacted promptly and instinctively: "All engines back full, emergency!"

The corvette passed clear, and *Kearny* slowed to a dead stop.

At this same moment, Joachim Preuss was squaring his sights on the "hostile" destroyer silhouetted by the convoy's flames. *U-568* unleashed three torpedoes.

Back on *Kearny*, Danis was set to order speed resumed when a starboard lookout shouted a warning. Danis reached the starboard bridge wing just in time to spot three white wakes. He shouted helm orders, then waited.

One of the iridescent trails passed just ahead of the bow, a second just behind the fantail. But the third struck squarely amidships. There came a bump below the waterline. Then a shudder as the torpedo penetrated *Kearny*'s five-eighths-inch-thick tempered-steel hull plates.

Finally, a devastating explosion.

The blast ripped out the side of a fire room, smashing lines and pipes and releasing gusts of steam that scalded living and dead. The seven firemen and water tenders in number 1 fire room died instantly.

Spreading upward, the force ruptured the starboard side of the main deck, heaving four sailors overboard. Higher up, *Kearny*'s deckhouse was crumpled, the starboard bridge wing torn away, the gun director stove in, the starboard whaleboat shattered, and the forward stack wrenched backwards.

Electrical power and radio communications were gone. Damage to the bridge destroyed the compass and severed linkages to engines and steering control. *Kearny* lost all headway. Her emergency siren, triggered by the backward lurch of the forward stack, screeched distress.

Though uninjured, Danis could do little except rally survivors on the bridge. "With the siren screaming and steam escaping," recalled Ens. Henry Lyman, "you couldn't hear yourself think." Lyman and two sailors tried to fire distress rockets. After two misfired, "we finally used a Very pistol."[19]

All might have been lost if not for *Kearny*'s sturdy design. The ship's reinforced bottom could withstand explosive shock, while its interior spaces were extensively compartmentalized to localize flooding. *Kearny* also boasted two entirely independent sets of engine rooms and fire rooms, which enhanced propulsion resilience.

Moreover, despite Captain Thebaud's worries about losing "beautiful ships" to "ignorance and lack of skill," *Kearny* possessed human resilience as well.

The fight to save *Kearny* was won in the forward engine room. Lt. Robert J. Esslinger, *Kearny*'s thirty-three-year-old chief engineer, and Aucie McDaniel, her forty-two-year-old chief machinist's mate, quickly took matters in hand. They directed damage control parties first to shore up the sagging bulkhead leading to the smashed number 1 fire room, then to plug leaks along the seams of the buckled door.

With one boiler in number 2 fire room lit and the other on standby, the black gang soon furnished steam to the port engine. Repair parties put out electrical fires, cauterized ruptured fuel lines, ran emergency cables, removed wreckage, and repositioned heavy gear to ease strain on *Kearny*'s starboard side.

Meanwhile, Alfred J. Booth, a quartermaster from northeast Pennsylvania, shifted emergency steering to manual control, enabling Harold E. McDougal, a chief quartermaster from Seattle, to regain steering at secondary control. Absent a compass, McDougal used the ship's flapping commissioning pennant as a wind sock.

With radio communications restored, Danis updated Thebaud. SOE ordered him to break off and head for Reykjavik. Next morning, *Kearny*'s speed was up to ten knots; that afternoon Danis rendezvoused with Jack Frost's *Greer*. The two ships reached Rekjavik Harbor on the morning of October 19.[20]

"She's one of our newest and best," Jack Frost boasted to a newspaper reporter as the two sized up *Kearny*'s damage. "She's got more horsepower under her hatches than a battleship and she's armed to the hilt. These new destroyers are practically light cruisers." The reporter asked *Greer*'s skipper how well his own "over-age" ship could withstand such a blast. "The skipper laughingly remarked that [his] old destroyer hull would 'keep out the larger fish.'"[21]

Kearny's hull had been sliced two-thirds of the way across. But her main deck plating, the source, in conjunction with the keel, of the ship's longitudinal strength, held, keeping her upright, holding her trim, throughout the entire ordeal.[22]

Sadly, the four *Kearny* sailors thrown overboard were never found. Combined with the seven fire room fatalities, this meant eleven sailors killed and twenty-two wounded—the first U.S. Navy casualties in the Battle of the Atlantic.[23]

Kearny's lost lives enraged politicians and constituents. Cries rang out for reprisals and the removal of remaining strictures in America's Neutrality Act. "Intervention need not be expressed in a declaration of war," counseled a more measured editorial in the *Chattanooga Daily Times* in Tennessee. "But if Congress does not act speedily to throw our sea resources in the struggle, we shall continue to suffer the disadvantages that the *Kearny* incident emphasizes."[24]

The *Kearny* incident also offered a bully pulpit to FDR as he navigated the shoals between war and peace. During an October 27 Navy Day address, FDR drove home his message. "America had been attacked. . . . The shooting has started, and history has recorded who has fired the first shot[;] . . . we do not propose to take this lying down. . . . Our navy is ready for action."[25]

8 | HOUSE, TOMB, AND SCHOOL

NEW WEAPONRY TECHNOLOGIES increasingly impacted the Battle of the Atlantic, but for the present, locating and avoiding U-boats came first. This priority put immense pressure on ships at sea. But just as thousands of people on the ground played vital roles in the Battle of Britain, so thousands ashore strove to outwit and evade Dönitz's U-boats.

Countering the work of Dönitz's French headquarters, for example, was the operations center of the Royal Navy's Western Approaches Command (WAC). Previously located at Plymouth, along the English Channel, WAC had relocated to Liverpool, to be both clear of German aircraft and closer to action in the Atlantic.

Derby House, a block of nondescript buildings near the Mersey River, was WAC's nerve center. Its boss was sixty-one-year-old Adm. Sir Percy Noble, now nearing fifty years in uniform. Noble combined a commanding presence with elegance (he was called "the best-dressed Admiral in the service"), charm, affability and an even temper—vital in times of high stress, enormous losses, and meager resources.[1]

From a glass-fronted office, Noble looked out on a massive table-mounted situation map displaying the latest positions of transatlantic convoys and the U-boats threatening them. Though the map and a companion wall chart were updated round the clock, "fixes" on U-boats were approximations, and their projected intentions were estimations.[2]

In this setting of imprecision and guesswork, Sir Percy made life-and-death decisions on how to best deploy warships under his command. To inject more confidence into his decisions, he looked to the Royal Navy Intelligence Division.

Much maligned during and after the Great War, NID saw its fortune improve dramatically in December 1938, when Rear Adm. John Godfrey took charge.[3] One key underling described Godfrey (whose respect for science and support of Anglo-American collaboration helped facilitate Sir Henry Tizard's 1941 mission) as both an "original thinker" and a "practical . . . seaman."[4] Said another:[5]* "Like the driver of a sports car . . . he saw no danger or discourtesy in acceleration."

NID comprised two thousand men and women, but the thirty-six assigned to NID's Operational Intelligence Centre (OIC) were chiefly responsible for tracking enemy ship movements. Information from field agents, code breakers, reconnaissance flights, and signals intelligence (SIGINT) sources flowed into OIC's four subsections, two of which, the D/F (direction finding) Plotting and the Submarine Tracking Room ("the Room"), were arguably the most critical.

Harnessing radio waves revolutionized OIC's job. Wireless radio, for example, afforded two-way global communication with Royal Navy ships. Meanwhile, RDF (radio direction finding) stations ringing North Atlantic seacoasts could detect and plot the bearings of radio transmissions from enemy ships.

Wartime exigencies prompted Godfrey to infuse NID with talent from unusual sources—law, history, finance, journalism, even art. And, as Royal Navy regulars left NID for combat commands, reservists took key roles. "Civilians in uniform" often invigorated operational intelligence. Unburdened by military rigidity, they could, as one outside observer quipped, "resist . . . cooking raw intelligence to make their masters' favourite dishes."[6]

*Ian Fleming, Godfrey's personal assistant, later reimagined Godfrey as "M," the Secret Intelligence Service Head in James Bond spy thrillers. ("Secret Agents, Secret Armies: Who Was the Real James Bond?" The National WWII Museum | New Orleans, May 21, 2020, https://www.nationalww2museum.org/war/articles/Ian-fleming-royal-naval-intelligence-department [accessed October 12, 2020])

One example was thirty-seven-year-old Rodger Winn, a successful London barrister educated at Cambridge, Harvard, and Yale. Winn had, like Sir Henry Tizard, once dreamed of being a sailor. But childhood poliomyelitis left Winn short in stature, with a twisted back and pronounced limp. He'd tried to volunteer for the Royal Navy but was deemed physically unfit even for the reserves. Instead, Winn became a civilian volunteer, expecting his legal and German-language skills would be employed interrogating POWs. But these very same skills found another, more pressing use: sifting through raw intelligence, much of it in German. Winn was instead assigned to the Room, then headed by an old-school RN captain named Ernest Thring.[7]

Winn proved an adroit amateur who learned quickly. However, during the first twelve months of the war, neither D/F Plotting nor Submarine Tracking could provide much actionable information. Because most German U-boats still operated independently, D/F Plotting simply couldn't intercept enough radio transmissions and plot enough bearings to pinpoint U-boats reliably. For its part, without definitive U-boat fixes, Submarine Tracking couldn't advise the Trade Division on how to reroute convoys.

By September 1940, however, with U-boat wolfpack tactics becoming common, Submarine Tracking's effectiveness improved. For his part, Winn, though still a civilian, was turning into a confident, outspoken advocate for anticipating enemy moves and responding accordingly.

Thring, though no slouch, was skeptical of his pathbreaking underling. For now, Winn lacked authority to apply forecasting, but he cultivated influential and like-minded advocates in the Royal Navy. In January 1941, with their support, Winn received a reserve commission and displaced Thring.

The Submarine Tracking Room's stature steadily climbed under Commander Winn's leadership. By summer 1941, NID's OIC war room, squeezed into a low-ceilinged concrete bunker known to its occupants as "Lenin's Tomb," was considered especially indispensable to safeguarding the convoy lifeline.[8]

It became an ever-expanding repository of vital U-boat information: the speed, endurance, and operating characteristics of each type; the backgrounds, personalities, and quirks of individual U-boat commanders; the details of favored patrol dispositions; even the meaning of signals related to sightings, positions, and weather conditions.

More than a repository, the Room was also a hive of activity. SIGINT supplied OIC trackers with enough bearings to plot lines that (for the benefit of Derby House) converged on actual U-boat locations. "Traffic analysis," evaluating patterns of transmissions to and from specific enemy radios, also helped—revealing the presence of a German resupply vessel, for example, or identifying the lead U-boat in a wolfpack.

Raw electronic data was not all. POW interrogations might produce misleading information, but summaries of them could confirm or discount other information. The same was true of aerial reconnaissance photos and clandestine spy reports.

The Room's hub was a square table, eight feet to a side, across which sprawled a chart of the North Atlantic peppered with tiny colored pins—red pins for firm fixes, white for visual sightings, blue for the convergences of radar and D/F data points. Winn and his deputy Patrick Beesly, a reservist in his late twenties, worked long hours in the smoke-filled dungeon. Whenever Winn found it difficult to stand unaided, he locked shoulders, arms, and fists and pinioned them to the tabletop.

With outward calm, Winn and Beesly eyed pin movements, calculated distances, computed speeds. Always mindful of air-cover boundaries—red arcs painted across stretches of ocean—the two also monitored wall graphs depicting the peaks and valleys of merchant ship construction, merchant ship losses, and U-boat destruction.

While accustomed to treating organizational superiors with deference, Winn never shied from expressing his convictions. Whenever challenged, he countered with supporting data: teleprinter output, telegrams, cables, telephone messages, and letters. And, though Winn drove staff relentlessly and rebuked mistakes harshly, he treated colleagues as individuals and professionals, regardless of pecking order.

Periodically, one piece of Lenin's Tomb equipment clattered insistently to life. It was a teleprinter hardwired to Bletchley Park (BP), a Victorian-era estate roughly fifty miles from London. BP housed the headquarters of Britain's Government Code and Cypher School (GC&CS). GC&CS supplied top secret "special intelligence" that could heighten Lenin's Tomb and Derby House effectiveness. Perhaps even tip the balance in the Atlantic.

German cryptologists confidently assumed Enigma ciphering to be unbreakable, but that didn't keep adversaries from trying. During the 1930s, for example, France and Poland collaborated to crack Enigma.

While French agents ferreted out crucial information on Enigma internal wiring and rotor settings, Polish scientists and mathematicians concentrated on high-level cryptanalytic research. After a Polish mathematician finally figured out the wiring for both the Enigma machine and its rotors, the Poles fully replicated a German Enigma. A big step, but German rotor settings still needed to be determined.

To accomplish this, the Poles tried to use "indicators" embedded in each Enigma message. Some settings had to be sent "in the clear" to give receiving operators a place to start. One German code clerk, for example, repeatedly used his girlfriend's name, Cillie. Such easily guessed settings soon became known as "Cillies."[9]

Even when shortcuts succeeded, code breakers inevitably "went blind" whenever Germans tweaked the system. To counter this, a Polish scientist devised an electromechanical machine that could work systematically through all possible rotor settings. The device, which resembled the guts of multiple Enigmas wired together, was called a "Bomba," supposedly because of the ticking noise it made.* The Bomba couldn't decode transmissions, but it could eliminate many rotor-setting combinations.

Bomba use, combined with code-breaking tricks, worked well enough until 1938, when the Germans turned the tables. Enigma code clerks continued using three rotors at a time but now chose three from a set of five.

On July 25, 1939, with Poland soon to be invaded, Polish, French, and British representatives met near Warsaw. At first the British were skeptical. But once the Poles presented their guests with Enigma replicates, doubt crumbled. In the end—and with little choice—the Poles turned over to them everything in their possession.[10] ("Bomba" now became "Bombe.")

---

*Other sources thought it derived from an ice-cream confection enjoyed by Polish cryptographers.

To master Enigma, Britain assembled a team of academics, linguists, and cipher experts. Alan Turing and Gordon Welchman, two Cambridge University mathematicians, stood out. Mobilized without uniform or ceremony, the young (average age twenty-three) Bletchley recruits continued their tweedy, pipe-smoking ways in a setting redolent of British elitism. BP operated round the clock in eight-hour shifts. Meticulous former schoolmasters proved ideal as watch supervisors.[11]

At first, BP's team knew only a few basics. Germans communicated in codes and ciphers tapped out using Morse Code. Encoded messages were sent by wireless radio—a means simultaneously fast and ripe for interception.

Once familiar with prior achievements, Turing and Welchman began thinking of better and quicker ways to solve "three-rotor" Enigma. Early on, Turing envisioned a machine that would identify "cribs"—text that cryptanalysts assumed would show up in a message. Turing's Bombe would look for rotor settings that allowed enciphered text to match cribs. Welchman, for his part, devised a means to defeat the stecker.*

Agnus Dei† (aka "Agnes"), the first British Bombe, built by British Tabulating Machine Company (BTM), reached Bletchley on March 14, 1940. Weighing a ton, standing over six and a half feet tall, and consisting of thirty-six three-rotors sets, Agnes was essentially an electromechanical finding aid. Guided by cribs, Agnes' "runs" could test millions of mathematical possibilities for the settings of three-rotor Enigmas.[12]

Setting up these runs was time-consuming work for the enlisted WRENS (Women's Royal Naval Service) ultimately assigned to do it. And though the hot, clattering, smelly, oil-spraying machines worked round the clock, demands for access vastly outstripped Bombe availability.

Even before Agnes arrived, breaks had already been achieved in German air force (Luftwaffe) and army (Heer) Enigma systems. Their code clerks tended to be lax about communications security. (The mistakes, once called Cillies,

*GC&CS's code-breaking efforts are dramatized in the 2014 film *Imitation Game*.

†The "Lamb of God," a designation of Jesus Christ in Christian liturgical usage.

were now "Sillies.")[13] What's more, Luftwaffe traffic provided "depth"—enough messages with identical rotor settings that code breakers could make better guesses.

Kriegsmarine Enigma, however, proved a much tougher nut. Its code clerks chose three rotors from sets of eight, not five, and BP didn't know the wiring of the other three. Two U-boat sinkings—one off Scotland in February 1941, another in the North Atlantic three months later—eventually yielded these three rotors. Still, much of Enigma's secrecy lay embedded in printed code books that expired monthly. Until up-to-date code books could be "pinched," Enigma's opacity would persist.

The long-awaited breakthrough came on May 9, 1941, when a British destroyer forced *U-110* to the surface. Before it sank, and unknown to BdU, a British boarding party retrieved up-to-date Enigma gear, signal books, and ciphering instructions.[14]

For now, BP had it all. Once naval signals were decrypted and translated into English, the messages (sometimes thousands each day) went to Lenin's Tomb by teleprinter. A lot might be chatter, but receiving it in "real time" helped Rodger Winn more reliably pinpoint U-boats and more presciently anticipate their moves.

But OIC also had to be careful not to overreach. Stamping Enigma-derived information "Top Secret Ultra," the British exercised care not to arouse German suspicions. There was particular caution about revealing too much to the Americans.

As early as December 1940, Britain and America had agreed to share cryptology breakthroughs. But a February 1941 exchange visit to Britain raised misgivings. The U.S. Navy's two representatives were junior officers lacking depth in cryptology; the U.S. Army's pair were civilian code breakers hastily promoted to high military rank. The Army did deliver a Purple Machine, a time-tested device used to crack Japanese diplomatic messages, but the Yanks learned few specifics on Bletchley's achievements.[15]

While the Admiralty maximized operational intelligence by establishing a centralized OIC, the U.S. Navy continued to balkanize. British observers were "shocked" by "inefficiency and irrelevance" in the Office of Naval Intelligence (ONI).

This assessment may have contributed to Admiralty reticence that February—though, in truth, BP progress on Kriegsmarine Enigma was still skimpy. Whatever the circumstances, NID's behavior apparently irked U.S. Navy commander Laurance Safford head of OP-20-G (Operations Branch 20, Communications Subsection G), the Americans' GC&CS counterpart. Safford decided to solve Kriegsmarine Enigma on his own. Despite Safford's determination, OP-20-G staff attacked Enigma the hard way, trying to divine its inner workings without access to either an Enigma machine or examples of decrypted messages.

In August 1941, just before the Tizard Mission, Royal Navy commander Alastair G. Denniston, the congenial sixty-three-year-old Scot who then headed Bletchley, visited OP-20-G, intent on dissuading Safford from having ONI attack Enigma by itself. Denniston apparently got a cold shoulder, and Safford's underlings soldiered on.

9 | WHAT WERE THEIR NAMES?

AIDED BY BLETCHLEY, Rodger Winn's Submarine Tracking Room orchestrated "evasive routing": altering convoy routes to avoid U-boats. Even if imminent threats couldn't be dodged, endangered convoys might still be reinforced. Winn became so adept that higher-ups routinely rubber-stamped his recommendations.

Though not directly sharing, the Admiralty, using the Royal Canadian Navy (RCN) as conduit, did update the U.S. Navy on U-boat positions. As cover, it claimed the information had been gleaned by other means.

Washington first began receiving updates "as estimated by Admiralty" in late August 1941. In effect, the U.S. Navy benefitted from Ultra months before knowing its full details.[1]

Of course, "crystal-balling" had limits. On October 9, for example, four days after Convoy SC-48 left Nova Scotia, the Room realized that seven German U-boats were gathering at the "CHOP" (change of operational control) line, where Canadian, American, and British escorts rendezvoused. The Room promptly recommended rerouting south. SC-48 complied, only to cross paths with Karl Thurmann's *U-553*.

Even as SC-48 escorts battled U-boats, planners devised evasive routing for HX-156: forty-four merchants departing Argentia on October 23. HX-156 would first steam 1,900 miles due east, then northeast for six hundred miles to reach MOMP (the CHOP line). From MOMP, HX-156 and its British escorts need only turn slightly southeast for the final 480-mile leg to safety. The path, the Room believed, should keep HX-156 clear of menace.

At about 3 a.m. on October 31, 1941, *Kapitänleutnant* Erich Topp peered into the darkness from the bridge of *U-552*. Six days out of St. Nazaire, *U-552* had just reached its assigned grid on a patrol line extending southeast from Greenland.

One of Topp's lookouts spotted oncoming ships—an eastbound convoy. Following protocol, Topp radioed the sighting coordinates to Dönitz's forward command post in Kerneval, France, where, much like the Admiralty's Submarine Tracking Room, wall-mounted maps, charts, diagrams, pins, and flags tracked the current situation in the Atlantic.

While certain Enigma remained secure, Kerneval staff knew the British monitored U-boat radio transmissions. They debated what Dönitz called "appreciations"—their version of what Rodger Winn called "useful fictions." Would the enemy reroute convoys on the basis of radio intercepts? Or would convoys stick to planned routes, expecting that BdU would shift U-boats?

Topp, then twenty-seven and a member of Crew 34, had shown early promise. In August 1940, while commanding *U-57*, one of Germany's small prewar Type II U-boats (nicknamed *Nordsee Enten*—"North Sea ducks"), Topp sank three ships for 12,000 tons, only to have his boat accidently rammed by a Norwegian steamer.[2] The near calamity (*U-57* was salvaged and eventually returned to service) behind him, Topp took command of *U-552* that December. Topp earned *U-552* its first success in March, sinking a 12,000-ton British tanker. By mid-September 1941, combined sinkings soared to at least eighteen ships, well over 100,000 tons.

Five American destroyers met up with HX-156 on October 24. Responsible for protecting the merchants all the way to MOMP, U.S. Navy commander Richard E. Webb stationed two of his three new radar-equipped tin cans off the convoy's port and starboard bows.

The third, *Niblack*, patrolled astern, while four-stackers *Reuben James* and *Tarbell* took the port and starboard flanks, respectively. "The *Rube*" was first commissioned in 1920.[3] After a March 1939 overhaul, she joined the Neutrality Patrol but only seven months later ran aground off the north coast of Cuba. In April 1941, after completing drydock repairs, *Rube* received a new commanding officer (CO), Lt. Cdr. Heywood L. "Tex" Edwards, a 1926 Naval Academy graduate and 1928 Olympic wrestler.[4]

Up until Halloween, a full week out and just shy of MOMP, HX-156 enjoyed generally uneventful sailing. Aware of SC-48's plight, escort crews were on edge. But only two suspected targets were detected: the first on October 25, the second four days later. In each case, nothing more than fish.

Steaming at nine knots, the ships of HX-156's eight columns had mostly held station, though merchants (as usual) made too much smoke. The newer destroyers patrolled vigorously, but the four-stackers couldn't—not if they hoped to conserve fuel and stick with the convoy.

Throughout the passage, the Room used BP decrypts to gauge U-boat movements. On October 28, after detecting five submarines moving west on a collision course, the Admiralty diverted HX-156 southward. That same day, though, RDF stations ashore pinpointed U-boat broadcasts in the convoy's vicinity. Despite Winn's best efforts, HX-156 faced imminent attack.

Tarbell, despite its age, boasted a piece of new gear: an onboard direction-finding (D/F) set. At roughly 5 a.m. on October 31, the set picked up a U-boat radio transmission off the convoy's port quarter. *Reuben James*, nearest to the suspected position, set off to investigate.

Rube's Edwards, still clad in a bathrobe, stepped from his emergency cabin onto the bridge. He ordered the OOD, James M. Belden, to come left. A yeoman, meanwhile, began "pinging" the bridge sound gear to pick up the contact.

As Edwards went below to dress, *Rube*'s helmsman, twenty-year-old Fireman Parmie G. Appleton, heard someone summon Lt. Benjamin Ghetzler, *Rube*'s executive officer (XO). Belden, by Appleton's account, was then writing up a radio report and asked the time. Appleton checked a bulkhead clock—"0549."[5]

In Erich Topp's estimate, *U-552* had been stalking its prey for two and a half hours. Through early morning overcast a lookout spotted the telltale stacks of an old destroyer. Topp decided that first light was too near to steer clear and make a new approach. Better to make sure of at least one target.

U-552 launched two torpedoes from a thousand yards off the destroyer's port beam. The target was then swinging to port, puffs of black smoke rising from its stacks. The first torpedo struck its port side, just forward of the first funnel and below the bridge.

In what Topp described as a horrible explosion, members of the destroyer's crew flew skyward like flecks of dust.

Unlike the *Gleaves*-class *Kearny*, the *Clemson*-class *Reuben James*, even with recent repairs to its hull, was not designed to absorb and survive the German torpedo that smacked its port side. A triggering blast followed by another—perhaps the second torpedo, more likely *Rube*'s forward magazine—hurled more fire and debris skyward.

One of the "flecks of dust" Topp saw may have been Parmie Appleton. The first blast lifted Appleton off his feet, slammed him skull-first into the overhead, and caromed him off the after bulkhead. No sooner had Appleton regained his feet and grabbed the wheel than the second, bigger explosion propelled him through the top of the wheelhouse, which seemed to open "like the petals of a flower." Landing in the water near the bow, Appleton found himself being sucked downward.[6]

Meanwhile, Pittsburgh native William Bergstresser, a thirty-five-year-old chief machinist's mate just off watch, felt the ship shake, shiver, and begin to sink.[7] In the after engine room, Fred Zapasnik, a shipfitter first class from New Castle, Pennsylvania, was knocked off his feet. Lights went out; when Zapasnik tried to reach the main deck, a cascade of water pushed him back.[8]

Still farther aft, Lawrence Sills, a ship's baker from Jackson, Mississippi; Roy V. Bush, a fireman second class from Ashtabula, Ohio; Fireman Third Class Leland E. Tyger, Bush's buddy from Detroit;[9] and Danny Del Grosso, a seaman from Galeton, Pennsylvania[10]—all fell from their bunks. Bent lockers lay askew. Toppled bunks and mattresses crowded a narrow passageway. The men climbed the ladder to the ship's stern, Sills wearing just underclothes and a life belt.[11]

It was still short of first light as survivors got topside. *Reuben James*' after three stacks were completely gone. The fourth still stood, but orange flames crackled high around it. Thick curls of smoke streamed aft. *James*' bridge—the ship's nerve center—had vanished. What remained afloat couldn't last long.

James carried two lifeboats, but one was partly demolished and the other, the captain's gig, was impossible to lower. Bergstresser, taking charge, ordered balsa life rafts thrown overboard. One machinist's mate, removing his shoes to test the water, pronounced it cold. Lawrence Sills saw a raft in the water off the port side. Then, noticing someone else cutting another loose, Sills ran over to help. Together, the two got it—and themselves—over the side.

With flames rushing aft and the fantail sinking, many now half-slid or jumped into the slimy water. Some, though, still hesitated. Bush and Tyger readied to jump for a raft directly astern but then saw *Rube*'s propellers spinning just below the surface. Afraid suction might pull the raft under, the pair instead jumped over the side.

Like Fred Zapasnik, Bill Appleton had escaped the after engine room. But he feared that older brother Parmie might have been on the bridge. The two Mississippi natives had enlisted together just that February, Parmie at age twenty, Bill at only sixteen. Bill looked for his big brother as long as he dared, then entered the water alone.[12]

Brent N. Bridges, meanwhile, a twenty-year-old radioman from Garfield, Utah, wore his dungarees over the side. One pocket contained $120, but he soon kicked the pants off to make headway through the jelly-thick oil.[13]

Fireman Second Class Robert Carr swam to a raft about seventy feet away, joining men clinging to its sides. All were shivering and black with oil. Some vomited oil and saltwater.[14]

Danny Del Grosso didn't feel cold as he swam away, thinking maybe the oil scum warmed the water. More likely he was too numb to feel. Del Grosso reached a raft but couldn't climb up—his body was too slick. Someone finally pulled him on board.

Fred Zapasnik reached a raft already crowded with men, so he and others gripped ropes dangling over the side. Some prayed aloud, others, wounded, screamed. Fireman Les Richardson from Center, Alabama, Zapasnik's closest shipmate, unable to stand the wailing, left the raft.[15]

Brent Bridges, still alone and about sixty feet from the ship, glanced over his shoulder. From his vantage, *James*' stern still loomed against the horizon. But moments later it upended and went down, a gurgle of sea its only marker.

With *Rube* now vanished, men on the rafts noticed lifeless bodies bobbing in the black swells. Some believed they heard screams from men trapped inside the hull.

Then, suddenly, depth charges that had been stowed ready for instant use exploded. There were two blasts, though some thought more. (Wrote Topp: "Wreck atomized by powerful detonation of her own depth charges.")[16]

One explosion spun Robert Carr's life raft like a top. He felt like he was swimming—only up in the air. Upon landing, Carr managed to climb back onto the raft—one of only a handful who did.

This (or the second) blast lifted Fred Zapasnik's raft clear from the water. Splashing down, Zapasnik got sucked down, losing all sense of position. Months before, Tex Edwards had ordered that all crewmen keep life preservers and belts close at hand. Many routinely ignored the edict, but Zapasnik, with a wife and two-year-old daughter in Boston, paid heed. Now his life jacket popped him back to the surface.

Lawrence Sills managed to cling to his raft through what to him was a first blast. Screaming and yelling became the prelude to a second. Afterwards, Sills lost his grip but soon found a floating ammunition box to cling to.

Men still on board rafts were now dazed, disoriented. Those in the water bled from mouths, noses, ears, rectums. It became hard to distinguish living from dead.

While two destroyers guarded the convoy, a third made a sonar sweep, and *Niblack* searched for survivors. Her sailors spotted rafts astern crowded with men and, bobbing farther out, what looked to be life-jacketed seals. *Niblack* backed cautiously through the area, as crewmen rigged cargo nets and heaved lifelines. Young sailors went down to the lead raft to help survivors up, while chiefs clung to the nets and tried to fasten lines around men in the water. Oil, lingering darkness, and the survivors' horrid condition prolonged the task.[17]

Roy Bush and Leland Tyger were rescued early. So was Bill Bergstresser. ("It would have had to be quick," he recalled. "But it didn't seem quick.")[18] And so, ironically, was Fred Zapasnik's friend Les Richards. Meanwhile, by the time rescuers hauled in Zapasnik, Sills, and Sims, all were too numb to grasp—never mind climb—the nets.

And, for his part, Water Tender First Class Lloyd Sims—who'd worn a life jacket only to have it ripped away by a depth charge blast—struggled almost four hours before being reeled in, barely alive.[19]

The rescue was nearly complete when, a little after 7 a.m., sonar reported a contact dead astern. Though three men were still in the water—one definitely dead, one possibly, a third semiconscious—*Niblack*'s CO rang up full speed. As the three bodies drifted astern, another destroyer dropped depth charges.

From *Reuben James*' crew, just forty-five sailors—and no officers—were saved. Uncannily, both Appleton brothers escaped the ocean's icy grip. And, despite initially being reported lost, so did Danny Del Grosso.

The disaster, so soon after the *Kearny* incident and so much worse, dominated the news back home. Said *The New York Times*: "Whatever the German motive . . . the attack upon the *Reuben James* drives home more forcefully than ever before the fact that Germany and the United States are pitted against each other in the Atlantic in a struggle for mastery of the seas. . . . The time has come to take off the shackles."[20] Despite the furor, America's resistance to intervention in Europe's war remained strong on Capitol Hill. Though FDR was still willing to wage war, *Reuben James*' loss brought him no closer to declaring it.

Months later, Depression-era Dust Bowl balladeers Woody Guthrie (himself a merchant mariner) and Pete Seeger, borrowing a traditional tune, mythologized ship and crew in "The Sinking of the *Reuben James*." Its haunting refrain, crafted by Seeger, asks: "What were their names, tell me what were their names? Did you have a friend on the good *Reuben James*?"

Having already obtained victim names from casualty lists, reporters sought out family members and unearthed premonitions. "We're asking for it," James

Walton Rogers, a twenty-four-year-old seaman from Chattanooga, Tennessee, had written his father on October 15. Alton W. Cousins, a forty-four-year-old chief machinist's mate visiting family in Cranston, Rhode Island, two weeks before, had left his gold watch behind. "I'm going to leave this here," Cousins told his wife. "It's not going down with me."[21] And, in an October 11 letter to his parents in Vero Beach, Florida, Boilermaker Second Class Gene Guy Evans described *Rube*'s mission: "We are convoying British supply ships and it looks like we will be having a hot time pretty soon."[22]

Reporters, of course, also quoted survivors. Said Bergstresser about the crew: "They felt there was something there as long as the ship was floating," then added, "They felt lost when she went down." And while Brent Bridges "had no qualms about going back to sea," he "didn't want any more 'four-stack destroyers.' I saw what a torpedo could do to one."[23]

10 | WE KNEW ABOUT YOU

***BORIE* WAS PATROLLING** the Pacific when the first radio reports of the disastrous December 7 attack on Pearl Harbor came in. A war that appeared so distant and far-fetched, at least from the Panama Sea Frontier, suddenly appeared at the doorstep. Even as scuttlebutt (rumor) about damage to the Pacific Fleet spread among the crew, individual anxieties hid behind posturing—"How dare those Japs?"—and bravado—"It won't last six months!"

The ship immediately turned backed for Balboa with orders to refuel, reprovision, and go right back out. There was fear—unfounded but not unreasonable—that Japan might attack the canal.

En route, war-induced anxiety exposed just how edgy *Borie*'s crew could be. Early each morning Pete Miller customarily left his cabin, stepped out onto a bridge wing, and stretched himself while slowly scanning the horizon. Miller's December 8 routine seemed unchanged until he leapt back into the wheelhouse, grabbed a pair of binoculars, and ordered, "General Quarters!"

A seaplane circled low in the sky, distinct yet unreported by *Borie* lookouts. Once the intruder disappeared, Miller secured from GQ, then ordered all not on watch—about two-thirds of the crew—to assemble on the forecastle for a "pep talk." Miller had barely begun when someone shouted, "Pete, for Chrissakes, look out forward!"

The destroyer squadron commander, who happened to be on board, thought he saw a spread of torpedoes heading directly for the bow.

"Hard right!" Miller screamed as he scurried back to the bridge. "General Quarters!"

What followed would have been comical were it not so fraught. Men who moved assuredly during drills now collided, went the wrong way, or simply forgot what to do.

If torpedoes not porpoises, *Borie* would have been doomed.

False alarms persisted. Once, as *Borie* approached a squall line, a lookout spotted a huge bow knifing through low clouds. "All hands, battle stations! All engines full ahead! Stand by for torpedo attack!" To be sure, the oncoming ship was huge. And menacing. But an exchange of signals revealed it to be *Trenton*, an aging U.S. Navy cruiser from Balboa, also on patrol.[1]

Confusion was owing to the many inexperienced personnel coming on board. It was November 1940 redux, only this time the latest arrivals were new ensigns, not enlisted recruits. Not only did Pete Miller rank highest on *Borie*, he was also its longest-serving and only career (regular USN, not reserve, USNR) officer. Fully seven of *Borie*'s current roster of nine officers had been on board far less than a year. More than ever, *Borie*'s survival depended on veteran petty officers, many themselves raw recruits in 1940.

Patrols now extended for weeks. The ship once returned from the Pacific to find supplies simply piled on the dock. After loading, it was back to patrol, without respite ashore. Panama's sea frontier was then packed with warships bound west to help restock the Pacific Fleet. Many *Borie* sailors longed to join them—just to escape Panama's tedium.

⌖

In mid-February 1942, the ship went into dry dock at Balboa. During a previous stay, with the ship "up on blocks," *Borie* sailors equipped with long-handled scrapers had immediately been lowered over the side. The removal of accumulated barnacles and rust was dreadful work. Each push of the scrapers moved scaffolds away from the hull. Though the barnacles came off more slowly than the dry-dock water level dropped, some men still got soaked. This time, much to the crew's relief, local workers stood by on floating platforms, scrapers ready, as *Borie* entered the basin.

One evening, Bob Maher stood at the rail talking with Chief Boatswain's Mate Herman Brown, an old salt with bad memories of this same dry dock. Once before, "Boats" told Bob, he had come back from liberty drunk and riding a motorcycle. Boats had run right over the edge of the dry dock, tumbling to the concrete below.

Though long since recovered from his injuries, Boats worried it might happen again. Ridiculous, Bob assured him. The odds were all against it. Besides, Brown didn't have a motorcycle.

A day or so later, though, a sailor shaving next to Maher in the crew's wash room asked, "Hear what happened to Chief Brown last night?" Coming back from liberty, this time on foot though just as drunk, Boats had fallen off *Borie*'s gangway, landing headfirst on the basin concrete, crushing his skull.[2]

Herman Brown's death was just one more cautionary tale to absorb. After more than a year in the U.S. Navy and plenty of it at sea, Maher had absorbed quite a few.

Bob understood that "mentors" like Boats Brown offered lopsided lessons—things *not* to do as well as *do*. Still, all the lessons contributed to his growth, both as a man—Bob was now twenty-three—and a sailor.

In a flawlessly typed two-page letter dated February 17, 1942, Gully Brown updated her husband's parents on life in Panama: "We had the best time last week—Wed. night went to a dinner dance at the Tivoli Hotel given by my office. Thurs. nite had Curly Dietz out for dinner and then Sunday night we were invited to the Union Club for the Carnival . . . like the Mardi Gras on a smaller scale."

"Have we told you about the car we finally succeeded in renting?" Gully continued. It belongs to Curly Dietz the newest Ens. on the ship and is an old dump but has good tires and gets us where we have to go. . . . Brownie shined her all up[,] . . . painted over the rusty spots and we look quite presentable."[3]

Twenty-three-year-old Walter H. "Curly" Dietz Jr. had reported on board *Borie* in late December 1941. Brownie and Curly shared Bay State origins. Dietz's father had established Dolly Madison Bakeries in central Massachusetts. Later, after Dolly Madison merged with Hathaway Bakeries, Walter Sr. had moved the family to Newton Center, just outside Boston.

Walter Jr. attended his father's alma mater Yale University but didn't graduate. "He just wasn't a student," recalled younger brother John. "Only interested in fraternities and parties." After working at a Boston printing firm, Walter Jr. successfully enrolled in V-7 and, after completing *Prairie State*, married Betty, a girl he'd met at church. With Betty accompanying, Ens. Curly Dietz shipped out to Panama and joined *Borie*.[4]

⌖

Brownie and Curly were two of a trio of new ensigns. The third was Philip B. Brown, a twenty-six-year-old Carolinian. Though born in North Carolina, Phil had grown up in Dillon, South Carolina, where his father was a textile mill executive. After attending local schools, Phil graduated from Darlington, a Georgia boarding school.

Aiming for a Naval Academy appointment, Phil next enrolled at Severn, a Maryland prep school for Annapolis aspirants. Meanwhile, his parents rallied influential friends and business contacts to back Phil's candidacy. It took time, but Phil finally received an appointment to the Annapolis class of 1939.

Then-CNO William D. Leahy spoke at Phil's Academy graduation. Telling the 579 graduates that a "grave emergency" would soon confront them, Leahy admonished them "not to waive their commissions" unless they "aspired to . . . the usual comforts of life ashore."[5]

A North Carolina newspaper account conveyed the sense of urgency. "Middies received orders of assignment to various naval vessels effective June 24, thus reducing the usual days at home by six days." It went on to list North and South Carolinians being assigned to battleships *Arizona*, *Idaho*, *Oklahoma*, *Pennsylvania*, and *Tennessee*; aircraft carriers *Enterprise* and *Ranger*; and cruisers *Columbia*, *Indianapolis*, *Memphis*, and *Savannah*. For "Philip Bosche Brown of Dillon," meanwhile, the entry simply read, "Unassigned."[6]

Shaky academics may account for Phil's failure to find a billet. Commissioned but without a ship, Phil Brown instead joined the Burch Corporation, an Ohio manufacturer of farm machinery. The interregnum lasted until

May 1940, when the Navy activated Phil, first as a V-7 recruiter and then, in September 1941, as *Borie*'s signal officer.[7]

Having two "Ensign Browns" on board risked confusion. Navy regulations required that subordinates address each as "Mr. Brown." Among themselves, however, the crew employed a simple distinction. Since Phil worked topside, he became "Light Brown." Morrison, who worked below decks with the engineers, became "Dark Brown."[8]

During one Atlantic patrol, Bob Maher happened to be at the helm when *Borie* received a sudden jolt. As he eased the ship back on course, Bob spotted a whale, head to port, tail to starboard. It must have been forty feet long. A bright pink wake revealed the whale had been wounded in the collision, but *Borie* had sustained damage, too: a dent in the sound dome, the cover protecting the sonar gear. Unable to detect submarines—or whales—*Borie* went in for repairs, the crew got liberty, and Bob Maher became something of a hero.

By then, however, even time ashore in Panama had become tedious. Bob and his friends jumped at the opportunity to do something different. Once they ventured to a remote town called Las Arraijas (Arraiján). As they entered Las Arraijas' only bar, its proprietor motioned them to a small interior room where a disheveled American sailor, a radioman, lay passed out.

He had been there many days, the proprietor explained, and must be in great trouble. Apparently, the radioman had shacked up with a local girl. Ever since finding her in bed with another man, he'd been drinking himself into a stupor. The *Borie* men felt sorry but declined to intervene. Up to him, not them, to sober up and face the music. But "being UA" so long was definitely bad news.

While few *Borie* sailors considered going UA themselves, many repeatedly applied for transfer. But Pete Miller was not about to let veterans go. With so many inexperienced ensigns on board, he blocked defections.

Once, when *Borie* received a directive inviting men above a certain rank to apply for aviation training, Bob Maher and two dozen others tried signing up. Bound by the directive, Miller couldn't prohibit them from going to a naval hospital for qualifying physicals. But that didn't keep him from exerting influence.

After Bob and several buddies completed physicals, they were waiting for transport back to the ship when a jeep sped by, screeched to a halt, swung around, and pulled alongside. The driver, a hospital corpsman, just happened to be a high school classmate of Bob's.

"Are you guys from the *Borie*?" he asked.

All nodded.

"Hell, we knew about you," laughed the corpsman, "and we heard that everyone was going to fail!"

Indeed, no one passed. All suspected it was Miller's doing.[9]

11 | TARGET AMERICA

RIGHT AFTER PEARL HARBOR, Karl Dönitz pushed to exploit America's vulnerability. To send U-boats across the Atlantic and make America pay the price for aiding Britain.

American factories depended on raw materials and, as America mobilized to supply its allies, that dependence would only deepen. Thus far, Adolf Hitler had avoided war with the United States. Having invaded Russia, moreover, the Führer hardly needed more enemies. But, as Dönitz's boss, Grand Adm. Erich Raeder, the austere and blindly patriotic sixty-six-year-old head of the Kriegsmarine insisted, America was already waging naval war. Supplying Great Britain and the Soviet Union with war material, escorting North Atlantic convoys, even arming its own merchant ships and allowing them to enter the war zone. Restraining Dönitz's U-boats only upped America's advantage. Time now to strike.

Japan's sneak attack changed the equation. It surprised Hitler and signaled that the Rising Sun would fight on its own terms. Still, Japan's preemptive strike might yet benefit the Third Reich. For one thing, it was bound to siphon Allied sea and air forces from the Atlantic and Mediterranean, enhancing Axis opportunities there. For another, should Japan decide to attack Russia in the Far East, it might take pressure off the Eastern Front. Weighing these variables and Raeder's pleadings, Hitler declared war on America and lifted restrictions on U-boats.[1]

Dönitz was ecstatic. U-boat productivity in the North Atlantic was declining sharply. Here was an opportunity "of getting at enemy merchant ships in conditions which elsewhere have ceased almost completely."[2] Without delay, BdU began organizing a U-boat expedition to America's East Coast.

Though Dönitz portrayed his U-boat assault on North America as Operation *Paukenschlag* ("Roll of the Drums"), he was hard put to assemble enough boats to execute it. Battle losses, diversions to the Arctic and Mediterranean, and mounting production delays reduced available U-boats to just sixty-four. Worse, in the months ahead only thirty-four more would join the Atlantic force.[3]

The voyage to America's Eastern Seaboard—three thousand miles or more—required deploying Type IX *Seekühe* (sea cows). These boats were nearly a third bigger than the Type VIIs. Their newer versions (Type IXCs) had a range of 11,000 miles, nearly twice Type VIIC's. Sea cows were roomy and could carry fourteen torpedoes but also had drawbacks; they were slower to dive, more difficult to maneuver, easier to spot.[4]

Of BdU's twenty sea cows, moreover, only six could be readied in time to join *Paukenschlag*. To these, Dönitz added ten Type VIICs expected to operate near Newfoundland and Nova Scotia.[5]

Altogether, sixteen U-boats seemed a meager force for such an ambitious endeavor. But not unprecedented. In October 1940, during what U-boat veterans celebrated as the "Happy Time" (*glückliche Zeit*), a force averaging just thirteen U-boats sank sixty-six ships with only one U-boat lost. Triumphant crews returning to French ports were personally welcomed by Dönitz, serenaded by bands, and showered with bouquets, congratulations, medals, and promotions.[6]

Dönitz understood the *Paukenschlag* U-boats were simply too few and too widely scattered for pack tactics. Instead, to inflict the most damage and spread the most terror, they were to strike simultaneously on signal from Kerneval. The six *Seekühe* would range from New York south to Cape Hatteras, lying quietly near the bottom on the continental shelf by day then surfacing by night. They were to strike the largest, least protected targets, especially loaded tankers steaming independently. Even deck guns could be used when conditions permitted.

Paukenschlag's first wave departed France between December 18 and December 27. One sea cow turned back after developing a telltale oil leak. The others encountered hideous weather, brutally cold temperatures, and mountainous seas. These conditions made passage grueling, especially for the Type VIIs. Crew clothes, always wet and heavy, iced over. Frozen jacket collars scraped necks until they bled. Bones succumbed to aches and rheumatism.[7]

A topside watch officer on one Type VII who failed to secure his safety harness was washed overboard and lost. Several Type VIIs ran headlong into a winter hurricane. "The waves were as high as houses," striking the deck "like an avalanche," recorded *U-333*'s *Kapitänleutnant* Peter-Erich "Ali" Cremer. Seas washed away fenders and lines and splintered wood supports.

U-333 rolled on the surface like a pendulum—120 degrees from port to starboard and back. At either extreme, Crew 32's Cremer estimated, "one could plunge one's bare hands in the water." Simultaneously, after climbing a wave and tunneling through its crest, Cremer's boat "hung for a moment with its stern in the empty air and plunged down into the trough." When the boat was sliding down, its twin screws spun like airplane propellers.[8]

At last, with *U-333* shuddering "like a steel spring," Cremer gave up traveling on the surface. He and other exhausted *kommandanten* ran submerged, surfacing only to recharge batteries and ventilate boats. Progress slowed to just twenty or thirty miles a day, spoiling plans for simultaneous attacks on January 13. Indeed, the first blow—the January 14 sinking of a 9,600-ton Panamanian tanker in the shallows off Long Island—came four full days before the last boats reached the station.[9]

At first, *Paukenschlag* didn't wreak the devastation that BdU envisioned. Still, *kommandanten* were struck by the opportunities they saw. Most ships steamed independently, many with running lights on. Even darkened ships were clearly silhouetted by lights ashore.

Boats patrolling off New York carried Manhattan street maps marking inlets and harbors as well as famous tourist sites. One sea cow *kommandant*, surveying New York Harbor with binoculars, joked to his crew of seeing dancers atop the Empire State building. *U-333*'s Ali Cremer "could distinguish equally the big hotels and the cheap dives and read the flickering neon signs."[10]

Not until April and May would authorities impose blackouts on waterfronts and coastal skylines.[11]

Allied political and military leaders were just then gathering in America's capital for the First Washington Conference, code name Arcadia, set to convene December 22. Now united on full war footings, it was time for them to formulate war production schedules and lay out a war-winning global strategy. It was agreed—in line with Plan Dog and subsequent ABC-1 Staff Agreements—that defeating Germany came first, defeating Japan second. But how were they to pull it off?

America's reaction to Pearl Harbor had been swift and dramatic. The U.S. Navy shifted from obsession with the Atlantic to obsession with the Pacific. Blame spread like contagion. Adm. Husband Kimmel, Commander in Chief Pacific Fleet (CINCPAC), had been promptly relieved, on December 17. After repeated offers to resign, Kimmel's boss, CNO "Betty" Stark, would eventually step aside as well.

Yet despite the evident turmoil, there was no leadership vacuum. Having impressed as CINCLANT, Adm. Ernest J. King step by step assumed overall command. First, effective December 30, 1941, came promotion to Commander in Chief United States Fleet (COMINCH),* an overarching job giving him control of the Navy Department's bureaucracy as well as America's battle fleets. Later, on March 18, 1942, King assumed concurrent duty as CNO.† Because he reported directly to the president rather than Navy secretary Frank Knox, King wielded considerable clout. But ahead lay the formidable task of harnessing and supporting Anglo-American strategy. Difficult enough in the best of times—and these were the worst.

Indeed, from the start, Arcadia's delegates shouldered cascading setbacks as Allied bases and possessions in the Pacific and Far East tumbled like

*King refused the title "CinCUS," because—though inadvertently—the acronym, pronounced "Sink us," sounded outright defeatist.

†Stark then reported to London, becoming Commander U.S. Naval Forces in Europe.

dominoes. *Paukenschlag* compounded these setbacks while cleaving Anglo-American amity.

Prime Minister Churchill led Britain's delegation, but accompanying him was Admiral Pound. Accordingly, there was intense discussion of merchant convoying. Losses off America's Eastern Seaboard made clear, at least to the British, that coastal convoying should begin at once.

Both Allies had once flirted with consolidating Atlantic convoy protection under American aegis. Now, Churchill and Pound called for a unified escort command under Western Approaches commander Adm. Percy Noble.

Unity of command seemed to be the order of the day, but pressed on the matter, King, who was now Pound's American counterpart, vigorously disagreed. King certainly appreciated the U-boat threat. After all, *Greer*, *Kearny*, and *Reuben James* belonged, or had, to the Atlantic Fleet. Moreover, he wasn't short on experience or insight. During a four-decade career, King had served on board surface ships and submarines, qualified as a naval aviator, and commanded the aircraft carrier *Lexington*.

Just like the Royal Navy, the U.S. Navy lacked the sea and air resources to protect shipping adequately. In the wake of the Destroyers-for-Bases deal, King had just 177 destroyers at his disposal, only half of them modern.[12] Many were already committed to transatlantic merchant convoys, troop lift, or coastal frontier defense. The balance was desperately needed in the Pacific. With warship construction focused on big ships—aircraft carriers, battleships, and cruisers—just eight new destroyers would join the fleet between January and March.

Under such circumstances, COMINCH believed coastal merchant ships were simply better off sailing alone. The Germans could only send a few boats at a time to the United States. Large convoys would be easier for these few to spot.

For now, King was prepared to assume the risks and consequences. What he wasn't about to yield was command and control of an ascendant U.S. Navy to a Royal Navy in decline.

King held his ground, but this didn't prevent Churchill, a consummate schemer, from trying to outflank him. Days later, when the prime minister left Washington for a side trip to Canada, he left behind a draft telegram to be sent to Britain's war cabinet.

The telegram purported to be a summary of Arcadia's proceedings, but King sniffed overreach. Britain would, Churchill blithely asserted, "assume responsibility for the security of the Atlantic Ocean in the existing close collaboration with the United States naval forces there assigned."

King wrote to a colleague at the time: "I have no intention whatever of acceding to any unity of command proposals that are not premised on a particular situation in a particular area at a particular time for a more or less particular period." During his short tenure at the top, King went on, "I have found it necessary . . . to point out to some 'amateur strategists' in high places that unity of command is not a panacea for all military difficulties—and I shall continue to do so."[13]

King was tall, spare, and taut in appearance, intolerant, coarse, and profane in manner. He combined a superior intellect, a firm grasp of strategy and tactics, an encyclopedic knowledge of naval minutiae, and an immense capacity for work, on one hand, with ill-concealed penchants on the other for carousing and womanizing and a haughty disdain for lesser mortals, especially politicians and other civilians. King was feared and respected, rarely admired. While Admiral King did not think he was God, some joked, God thought he was Admiral King.* Certainly, King was nobody's courtier. But now, in military, political, and diplomatic forums such as Arcadia, his forthrightness cast him as an Anglophobe bent on disrupting Anglo-American cooperation.

Someone altogether more focused on the war in the Pacific than he was on the war in Europe.

Though their nations were figuratively on the ropes across the globe, Arcadia delegates were determined to go on the offense as soon as possible. What

*As portrayed in rhyme by *The Saturday Evening Post*:

No merry old soul of a King is he
He's six-foot-two of TNT,
With a glacial eye and a granite jaw,
And he loves to eat young ensigns raw.

(Ethel Jacobson, "People You Know: No. 27 of a Series," *Saturday Evening Post*, September 18, 1943, 34)

each proposed—or counterproposed—established a lexicon of operational code names that henceforth dominated Allied agendas and cable exchanges.

Winston Churchill took the lead by proposing Gymnast, an Allied invasion of Northwest Africa, designed to trap German forces fighting the British. Thinking Gymnast too much of a detour, U.S. Army Chief of Staff George C. Marshall countered with a late-summer 1942 invasion of France in Brittany or the Brest Peninsula.* In Marshall's estimation, such a move would strike closer to the heart of the Nazi war machine. To King, who supported Marshall's objections, it would also eliminate U-boat bases on coastal France.

In the end, FDR overrode Marshall and King. Sensing Gymnast's potential for seasoning American troops ahead of confronting German forces in Continental Europe, the president sided with the prime minister. So, Gymnast it would be—no later than May 25. Marshall's priority was deferred. Instead, there would be Bolero, the buildup of Allied forces in the British Isles as a prelude to Roundup, a larger Northern Europe invasion in 1943.[14]

Gymnast, Bolero, and Roundup demanded nearly boundless sealift: the massed, coordinated transport of men, equipment, supplies, and fuel. This necessitated shipping of all kinds: troopships, freighters, tankers, and landing craft, large and small.

"Ships! Ships! All we need is ships! What a headache!" Maj. Gen. Dwight D. Eisenhower, newly installed as U.S. Army chief of plans, confessed to his diary.[15] Or, as Winston Churchill later (and more eloquently) described the conundrum: "Shipping was at once the stranglehold and sole foundation of our war strategy."[16]

In an emergency step, delegates agreed to pool merchant shipping. This helped but didn't solve the inevitable shortfall. For now, they had no choice but to curtail their grandiose plans: postpone Gymnast indefinitely, trim back and stretch out Bolero. Over the longer term, to accomplish anything, merchant ships would have to be built on a massive scale.

Already, FDR had directed the once-somnolent U.S. Maritime Commission to build 12,000,000 tons of new merchant shipping. During Arcadia, he raised the goal to 18,000,000 tons. Finally, on February 19, once Arcadia concluded,

---

*To be code-named Sledgehammer.

he committed to 24,000,000 tons. Assuming all this was achieved, the combined Anglo-American merchant fleet would swell to nearly 50,000,000 tons.[17]

An impressive total, but one that begged the continuing question: How would the Allies protect that massive fleet against U-boats? Arcadia delegates passed this buck to a simultaneous and subsidiary Anglo-American "Convoy Conference." To no one's surprise, the Royal Navy representatives used this forum to make their case for a single North Atlantic (British) convoy escort commander. This time, though, the American delegates countered with a specific (Ernest King–sanctioned) scheme.

Surprisingly, matters here moved swiftly, at least at first. By January 24, using the American template, conferees hammered out, endorsed, and circulated a new Atlantic convoy escort scheme. But five days later, when Dudley Pound returned to Britain and saw the result, he fumed. Pound immediately cabled Washington. In his opinion, "divided control" of escorts "was wasteful of our resources." Rather, the First Sea Lord insisted, Britain should assume "strategic direction" at "the earliest possible moment."[18]

Rounds of testy cross-Atlantic exchanges followed. Finally, on February 4, after further modifications, a new "divided control" plan took effect. Canadian escort groups would protect merchant convoys from North America to and from longitude 45 degrees west—what was called the West Ocean Meeting Point (WOMP). From Europe, to and from longitude 22 degrees west (the East Ocean Meeting Point, or EASTOMP), Royal Navy escorts would do the same.

For the longer (1,800 miles) and more vulnerable passage between WOMP and EASTOMP (and beyond), the plan created a Mid-Ocean Escort Force (MOEF), composed of fourteen close-escort groups—five American, five British, and four Canadian.

Eastbound MOEF escorts would protect convoys from WOMP all the way to Londonderry, Ireland, westbound MOEF escorts from EASTOMP all the way to St. John's, Newfoundland. To make this "straight across" system work, however, the escorts would have to adhere strictly to Great Circle Routes (the shortest tracks between two points on the surface of the globe). Rerouting would have to be avoided, and escorts, particularly the "short-legged" corvettes, had to economize on speed.

As conceived that February, MOEF numbered altogether 143 ships: 42 destroyers (15 American, 15 British, 12 Canadian) and 101 corvettes (52 British and 49 Canadian).[19]

It didn't take long, however, for conflicting priorities to whittle away at MOEF's strength.

12 | ROOTS OF EVIL

ONE SUBSTANTIVE CONCESSION COMINCH had wrung from Arcadia deliberations was for America to keep open a "line of communication" between Hawaii and the Southwest Pacific, meanwhile stockpiling for counterattacks there. Important first steps but little solace to a nation still writhing in pain from Pearl Harbor—and hungry for revenge.

All this pressure fell on King as he set up shop in the Navy Department. "I had to start with nothing," he recalled later.[1] Indeed, the office's prior occupants had left nothing behind. Several of COMINCH's principal staff came directly from the Atlantic Fleet. Among them, working at a table commandeered from another office, was U.S. Navy captain Francis S. "Frog" Low, King's forty-seven-year-old operations officer.

Frog—a Naval Academy nickname*—was a career submariner who seldom crossed paths with King but knew his fulsome reputation. Nevertheless, when invited to serve directly under King—and forfeit a cherished opportunity to command a submarine squadron—Frog promptly accepted.

In time, Low gained perspective on King's harsh behavior. One evening, as the two dined alone, King "divulged the only bit of personal information" Low ever recalled receiving. "He said that as a young ensign he early realized that he had a tendency to be 'soft' and that he knew, if he was to progress in

*The sobriquet was attributed to Low's facial expression and his baritone voice.

the Navy, he would have to get a grip on himself." King, in other words, was "building himself a suit of armor . . . and rarely stepping out of it."[2]

King's growing confidence in his operations officer was rewarded after Lowe went to Norfolk, Virginia, to inspect *Hornet*, the Navy's newest aircraft carrier. America's carriers had been spared the ravages of Pearl Harbor by happening to be out to sea. Fast fleet flattops were destined to become the U.S. Navy's dominant seagoing weapons, especially in the Pacific. But, in early 1942, questions remained on how best to employ them.

Radar was still new, so carrier aircraft (along with battleship and cruiser float planes) were often used as airborne scouts. Japan's stunning carrier aircraft assault on Hawaii had removed lingering doubt about carrier capabilities. At the same time, though, advances in submarines pointed to vulnerabilities. Already, U-boats had claimed two Royal Navy carriers—*Courageous* and *Ark Royal.*

On the return flight from Norfolk, Low first hit on a new possibility: using a carrier as strike platform for U.S. Army Air Forces (USAAF) medium bombers. Frog knew King's interest in carrier tactics and his obsession with revenge on the Japanese. Still, as he met with his boss back in Washington, Frog understood that proposing interservice cooperation with the USAAF would be risky.

The two branches fiercely disputed preeminence in military aviation. The U.S. Army Air Corps—since June 1941, the USAAF—had won a key victory in this struggle: all land-based aircraft—notably bombers—belonged to it. In an arrangement that had the effect of law, the U.S. Navy was limited to ship-based aircraft, plus seaplanes and blimps. Thus, it was the USAAF, not the USN, that protected America's coastal airspace. Even now, with German U-boats roaming the Eastern Seaboard, FDR, influenced by Secretary of War Henry L. Stimson, resisted Navy pleas to loosen restrictions. The war secretary, backed by George Marshall and the USAAF commanding general, Henry H. "Hap" Arnold, believed that Army pilots were as capable of battling U-boats as Navy aviators. Maybe better.

Explaining what he'd seen over Norfolk, Frog got to the point: "If the Army has some plane that could take off in a short distance, I mean a plane capable of carrying a bomb load, why couldn't we put a few of them on a carrier and bomb the mainland of Japan?"

As King tilted back in his chair, Low wasn't sure what to expect. He understood King's volatility. The scorn he could unleash without warning.

"That might be a good idea," King finally said.[3]

Frog's seed of an idea, brought to fruition in USAAF Col. Jimmy Doolittle's April 1942 bombing raid, stunned Japan's warlords and electrified America. But even as plans for this audacious blow in the Pacific progressed, *Paukenschlag*'s devastation off America's Eastern Seaboard mounted.

In the last two weeks of January, U-boats sank twenty-three Allied ships, thirteen of them tankers, many in sight of shore. Counting losses farther north, the total climbed to forty-one. For the U-boat crews, it was indeed a second "Happy Time." In Dönitz's reckoning, by going "for the hub, and particularly the oil supplies," his wolves were "getting to the root of evil."[4]

After feasting first on shipping off Long Island, New York City, and New Jersey, Dönitz's Type IXs headed south towards Cape Hatteras. One *kommandant* arrived with only five torpedoes to spare but was astounded by the bounty of targets. In just seven hours he sank two freighters by torpedo and deck gun.

Dönitz's inclination was to send every boat possible west to America. Instead, Hitler's strategic "intuition"—his certainty that Norway was the "zone of destiny"—combined with vacillation by other high military authorities, diverted BdU's precious boats elsewhere. Sometimes as few as half a dozen U-boats operated simultaneously off America.

In April, Dönitz reinforced *Paukenschlag* with the first submersible supply vessels, U-tankers—or what U-boat sailors called *Milchkuhe* (milk cows). Many were converted minelaying U-boats, designated Type XB. But others—designated Type XIV, eventually eleven in all—were purpose-built. Extra storage and fuel space supplanted torpedo tubes. Their crews usually included medical staff. *Milchkuhe* also furnished replacements for sick or wounded crew. In sum, they enabled the Type VIIs to range farther and operate longer.

Paukenschlag hit its peak that month. A total of 31 U-boats—14 Type IXs and 17 VIIs—sank 133 ships displacing over 640,000 tons.

Shouldering the blame was Vice Adm. Dolly Andrews (the same Dolly Andrews who had addressed Morrison Brown's *Prairie State* June 1941 graduating class). A native Texan, personal friend of Franklin Roosevelt, and Annapolis classmate of Ernest King, Dolly had the thankless, near-futile job of protecting America's Eastern Sea Frontier, from the Canadian border to Jacksonville, Florida.

The tonnage losses there were certainly devastating. But the human details appalled: men swimming for their lives through thick oily goo and intense flame or (purportedly) strafed by U-boat machine-gun fire.

Working out of headquarters in lower Manhattan, Andrews scrambled to corral enough air and sea escorts to protect coastwise shipping. He had altogether less than one hundred surface vessels, many of them small, some even powered by coal. Perhaps as many as 170 multiengine military aircraft swept the coastal skies. None of the half belonging to the AAF were equipped with radar; they carried bombs, not depth charges. The Army pilots were keen but green, scarcely prepared to find or track, never mind sink, a U-boat.

To avoid nighttime attacks, coastwise merchants traveled "bucket-brigade" style: steaming by day then anchoring overnight in protected bays. Tanker losses were so bad in March and April that all remained in port until further notice.

In February, newspapers howling for action, a handful of destroyers was dispatched on roving patrols. Their patrol cycles were predictable, and, in good weather, U-boats could easily spot them. Moreover, these ships were still ill-fitted for effective search.

On February 28, at about 5 a.m., while patrolling calm waters under clear skies off the Delaware Capes, four-stacker *Jacob Jones*—unaware of imminent peril—steamed into the crosshairs of *U-578*. A day before, thirty miles off New Jersey, *U-578*, a Type VIIC midway through its first *Paukenschlag* foray, had sunk a 7,500-ton fuel oil–laden American tanker.

U-578's forty-year-old Crew 23 skipper, *Fregattenkapitän* Ernst-August Rehwinkle, waited in patient disbelief as the range closed. At last, Rehwinkle fired two bow torpedoes, both of which hit *Jacob Jones*. The first tore away the ship's bow. The second, striking less than minute later, set off "Jakie's" depth charges, blowing its stern to smithereens.

The truncated wreck stayed briefly afloat as survivors scrambled to evacuate. Twenty-two-year-old Joseph Tidwell, a machinist's mate from Tuscaloosa, Alabama, had left the aft engine room and gone up to the galley when the ship "seemed to bog down." Then, a huge explosion. Tidwell ran up "to see what I could do and saw some of the boys cutting rafts away. I jumped in the water and climbed on one."[5]

When four crewmen, among them Thomas Moody, a twenty-two-year-old machinist's mate from Franklin, Kentucky, tried to launch a lifeboat, they found necessary gear blown away. Unwilling to "go out in that cold water without getting something warm," the four lingered on board. Finding coffee, some sugar but no cups, they took turns with a soup ladle to slurp it down. In an open storage locker, they found stacks of thermal underwear. Each donned three sets before leaving the ship.[6]

After escaping Jakie's forward engine room, Richard Dors, a twenty-five-year-old machinist's mate from Brockton, Massachusetts, found himself on an overcrowded life raft. As the raft drifted close to the wreck, Dors decided to climb back and look for other flotation. Finding nothing and with the main deck awash, he jumped back. After swimming to another raft, Dors "saw the last of the Jakie go down," followed by a "big explosion." The blast "knocked some of the fellows off their rafts and almost blew me out of the water, but I held on. The water was . . . plenty cold."[7]

Later that morning, a search aircraft spotted debris, and a patrol boat was dispatched to the scene. Rescuers found just two life rafts containing eleven survivors, including Tidwell, Moody, and Dors.

Throughout the crisis, Dolly Andrews never lacked for advice, not least from the president. "If I were in your place," FDR wrote Andrews on March 9, "I would buy (for junk prices) a lot of old ferry boats. . . . Cut off their overhangs, build up a wooden bow, put a bulwark around the stern, take off the top hamper, and the silly looking things will be able to patrol. . . . All it [*sic*] needs is one radio, one light gun and half a dozen depth charges."[8]

Pressured on all sides, Andrews eventually instituted what was dubbed "Hooligan Navy," a collection of civilian fishing and sailing vessels whose crews looked for U-boats. According to historian Craig Symonds, the best the ragtag flotilla could do was provide "some excitement and gratification to a handful of eager volunteers"—among them author Ernest Hemingway.[9]

All the while, the Brits harped on King's failure to organize convoys and antisubmarine warfare (ASW) defense. As early as February 6, Churchill privately warned FDR intimate Harry Hopkins: "It would be well to make sure the president's attention has been drawn to the very heavy sinkings by U-boats in the Western North Atlantic." The prime minister followed up in March, this time distressed over "the immense sinkings of tankers" in the Caribbean Sea. "The situation is so serious that drastic action of some kind is necessary."[10]

FDR did his best to mollify Churchill, reassuring him that promised shipments would somehow make their way to Britain. Having settled on King to "kick the U.S. Navy into the midtwentieth century," however, the president ignored, for now, all calls to sack COMINCH, instead directing his wrath at Navy secretary Frank Knox.[11]

Knox, a former newspaper publisher, tried to placate FDR and the American people, sometimes by playing fast and loose with the truth. In February, as one instance, he announced that at least three U-boats had been sunk, four more damaged. All such claims were uncorroborated. It was not until April 14—four days before Doolittle's raid—that an American warship successfully cornered a U-boat.

The ship was *Roper*, a *Wickes*-class destroyer temporarily assigned to Andrews. Since commissioning in 1918, *Roper* had been in and out of mothballs twice. *Roper* was armed with 4-inch guns, torpedo tubes, and depth charges. But, unusually for such an old tin can so early in the war, *Roper* was also equipped with British-built radar.

On April 1, while returning to Norfolk from convoy duty, *Roper* had picked up sixty-nine survivors from the American cargo-passenger vessel *City of New York*, torpedoed off the Outer Banks.[12] The youngest survivor was a baby boy born in a ship's lifeboat to the wife of a Yugoslav diplomat.*

Roper departed Norfolk on April 13. Just after midnight on the 14th, near Bodie Island Lighthouse, *Roper* picked up a radar contact, distance 2,700

*Desanka Mohorovicic named her son Jesse Roper Mohorovicic in honor of Jesse M. Roper, the heroic U.S. Navy officer for whom the destroyer was named.

yards. Lt. Cdr. Hamilton W. Howe, the ship's thirty-six-year-old skipper, had just turned in for the night. As Howe described it in a postwar interview: "I got word from the officer of the deck that a contact had been made" and that "he was going to investigate."

Howe "somewhat reluctantly" left his bunk and went to the bridge. At first there seemed little cause for concern in waters teeming with small patrol boats, fishing trawlers, tugs, and salvage craft. But, said Howe, "It seemed to be moving very fast. That was a little suspicious. I decided to call general quarters, man all stations—torpedo tubes, guns, machine guns."

Roper had drawn a bead on *U-85*, a Type VII on its second patrol to America. Greger Eberhard, *U-85*'s twenty-six-year-old *kommandant*, surfaced in continental-shelf waters barely a hundred feet deep. "American beacons and searchlights visible at night," read a *U-85* sailor's diary entry recovered later.[13]

Crew 35's Eberhard knew crash-diving was futile—*U-85* would only be ripped apart by depth charges in the shallows. The alternative: stay surfaced and run for deeper water. Greger, unaware his pursuer used radar, hoped to shake free before daylight.

Roper gradually overhauled what Howe still assumed was a "small U.S. vessel." Just in case, "it was my decision to turn on our big searchlight," all the while "being ready . . . to open fire . . . if . . . mistaken."

Just then, "a wake . . . went down our port side."

It had been left by a torpedo fired from one of *U-85*'s stern tubes. "By the grace of God," recalled Howe, "we were spared."

Roper was now three hundred yards from the contact. Its powerful arc lamp spot lit a U-boat turning to starboard. *Roper*'s gunners scarcely hesitated.

As described in *Roper*'s war diary: "Number 1 machine gun . . . cut down German sailors as they hurried to man their guns." One *Roper* gun "got the range quickly and scored a hit on the conning tower[;] . . . soon after, the submarine began to sink. Orders to fire a [*Roper*] torpedo were immediately given . . . but the U-boat disappeared before the order could be obeyed."[14]

What happened next fueled second-guessing.

According to *Roper*'s war diary: "About forty of the [U-boat] crew were left swimming about in the water, but Roper was more immediately concerned with the certain destruction of the enemy than with the rescue of personnel."

"We lost temporary contact," Howe recalled in his postwar account. "We circled around and dropped depth charges." Then: "We came back and made what we thought was a new [sonar] contact. So, we made another depth charge attack. And, just as we were in the midst, we heard some shouts in the water." But, Howe continued, "we had to carry through with our attack."

Almost certainly, *Roper*'s point-blank gunfire had spelled *U-85*'s end. Eberhard's vessel was probably already settling stern first as *Roper* dropped depth charges. During the subsequent run, depth charges, preset to explode at fifty feet, blasted the *U-85* survivors.

With guns silenced and depth charges expended—but still wary of U-boats—Howe hauled *Roper* away. "When day broke," the war diary continued, "a PBY [twin-engine Catalina flying boat] appeared to assist in the work. The plane dropped a depth charge over an oil slick and a mass of debris. . . . The *Roper* added two more." When it was all over, "Boats were put off from the destroyer to pick up the men and any articles that could be found."

"We knew we had gotten a U-boat," summarized Howe a quarter-century later. "We recovered dead German seamen—twenty-nine to be exact."[15]*

Historian Clay Blair, writing decades after *U-85*'s sinking, disputed the *Roper* account and suggested culpability. In his opinion, "excited Americans" botched an opportunity to save lives, capture prisoners and valuable intelligence, including a precious Enigma machine."[16] But it is equally compelling to see that Howe's actions drew from the fates of *Greer*, *Kearny*, *Reuben James*, and, most recently, *Jacob Jones*.

To Allied destroyer skippers, U-boats were the "root of evil." Presuming they gave no quarter, they got no quarter.

---

*On April 15, 1942, the sailors' remains were buried with full military honors in Hampton National Cemetery. On July 22, the Navy acknowledged the burials but withheld *U-85*'s identity and the date of its sinking.

13 | SAFE DUTY AREA

THAT SAME APRIL, singly and collectively, morale on board *Borie* dipped to a low ebb. Morrison Brown's hopes that Gully might stay on in Panama, for example, were dashed. As he lamented to his parents in a midmonth letter, "My dear wife had to leave. . . . A regular London fog came over me[;] . . . half of me went home and the other half had to stay."[1]

Meanwhile, over the previous eighteen months, neither had *Borie* visited a U.S. port nor had her sailors taken home leave. Though Bob Maher considered Miller an excellent officer, someone he trusted with his life, the captain didn't seem to worry about things like liberty and leave.

Then, in early May, to Maher's mind, "one of the best things . . . occurred. Lt. Cdr. Phil Osborn came aboard and relieved Captain Miller as commanding officer."[2]

Philip R. "Phil" Osborn was a 1929 Annapolis graduate. In 1936, following stints at sea, Osborn became a Naval Academy English instructor. In 1938, though slated to become gunnery officer on a new destroyer, Osborn went instead to China, serving first on a Yangtze River patrol boat and then as XO on a submarine tender. Osborn's final stop before *Borie* was cruiser *Augusta*, where he probably witnessed Roosevelt's and Churchill's August 1941 Argentia rendezvous.[3]

Now a thirty-five-year-old commander, Osborn landed his first full-fledged seagoing command. Pete Miller, meanwhile, was going off to skipper a bigger, newer destroyer in the South Pacific—the very type of billet that many *Borie* officers and sailors dreamed about.*

From the start, Osborn strove to win over *Borie*'s homesick crew. A few days after command changed hands, the ship set out with a small convoy to Cuba. Only this time, instead of anchoring in Guantánamo Bay, *Borie* immediately headed north.

"What a thrill to see home again," Maher recalled, "as we rounded the southern tip of Florida and sailed up the western coast, always keeping land in sight. We entered Tampa Bay about May 20 and headed toward St. Petersburg."

Because "St. Pete's" docking facilities were limited, *Borie* anchored in the channel. But even from there the crew could see a cheering crowd waiting on the dock. *Borie*, it turned out, was the first U.S. Navy warship to visit since Pearl Harbor.

Decked out in tailor-made whites (custom attire usually forbidden on bigger ships) niftily accessorized with service ribbons, Maher, Jim Allegri, and Jim Aikenhead went ashore with the first liberty party. As the motor whaleboat approached the dock, the cheering reached full crescendo. And, as the sailors wobbled ashore on unsteady sea legs, the crowd surged forward. Arms reached out to grab them, many in hopes of taking them home for a meal or to a bar for free drinks.

Over the next days, St. Petersburg took on a carnival atmosphere. At first, its patriotic citizens just couldn't get enough of *Borie* and its crew. Invitations to homes, bars, restaurants, churches, parties, and picnics poured out. To Maher's mind, however, the nicest thing was to be able to sit with young American girls "who were having as much fun as we were."

A stint on Shore Patrol (SP) gave Maher a better appreciation of how young sailors too long at sea and on distant outposts could test the boundaries of civilized behavior. His partner was twenty-four-year-old Edgar T. "Eggs" Robertson, a carpenter's mate and one of thirteen *Borie* sailors hailing from Lyndhurst, about six miles northeast of Kearny.[4]

---

*As captain of *Jenkins* (DD 447) Miller received a Navy Cross and Silver Star for actions in the Solomon Islands. ("Harry Fanker Miller" [Navy Cross, Silver Star], n.d., The Hall of Valor Project, https://valor.militarytimes.com/hero/21391 [accessed 8/2/20])

Normally there were few problems, even when it was time to return to the ship. That's when Bob and Ed would make a sweep of St. Pete's bars, lounges, and restaurants, making sure every sailor they saw started back. Usually a simple "Let's go, sailor" or "Time to go" did the trick. Few protested, though once, to the pair's bewilderment, an elderly matron did. "Why are you spoiling their fun?" the woman demanded. "You should be ashamed of yourselves!"

Several days in, however, St. Pete's welcome mat began to fray. Untoward incidents—some true, some exaggerated, some apocryphal—piled up. *Borie* sailors, drunk or sober, insulted or propositioned local girls. One man returned to the ship sloshed, hatless and barefoot, leading two large ducks on leashes. Another sailor, equally sloshed but more obstinate, climbed a tree and refused to descend. When local police declined to intervene, an officer's threat of court-martial finally coaxed him down.[5]

In the end, no cheering crowds were on hand when *Borie* finally weighed anchor.

As *Borie* sailors were wearing out their welcome on Florida's Gulf Coast, the U.S. Navy finally put in place a convoy system between Key West, Florida, and Hampton Roads, Virginia. Each convoy numbered roughly forty-five merchants and tankers, protected by seven or eight surface escorts—U.S. Navy destroyers and Coast Guard cutters augmented by borrowed Royal Navy corvettes and trawlers. By June, escorted convoys extended as far north as Halifax. And, with New York Harbor as nexus, coastwise merchant shipping now interlocked seamlessly with transatlantic convoys.[6]

These stiffening defenses curtailed the "Second Happy Time" but didn't entirely end *Paukenschlag*. Compelled to adapt, Karl Dönitz probed weaknesses in the Caribbean Sea and the Gulf of Mexico. Among his boats scouring the tropics was *U-107*, a Type IX sea cow bearing a storied reputation. *U-107* had been commissioned in 1940 with a noteworthy *kommandant*, Crew 27's Günter Hessler, Karl Dönitz's thirty-one-year-old son-in-law.

When Hessler notched four kills during *U-107*'s maiden patrol, Dönitz lavished warm praise on him. A spring 1941 foray to the waters off South Africa cemented Hessler's standing: *U-107* accounted for fourteen sinkings totaling

87,000 tons, the highest tonnage yet for any single U-boat patrol. Early that fall, again in the South Atlantic, Hessler continued to shine. Though pitted against five armed escorts, he accounted for three freighters in an eleven-ship convoy.

Credited now with twenty-one sinkings totaled 119,000 tons, Hessler became first staff officer to Dönitz.[7] *U-107*'s command, plus its reputation, passed to twenty-six-year-old Harald Gelhaus, a first-time *kommandant* from Crew 35.

As if jinxed by *U-107*'s legacy, Gelhaus' first patrol turned into a fiasco. In mid-December, when a wolf pack joined by *U-107* set upon fifty-eight merchants westbound from Gibraltar, the wolves met their match. British escorts—thirteen in all—struck back with teamwork and dogged persistence. By December 22, when Dönitz finally called off this Pyrrhic endeavor, only two small merchants and one escort had been sunk, while three U-boats had been lost.[8]

The strain of this battle kept *U-107* out of *Paukenschlag*'s vanguard. But once Gelhaus joined at the end of January 1942, he built his own credentials. *U-107* sank two vessels, one a 7,400-ton British tanker.

Homebound in mid-February, however, Gelhaus blundered. While maneuvering to refuel another U-boat, he steered *U-107* into a collision. The blow ruptured the other U-boat's starboard fuel tank, crushed its bow tubes, and left both boats hobbling. They just barely reached safety.

Prospects looked dim when *U-107* returned to America's Eastern Seaboard in May. After patrolling unsuccessfully off Cape Hatteras, *U-107* and two other boats set course southward. On May 29, *U-107* entered the Caribbean.

Gelhaus' fortunes quickly improved. During the first week of June, *U-107* sank three merchant steamers: one Panamanian, one Honduran, one American. Then, late on June 9, south of the Yucatan Channel and about sixty miles southeast of Cozumel Island, *U-107* intercepted another American merchant.[9]

Steaming alone at eleven knots, the 2,600-ton U.S. Army Transport (USAT) *Merrimack* carried military stores from New Orleans to Cristobal. Though unescorted, *Merrimack* wasn't completely defenseless. On board was a Navy armed-guard detachment.

Arming American merchant ships was first considered in June 1941 after the loss of *Robin Moor*, a vintage American-built freighter carrying general cargo and passengers from New York to Mozambique. But it was November before Congress finally repealed portions of the Neutrality Act forbidding the arming of U.S.-registered merchantmen. The Navy hastened to equip vessels with cannons and machine guns, but training enough reservists to operate and maintain them took time. Beyond that lay another hurdle: fractious relations between the Navy and the America's merchant marine. Navy sailors, accustomed to regimentation, often locked horns with National Maritime Union stalwarts. Salty merchant mariners mocked the Navy "sea scouts," while armed guards joked about the civilians' three shifts: "sack time, coffee time, and overtime."[10]

Responsibility for bridging this gap fell on young, inexperienced Naval Reserve ensigns. The novice put on the spot on board USAT *Merrimack* was twenty-four-year-old Ens. Hunter Marshall III.

Marshall, a native of Charlotte, North Carolina, and a 1939 Davidson College graduate, joined the Naval Reserve in July 1941. On January 16, 1942, he was one of eight hundred midshipmen commissioned from Northwestern University's first V-7 class.

Marshall belonged to a prominent cotton manufacturing family. In the April 12, 1942, edition of the *Charlotte Observer*, Hunter, wearing his dress blues, was pictured standing shoulder to shoulder with his three brothers (all younger but equally tall) behind their seated parents. Less than two months later, Hunter faced battle.[11]

At about 10 p.m. on June 10, a *U-107* torpedo struck *Merrimack*'s starboard side just forward of the bridge. Lights went out, and *Merrimack* sagged to starboard, her engines running full speed, rudder jammed hard right.

Armed-guard sailors quickly manned stations aft. Though young Ensign Marshall took overall command, Gunner's Mate Third Class Howard Skaling captained the gun crew. A forty-three-year-old from Tampa, Florida, Skaling was a World War I veteran. Leaving a wife and a career as a house painter behind, Skaling had reenlisted on March 12.[12]

All eight of Skaling's gun crew were seamen deuces, the youngest age twenty, the oldest twenty-six. Six haled from towns bordering Lake Michigan, and their last names—Seivertson, Shipp, Shunk, Sieniki, Simbulan, Skrelunus,

Smutska—suggested they'd been assigned alphabetically. (The only one out of alphabetical order was Georgia native John J. Waller.)[13]

As Marshall's armed guardsmen unlimbered the fantail gun, *Merrimack*'s civilian crew (save for fifty-four-year-old master Wilbur Flowers) prepared to abandon ship. Thirty or more mates, engineers, seamen, cooks, firemen, oilers, wipers, and stewards mustered on the boat deck. Finding *Merrimack*'s starboard lifeboat demolished, men crowded into number 2 lifeboat. Those unable to fit began releasing *Merrimack*'s rafts.

Once lowered and cut loose, the lifeboat drifted astern. There, blocked by *Merrimack*'s jammed rudder, the craft got sucked into the spinning propeller. Many died instantly. Others struggled to keep clear.

Most carried police whistles. Men on the rafts heard whistles blow all around them. But once *Merrimack* sank and the rafts drifted away, the whistling faded, then stopped.

Daylight revealed nine survivors: eight merchant mariners and Seaman Second Class Waller. The men organized themselves, lashed together the two rafts, and settled on how to ration emergency supplies.

Food, oddly, didn't pose a problem. Supplies on hand included huge quantities of malted milk balls—a crude diet, but no one would starve. Water, though, was scarce, and days of merciless sun took a toll. Hope revived whenever they sighted an aircraft, but each was gone before spotting them. Once a destroyer came into view, but it too kept going. Ready to give up, a few took to the water, despite sharks.

A week before *Merrimack* sank, destroyer *Borie* had left Cristobal, escorting two British ships to Key West. An uneventful voyage, but these were troubled waters. Copies of daily reports on U-boat sinkings and attacks were posted on ship's bulletin boards. In the previous month alone, about forty ships had been sunk in the very area *Borie* was traversing. (A news account citing—but not naming—*Borie* painted a rosier picture: "This task unit leader . . . keeps intact a record of hundreds of ships convoyed safely, not a single ship lost[:] . . . proof once again that the U.S. is clearing the blue Caribbean of the menace of Nazi U-boats.")[14]

The crew got a few days' liberty in Key West, where, Bob Maher recalled, it was so hot "sleeping was almost impossible." Morrison Brown, though, had it much better. He left the ship at Key West and rushed to Miami. As he afterwards wrote his paternal grandmother in Swampscott, Massachusetts: "I actually spent a night in Miami. . . . Didn't even call on the phone. Just walked in on Gully."[15]

Out again from Key West, *Borie* took charge of an eleven-ship westbound convoy traveling at barely eight knots. This was cause for tension, and sure enough, just a day into the passage, a Navy plane reported a sub close by.

Seizing the moment, Phil Osborn took *Borie* off in pursuit. "Whoop, whoop, whoop!" *Borie*'s emergency horn blared. At full speed her fantail dug in, and her bow rose like a speedboat's.

Seeing what looked like a periscope, *Borie* dropped depth charges, then fired its forward 4-inch gun at it. As the ship sped past a troopship, Army men lined the rails yelling and waving. Excitement and exhilaration were followed by deep embarrassment; the "periscope" was just metal jutting from submerged wreckage.

As usual, one false alarm begat more. Twice after dark, Navy planes dropped flares that lit the convoy. Ships milled around as if having their pictures taken. It was more circus than convoy. Fortunately, no subs took advantage. And thankfully, early in the afternoon of June 15, the escort commander detached *Borie* to investigate an aerial sighting of rafts with survivors.[16]

This wasn't *Borie*'s first rescue mission. Back in early January in the Pacific, the ship searched for a downed seaplane. That quest had lasted days. Finally, a crow's nest lookout had hailed, "Object on the horizon, off the port bow!" Indeed, it had been the plane wreckage, its crew sitting on the wings, waving, and cheering.[17]

Now, five months later, in what Bob Maher's mother's letters blithely called a "safe duty" area, *Borie*'s crew combed the sea for survivors of a U-boat attack.

Borie found *Merrimack*'s nine shriveled survivors on June 16. It drove home a realization. It seemed the war had been searching for *Borie* and had now found it.

14 | OUT OF FOCUS

WELL INTO 1942, despite cooperation elsewhere, America and Britain shared little operational intelligence about German U-boats. Not that there weren't exceptions. NID's John Godfrey, for example, trusted Vice Adm. Robert L. Ghormley (then FDR's special naval observer at the Admiralty) enough to share closely held secrets. And as early as April 1941, Britain's naval attaché in Washington had been passing summaries on German and Italian surface navies to Capt. Laurance Safford in OP-20-G. While Safford welcomed these, he also deeply mistrusted Bletchley Park, residue of the botched February 1941 exchange visit.[1]

Bletchley's "loss" of Enigma, coupled with America's entry into war, eventually altered Anglo-American code-breaking dynamics. Sometime in 1941 the Kriegsmarine made major changes to Enigma, introducing a four-rotor model, called M4, that greatly increased enciphering possibilities. M4 was initially installed on board capital ships, but by February 1942 it was in use on the Atlantic U-boat networks.[2] BP personnel called the resulting cipher "Shark." Lacking the technological capacity to unravel it until timely code books could be snatched, BP "went blind."

This proved a crushing setback for Rodger Winn, severely curtailing OIC's capability to track U-boats. "Since the end of January," Winn admitted (with typical British restraint) on February 9, "the Atlantic is 'out of focus.'"

The blackout held major implications, not only for North Atlantic convoys but also for the U.S. Navy's struggles to contain *Paukenschlag*. Though the Americans weren't privy to specific Enigma intercepts, alerts from OIC (had they not been "blacked out") might have revealed the full scope of BdU's ambitions, the introduction of milk cows, and the fact that U-boats were operating singly, not in packs.[3]

A distressed Winston Churchill decided to sack NID's John Godfrey. Churchill also expressed his willingness to lift the veil on British cryptography. In a late February letter hand-carried to FDR, Churchill wrote: "You spoke of the importance of our cipher people getting in close contact with yours. I shall be glad to put any expert you care to nominate with my technicians."

The curtain was about to rise—with new American players pacing the stage.

⌖

Post–Pearl Harbor reverberations included a shake-up in the Office of Naval Intelligence. Considering ONI culpable for not detecting Japan's carrier advance on Hawaii, King shifted OP-20-G's code breakers from ONI to the Office of Naval Communications (ONC).

The shift also meant the sidelining of Laurance Safford and his key deputies. Past feats notwithstanding, Safford's ill will towards BP made him a liability. Over fierce objections, Safford was reassigned, but not before making a baleful prediction: "Our prospects of ever breaking the German 'Enigma' cipher machine are rather poor."[4]

Control of OP-20-G passed to Cdr. Joseph "Buzzard" Wenger, a tall, skeletal 1923 Naval Academy graduate who happened to be a Safford protégé.

In the backwash of Churchill's offer, a Bletchley delegation already in the United States to evaluate RDF and radar networks contacted Capt. Joseph Redman, Wenger's boss, to arrange a "wireless conference." Having toured British RDF installations in Bermuda two years before, the fifty-year-old Redman had already made personal inroads with the British.

Beginning April 6 in Washington, OP-20-G and BP representatives met for nearly two weeks. Both sides were cautious but also candid. After Wenger explained OP-20-G's successes—and shortfalls—the lead British representative explained how the Admiralty intercepted German radio traffic, how

BP (he called it "Station X") deciphered those intercepts, and how the Admiralty's Submarine Tracking Room put them to cautious use.

The British hoped to discourage the Yanks from duplicating work already under way. In the process they ended up revealing some of BP's most technical and secretive matters, including their progress—and blind spots—with Enigma. In return for staying out of Enigma the Brits even offered specific concessions, including the promise that two OP-20-G liaison officers could be assigned to GC&CS.

To some extent, both delegations believed they'd laid the groundwork for future Anglo-American cooperation on SIGINT. A month later, Edward Travis, then a rising GC&CS deputy, promised in writing that "by August or September" Americans would receive a Bombe plus "a mechanic to instruct in the maintenance and operation."

Travis—no fool—also included an escape clause. If, for some reason, his promise fell through, Americans would at least receive "a detailed statement as to why this [Shark] traffic cannot be read."

But if the British expected OP-20-G to back away from Enigma based on such a promise, they were mistaken. After taking over from Safford, Wenger spun off a new unit, called OP-20-M, put thirty-nine-year-old reserve Cdr. Howard T. Engstrom in charge, and ordered him to defeat four-rotor Enigma as soon as possible.[5]

Wenger and Redman agreed with the British that the U.S. Navy lacked an organization to exploit operational intelligence effectively. Indeed, the latter had nothing that could be credibly called a "war room."

It was March before Admiral King established the Combined Operations and Intelligence Center (COIC), under Cdr. George C. Dyer, Ernest King's flag secretary and confidant. Despite the ravages of *Paukenschlag*, Dyer and COIC faced bureaucratic barriers. COIC could neither redirect convoys nor keep tabs on merchants gathering at staging points. Even if fresh intelligence pinpointed a U-boat menace, COIC lacked authority to sound the alarm.

Worse, most COIC personnel weren't cleared to see the information on COMINCH Atlantic Section's plot boards. COMINCH Atlantic Section, meanwhile, was drowning in conflicting information about enemy locations and activities.[6] Neither unit could approximate Admiralty OIC's efficiency or match Rodger Winn's bag of tricks.

But now, as OP-20-G and BP delegations negotiated better cooperation on SIGINT, Admiral Ghormley tipped off Ernest King about Rodger Winn's unorthodox U-boat tracking methods. After touring Winn's bailiwick (courtesy of John Godfrey), Ghormley remarked that "only about twenty-five of the British navy are admitted."[7]

OIC's combination of efficiency, effectiveness, and tight security piqued King's interest. Arrangements were made for Winn to visit America. Under other circumstances, Winn's trip might have masked another attempt to school King on the British way. Indeed, it seemed to be just that when Winn locked horns with one of King's flag-level gatekeepers.

America, the rear admiral asserted, didn't need any advice from the British. "The trouble is, Admiral," Winn replied tartly, "it's not only your bloody ships you're losing; a lot of them are ours!"

Winn's straight talk won the day, earning him a "full and friendly" hearing from King and a concession that COIC lacked effective submarine tracking. COMINCH instructed Rear Adm. Russell Willson, his chief of staff, to designate someone to understudy Winn. Frog Low, then Willson's assistant, thought he had just the man.[8]

⌖

Kenneth A. "Ken" Knowles, a brilliant, reclusive Naval Reserve lieutenant, had strung together a peripatetic boyhood and disappointing military career. Born outside Milwaukee in 1901, Ken had been raised in Nevada and New York State before his family settled in Denton, a Maryland farming community. Graduating from high school there in 1921, Ken attended Cornell University until illness forced him back home.

Recovered but short of prospects, Knowles decided to enlist. Rejected by the Navy and Army, he joined the Marines and, after completing boot camp in 1923, passed a competitive exam to enter the Naval Academy. Ken did well there, captaining the Academy's rifle team and graduating near the top of his class. Still, according to the 1927 yearbook, Ken was "quiet and unassuming" and "makes friends rather slowly."

Knowles set out on a traditional sea/shore career. After tours on board two *Clemson*-class four-pipers, he was posted to the Naval Academy in 1934. In April 1936, having married and settled his bride (Velma, the daughter of a Texas physician) in Annapolis, Knowles received orders to report to battleship *Pennsylvania*. Soon, though, his career faltered.

In October 1937, Knowles received three months' sick leave, owing, by his own account, to problems with vision and hearing. The final blow hit in July: "On discharge treatment Naval Hospital, San Diego," the orders read, proceed "to home relieved all active duty."

Retired as a lieutenant, Knowles nonetheless maintained sea-service ties. As civilian editor for *Our Navy*, a professional magazine with offices near the Brooklyn Navy Yard, Knowles kept current on Navy policies and trends, building a reputation as an astute authority on naval matters.

As war approached, Knowles welcomed a call back to active duty, accepting a position in the University of Texas's Naval Reserve Officers Training Corps detachment. The Austin posting brought Velma closer to family. Knowles preferred going to sea, but Navy medicos refused.

Fortunately, during his tour on board four-piper *Paul Jones*, Knowles had impressed her XO, Francis Low. Knowles lacked intelligence background, but Frog remembered how Ken organized mountains of information and prepared clear, concise recommendations. Thus, when King okayed sending someone to visit Admiralty OIC, Low suggested Knowles. In late June 1942, Ken received orders to report immediately to Washington, DC; within a month, he was dispatched to visit Rodger Winn's Submarine Tracking Room.[9]

For his part, Frog Low soon left King's inner circle. Senior Navy officers customarily took on COMINCH staff roles, held them briefly, then went back to sea.[10] Assigned command of heavy cruiser *Wichita*, Frog left for New York to join his ship.

Before departing, however, Frog made a fateful suggestion: "I thought, regardless of the paucity of our present forces, that our organization was basically wrong. . . . We should have a completely separate organization to deal with the U-boats."

Low later said of this suggestion: "It came back to bite me."[11]

15 | STUCK IN LIMBO

ALL THAT SUMMER, Phil Osborn pursued his winning ways with *Borie*'s crew. "Our Capt. is still the swell guy he started out to be," Morrison Brown wrote his father in late June. "We sure do have a happy ship now."

Bob Maher reckoned Osborn a "Hollywood skipper"—worth bragging about to other crews stuck with hard-nosed captains. Not only did Osborn grant "quality liberty," he seemed to relish his own time off the ship. Even before *Borie* docked, the skipper customarily appeared in dress whites, ready to go. Once lines were secured and brow (gangplank) in place, he ordered "Liberty begins at once" and scurried ashore.[1]

But happy ship or no, many still applied for transfer. Some succeeded, though usually not those of most value to the ship. In Kingston, for example, Bob Maher visited a cousin on *Duncan*, a newer destroyer bound for the Pacific. He tried to arrange an on-the-spot transfer but had no luck.*

Morrison Brown likewise displayed restlessness. "I'm ready to move anytime now—that is to some other duty," he confided to his parents. "I expect the old 'B' will be doing the same thing we have for the duration." Without doubt, seeing all the warships passing through the canal heading for the

---

**Duncan* (DD 485) was sunk by Japanese gunfire near Guadalcanal on October 12, 1942, with the loss of forty-eight crewmen. (MaritimeQuest, http://www.maritimequest.com/warship_directory/us_navy_pages/destroyers/pages/alpha_pages/d/duncan_dd485_roll_of_honor.htm [accessed March 25, 2022])

Pacific heightened the sense of being stuck in limbo—neither safe at home nor part of the real war.

Prospects for home leave were also on Son's mind. Each letter now included an update—each with a bit more promise. On August 19: "Don't know exactly when my leave will come off, but I hope within the next four or five months anyway—but I'm not getting my hopes too high." And on August 30: "As I wrote Gully . . . I think probably between now & Xmas I'll be home. . . . If we get some more officers maybe it will be sooner."

That month, his parents fled Florida's late summer heat and humidity for the cool, rustic ambience of "Brown's Hill Billy Cabin," their mountain retreat in North Carolina. "To say I envy you," Son wrote on August 10, "is putting it mildly. The heat of this d—— place [Panama] sure gets you down."[2]

Panama's climate must have seemed particularly oppressive with *Borie* laid up in Balboa's dry dock for more refit. The ship's crew, Bob Maher recalled, spent "weeks living on a ship out of water."[3]

The most visible alteration was the shortening of *Borie*'s signature stacks. Though it afterwards made the ship appear sleeker, the change was not merely cosmetic. A lowered profile made *Borie* a less conspicuous target, as did a new camouflage paint job. And while *Borie* left Balboa as thin-skinned as ever, workers applied a few protective touches: plating over hull portholes and fully enclosing the bridge.

Another major change required removal of *Borie*'s distinctive crow's nest. The perch (the bane of *Borie* lookouts) gave way to a three-hundred-pound radar antenna, in effect an entirely new—and better—way to "see."

The cavity magnetron—Sir Henry Tizard's transformative gift—made it possible to upgrade even small warships with compact radar gear. *Borie* received what was called "SL" surface-search microwave radar.

The first American-built shipboard radars used long-wave technology. The gear took up lots of space, and mast-mounted antennae didn't revolve. To pick up a surface contact, the entire ship had to be turned in its direction. Little wonder that warship captains resisted using radar.

Microwave (also called centimetric) radar permitted smaller antennae—roughly half the size and a third lighter than earlier versions. Below decks, SL's circular "PPI" (plan position indicator) screens could "paint" (display) the range and bearing of a surface contact up to twenty miles away. Radar operators could also "see" merchant ships at night or in thick weather. With radar's proliferation came acceptance and less reluctance to use it.[4]

Sometime that October, as *Borie* emerged from Balboa's dry dock, a new XO, Lt. Charles "Hutch" Hutchins, joined the ship.

Hutch's prewar naval career, which had begun with his 1936 Naval Academy graduation, had lasted just two years. Born in Rhode Island, he grew up an only child in Terre Haute, Indiana. After high school, Hutch attended a local technical institute where his dad taught engineering. He then enrolled briefly at Indiana University before receiving a congressional appointment to Annapolis.

Once commissioned, Hutchins served on board battleship *Nevada* in the Pacific and then, in May 1938, received orders to *Wickes*-class destroyer *Dorsey*. The ship was probably a poor fit for an ambitious junior officer: *Dorsey* towed gunnery targets off the Canal Zone and in the Caribbean.

But it's also likely Hutch heard Indiana's siren call.

Since 1932, Academy graduates had been forbidden to marry until completing two years of sea duty. Sensitive to social conventions of the time, officials worried that some aspiring brides took advantage of graduates who'd had limited experience with female companionship.* The constraint might indeed have prevented hasty unions, but it also frustrated couples sure of their intentions. In June 1938, having satisfied the rule, Hutchins married Ann Hubbard, a Terre Haute native whose father owned Wabash Fibre Box, a manufacturer of corrugated packaging.

---

*In 1931, twenty-two weddings were performed in Annapolis right after graduation, and most brides were city natives. A year earlier, according to the *New York Times*, "of the twelve newly created officers to wed, ten married girls several years older than themselves." ("Ban on Annapolis Weddings to Break an Old Tradition," *New York Times*, June 5, 1932)

Hutch considered his new bride and their future together. That same November, he resigned his regular commission and, by year's end, was back in Terre Haute, working at Wabash.

It took Pearl Harbor to uproot him. Recalled to active duty as a reserve lieutenant (junior grade), Hutch found himself posted (after all) to the Canal Zone. First as an ordnance officer ashore but then, within the year, as a full lieutenant and *Borie*'s second in command.[5]

The new XO's resume was arguably slim: an Annapolis degree, a little over two years at sea, and most recently, a dockside desk job. But now, at twenty-nine, Hutch also boasted three years of maturity and business acumen—steps ahead of *Borie*'s V-7 reservists.

⌖

Morrison Brown's mid-October letter to his sister Mary and her husband George Creighton, proprietors of a cattle ranch near Gainesville, Florida, offhandedly envisioned postwar life. "From all the magazines I read here, Fla. is the coming state as far as raising cattle is concerned. . . . How about a partnership after the war?

"As some of the enlisted men on board say—after the war is over, I'm going to sling an anchor over my shoulder and start walking inland. When someone stops me and asks me what I have on my back, that is where I intend to settle down."

"Please drop me a line & tell me about the kiddos," he signed off, in reference to Mary and George's brood (two daughters and a son, the oldest four years, the youngest ten months). "Give them all a big hug & kiss from 'Mad Mike' or 'Mike' as everyone now calls me. Remember I don't want my nieces and nephews calling me uncle—just plain 'Mike.'"

By now, it seemed, *Borie*'s wardroom had crafted its own nicknames for Light Brown and Dark Brown. Phil was now "Brownie," while Morrison, the man of many nicknames (Brownie, Morie, and Son in addition to Dark Brown), was now "Mad Mike"—a nod, perhaps, to the auto enthusiast's growing mastery of *Borie*'s propulsion plant.*

---

*Henceforth, for clarity, Morrison R. Brown will be referred to as "Mike" rather than "Brownie," "Morie," or "Son."

16 | CARTE BLANCHE

THAT SAME AUGUST, as America's U-boat defenses stiffened and *Paukenschlag* ebbed, Britain's First Sea Lord, Dudley Pound, assessed the "critical situation" in the Atlantic. With America's interlocking convoy system in place, Pound saw trouble brewing elsewhere, predicting, for example, "a heavy scale of attack . . . east of Trinidad."

He also predicted nothing less than "another turning point" in the U-boat war. Dönitz must surely realize, Pound reasoned, that better opportunities now lay (as before) in the Eastern Atlantic. For every U-boat sent to America, Dönitz could keep three working more profitably in the Western Approaches.

Pound despaired that British and American navies had yet to make "our dual control" into a "single control." Both Allies would suffer the consequences of not "fighting on the basis of a unified strategy."[1]

Despite Pound's time-worn critique, Ernest King was, if anything, less inclined than ever to subordinate his resources. Rather, eyeing the long term, he steadily revamped American fleets for a two-ocean war. To counter British complaints about lax security he centralized control and consolidated staff. And while he opposed unified Anglo-American *control*, he allowed closer *collaboration*. One example was bringing together the U.S. Navy's Lieutenant Knowles and the Royal Navy's Commander Winn.

Winn and Knowles appeared kindred souls, each having overcome physical setbacks to gain wartime stature. Of course, Winn, not Knowles, boasted a track record. It was up to Knowles to learn from the master.

Once Knowles arrived in Britain, Winn introduced him to Lenin's Tomb, first as an observer. Then, having grasped what Winn's team did—and why—Knowles gained insight into Ultra. Though never visiting Bletchley Park, Knowles intuited Ultra's potential for fighting U-boats. He must have witnessed Winn's judicious use of it, never overplaying his hand.

Because he returned with much still to learn, Knowles prioritized a "close personal relationship" with Winn. Opening shop at Main Navy Building on Constitution Avenue in late December 1942, he assembled a team drawn primarily from existing COIC staff—most of them reservists. Their responsibility was to track U-boats in the Atlantic and Indian Oceans. A 24/7 watch divided into four sections updated estimated U-boat positions on four large wall charts. The two biggest tracked U-boats in the North and South Atlantic, respectively. One auxiliary chart kept tabs on portions of the Pacific from which the Kriegsmarine might intrude. The fourth displayed a continuous fifteen-day plot of all known U-boat activity across the globe.[2]

Even as Knowles built his operation, two obstacles hampered effectiveness. Four-rotor Enigma had yet to be solved. And code breakers on both sides of the Atlantic remained at odds on how to collaborate.

The British still considered Kriegsmarine Enigma their domain. GC&CS personnel were thus alarmed that summer to learn that OP-20-G was investing heavily in solving M4 Enigma. Intending to reassert control and set the stage for an ironclad agreement on U-boat intelligence, a GC&CS liaison officer met with Buzz Wenger, disclosing Bletchley's difficulties faced and revealing possible options to solve M4 Enigma.

While appreciating this candor, Wenger wasn't swayed. Since July, reports from the two American naval liaisons assigned to Bletchley painted a bleak picture. Three-rotor Bombes were scarce, "maddeningly slow," and making little progress.

Then, in September, Edward Travis returned to Washington, this time hoping to convince the Americans to consolidate all Enigma work at Bletchley. Both sides remained cordial, but Wenger knew full well King would squelch single control.

The upshot was a grand but tenuous bargain: "full collaboration upon the German submarine and naval cryptanalysis problems." Outwardly, the agreement, struck at the beginning of October, assured a partnership aimed at defeating the enemy. But it didn't account for the reticence of Bletchley scientists nor for the lopsided advantage in resources now at Wenger's disposal. OP-20-G had just received carte blanche to produce American Bombes by the hundreds—wielding heft the Brits couldn't hope to match.[3]

Howard T. Engstrom, Wenger's pick to lead the American Bombe project, was a balding, mustachioed Massachusetts native. Brilliant, precocious, and adept in languages and math, he graduated from high school at sixteen and earned a Northeastern University chemical engineering degree at twenty. Choosing an academic path, Engstrom received a Yale doctorate in mathematics in 1929. Then, after two years as a research fellow at the California Institute of Technology (part of it spent abroad, where he became fluent in German), Engstrom joined Yale's mathematics faculty.

Engstrom was living proof that Laurance Safford's efforts to crack Enigma were not altogether wasted. Responding to Safford's 1936 recruiting drive, Engstrom received a reserve lieutenant (junior grade) commission. From 1936 to 1940, during summer active-duty stints, he worked occasionally with Safford. And, while teaching and researching at Yale in early 1941, Engstrom and colleagues began preliminary theoretical work on Kriegsmarine Enigma. In July 1942 he was called to active duty, first as a lieutenant but four months later a lieutenant commander.[4]

In technical terms, Kriegsmarine four-rotor Enigma complicated deciphering by a factor of twenty-six. This left OP-20-G two choices. Either harness twenty-six three-rotor Bombes or produce an entirely new "high-speed" Bombe running twenty-six times as fast.

Only two companies could possibly produce such a marvel: International Business Machines (IBM) and National Cash Register. Dayton, Ohio–based NCR proved the logical choice. First, NCR's board chairman had long-standing ties with both MIT and the Navy. But a second determinant was the presence of Joseph R. Desch, a remarkable thirty-five-year-old electrical engineer. Desch had made a particularly strong impression during a December 1941 conference where he demonstrated expertise in high-speed electrical counters.

Desch's acumen for designing miniature, fast-firing gas tubes enthused Engstrom. These would be essential in producing super-high-speed Enigma-busting machines. Desch's participation was considered so essential that Navy brass pulled whatever strings necessary to make it happen. Learning that Desch was an officer in the Army infantry reserves, they prevented his being called to active duty.

Already, well ahead of striking the grand bargain with GC&CS, OP-20-G had contracted with NCR to design Bombes.

Born in 1907, Desch belonged to a family of German immigrant wagon makers. Living the boyhood idylls of the turn-of-the-century Midwest, Desch made straight *A*s and became a Catholic altar boy. Math and science were his schooltime interests, but radio technology became Desch's passion. His grandfather, father, and uncles were adept at fashioning wood and metal. In similar fashion, Desch became hands-on with electrical technology. Earning a scholarship to the University of Dayton's prep school, Desch then balanced work and study to earn an electrical engineering degree from that university.

After graduation, Desch supervised testing at Day-Fan Electric Co., a fan manufacturer turned radio-receiver producer (and soon to become a General Motors subsidiary). In 1938, after subsequent jobs at Dayton Electric and Frigidaire, Desch was hired by NCR ("Cash" to insiders) to head the company's new electronic research division and design the first electronic adding machines.

Still lean and muscular on the fringes of middle age, Desch enjoyed a reputation as something of a bruiser—he'd won boxing medals as an Army reservist. Yet Joe remained a deeply religious Catholic with a strong sense of ethics. Although a fourteen-year Army Reserve veteran, Joe (along with several NCR colleagues) took exception to a local bishop's exhortation that "we support the Allies with 'lives' if necessary." His June 3, 1940, open letter, published in *The Dayton Herald*, took the prelate to task. Rather than "preaching justifiable self-defense . . . you . . . advocate torture, misery and death for great numbers of American youth."

Such rock-ribbed principles infused his life. Though an outdoorsman, Desch rejected hunting in favor of gardening. Desch also adored ballroom dancing, particularly waltzes, with his wife Dorothy.

Desch never hid his badges of domesticity, but he also knew when to check them outside the shop floor. He smoked Chesterfield cigarettes, two packs a day, and at closing time liked his Scotch and water. And when circumstances warranted, Joe could curse with the best of them.[5]

The concept the Navy envisioned was an Enigma machine working in reverse. Fed a "crib" (a hunch about the plain-text meaning of a tiny portion of an intercepted message), the Bombe's rotors would cycle through all the billions of possible rotor combinations to find the settings that produced the crib. With these rotor settings determined, the balance of the message could be deciphered (if the hunch that underlay the crib was correct) using an Enigma machine with identical rotor and plugboard settings.

But after scouring Navy blueprints for a totally electronic Bombe, Desch identified a big problem. Such machines' specifications required an astounding 70,000 gas tubes—enough, effectively, to burn out the Bombe with extended use. He reached an undeniable conclusion. The NCR Bombe would have to be electromechanical. If time was so crucial to the war effort, the result couldn't be elegant. Instead, brute force would have to solve the problem.

That September, Joe Desch presented the Navy with a Bombe concept that would be mostly mechanical. Producing an all-electronic Bombe, he argued, would take years, time the Navy couldn't spare. Given the necessary resources and the removal of unnecessary red tape, NCR's ugly, powerful, high-speed Bombe, Desch estimated, could be rolled out in months.

Trusting in its relationship with NCR, the Navy promised Desch all that he needed: millions in funding, hundreds of trained personnel, and highest priority. As the project got under way, requests were approved and mounting cost overruns were accepted without question. The original two-million-dollar budget (more than $30 million in 2022 dollars) doubled in a few months.

But the U.S. Navy's blank check, Joe Desch soon learned, didn't come without strings.

⌖

While Americans of German heritage didn't undergo near the same scrutiny and hardship as did those of Japanese heritage, *Paukenschlag*'s assault on American shores generated fears about other possible nefarious Nazi plots. That summer, as Joe Desch was designing a Bombe to crack four-rotor Enigma, just such a plot made headlines nationwide.

In June 1942, U-boats landed two teams of saboteurs, both on East Coast beaches. All were former American residents. Two were naturalized citizens; two others had married Americans. The eight were split into two teams of four, each team equipped with crates containing explosives, incendiaries, fuses, detonators, and timing devices—all meant for an extended campaign of sabotage to aluminum plants, vital railroad areas, water supplies, and bridges. Altogether, the men were bankrolled $154,000 (about $2.5 million in 2022 dollars) to cover travel, bribes, and living expenses.

One four-man team, carried on board *U-202*, landed near Amagansett, Long Island, early on June 13, the other, on board *U-584*, five days later on a beach seven miles south of Jacksonville, Florida. After burying crates and changing into civilian clothes, the Long Island team was to meet in New York City with prearranged contacts. Meanwhile, the Florida saboteurs were to board trains for the Midwest.

Things immediately went wrong on Long Island when a Coast Guardsman stumbled across the Germans. First, the team's leader, George Dasch, a former New York waiter, threatened the guardsman. Thinking better of it, Dasch then offered him money to "forget" the encounter.

Unarmed and outnumbered, the guardsman took the money and pretended to agree, only to raise the alarm. Other guardsmen, rushing to the scene with orders to "resist invasion," instead found German cigarette butts and the area where the saboteurs had buried their cache.

Though *U-584*'s Florida team landed undetected, the overall plot soon unraveled. The eight were to rendezvous in Cincinnati on July 4 to coordinate attacks in Illinois, Kentucky, New Jersey, New York, and Pennsylvania. But instead, on June 19, George Dasch turned himself in to the FBI. The case blew open on June 27, when FBI head J. Edgar Hoover announced the landings and arrests (making no mention of Dasch's voluntary surrender).

The eight would-be saboteurs went on trial in July before a military commission, the first such tribunal since Abraham Lincoln's assassination. Given a glimpse of the defendants, one news reporter concluded they "were no Nazi supermen but merely a group of most ordinary looking individuals." All were found guilty and sentenced to death, though the sentences for Dasch and Ernst Burger, another Long Island infiltrator who turned himself in, were commuted to lengthy prison terms.* The remaining six were executed by electric chair on August 8.[6]

The trial and the backgrounds of those implicated dominated news all that summer. The plot's code name was Operation Pastorius, meant to honor the seventeenth-century immigrant founder of Germantown, Pennsylvania, America's first permanent German settlement. Among accomplices caught up in the FBI net were friends and family of German heritage residing in the Midwest. The saboteurs' rendezvous would have been just fifty miles south of Dayton, itself a prewar hotbed of pro-German Bund activity. Not least, one team leader was named Dasch.†

Under the circumstances, rightly or wrongly, directly or indirectly, Joe Desch and his family received close scrutiny. Particularly Augusta, Joe's

*In 1948, President Harry S. Truman had both Burger and Dasch released and deported to Germany.

†On family documents and death records the "Desch" surname got various spellings, including "Dasch."

mother. Augusta, whose maiden name was Stoermer, had emigrated from Germany at age thirteen, working her way from Liverpool, England, to Pittsburgh, where she lived with an uncle. Moving finally to Dayton, Augusta met and married Joe's father, Edward Frank Desch.

American-born Edward had died in 1937. Meanwhile, Augusta kept in touch with European relatives and even visited Germany twice before the war. More worrisome was Desch's half-cousin, also named Augusta but nicknamed "Gusty." Gusty Zimmerman's father, an ardent Nazi supporter, still lived in Germany. Gusty's husband in Dayton, meanwhile, admitted he tuned into prewar Hitler broadcasts.*

Background checking dragged on under an aura of suspicion. Desch's long service in the Army Reserve favored him. But what about that provocative, arguably pacifist, 1940 letter to the Dayton bishop? America was clearly defending itself now, but could Joe Desch countenance the German deaths that might well result from this top-secret project?

At some point, apparently, Joe Desch told the Navy he no longer wanted the job. But, when his security clearance finally came through, he was simply ordered to get to work.

---

*According to daughter Deb Anderson, her dad, who was fluent in German, had installed a powerful radio transmitter and receiver in the basement of his own home. Certain that all his radio traffic was already being monitored by federal authorities, Joe Desch never considered it an issue of particular concern. (E-mail communication with Joseph Desch's daughter Deb Anderson, January 12, 2021)

17 | GRIM IMBALANCE

DUDLEY POUND'S worst fears materialized that autumn. North Atlantic U-boats mounted fierce attacks on three eastbound convoys, sinking twenty-nine merchants loaded with food and war matériel. Equal disaster lurked to the south.

Beginning October 25, ten U-boats converged on Convoy SL-125, forty-two ships steaming north from Sierra Leone (*S*) to Liverpool (*L*), many transporting homebound troops. During a seven-day battle, much of it near Portugal's Madeira Islands, U-boats overwhelmed SL-125's inadequate escort force, sinking thirteen ships without losing one of their own. Casualties soared.[1]

Surveying October's carnage, Winston Churchill cabled Franklin Roosevelt to confess that "the spectacle of all these splendid ships being built, sent to sea crammed with priceless food and munitions, and being sunk—three or four every day—torments me day and night."[2]

Matters turned worse in November. U-boats sank over 800,000 tons of shipping—the highest monthly total in the war so far.[3] While Allied shipyards were now on pace to produce seven million tons of merchant ships annually, U-boat sinkings might well surpass that total by year's end. A grim imbalance.[4]

All this gave Karl Dönitz cause for optimism—if he were so minded. His U-boat fleet now numbered three hundred, the requisite, he'd once asserted, for a "mortal blow" to the enemy. By year's end he expected to have more than four hundred. Though, owing to repairs and overhauls, only half were operational at any one time, this was a crucial achievement.

Also, troublesome technical issues plaguing U-boat torpedoes since the onset of war were finally resolved. Torpedo warheads had once been equipped with magnetic triggers that too often exploded either prematurely or not at all. Cold northern weather was thought to be the cause, but the U-boats operating farther south reported the same problem.

Once faulty magnetic triggers were replaced by reliable contact triggers, another problem—defective torpedo "depth keeping"—emerged. Though this was not so quickly remedied, a solution (sealing leaks in a pressurized balance chamber) arrived just in time for *Paukenschlag.* Dönitz was now confident that U-boat torpedoes ran true.[5]

Meanwhile, big problems plagued the Allies. The limited operational ranges of surface escorts and antisubmarine aircraft forced Atlantic convoys to follow predictable Great Circle routes. And (unknown to them) B-Dienst experts were decrypting such a bounty of sailing route, course, and position data that Dönitz was using it for tactical decisions.

Dönitz, however, a realist, remained far from content. While the autumn surge in sinkings was impressive, too few occurred in the North Atlantic. It was there that "tonnage war" (*Tonnagekrieg*), his preferred tactic, was best waged. To BdU's mind, *Tonnagekrieg*—put simply, sinking more tonnage than the Allies could launch—held the key to foiling Allied hopes of using Britain as an invasion springboard.

Tonnagekrieg's window of opportunity was closing. At a stroke, America's entry into the war added substantially to Allied merchant tonnage—as did tonnage from friendly Latin American countries. To his *kommandanten,* more tonnage meant more opportunities. But those same opportunities ran up against improved Allied defenses, not least the incremental growth and reach of Allied airpower.

To optimize current opportunities, BdU strung wolf-pack echelons—sometimes totaling between ninety and a hundred U-boats—across all possible routes from Iceland south to the Azores. In the longer run, to capitalize on *Tonnagekrieg,* Dönitz needed unlimited authority to dispatch his burgeoning fleet wherever it could sow the most devastation.

Such authority would soon be his, but not before a potentially significant shift in the war's balance.

In the last days of October 1942, even as U-boats pounced on SL-125, BdU's *kommandanten* failed to spot (and B-Dienst failed to detect) Allied task forces and convoys penetrating adjacent waters. Their armada—five hundred vessels strong—converged on North Africa from Norfolk, Virginia, and multiple ports in the British Isles.

Ships carried supplies and upwards of 100,000 troops for Operation Torch (the new code name for Gymnast, now finally under way), the Anglo-American assault on beaches in Morocco and Algeria. Torch's successful November 8 D-day landings triggered the dispatch of as many as fifty U-boats to positions inside and outside the Mediterranean.

In early going, with Torch invasion vessels disgorging troops and cargo, BdU's marauders slipped in for some easy kills. But, in return for the sinking of eleven Allied ships, Dönitz lost three U-boats. Moreover, against his protestations, Atlantic-force submarines were diverted to the Mediterranean—destined to be bottled up and never to return. In Dönitz's view, the U-boat arm was thereby denied the opportunity to strike decisively—at minimal risk—at North Atlantic convoys.[6]

For their part, America's Joint Chiefs of Staff (and particularly Ernest King) had dragged their feet on Torch, seeing it as the unnecessary diversion of men, ships, aircraft, and matériel. The chiefs acceded to the landing only after considerable arm-twisting from FDR, who was convinced that an offensive must somehow be "laid on" in the Atlantic Theater in 1942.[7]

As expected, Torch preparations monopolized logistics—delaying, rerouting, or cancelling merchant convoys; stripping non-Torch convoys of protection; and draining strategic stockpiles. Even Torch's successes offered mixed blessings. Troops held beachheads but consolidating and advancing required massive reinforcements.

Allied convoys from the United States arrived regularly. The first left New York on November 2, arriving November 18 with 30,000 more troops and 161,000 tons of supplies.[8] But Torch's insatiable appetite jeopardized future offensives. In particular, the dwindling of fuel stocks and the shortage of tankers to replenish them reached crisis proportion.

British oil stocks dropped from seven million tons to five million. Worse, the RN, which consumed 130,000 tons of commercial fuel monthly, saw its ready reserve decrease to 300,000 tons. The Admiralty held another million tons for emergencies, but once these ran out, RN bunkers could run dry.[9]

The reasons were evident: U-boats sank 185 Allied tankers during the first nine months of 1942. America's interlocking convoy system lengthened shipping routes and consequently slowed tanker passages. Hideous North Atlantic weather had laid up over 20 percent of Britain's tanker fleet for repair. And, not least, petroleum used by British forces in North Africa was siphoned from home stores.

"This does not look at all good," Winston Churchill scribbled in the margins of statistical summaries. Then, always a man of impulse, Churchill cabled Franklin Roosevelt, proposing drastic measures. Divert U.S. Navy escorts from the North Atlantic to protect special oil convoys from the Caribbean to the British Isles. Organize a special new detachment of modern U.S. Navy destroyers to escort other oil shipments from the Caribbean to Torch ports in the Mediterranean.

To Ernest King, this was more Churchillian overreach. Why did the British need seven million tons? Five million represented a six-month supply. No American war zone possessed more than ten weeks of aviation gasoline. America's Northeast had just four weeks' fuel oil reserves.

Unwilling to disrupt current convoy schedules, Roosevelt demurred. But distress now prompted Churchill's War Cabinet to act. Beginning in December, Dudley Pound was to organize at least three British-protected special oil convoys sailing directly from Trinidad.[10]

Early on November 19, eleven days after the Torch landings, U.S. Navy cruiser *Boise* entered Delaware Bay, gliding up the Delaware River past Wilmington towards Philadelphia. Once the ten-thousand-ton cruiser had warped alongside a pier, the scars, shell holes, and flame-scorched bulkheads of a furious fight went on full display. Off Guadalcanal on the night of October 11–12, *Boise*, leading three other U.S. Navy cruisers and five destroyers, had ambushed a column of Japanese warships. Now, emblazoned on *Boise*'s bridge were six ship profiles (each accompanied by a miniature Rising Sun flag) representing *Boise*'s share of the total claimed sinkings.*

Ernest King was piped on board to congratulate *Boise*'s skipper and crew. "I want you men to know your job was well done," said King after examining the ship's scarred gun turrets. "Now I want you to get your ship in shape and get back there for the next round."

Notwithstanding COMINCH's eagerness to return *Boise*'s sailors to the Pacific, what they wanted most was shore leave—the first in five months. Sailors with no home-going plans found embrace in the City of Brotherly Love. The *Boise* boys swung arm and arm along crowded streets. Sailors were feted in hotels, bars, restaurants, movie theaters, USO centers†, and the Stage Door Canteen.[11]

Meanwhile, after their own night on the town in Philly, Gully and Brownie composed a joint letter to her mother and his parents. Gully went first. "You probably saw in the paper about the cruiser Boise damaged in the Solomons [Islands, of which Guadalcanal is one] after sinking a whole bunch of Jap ships, well our B [*Borie*] brought them up [north along the Eastern Seaboard]."

"Thought at first," she continued, "[*Borie*] would be in for just a day or so but . . . news came of *3 more days* reprieve." To this happy news Brownie added even better tidings. Come the end of December, *Borie* would be leaving Panama for extended shipyard work in New Orleans. "There may be a chance that I can get leave 2 weeks before N.O. If so, will be home for Xmas. Just keep your fingers crossed."[12]

Borie's extra days in Philadelphia were welcome news also for New Jersey natives like Bob Maher. Making the most of three days' liberty, Bob hopped

---

*U.S. ships actually sank one enemy cruiser, damaged another, and sank a destroyer. In turn, the Americans lost destroyer *Duncan* (see footnote, chapter 15) and suffered damage to another cruiser.

†The USO (United Service Organizations), founded in 1941, was and is a nonprofit that supports armed forces personnel with facilities like canteens and, famously, live entertainment overseas.

a train to Newark's Pennsylvania Station. From there he called his parents, announcing, to their complete surprise, that he'd be home in ten minutes.

Bob's brother Ed, a singing bartender at a local pub, was at work when Bob arrived. No matter, it gave Bob an inspiration. Unknown to Ed, Bob left home and slipped quietly into the pub. Then, when a patron (alerted to the surprise) requested that Ed sing a special song, Bob snuck up from behind to harmonize as Ed belted out the first notes. The two brothers hugged and cried yet somehow managed to finish the song together.[13]

18 | LAND OF IMPROVISATION

LT. CDR. BILL DRANE, a thirty-five-year-old Tennessean, was certain *Bogue* was bound for the Pacific. Since forming at Sand Point Naval Air Station, Washington, in June 1942, Escort Scouting Nine (designated VGS-9), the carrier aircraft squadron he commanded, had been preparing to fight the Japanese. In a freewheeling unofficial unit history tracing Scouting Nine's sojourn from Sand Point to Long Beach and San Diego, squadron operations officer Lt. Roger "Stomp" Santee, wrote, "Shaped up finally and ready to do battle . . . we . . . set course . . . to sink the Rising Sun."

Auxiliary aircraft carrier *Bogue* (ACV 9, or as Santee dubbed it, the "Reluctant Dragon") weighed anchor on November 22. *Bogue* wasn't much on looks: viewed in profile, it resembled an inverted hat. *Bogue*'s smokestacks, rigged like auto exhaust pipes, jutted from either side, their mouths turned up and flush with the flight deck. Its island structure (five feet wide, twenty-five long, fifteen high) seemed both obstacle and oversight. However, to *Bogue*'s crew and its complement of aviators, altogether more than nine hundred men, the ship's destination mattered more than looks. Many of the crew were veterans of carrier *Lexington*, lost during the May 1942 Battle of the Coral Sea.[1] Now, on board a new ship, they thirsted for revenge, just as VGS-9's aviators thirsted for glory.

"We sailed exuberantly through the night," Stomp recalled, "out from Point Loma's fog-filled bay." The next morning, however, was quick to disappoint. "Now hear this! This is the [*Bogue*] Executive Officer speaking. We have been ordered to proceed to the Panama Canal. On arrival there, we will receive further orders."

As *Bogue* neared Panama, squadron pilots flew their barrel-chested TBF Avenger torpedo bombers and stubby F4F Wildcat fighters to the AAF base on the Atlantic side of the canal. According to Santee: "Many of the Army pilots wondered why in the hell we didn't spin out while making those steep banked turns in to the landings."

The reason, explained Santee, was simple. "We concentrated . . . on carrier landing practice because most of the pilots were fresh out of flight training. . . . Coming aboard a carrier . . . in rough seas and bad weather was certain to require confidence and skill."* Landing on board *Bogue* added another frisson of risk. The Reluctant Dragon was, as Santee described it, "a four hundred and twenty-three foot [former] oil tanker† supporting a flight deck." Takeoffs and landings at sea required flattops to steam into the wind, adding speed—and airfoil lift—to oncoming gusts. Yet "this mighty man of war was capable of top speeds of [only] twenty to twenty-five miles per hour."

But even practice held consequences. On December 4, Ens. James O. Pfeffer, a twenty-one-year-old Avenger pilot from Missouri, died, along with his radioman and gunner,‡ in a midair collision.[2]

A month later, after *Bogue* reached Norfolk, Virginia, Bill Drane checked in with Naval Air Force, U.S. Atlantic Fleet (ComAirLant) to report VGS-9 ready for duty. ComAirLant, a consolidation of three other commands, was itself just three days old. When Santee went there to obtain some tactical instructions, "I was informed that there were none. We were in the land of improvisation and trial and error."[3]

Not being a genuine submarine was the U-boat's Achilles' heel. Like all World War II submarines—Allied or Axis—the U-boat was actually a submersible torpedo boat reliant on dual propulsion: diesel engines on the surface, electrical

*Particularly for Avenger pilots. At five tons, the TBF was the heaviest single-engine aircraft produced during the war.

†*Bogue* was converted from a cargo ship, not a tanker.

‡ARM 3c C. M. Marlette Jr. and S1c G. S. Laughlin.

motors submerged. Huge onboard storage batteries supplied electrical power. Their daily recharging required several hours cruising on the surface.[4]

A U-boat traveled nearly twice as fast on the surface as it did under water.* At top speed—roughly seventeen knots—a U-boat could easily overtake a merchant convoy and even outrun some slower escorts. But surface cruising, whether for speed, maneuvering, replenishment, or battery charging, risked being seen.

The risk was acceptable if lookouts stayed alert and opponents lacked effective radar. By mid-1942, however, many Allied convoy surface escorts carried microwave (centimetric) radar, and their crews were mastering it.

For now, airborne radar gear was usually not as advanced. The first sets crammed into aircraft cockpits employed long-wave technology, and to counter them German scientists had devised a simple radar-detection device called "Metox." Metox could reliably sniff out primitive airborne-radar pulses. When an alarm tripped, the U-boat simply slipped beneath the waves.[5]

While Metox stymied stealth attacks by Allied aircraft, a more vexing deterrent to them was distance. Heading east (usually heavily laden) from Canadian waters or west (usually in ballast, what merchant mariners called "flying light") from Britain's Western Approaches, North Atlantic convoys plied stretches of ocean dominated by the collision of the warm Gulf Stream and cold Labrador Current. Storms and icebergs menaced, and even when they didn't, fogbound calms endangered every vessel afloat and any aircraft aloft.

British antisubmarine air squadrons flew from Northern Ireland, Western Scotland, and Iceland. Royal Canadian and U.S. Navy aircraft from Nova Scotia, Iceland, and Newfoundland. But the twin-engine planes at hand—Whitleys, Beaufighters, Wellingtons, Blenheims, Catalinas, and Hudsons—could only fly so far and patrol so long.

Beyond the limits of air cover, merchant convoys traversed what was variously called the Air Gap, Greenland Gap, Black Hole, or Black Pit. During

*At a maximum submerged speed of eight knots, a U-boat's batteries would expire after just fourteen hours. If forced to stay down longer than twelve hours, speed had to be cut to four knots.

four to five tense days, the convoy and its surface escorts ran a U-boat gantlet without help overhead. BdU exploited Air Gap boundaries. German U-boats located convoys before they entered the gap, preyed on merchants traveling inside, then withdrew when air cover resumed.

While the North Atlantic contained the biggest void, there were gaps, holes, and pits elsewhere as well. Convoys transiting between Gibraltar and West Africa, for example, braved "no-fly zones" west of the Canary Islands and east of the Azores. The Azores Gap was a particular favorite of Dönitz's U-boats—a place to hunt and replenish safely.

By the end of 1942, Atlantic air umbrellas stretched roughly four hundred miles east of Newfoundland, five hundred miles south of Iceland, and seven hundred miles west of the British Isles. This represented real progress, but progress that was regularly confounded by Allied division and indecision.

Despite collaborating on the Doolittle Raid, Ernest King and Hap Arnold diverged over tactics and jurisdiction for fighting U-boats. By ironclad arrangement, the USAAF operated practically all land-based, multiengine aircraft. Arnold was willing to employ his bombers against U-boats—but not on King's terms.

COMINCH wanted AAF antisubmarine aircraft to help escort convoys. But Army pilots loathed such "babysitting," and Hap Arnold preferred organizing medium-range bombers into roving "submarine destroyer squadrons." King welcomed the bombers but insisted they be assigned to Navy sea frontier commands.

Across the Atlantic, interservice squabbles were no less fierce. Britain's RAF, independent of both the Royal Navy and Army, also disdained shepherding convoys. The RAF believed its "proper" priority was strategic bombing of Germany.

In May 1941, after much prodding, RAF bombers attacked U-boat pens under construction along the coast of France. The attacks were too late and too little. By autumn, concrete revetments with walls sixteen feet thick rendered U-boats inside them impervious to air assault.* It was not until the following

*Raids by AAF bombers from October 1942 to January 1943 likewise failed.

May that the RAF initiated a new anti-U-boat campaign: round-the-clock patrols of the Bay of Biscay, a choke point for U-boats entering and exiting the Atlantic from French bases.

Meanwhile, in the United States, Hap Arnold set up an autonomous USAAF antisubmarine command. While Army medium bombers assigned to Navy sea frontiers would continue babysitting convoys, Army long-range Liberators would stalk U-boats.

The Consolidated four-engine B-24 Liberator was a potent addition to the arsenal of aerial antisubmarine warfare. In its long-range (LR) configuration, the so-called Flying Boxcar boasted an operational ASW patrol radius of four hundred to six hundred miles. But a very-long-range (VLR) Liberator's reach, with some armor shed, gun turrets removed, and additional fuel storage added to the bomb bay, extended to a thousand miles.[6]

VLR Liberators could significantly shrink, but not completely close, air gaps. What's more, Allied bomber commands got first call on Flying Boxcars rolling off Consolidated assembly lines. Prof. Patrick M. S. Blackett, an eminent physicist (eventually a Nobel Prize winner) and the Admiralty's expert in a new science called operational research (OR), calculated that a combined force of two hundred LR and VLR bombers would have a more decisive impact protecting Atlantic convoys than they would bombing Germany.[7]

But Blackett's case fell on deaf ears and closed minds. Allied navies would simply have to devise other gap-closing measures.

Aircraft carriers seemed the obvious choice, but carriers were scarce, costly, and desperately needed to take on Japanese carrier forces in the Pacific. The losses of British carriers *Courageous* and *Ark Royal* demonstrated just how vulnerable these behemoths could be in U-boat-infested waters. But such setbacks didn't deter Winston Churchill or Franklin Roosevelt, both inveterate naval enthusiasts, from championing schemes to bring carrier aircraft to bear against U-boats.

By spring 1941, spurred on by Churchill, the Admiralty had equipped four vessels—a tender and three merchants—with catapult gear, producing what were called CAMS (catapult aircraft merchant ships).[8] A similar "make-do" invention was the MAC (merchant aircraft carrier), a tanker retrofitted with a small flight deck. In time, nearly twenty MACs would operate in the North Atlantic.[9] The problem with both, however, was that their aircraft could take off but not land. One way or another, CAMS and MAC pilots usually wound up in the drink.

However, Churchill and his Admiralty also pursued a third innovation. Early in 1941 the British had captured *Hannover*, a 567-foot, 5,600-ton German merchant vessel. Equipped by the British with a small but complete flight deck, *Hannover* became HMS *Audacity*, a cheap, expendable aircraft carrier capable of launching—and landing—six fighter aircraft.

Franklin Roosevelt too was inspired by the idea of bargain aircraft carriers. And, backed by America's expanding shipbuilding capacity, he pulled levers to produce them. In October 1940 FDR proposed transforming Maritime Commission ships already under construction into aircraft carriers stocked with as many as a dozen aircraft. By November 1941, two merchant hulls had been repurposed and commissioned as carrier prototypes: the U.S. Navy's *Long Island* and the Royal Navy's *Archer*.[10]

In the wake of Pearl Harbor, conversions of twenty more cargo vessels and four tankers—a dozen each for the Royal Navy and U.S. Navy—were fast-tracked. The second-generation small carriers incorporated more powerful engines, extra fuel capacity, longer flight decks, and bigger hangars. As American shipyards toiled on the two dozen conversions, pressure mounted to rush these "escort carriers"* into action—in no small part because of *Audacity*'s year-end exploits.[11]

Audacity's fighter aircraft—Wildcat models that the British dubbed Martlets—were intended primarily to shield convoys from Luftwaffe intrusions.†

*Designations changed over time. *Long Island*'s original designation was APV-1. Designations for subsequent models were AVG (aircraft escort vessel) and ACV (auxiliary escort carrier). Escort carrier (CVE) was not settled on until July 1943. Nicknames abounded as well: "jeep carrier," "baby flattop," and, by the British, "Woolworth carrier."

†As first envisioned by FDR, carrier-based aircraft would scout, not strike. After spotting U-boats and marking their positions with smoke bombs, aircraft would stand aside as surface escort guns and depth charges made the kill.

Indeed, on September 21, an *Audacity*-launched Martlet intercepted and shot down a four-engine German Condor—a notable first.[12]

Not quite two months later, on December 14, this time carrying four Martlets, *Audacity* joined sixteen British surface escorts (a combination of destroyers, corvettes, and sloops) to guard Homebound Gibraltar 76, a thirty-two-ship merchant convoy from the Rock to Great Britain. The number of escorts assigned was no fluke. U-boats and Condors continuously stalked this lucrative ocean corridor.

Beginning December 16, true to form, as many as a half dozen U-boats relentlessly assailed Homebound Gibraltar 76. Despite sometimes horrendous flying weather, *Audacity*'s Martlets fought with daring, not only against Condors (shooting down two and damaging a third) but also against U-boats. On December 17, for example, one Martlet, after spotting a U-boat twenty miles ahead of the convoy, made an ill-advised strafing run. The submarine's flak gunners promptly dispatched the aircraft, killing its pilot. But converging firepower from five surface escorts soon exacted fitting revenge.[13]

On December 21, after this U-boat and three more were forced to scuttle or sunk outright, BdU threw more submarines into the brawl. Dönitz, who knew nothing about *Audacity*'s origins, accepted one *kommandant*'s claim of being up against a full-fledged carrier.

Late that night, U-boat torpedoes cut short *Audacity*'s short, glorious—and eye-opening—career. Against the advice of the convoy's escort group commander, the aggressive—and soon to be celebrated—RN commander F. J. "Johnny" Walker, *Audacity*'s (more senior) skipper stationed his carrier on the unprotected starboard flank of Homebound Gibraltar 76. Jolted by a torpedo, *Audacity* sank at 11 p.m. with the loss of seventy-three crewmen.

Homebound Gibraltar 76 finally reached its destination on December 23, leaving BdU in despair at the week-long battle's tally. In exchange for sinking *Audacity* (what Dönitz concluded must have been some sort of aircraft tender, not a fleet carrier), a British destroyer, and two merchants, he had lost at least three (and possibly five) U-boats: an unsustainable ratio.

"The sinking of the aircraft carrier," Dönitz wrote in what doubled as understatement and premonition, "is of particular importance . . . in every future convoy action."[14]

For the Allies, the results were equally instructive but vastly more promising. Summoned to the Admiralty, Walker—RN's hero of the hour—made clear Homebound Gibraltar 76's foremost lesson: "Aircraft are absolutely invaluable for anti-submarine warfare. . . . ALL escorts should be used as striking forces for offensive lunges away from the convoy, attacking U-boats."[15]

In short, ASW forces, air and sea, would work better in tandem than at cross-purposes.

Meanwhile, unaware of Johnny Walker's epiphanic pronouncement, VSG-9's aviators labored on in Stomp Santee's "land of improvisation." Sadly, Santee could no longer be cavalier about squadron "trial and error" off the Virginia Capes: "We devised our own search and attack procedures, correcting errors as they occurred. There were many. . . . At times morale fluctuated like the tides among all hands and severely hampered operations."[16] With the February 7, 1943, deaths of three comrades, squadron morale must have plunged to a new low.

Two fatalities were young ensigns, both piloting Wildcats. The third was Lt. George S. Friend of Pasadena, California, a veteran aviator serving as *Bogue*'s landing signal officer (LSO)—responsible for coaxing pilots onto a short, rolling, pitching flight deck. "According to the official Navy telegram sent to his parents," reported a Pasadena newspaper, "Lieutenant Friend died as a result of being struck by an airplane."[17]

Carrier aviation fatalities are inevitable, even under the most controlled conditions. But to suffer three noncombat deaths on a single day was both distressing and ominous. The losses must have left VSG-9 personnel in doubt of their readiness for what lay ahead. In just two weeks *Bogue* was scheduled to leave Norfolk, bound for the North Atlantic.

19 | SEASON OF JOY AND PERIL

"**THE PHILADELPHIA TRIP** is probably now an old story," Morrison Brown wrote his mother on December 13, 1942, a couple weeks after *Borie*'s return to Panama. Still, "you can imagine how much fun it was. Sort of a second honeymoon."

Beyond its immediate pleasures, Philadelphia built anticipation for the coming holidays. "The Christmas leave is almost certain now," he went on. "Whether I'll be home on December 25 is a question—but any day before or after the 25th you can expect me. . . . It seems more like a dream.

"There's not much I can write you about the ship," Son concluded, "We now have three Ens. [ensigns, newly commissioned officers] on board and expect another any day now."[1]

Two of the new ensigns, thirty-year-old Richard Earl "R.E." St. John and twenty-three-year-old Lawrence S. "Larry" Quinn, were former high school football coaches.

During four seasons as a starting left halfback for Austin College, a small Presbyterian liberal arts school in northeastern Texas, R.E. built a reputation as a "consistent ground gainer and passing star." After earning a BA degree in 1936 and an education master's degree in 1937, R.E. (who was raised in Royse City outside Dallas) joined the faculty and football coaching staff at East Texas'

Kilgore High School. Rooming with two other coaching assistants in a big house across the street from the school, "Coach Saint" gained recognition in a community fanatical about its Bulldogs. In fact, after Kilgore's head coach left to join the FBI, Coach Saint took over for the 1941 football season, only to resign the following January, enlist in the Navy, and attend midshipman training in New York.[2]

Larry Quinn, seven years younger than R.E., had followed a similar trajectory in western New York State. After graduating from St. Lawrence University in 1941, Larry, a Saints' gridiron captain and three-sport standout, became assistant football coach at East Rochester High. In Quinn's "one and done" season, East Rochester's Bombers cruised to an undefeated, untied, and unscored-on season.[3]

St. John's and Quinn's shared background made them friends. But it also added a new dimension to *Borie*'s command dynamic. Though R.E. and Larry were *Borie*'s most junior officers, they had already proven, in the classroom and on the playing field, that they knew how to organize, coach, discipline, and mentor teams of young men.

Meanwhile, to *Borie* veterans "Mike" Brown, "Brownie" Brown, and "Curly" Dietz, the ensign influx meant two things. First, the veterans could enjoy home leave. Second, it raised hopes for transferring off the "B." As Mike framed it to his mother Marion: "Within a short time some of us old timers will be getting a change of duty. I hope so."

On December 22, as the ship readied to leave Cristobal for New Orleans, Phil Osborn received a new set of orders for *Borie*: "By ComPaSeaFron [Commander Panama Sea Frontier] dispatch . . . of December 1942, this vessel was detached and ordered to report to . . . ComSoLant [Commander South Atlantic Force]."[4]

Duty in the South Atlantic promised to push *Borie* closer to the war against U-boats. Reacting to bolstered convoy defenses along America's Eastern Seaboard and in the Gulf of Mexico, U-boats were concentrating off Brazil, South America's largest and most populous nation.

Although Getúlio Vargas, Brazil's autocratic president, had severed diplomatic ties with the Axis, he clung to neutrality. Brazil, while weak militarily, was geographically pivotal: the waters between Cape San Roque on Brazil's northeast coast and the Cape Verde Islands off North Africa constituted an "Atlantic Narrows" of strategic value to both sets of belligerents.[5]

Vargas, accordingly, kept above the fray, waiting to see how the "winds of war" blew. But his fence-sitting ended in mid-August after a pack of U-boats, sustained by *U-460*, a milk cow, sank five Brazilian merchant marine vessels. One carried three hundred Brazilian army soldiers and most drowned.

The disaster provoked widespread anti-Axis rioting and pushed Brazil into the Allied camp. Simultaneously, however, Vargas closed Brazilian ports and slapped an embargo on all its oceangoing commerce.

Desperate to lift Vargas' embargo, COMINCH dispatched Vice Adm. Jonas Ingram, Commander Fourth Fleet, to parley. Ingram's promises of military aid induced Vargas to lift the shipping ban. The U-boat blitz briefly receded, only to return with a vengeance. In November and December, U-boats sank twenty-one Allied merchants, totaling almost 120,000 tons. This hastened plans to organize escorted convoys (under Ingram's control) between Trinidad, an island just off the coast of Venezuela, and Bahia, a Brazilian port, four thousand miles to the south.[6]

Once New Orleans shipyard workers finished upgrades, *Borie* would sail for Port of Spain, Trinidad, to begin escorting "TB/BT" convoys.

⌖

As *Borie* left Cristobal for New Orleans on Christmas Eve, Joe Desch and his NCR engineering team largely disregarded the holidays to press forward with their work. That November, what was officially (and secretly) called the U.S. Naval Computing Machine Laboratory (NCML) took up quarters in Building 26, an art deco structure formerly used as NCR's night school. Air-conditioned and fireproof, Building 26 (it was the twenty-sixth building constructed on NCR grounds) contained 37,000 square feet of floors reinforced to accommodate heavy machinery. Conveniently detached from other Cash facilities, NCML also boasted a commodious loading dock right next to a Baltimore and Ohio Railroad spur line.

NCML security was particularly tight. Machine gun–wielding U.S. Marines guarded entrances and watched from rooftops. These combat veterans, many of them Purple Heart recipients, could be skittish. One door-slamming project engineer startled a Marine shaving at a bathroom sink. Before he knew it, the engineer was staring down the muzzle of a .45-caliber pistol.

Though cleared now for security, Desch found his routines and relationships in disarray. Joe was permitted limited visits with his mother and two younger sisters, but contacts with Gusty, her husband, and other distant relations were strictly forbidden. Meanwhile, Navy plainclothes agents began round-the-clock surveillance on Joe's movements. Agents sat in cars parked outside Building 26 and also Desch's home—always ready to tail him wherever he drove.

Even more intrusive was the proximity of Navy lieutenant commander Ralph I. Meader, the officer in overall charge of the Dayton project. Meader, a Dartmouth College graduate and something of an inventor, actually took up quarters in Joe and Dorothy Desch's modest two-bedroom Tudor cottage. Though married to a British-born actress, Meader, who reputedly fancied himself a ladies' man, flirted flagrantly with Dorothy. Moreover, Meader was an ever-present reminder that Desch's allegiance remained suspect.

December was also disrupted by the imminent arrival of Alan Turing. Turing, once GC&CS's driving force, had been sidelined. Despite his singular talents, Turing's eccentricities and administrative ineptitude had become intolerable as Bletchley operations expanded.[7]

For now, Turing was being shunted to America. Booked on board *Queen Elizabeth*, the luxury liner turned troop transport, he disembarked in New York City in November. He was to work at Bell Telephone Laboratories helping develop a more secure telephone link between Washington and London—what became known as a "scrambler." However, a side trip to NCML was also arranged.[8]

Joe Desch and his team were novices when it came to the fractious Anglo-American efforts to crack Kriegsmarine Enigma. To their credit, the Brits were providing useful information about their Bombes, information that gave NCML a good start. That said, Desch wasn't entirely comfortable with hosting another kibitzer. Turing would have complete access to NCML, while Desch expected to learn little about GC&CS's deepest secrets in return.

Of pressing curiosity was news that Bletchley had somehow broken four-rotor Enigma.

⌖

Since February 1942, GC&CS had endured recriminations for having "lost" Kriegsmarine Enigma. OIC had begged for a breakthrough. The Battle of the Atlantic was, OIC icily reminded Bletchley in November, "the only [campaign] in which the war can be lost unless BP do help."[9]

By now, frustration competed with determination at BP. November was on track to become the worst month of the war for Allied merchant shipping losses worldwide. Bletchley staff knew full well the current meagerness of their ability to help could be measured not only in lost cargoes but also in sunken ships and shattered lives.

Fortunately, deliverance neared.

On October 30, a radar-equipped British Sunderland reported a contact, "possibly a submarine," north of Port Said, the Mediterranean terminus of the Suez Canal. A British destroyer conducted a sweep but found nothing.

Seven hours later, however, just as four more British destroyers, including HMS *Petard*, arrived on scene, another aircraft sighted a periscope a few miles away. All five destroyers converged and, after ten hours of relentless depth charging, forced a severely damaged *U-559* to the surface.

Petard and *Hurworth*, closest to *U-559*, promptly raked its conning tower with 20- and 40-millimeter cannon fire, killing or wounding several Germans—among them the *kommandant*. Meanwhile, in their haste to scuttle and abandon ship, remaining crew failed to jettison *U-559*'s Enigma.

As *Petard* edged towards the wallowing submarine, a boarding party led by thirty-year-old Francis Fasson, the first lieutenant, scrambled on board. Fasson, stripped down, bearing a flashlight, wielding a submachine gun, and joined by sixteen-year-old Thomas Brown, a NAAFI* canteen assistant, hastened below.

Finding keys in *U-559*'s radio room, Fasson opened a locked drawer stuffed with papers and "confidential books." Twice, Brown carried stacks of these materials to other boarding party members topside. Returned from his second trip, Brown helped Fasson pry loose a "box" attached to a bulkhead. Most likely *U-559*'s four-rotor Enigma.

---

*Navy, Army and Air Force Institutes, a British government–sponsored company (analogous to the USO) running recreational facilities and shops used by its armed forces.

As he struggled to disconnect a welter of connecting wire, Fasson again dispatched Brown topside, this time ordering him to stay there. Meanwhile, Fasson, now assisted by Able Seaman Colin Grazier, lugged the mysterious box to the base of the control room ladder. Fasson and Grazier were busy securing a lift line to haul the box up when *U-559* started down by the stern.

"You'd better come up!" Brown shouted down the ladder, before leaping into a waiting whaleboat. Concerned that the towline attached to *U-559* might upend the whaleboat (drowning occupants and the trove of materials), *Petard*'s skipper ordered the line cut.

U-559 soon vanished, taking Fasson, Grazier, and the box down with her.[10]

The materials pinched by *Petard*'s intrepid boarding party included code books used to report weather conditions and ship sightings. The materials were rushed to Bletchley, but it was December 13 before code breakers discovered in them, much to their relief, an exploitable lapse in German security.

U-boat code clerks transmitted weather alerts using four-rotor Enigma as if it were its three-rotor predecessor, simply disengaging the fourth wheel. In short order, BP personnel could work out—for any given day—settings for the three rotors. BP's three-rotor Bombes, meanwhile, could determine the setting for the fourth.

The breakthrough was by no means final. Nor did it obviate the work under way in Dayton. Still, the weather code book was not due to expire for three more months. Until then, GC&CS possessed all the tools needed to help OIC once again.

"As the result of the most strenuous endeavor," Dudley Pound signaled Ernest King that same day, "a few days' U-boat traffic will be readable in the immediate future, and this may lead to better results in the near future." But Pound added a caution: "You will, I am sure, appreciate the care necessary in making use of this information to prevent suspicion being aroused as to its source. . . . It would be a tragedy if we had to start all over again."[11]

Meanwhile, the teleprinter in OIC's Submarine Tracking Room clattered back to life, delivering decoded U-boat intercepts. Understandably, this was cause for jubilation in Lenin's Tomb. After all, it put Rodger Winn's team back squarely in the game. The only missing element was Winn himself.

After two stressful years, Rodger Winn, whose commanding presence masked a frail physique, had succumbed to nervous collapse. There were suspicions and warning signs along the way. Whenever his hands shook, for example, Winn fortified himself with swigs from a pocket flask of whisky. But inevitably, Winn became so visibly rundown, drained, and distressed that doctors had no choice but to order complete rest.[12]

Tracking Room operations now passed to Winn's young acolyte Patrick Beesly. One of the room's more pressing challenges was to clear a path for "TM-1," the first of three special oil convoys sailing, at Churchill's insistence, from Trinidad to the Mediterranean.

The four vessels reaching Port of Spain in the afternoon of December 27 might, because of their gray paint schemes, have been mistaken for U.S. Navy warships. Actually, 1,350-ton destroyer *Havelock* and 950-ton corvettes *Godetia*, *Pimpernel*, and *Saxifrage* were all His Majesty's Ships. Seconded to America's Eastern Sea Frontier over the previous nine months, they'd simply conformed to Vice Adm. "Dolly" Andrews' appearance specs.

All four also belonged to Escort Group B-5, one of five British close-escort groups assigned back in February to what was called the Mid-Ocean Escort Force. As first conceived, MOEF escort groups were to protect convoys making "straight across" (nonstop) transatlantic runs. To pull this off without exhausting fuel, MOEF's vessels, many of them corvettes, would have to economize: adhere to Great Circle routes, decrease speed, and maneuver sparingly.

MOEF's fourteen escort groups (some American, some British, and some Canadian) had originally numbered 143 warships, but the demands of Operation Torch had trimmed their ranks. B-5's four warships—its full complement was nine—entered port rust streaked and worn down. *Godetia*'s malfunctioning boilers were B-5's chief disability, but after so long at sea and so far from home, every B-5 ship and sailor craved respite.

Waiting in Port of Spain were nine tankers constituting TM-1: two steam-powered and seven diesel-driven; five British, three Norwegian, and one Panamanian; all painted the same dull "crab-fat" gray. Both sets of crews,

Royal Navy* and merchant marine, must have been apprehensive about the task ahead. The transatlantic passage of vessels laden with aviation fuel, furnace oil, lubricants, and benzine under the scant protection of four beat-up escorts.

A mandatory conference of masters assembled ashore early the next morning. Sailing orders and operational instructions were distributed; Arthur Laddle, master of British steam tanker *Oltenia II*, was designated convoy commodore, and TM-1's senior officer escorts (SOE), forty-year-old RN commander Richard C. Boyle, was introduced.

During this meeting, Boyle likely learned that several of TM-1's tankers were DEMS (defensively equipped merchant ships), supplied with cannons, heavy machine guns, and the gunners to operate them.† He may also have discovered that two TM-1 motor tankers—*Cliona* and *Norvik*—carried gear to refuel other vessels at sea. This new capability could be a boon to MOEF escorts. But the process could be risky—especially in rough weather.

To a man, the conferees were unnerved by TM-1's scheduled departure. Urgent repairs and reprovisioning were still incomplete. Local authorities, however, seemed more concerned about Port of Spain's "loose lips" than Central Atlantic U-boats. TM-1 and Escort Group B-5 would sail that same afternoon.[13]

---

*Corvette *Godetia's* captain was British, but its crew was Belgian: fishermen, ferrymen, and tugboat hands who had escaped to England and joined the Royal Navy.

†Comparable to U.S. naval armed guards.

20 | HE WHO SEES FIRST

ON SUNDAY, JANUARY 3, 1943, *U-514*, a Type IX four weeks out of Lorient and Trinidad bound, cruised on the surface southwest of the Azores. This was *Kapitänleutnant* Hans-Jürgen Auffermann's second mission to the South Atlantic (a "Calypso Patrol"). On the first, *U-514* had left a Baltic port in August 1942 and not returned until November. Such extended cruises, made possible only by U-tanker support, were grueling under the best of circumstances.

Central Atlantic weather could be punishing, but today's conditions—a crisp northeasterly breeze kicking up a light chop, moderate visibility under a canopy of clouds, occasional showers—bordered on pleasant. By contrast, conditions near the equator exhausted the crew. Topside, scorching sun and blinding glare. Inside, hot, hammering diesels and a fetid miasma of sweat and condensation.[1]

Hunting in the tropics, meanwhile, required improvisation and risk-taking. While scouting Barbados during that first patrol, Auffermann spotted two freighters docked at Bridgeton, Barbados's capital. Finding Bridgeton's inner harbor blocked by antisubmarine netting, Auffermann ended up launching six torpedoes, two of which penetrated the net's steel mesh to sink the outermost vessel, a 5,500-ton merchant steamer. The vessel settled in the mud, doubtless stunning the populace.[2]

Searching for more targets, *U-514* went all the way to the equator. Brazil's ports were then sealed, so Auffermann infiltrated an Amazon River estuary. He sank two Brazilian freighters and was fortunate not to be trapped.

Auffermann's eighty-seven-day patrol claimed four ships for slightly more than 17,000 tons, hardly spectacular results. Indeed, given *U-514*'s long voyage and how BdU measured productivity—average tonnage sunk per day at sea—Auffermann's score was quite low.

Now, still far from its destination in the second patrol, technical and mechanical problems hampered *U-514*. Radio gear was acting up, and a malfunctioning diesel limited surface speed. Though *U-514*'s chief engineer hoped to repair the engine, Auffermann worried.

"He who sees first has won," went a U-boat maxim. As you scan a seemingly empty ocean, always bear in mind an enemy is looking and listening too. Inured to this dictum, Auffermann instantly raised binoculars when a lookout shouted, "Masts on the horizon!" Auffermann's practiced eyes picked out the contact, cross-hatched threads poking above the horizon. But the threads—merchant masts—were rising, gaining definition. Headed his way.

Equally axiomatic was a Dönitz edict: "He who uses fully the moment of surprise finds success."[3]

Auffermann ordered a course to intercept. Then: "Battle stations! Clear the bridge! Dive!" Auffermann secured the top hatch, slid into the conning tower, and stepped to the periscope.[4]

To be certain, he'd have to get closer. Auffermann hoped the boat's diesels could muster enough speed.

As *U-514* resurfaced, trimmed down to its smallest possible profile, Auffermann clambered back to the bridge, binoculars ready.

He saw tankers, five at least. But what about convoy's escorts? How many were there? How much threat did they pose?

It was well after dark on December 28 when TM-1 and B-5 finally cleared Port of Spain and moved into night steaming formation.[5] Eight tankers lined up in columns of two. From port to starboard: *Albert L. Elsworth* ahead of *Vanja*; *Oltenia II* (Convoy Commodore Arthur Laddle's ship) ahead of *British Dominion*; *British Vigilance* ahead of *Empire Lytton*; and *Norvik* ahead of

Cliona. Minister Wedel, the ninth tanker, became a "column of one," farthest to starboard, abreast of the other column leads.[6]

Meanwhile, B-5's escorts took stations at the convoy's "corners": *Havelock*, Boyle's flagship, off TM-1's port bow; *Pimpernel*, off the starboard bow; *Godetia*, the port quarter; and *Saxifrage*, the starboard quarter.

On December 29, barely a day at sea, a Catalina spotted a U-boat well astern of TM-1. After dropping bombs and depth charges, its pilot alerted *Havelock*. Boyle considered his options. He was, according to a fellow skipper, "slow, accurate and very meticulous." Everything was to be "weighed up and considered most carefully."[7] With this U-boat well astern, maybe even damaged, TM-1 would simply press on.

By December 30, TM-1 was in the Central Atlantic's "Black Pit"—beyond range of air cover until nearing Gibraltar. Operational instructions specified cruising at eight knots, but adverse winds and currents slowed the pace. Repairs to *Godetia*'s boilers were complete, but now the transformer powering *Godetia*'s radar broke down. This increased Boyle's concerns, but all in all, the last two days of 1942 and the first two of 1943 passed without incident.[8]

Then, on the morning of January 3, Admiralty OIC alerted Boyle that a U-boat was operating nearby. TM-1 should reroute south after dark. A more urgent warning followed. The U-boat had apparently transmitted a contact report to Dönitz headquarters.

Other U-boats would be gathering. Anticipate concentrated attack.[9]

Auffermann's convoy sighting reached Karl Dönitz as he mulled the plight of his North Atlantic U-boats. Through December—with no end in sight—fierce storms and high seas pummeled U-boats and disrupted patrol lines. With thick clouds blocking stars, navigation became guesswork and search for convoys all but futile. Topside watch standers could only hold on—and hope that safety harnesses didn't snap.

Dönitz faced a dilemma. Should he allow *kommandanten* to button up? Or should he insist they ignore the tempests? U-boats were routinely failing to intercept convoys Dönitz knew to be sailing. Horrid weather alone couldn't be blamed. British convoy routing, usually so conservative, appeared to be gaining flexibility. Allied convoys were dispersed more widely, diverted more frequently. Dönitz had B-Dienst's assurance that message security, if anything, was tighter than ever. What then?

In March 1942, in the wake of a British commando raid on coastal St. Nazaire, Dönitz moved U-boat Control, his command headquarters, from Kernevel to Paris.[10] The atmosphere in these new facilities remained informal and collegial. Though the Lion inspired awe, he encouraged staff to challenge his ideas and present their own.

For now, Dönitz reasoned, success might lie farther south. The Allies, after all, needed North African reinforcements. Gibraltar-bound convoys might run less often, but ton for ton, sinking them could prove more decisive. In December, prompted by such reasoning, Dönitz had deployed Group Dolphin athwart the Great Circle track between New York and Gibraltar. Keeping to this line, Dolphin's six U-boats were reconnoitering westward—so far without success.

Quite possibly, the convoy Auffermann sighted had originated in the oil ports of Curaçao-Aruba and was bound for Gibraltar. If so, it was apt to take the shortest track. Just an intelligent guess, but such guesses often determined U-boat operations.

Dolphin's southernmost U-boat was now about a thousand miles northeast of Auffermann. Auffermann's was just one sighting. There was yet no certainty about the convoy's actual route. Between Dolphin and *U-514* lay a vast expanse of ocean. At best, Dönitz could only make his guess—and act accordingly.[11]

Recalled one headquarters insider, "Dönitz very seldom 'ordered.'" Instead, he "convinced," and, when finally decided on the most logical move, "really convinced."[12] So it was now: Dolphin was to start southeastward. Meanwhile, Auffermann received confirmation that U-boat command "had completed arrangements for the concentration of boats."

Finally, having expressly reminded *U-514*'s *kommandant* to "shadow without fail," Dönitz authorized him to "attack when darkness falls."

At about 6:30 p.m. on January 3, TM-1 was roughly 960 miles northwest of Barbados, steaming at nine knots, when SOE Boyle ordered the formation to alter course southward. A simple maneuver but prone to mishap, especially after dark. Just then, *Havelock*'s ASDIC operator reported a submarine contact on the starboard bow five thousand yards ahead.

Even as *Havelock* raced to investigate, J. C. Butterwick, first officer on board *British Vigilance* (lead vessel in TM-1's centermost column), signaled its course change by one blast on the ship's horn. *British Vigilance* had just started lumbering to starboard when, without warning, a torpedo struck its starboard bow. *Vigilance* carried 11,000 tons of benzine—what the British called petrol, the Americans gasoline. Flames shot skyward, producing pillars of smoke and emitting the sickly-sweet aroma of a corner filling station.

The starboard turn positioned motor tanker *British Dominion* (and its nine thousand tons of aviation fuel) directly astern of *British Vigilance.* Joseph D. Miller, *British Dominion*'s master, at once swung his ship to port to avoid *British Vigilance*'s "burning mass." Having spotted the submarine, said Miller, "we immediately opened fire with our [20-mm] Oerlikon to indicate the position."

Someone on the bridge of *Empire Lytton*, the steam tanker off *British Vigilance*'s starboard beam, also saw the U-boat: "a dark shape with a 'V' bow wave . . . about 400 yards away."

Seemingly heedless of his cargo (12,000 tons of aviation fuel) *Empire Lytton* master John Andrews attempted to ram the U-boat. Its helm turned hard to port, its engines at full speed, *Empire Lytton* came close, only to see *U-514* slide by under the bow. With the submarine pulling away yet still visible, *Empire Lytton*'s Oerlikons opened fire. A stream of 20-mm rounds interspersed with tracers—Andrews claimed as many as three hundred—streaked low across the water. Some, according to eyewitnesses, "bouncing from the conning tower."

Meanwhile, with flames enveloping *British Vigilance*'s port side and smoke filling its bridge, First Officer Butterwick ordered cargo tanks flooded with steam. Groping his way to the engine order telegraph (EOT),* the ship's master, Evan O. Evans, rang "Full astern." Hoping someone still below would execute his command, Evans headed for his cabin to retrieve ship's papers.

---

*Communications devices mounted in pilothouses and engine rooms. Moving a handle on the pilothouse EOT transmitted desired speeds ("bells") to the engine room EOT; personnel there acknowledged the "bell" by moving their EOT handle to the same position.

Unable to find the papers, Evans went to the main deck. The midships section appeared deserted, but chaos reigned on the after boat deck. The ship was only now losing headway (someone indeed had answered Evans' EOT command), but men were already jammed into lifeboats, screaming to be lowered.

Evans shouted to belay lowering until *British Vigilance* stopped, but there was no calming the situation. Jets of flame spurted from engine room ventilators. Ammunition used in the ship's guns began to pop.[13]

⌖

Revised Royal Navy antisubmarine warfare tactics decided Boyle's response to the torpedoing of *British Vigilance*. Rather than splay out from the convoy, dropping depth charges at random, B-5's escorts would employ "Raspberry," a convoy-defense tactic developed at what was called "WATU," the Western Approaches Tactical Unit.

Using the lessons of earlier convoy attacks and U-boat sinkings, WATU's war-gamers* realized most U-boats attacked from *within* the columns of a convoy. Approaching on the surface at night and from astern—where lookouts were fewer and less vigilant—a U-boat sped forward between two columns. Then, after firing torpedoes, submerged, reloaded tubes, and waited below until the convoy and its escorts rolled by.[14]

Boyle now executed Raspberry. As *Havelock* raced back from its fruitless chase, Boyle ordered *Godetia* and *Pimpernel* to illuminate the scene while *Saxifrage* retrieved *British Vigilance*'s survivors. Once back in position, *Havelock* zigzagged across the "bow" of the convoy to scatter any U-boats lurking ahead. Meanwhile, *Godetia* and *Pimpernel* swept astern, ready to pounce should the U-boat skipper resume the attack. Should he stay down, TM-1 would at least gain time and distance.[15]

⌖

Meanwhile, the last three men on board *British Vigilance*—Master Evans, his second officer, and a badly injured seaman—reached a midships lifeboat

*WRENS volunteers led by forty-one-year-old RN commander Gilbert Roberts, a former destroyer captain coming off convalescence for tuberculosis.

still on its davits. After hoisting the seaman on board, Evans and the second officer boarded as well, lowered the boat, and began rowing. Nearing the tanker's bow, they saw a huge hole—the torpedo's exit wound. Lest they be sucked in, the two men leaned into the oars, pulling the lifeboat slowly, agonizingly clear of danger. No sooner had they eased up than a huge blast ripped *British Vigilance* apart.

As Evans later described it to a board of enquiry, "Flames on the fore deck increased into a solid mass, rising to great height." When last seen at 10:30 p.m., *British Vigilance* was still "blazing fore and aft." And, later, with Evans and fellow survivors* on board *Saxifrage*, "the whole horizon was lit by the flames."[16]

*The final casualty totals were twenty-seven crew rescued, twenty-seven dead or missing.

21 | TUMULT TO AVOID

THAT JANUARY an unsigned report titled "Offensive Action against U-boats" circulated within COMINCH. A month before, in a cable to Ernest King about the latest Enigma breakthrough, Dudley Pound had struck a schoolmasterly tone, emphasizing "the care necessary" to safeguard special intelligence.

Attuned to how much could be lost, Britain was circumspect about exploiting Ultra. Because warships were scarce, technology and tactics primitive, and "air gaps" immense, its Admiralty used Enigma decrypts to evade U-boats, not attack them.

From the Admiralty's perspective, convoy rerouting also offered what today we call "plausible deniability." Abrupt changes in timetables, dispositions, and courses might raise Germans' suspicions but afforded many explanations *other* than a breach of Enigma. At the same time, rerouting didn't directly controvert COMINCH's "convoy vicinity" strategy.[1] Convoys, after all, attracted U-boats like chum attracted fish.

Neither "convoy rerouting" nor "convoy vicinity," however, seized the initiative. U-boats denied kills by rerouting survived to kill another day. Moreover, the sheer number of U-boats at sea made evading wolf packs ever more difficult. And, while "baiting" U-boats conveyed the notion of springing a trap, it really amounted to an attrition strategy.

Now, a new gambit was proposed: targeting U-tankers, the so-called milk cows so vital to U-boat operational endurance. Access to milk cows reduced U-boat transits across the Bay of Biscay, a choke point inviting air attack. Yet milk cows, while indispensable, were scarce. "With seven refueling submarines the enemy is barely able to provide effective logistic measures for the 100-odd [U-boats] now at sea. The loss of several . . . would decrease [U-boat] effectiveness out of all proportion."

One difficulty in pinpointing U-boats arose from the hours and often days required to decrypt U-boat messages. Information more than forty-eight hours old was all but useless. By contrast, the time and logistics required to schedule a U-tanker refueling opened a wider window of opportunity. "With the information currently at our disposal," asserted the report's author, "we are now able to determine up to a week or ten days in advance the exact position of their fueling area."[2]

Even before "Offensive Action against U-boats" made the rounds, *U-boat Situations*, Admiralty OIC's weekly update of U-boat dispositions, had forecasted peril for Convoy TM-1. *Situations* for the week ending January 4, 1943, advised: "A patrol line of six U-boats [Group Dolphin] was established on the 29th of December apparently to intercept convoys between U.S.A. and Casablanca between 32° N and 35° N near either 23° W or 33° W. . . . They [the U-boats] constitute a threat to the tanker convoy from Trinidad to Gibraltar which was attacked by a passage boat [in transit] on the 3rd of January with the loss of one ship."

U-boat Situations contained "appreciations," not directives. Still, *Situations* warned of a tumult to avoid.

On January 4, *Havelock*'s Boyle received an actionable signal, originating in Admiralty OIC, relayed by COMINCH: "U-boat estimated in your vicinity by D/F has made a sighting report of a convoy or important unit."

The recommendation—reroute TM-1 farther north—posed a quandary for SOE Boyle. Though not yet halfway through a projected fourteen-day transit, Group B-5's escorts, particularly corvette *Saxifrage*, were dangerously low on fuel. Refueling couldn't wait, and rerouting would carry TM-1 squarely into the fulsome winds of the northeast trades.

Exercising discretion owing to "unforeseen circumstances," Boyle declined the recommendation. Instead, he held course for the prospect of calmer winds and waters. Afterwards, he advised, "This course was necessary to obtain calm waters before escorts ran out of fuel."

Havelock refueled from *Norvik* in the afternoon but in the process sideswiped the tanker. Damage to the destroyer's bow was minor, but a fueling line fouled its starboard propellor, forcing *Havelock* to drop back and clear the snag. Topping off *Saxifrage*, *Pimpernel*, and *Godetia* went more smoothly next day but required transfers from both *Norvik* and *Cliona*.[3]

Hans-Jürgen Auffermann, believing he had torpedoed a 17,000-ton tanker on January 3, marveled at *U-514*'s torpedo handiwork: a sharp blast culminating in a cataclysmic fireball. But reverie was brief. First, converging tracer rounds convinced him he'd been seen. Then, after crash diving, the crisscrossing cavitation of escort propellors persuaded him to stay down. Finally, when *U-514* [the "passage boat" mentioned in *U-boat Situations*] at last broke the surface, its balky diesels faltered, and Auffermann lost contact with the tankers.

Dönitz seethed over Auffermann's lapse. "Seek the convoy to the northeast," he instructed *U-514* and another U-boat nearby. And, if the targets were found, "maintain contact at all costs but . . . do nothing more."

Group Dolphin, meanwhile, had just barely begun its thousand-mile journey towards *U-514* when a Cape Town–bound U-boat spotted another convoy—this one steaming straight for Dolphin. Sure enough, early on January 5, two Dolphin boats spotted what could only be that convoy.

It presented a tempting "bird in the hand," but BdU foresaw problems. This convoy's vessels were moving fast—probably "flying light"—and well protected: a battleship, cruiser, and nine destroyers. At best, it would take other Dolphin boats hours more to converge. The prize simply didn't merit the effort and risk.

Despite pleas to the contrary, Dönitz "convinced" staff to keep Dolphin on track for the eastbound tankers. Vindication came on January 8. At first light, the tanker convoy steamed directly into the middle of Dolphin's patrol line. As the rest of Dolphin converged, several boats then in transit also joined the hunt.

"Be hard in the attack," Dönitz exhorted his wolves. "Operate tenaciously. Go after the slightest opportunity with all your energy!"[4]

A week before Dolphin's interception of TM-1, Adolph Hitler had been boasting to New Year's guests of the utter destruction of a Barents Sea convoy. Then, to his consternation, a broadcast from London contradicted him: Allied convoy escorts had beaten off German cruisers and destroyers. Every merchant vessel had escaped.

The Führer lurched into a tirade. Germany's surface navy was a national disgrace! Its big ships should be scrapped, their big guns sent ashore, and their men transferred to submarines. Hitler summoned Erich Raeder, but feigning illness to avoid confrontation, the Kriegsmarine chief asked for a few days' delay.

When first assuming command of Germany's navy (then the Reichsmarine) in 1928, Grand Adm. Erich Raeder, the personification of God-fearing Prussian rectitude, vowed to remain apolitical. Once the Reichsmarine became the Kriegsmarine, however, Raeder found himself serving a man who personified the state.[5]

Despite Napoleonic ambitions for territorial conquest, Hitler became enamored of Raeder's oceanic Z-Plan: a grand fleet of German battleships, cruisers, and aircraft carriers slated for completion by 1948. Once his aggression outran Z-Plan's timetable, however, an impatient Führer pressed Raeder to pick up the pace: "If I can build the Third Reich in six years, then the Navy can surely build these ships in six years!"[6]

Raeder knew better. As war with Britain loomed, he understood his Kriegsmarine could do little more than "die gallantly." Forced to improvise, Raeder recast Z-Plan battleships and cruisers as surface raiders capable of starving the British Isles into submission.

During the Great War, Germany's U-boats—despite a late start—had come close to pulling this off. But under Raeder's *guerre de course*, Dönitz's U-boats held a subordinate role: scattering Royal Navy ships so big commerce raiders could roam free.

Setback on setback followed early successes. In September 1939, pocket battleship *Admiral Graf Spee* scored five sinkings, only to be cornered by hastily assembled RN hunter-killer groups. After scuttling his ship in Uruguay's River Plate estuary, *Graf Spee*'s captain committed suicide. Enraged, Hitler proclaimed that German ships must henceforth fight "to the last shell." Score victory or go down "flag flying."[7]

Raeder's next misstep was persuading Hitler to conquer Norway—a means to gain unfettered access to Atlantic sea-lanes. German forces succeeded but at great cost to the Kriegsmarine: three cruisers, ten destroyers, and a dozen smaller ships sunk. Raeder got his ports but found his much-reduced force overmatched in the North Sea.[8]

As Hitler watched with jaundiced eye, Raeder's persistence seemed at last to pay off. Late 1940 raids by battleship *Admiral Scheer* and battle cruisers *Scharnhorst* and *Gneisenau* destroyed close to forty Allied ships. His confidence renewed, Raeder hatched an even grander scheme: combine *Scharnhorst*, *Gneisenau* with new battleships *Bismarck* and *Tirpitz* for a rampage that would render the Atlantic impassable to British shipping.[9]

But *Scharnhorst*, *Gneisenau*, and *Tirpitz* were sidelined, and the grand mission, set for May 1941, was doomed. Undeterred, Raeder sent *Bismarck* into the North Sea, screened by a heavy cruiser and three destroyers. The German flotilla sank one British ship and crippled another southwest of Iceland. But *Bismarck* also sustained damage. Shadowed by British warships, the wounded giant lumbered towards sanctuary off the French coast. It looked like *Bismarck* might escape until an *Ark Royal* aircraft's torpedo jammed its rudders. On May 27, after being pounded by the guns of RN battleships and cruisers, *Bismarck* rolled over and sank, taking all but 115 crewmen with it. For the next year and a half, Erich Raeder's surface fleet sat in port, tethered and rusting even as Karl Dönitz's U-boats gained ascendency—and the Führer's favor.[10]

When Erich Raeder finally met with Hitler on January 6, he offered facts and logic: the Barents Sea flotilla commander had simply followed Hitler's orders not to lose another big ship. They were saved for forthcoming raids. Hitler listened but would have none of it, ordering Raeder to submit a plan to retire all the big ships and place their guns ashore.

Not easily intimidated, Raeder asked to speak with Hitler alone. Twice before, Raeder had tendered his resignation, only to have the Fuhrer balk. But if Hitler no longer had confidence in him, the time had come to part ways. He would step down on January 30, 1943, the tenth anniversary of the beginning of his tenure under the Führer.[11]

Asked for the names of two subordinates best qualified to replace him, Raeder nominated Rolf Carls, a battleship man, and Karl Dönitz. Carls was Raeder's clear favorite but choosing Dönitz (as Raeder would write in an otherwise equivocal recommendation) "would have the advantage of stressing . . . the U-boat campaign as of war-decisive importance."

On the evening of January 8, now ten days out of Port of Spain, TM-1's eight tankers and Group B-5's four escorts plowed northeast, speed nine knots, on gentle seas under cloudy skies and with light southeast breezes. Destroyer *Havelock* was stationed about three miles off TM-1's port bow when radar displayed a contact off to starboard.

Cdr. Richard Boyle ordered a quick course change and full speed ahead. Before long, despite darkness and cloud cover, alert lookouts spotted a surfaced submarine, two thousand yards dead ahead. Determined to ram, Boyle kept *Havelock* at full throttle. The U-boat deftly crash-dived—robbing Boyle of his chance—but *Havelock* ASDIC picked up the scent.

Moments later, five *Havelock* ashcans tumbled into the U-boat's residual turbulence. But even as undersea explosions rumbled, another blast pierced the night. *Albert L. Ellsworth*, lead ship in TM-1's portside column, had taken a torpedo.

Several heartbeats later, the blast sparked *Ellsworth*'s cargo—11,000 tons of fuel oil. On the bridge of *Oltenia II*, the tanker closest to starboard of *Ellsworth*, watch officer Kenneth Bruce rang the engine room to stand by. But, even as he did, *Oltenia* was struck too—also portside but farther aft. A heavy jolt aft unloosed a tower of flame "as high as the funnel." Then came a "great roaring noise"—the destruction of *Oltenia*'s boilers.

Bruce knew *Oltenia* was doomed. Dashing to the boat deck, assisted by another officer, Bruce got the portside lifeboat loaded, cleared away, and lowered. Bruce saw Arthur Laddle, *Oltenia*'s master (and TM-1's commodore), doing the same with the starboard boat. By now, *Oltenia*'s after deck was awash.

As Bruce and others put out oars and began to row away, *Oltenia*'s bridge collapsed into the sea, stirring a vortex that capsized the lifeboat and pulled men under. When Bruce resurfaced, he found himself underneath the overturned boat. Scarce recalling later how he managed it, Bruce dove down, resurfaced, and hoisted himself atop the inverted hull.

One of *Oltenia*'s life rafts floated not far off, as did an *Ellsworth* lifeboat. Their occupants picked up twenty more *Oltenia* survivors—all blackened with fuel, some suffering horrific burns. Arthur Laddle was among the missing and presumed dead when *Oltenia* "sank like a stone."[12]

Midnight January 8 came and went. *Ellsworth*'s and *Oltenia*'s castaways were transferred to *Havelock*, where medical personnel tended wounds, burns, and oil-ravaged lungs.

Meanwhile, TM's six tankers reordered themselves. Four took the front row (port to starboard: *Vanja*, *British Dominion*, *Empire Lytton*, *Minister Wedel*); two steamed behind (*Norvik* astern of *Empire Lytton*, *Cliona* astern of *Minister Wedel*). Merchant seamen were fearful and suspicious. Were Port of Spain's "loose lips" indeed sinking TM-1's ships? Why had the British provided so few escorts, and in such poor condition?

Indeed, SOE Richard Boyle had lost a third of his flock and was apt to lose more. *Pimpernel*'s and *Godetia*'s British-built radars, long overdue for overhaul, barely functioned. Group B-5 was going blind.

TM-1 now lay about five hundred miles from Tenerife, westernmost of the Canary Islands—still far from air cover. The latest Admiralty update—"From D/F activities . . . 6 or 7 U-boats estimated probably in your vicinity"—effectively told Boyle, "No letup in sight."

Sure enough, three torpedoes—a pair to *Minister Wedel*, the third to *Norvik*—renewed the feeding frenzy. Neither ship sank, but flames engulfed *Minister Wedel*, and the explosion on board *Norvik* killed two men. Crews on both ships took to lifeboats.

Afterwards, *Empire Lytton, Cliona, Vanja* and *Norvik* received orders to zigzag independently. With any semblance of protection gone, each merchant master scanned the horizon for a dawn that might never come. Each supposed his ship could be next.

That fate fell to *Empire Lytton*. At 4:30 a.m., a torpedo opened a gaping hole near its stem. The blast heaved up the forecastle deck, twisted *Lytton*'s goalpost masts, and splayed hull plates. The hatch to *Lytton*'s forward fuel bunker blew off, releasing a torrent of fuel oil that splashed the bridge.

Lytton carried 12,500 tons of aviation fuel—altogether, TM-1's most incendiary cargo. As soon as survivors were accounted for, TM-1 cleared the scene.

Afterwards, Boyle signaled: "On leaving position 028 18n 027 20w . . . the following were afloat: Norvik, badly damaged probably sinking. Minister Wedel not so badly damaged may be afloat. Empire Lytton easily salvageable. Albert Ellsworth was burning in position 027 59n 028 50w."

It ended with a postscript: "About 30 minutes after Havelock left Lytton was again torpedoed and blew up, aviation spirit."[13]

⌖

That same day, Prime Minister Churchill was immersed in arrangements for Symbol, a joint strategy meeting of Roosevelt, Churchill, and their respective staffs, scheduled for mid-January outside Casablanca.

An invitation for Russia's Joseph Stalin to make Symbol a three-power conference had fallen through, but that didn't stop "Uncle Joe" from sniping about his allies' failures to support Soviet needs. A claim from Stalin's London ambassador that Britain had "promised convoys of thirty ships in January and February" so roiled Churchill that he promptly responded in kind.

"[Ambassador] Maisky should be told," Churchill wrote Dudley Pound and Foreign Secretary Anthony Eden, "that I am getting to the end of my tether with these repeated Russian naggings, and that it is not the slightest use trying to knock me about. Our escorts all over the world are so attenuated that losses out of all proportion are falling on British mercantile marine.

"Only this morning news has come in of six of nine great tankers being sunk, full of oil and greatly needed, because we can only provide an escort of one destroyer and a few corvettes for this vital convoy."[14]

⌖ *Newton* (IX 33) at Jersey City, New Jersey, in 1935 *Naval History and Heritage Command*

⌖ *Borie* (DD 215) alongside the pier at Naval Operating Base Norfolk, Virginia, in 1923 *Naval History and Heritage Command*

Eddie Johnson (*left*) and Bob Maher in Panama *Courtesy Dianne Kropp*

Jim Allegri in Panama *Courtesy Dianne Kropp*

Bill Schmalberger in Panama *Courtesy Dianne Kropp*

Borie forward crew compartment *Courtesy Dianne Kropp*

Henry Thomas Tizard (*center*), British head of the Tizard Mission, visits with MIT researchers. The resonant-cavity magnetron is held by the researcher at right.
MIT Museum

Atlantic Conference leaders on the afterdeck of HMS *Prince of Wales* in Placentia Bay, Newfoundland, August 1941. President Franklin D. Roosevelt (*left*) and Prime Minister Winston Churchill are seated in the foreground. Standing directly behind them are (*left to right*) Adm. Ernest J. King, USN; Gen. George C. Marshall, USA; Gen. Sir John Dill, BA; Adm. Harold R. Stark, USN; and Adm. Sir Dudley Pound, RN. *Naval History and Heritage Command*

Part of the U.S. fleet moored in Balboa harbor before World War II *NARA*

Brown and Gullion wedding portrait: bride's uncle Allen W. Gullion (*far left*); unidentified bridesmaid; groom's brother-in-law, George Abbott Creighton (*back, third from left*); bride's friend and maid of honor, Lucy Powell; bride, Frances Gullion Brown; groom, Morrison Ropes Brown; groom's niece and flower girl, Carol Creighton; groom's father and best man, Carroll Ropes Brown (*third from right*); bride's cousin and bridesmaid, Fan Castleman Benjamin; unidentified groomsman *Courtesy Brown and Creighton families*

USS *Kearny* (DD 432) at Reykjavik, Iceland, in October 1941, showing torpedo damage amidships *Naval History and Heritage Command*

Sinking of the Reuben James; drawing, pencil on paper, by Griffith Baily Coale. Notice the exposed propeller guards *Naval History and Heritage Command*

Enigma machine
Britannica.com

Rodger Winn
Courtesy David Kohnen

Karl Dönitz
NARA

Erich Raeder
IWM Collections

Type VIIC U-boat returns to base after a war patrol, welcomed by a naval band.
Naval History and Heritage Command

⌖ Walter H. Dietz Jr. as V-7 midshipman
Courtesy Dr. Judith Dietz Win

⌖ Philip B. Brown
Courtesy Dr. Michael N. Brown, MD

⌖ Francis S. "Frog" Low
NARA

⌖ Kenneth Knowles
Courtesy Kenneth A. Knowles Jr.

⌖ Joseph Desch (*second from left*) shown at a wartime event with spouse Dorothy and U.S. Navy officer Ralph Meader *NCR Archive at Dayton History*

⌖ Mug shots and sentences of saboteurs landed by U-boats on East Coast beaches in June 1942. George Dasch is pictured at lower right. *NARA*

USS *Bogue* (ACV 9, later CVE 9) under way in Puget Sound, November 1942
U.S. Navy photo, Naval History and Heritage Command

USS *Card* Wildcat fighter over the Atlantic *NARA*

Avengers in flight *Naval History and Heritage Command*

USS *Borie*, January 1943 *U.S. Navy*

⌖ *Left to right*: Robert Jefferis, Lawrence S. Quinn, and Richard Earl St. John, pictured in Broadway Brewery, New York City, in 1943 *Courtesy Chip Quinn*

⌖ Donald F. Fennessey
Courtesy Donald B. Fennessey

Jonas H. Ingram at Recife, Brazil
U.S. Navy photo, NARA

Arnold J. "Buster" Isbell
U.S. Naval Academy Virtual Memorial Hall

Philip McCord Morse
American Institute of Physics

Henry H. Babson
Courtesy Babson family

⌖ Crew of *U-664* prepare to go over the side during attack by *Card* aircraft, August 9, 1943. *U.S. Navy*

⌖ *U-664* survivors on *Card* hangar deck. Adolf Graef is in the front row, fourth from the right. *U.S. Navy*

VC-9 officers on *Bogue*, August 1943. *Front row, left to right*: Roger C. "Bud" Kuhn, Robert J. Johnson, McSorley,* E. W. "Joe" Biros,# William M. Drane (CO), Howard S. Roberts, Harding,* Letson S. Balliett, W. S. "Munk" Fowler; *middle row*: Don Horn, Stewart E. "Kid" Doty,# Robert L. Stearns,# Donald E. Weigle, O. J. Donohoe, Killefer,* Harry F. Fryatt, Alexander C. McAuslan, Edwards R. Hodgson, William F. Chamberlain;# *back row*: Frank D. Fogde, Melvin Connley, Elbert S. "Stu" Heim,# Stewart,* David O. Puckett, Paul Walker, Jack Menary, Barton C. Sheela, Phil Perabo *U.S. Navy*

---

* Unknown first name
# Subsequently killed

A WAVE sets Bombe rotors prior to a run. *Allesmüller, via Wikimedia Commons*

Rolf-Heinrich Hopmann
U.S. Naval Institute photo archive

Crew on foredeck of *U-405*; note polar bear image on front of conning tower
U.S. Naval Institute photo archive

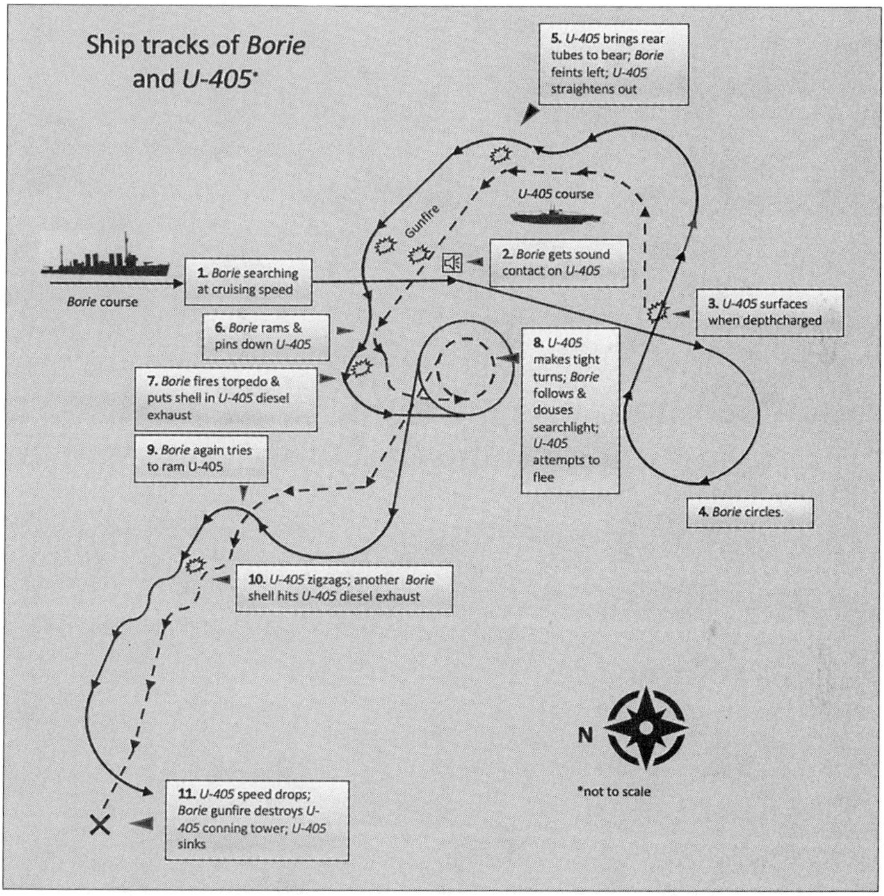

The course of action in the battle between *Borie* and *U-405*.

Illustration by David Sears 2023

Painting by U.S. Coast Guard artist Hunter Wood of the action between *Borie* and *U-405*, November 1, 1943 NARA

Borie survivors on *Card* flight deck NARA

Borie abandoned and sinking on November 2, 1943 *NARA*

⌖ *Borie*'s battle flag carried by Charles Hutchins (*second from left*) when he abandoned ship. Also pictured are Bill Green (*third from left*) and Walter Kurz (*fourth from left*).
Courtesy Dr. Michael N. Brown, MD

⌖ Royal E. Ingersoll pins the Navy Cross on Hutchins.
U.S. Navy photo, NARA

22 | CONSEQUENTIAL FORCES

BY JANUARY 1943, just two months into the Bombe project, Desch's team was behind schedule. Pressure, always intense, tightened with news that the British soon expected to have a fully operational four-rotor Bombe. After one especially testy meeting with Meader and Engstrom, Desch climbed atop a shop-floor table. Everyone, he shouted, had to start working harder and faster to get this machine out.

To say the least, progress had been complicated by Alan Turing's December visit. His arrival in a Dayton bustling with wartime production and military activity made finding short-term accommodations impossible. Turing ended up sleeping on Joe and Dorothy's living room floor.

Despite having little in common, the pair got along remarkably well. Still, Desch felt Turing had come to second-guess and eavesdrop. In fact, Turing's postmortem dripped with condescension. While allowing that "starting from scratch[,] . . . [Desch's] method is about as good as our own," Turing found much to pick apart, everything from machine gearing to wheel size. He dismissed a design feature Desch's engineers greatly prized: the machine's ability to brake, then backtrack to the precise rotor positions matching a crib. "It seems a pity," Turing wrote, "for them to go out of their way . . . to do all this stopping if it is not necessary."

Yet, despite prospects that NCML's Bombe might be flawed—even superseded—the Navy pressed on. To accommodate future Bombe operations,

Navy brass commandeered Mount Vernon Seminary, a former girls' school in Northwest Washington, DC.[1]

Bob Maher judged New Orleans "the best liberty port ever." Still, because the French Quarter was strictly off-limits to sailors, "it could have been better."

Maher and several shipmates were on leave in New Jersey when *Borie* reached the Crescent City in late December. To enjoy their return train trip from New York, they brought an ample supply of liquor. After a glowering MP (military policeman) warned "get that shit out of sight," however, their bacchanal shut down. Hopes to reopen it during a layover in Atlanta ran up against the strictures of a dry town. Only after a sympathetic cop steered them to a speakeasy did the revelry finally gain steam. So warm was the welcome they reached New Orleans a day late.

When in dry dock, *Borie* enlisted men still lived on board ship, enduring the noise and discomfort. Misery, though, was tempered by better shore facilities, including the base mess hall. "I had steak," Bob raved, "and we had real breakfasts every morning." The fare was an "eye opener," but so was ambience: "I was eating without having a foot hanging in my face from the bunk over my head."[2]

Following his own leave in Miami Beach, Mike Brown drove with Gully to New Orleans. "The first person we saw on our arrival," Mike wrote his parents on January 14, "was the Capt. coming out of the Jung. He had made the wonderful arrangements. We now have at $1.50 per day [about $25 in 2022] our room."

The Jung Hotel, then a fixture on Canal Street, was the gateway to the French Quarter. Save for the war, the Jung's comforts would have been beyond reach. For much of January, New Orleans hosted a festival of track, baseball, basketball, tennis, boxing, rowing, and yachting competitions. Just as venues scrambled to fill seats, hotels scrambled to fill rooms.

The next day, in a letter on Jung letterhead, Gully updated Mike's parents and grandmother on their boy's doings. "Hutch, the 'exec,' is off on leave for a few days and Morrie . . . is acting exec. That's next to the Captain! Even tho it only lasts a few days it'll be good for him."[3]

⊕

Erich Raeder's mid-January call to U-boat Paris headquarters was, in Dönitz's postwar recounting, "a complete surprise to me. I had no idea . . . Raeder was contemplating retirement. . . . He asked me to let him know within twenty-four hours whether I felt fit enough, from a health point of view, to assume the appointment."

There was no question as to his fitness, Dönitz assured Raeder by phone the next day. As for Dönitz's professing "complete surprise," there was also no question that Dönitz had schemed to supplant Raeder. Ever since spring 1942, when Nazi insider Albert Speer became minister of armaments, Dönitz had curried Speer's favor. Speer became an ardent believer in *Tonnagekrieg* and the need to expand the U-boat fleet further.

Dönitz left it to Speer to shape Hitler's choice. If Raeder's nomination of Dönitz was lukewarm, Speer's advocacy was single-minded. To achieve what he wanted, "the replacement of Raeder," Speer "merely hinted that all obstacles standing in the way of our U-boat plans could be eliminated were [Dönitz] given his head."

Certainly, Group Dolphin's recent triumph burnished Dönitz's prospects. Altogether, ten U-boats had partaken in the feast, with only one sustaining battle damage. *Kommandanten* claimed hits on twenty-five ships, producing fifteen sinkings. Dönitz assumed inflation but let the results stand. German propagandists touted fifteen sinkings for 142,000 tons,* and Dönitz readily accepted congratulations on a "brilliant joint success."

⊕

Symbol marked the fourth face-to-face encounter between Churchill and Roosevelt. On January 9, FDR was to begin a historic yet furtive seven-thousand-mile journey: first by train to Miami; then by Pan American Clipper to Gambia in West Africa via Trinidad and Brazil; finally, on January 14, by AAF transport to Casablanca.

---

* *British Dominion* was sunk on January 10, making TM-1's final confirmed loss tally seven tankers for 56,543 tons.

Two days before leaving, FDR assembled his three service chiefs. Reminding them the British would reach Casablanca with a plan and stick to it, he urged Marshall, King, and Arnold to define America's position on future strategy.

FDR asked too much: each chief was accustomed to crafting plans for his service alone. By custom, JCS decisions had to be unanimous. All they could finally agree to was contained in a short position paper advancing separate agendas: invasion across the English Channel in 1943 (Marshall); an offensive in the Pacific (King); a strategic air offensive against Germany's heartland (Arnold).

As at Arcadia a year before, Allied shipping shortages made the JCS position paper little more than a wish list. During 1942, the Allies had lost nearly eight million tons of shipping—three-quarters to U-boats. The six million tons produced in Allied shipyards, in other words, barely offset losses to U-boats.[4] Shortages of freighters, tankers, transports, and escorts constrained any single strategic initiative, let alone three.

Churchill and his chiefs—constituting the Imperial General Staff (IGS)—realized King's role at Symbol was crucial. King controlled essential inventories of ships without which their preferred strategy—to follow up the North African offensive by invading Sicily—would be impossible. They needn't concur with "Uncle Ernie's" priorities, but they had to hear him out.

As FDR predicted, the Brits came with a plan and stuck to it. While Churchill set about wooing Roosevelt, the CIGS (that is, the chiefs on the IGS) relentlessly assaulted the JCS with studies and position papers. But, on January 14, two hours before first meeting with the IGS, King, Marshall, and Arnold gathered for a "pregame huddle."* Despite British efforts to wear them down, the JCS vowed to maintain a united front.

Progress came at a glacial pace, in no small part because of King's stubborn focus on the Pacific. While invading Sicily made sense—Allied soldiers already in Africa were, for now, best employed against Sicily—getting America's sign-off hinged on mollifying King.

---

*Adm. William D. Leahy, FDR's personal chief of staff, had started for Casablanca, but influenza grounded him in Trinidad.

In the end, King proved his ability to hold his ground. While the Americans accepted Sicily (Operation Husky) as the next invasion target (thus postponing a cross-channel invasion until 1944), the British agreed to give King a freer hand against Japan. This victory was more symbolic than substantive, but it established King as a consequential force.

Churchill and Roosevelt held a formal press conference at noon on January 24, unveiling their Casablanca communiqué. The headline was Roosevelt's announcement that nothing less than "unconditional surrender" would end the war with the Axis. Details of means and methods remained secret.

"The Conduct of the War in 1943," the final output of the heated discussions of the Combined Chiefs (the IGS and JCS), stressed a foremost priority: "The defeat of the U-boat must remain a first charge on the resources of the United Nations." Here, too, means and methods stayed under wraps. Final decisions were postponed to a March 1 Convoy Conference in Washington, DC—Ernest King's bailiwick.[5]

Karl Dönitz, meanwhile, scarcely missed a beat. Just as the last words of Erich Raeder's January 30 announcement of his "reassignment" faded from the airwaves, Dönitz's first words of ascendency rang sharp and clear: "At the order of the Führer, I today take over the high command of the Navy."

To his U-boat arm, Dönitz proffered "thanks for its courageous readiness to fight to the death and for its loyalty," while in the next breath reassured them, "I shall personally command the U-boat war."[6]

It was a bold assertion of Dönitz's new status and prerogatives. Allowed at last to fight at sea on his own terms, he planned to give his utmost. To ensure proximity to Hitler, the new Oberbefehlshaber der Kriegsmarine relocated to Berlin, installing his family in a palatial suburban residence. But even as he enjoyed new luxuries—traveling by limousine, private train, and aircraft, under constant SS* protection—Dönitz remained upright and duty bound, projecting a fervency akin to the Führer's.

*The Shutzstaffel, "Protection Squadron," the feared Nazi paramilitary arm.

Dönitz knew that "personally commanding the U-boat war" would be difficult. Immense new responsibilities included fostering close relations with Hitler, deepening ties to Speer, and avoiding rivals' traps. But it was up to him to deliver victory—or at least prevent the type of defeat the Allies envisioned. And Dönitz's only chance to do that was to sever the Allies' indispensable lifeline of seaborne supplies, fuel, and manpower.[7]

Dönitz clung to the conviction that he would receive the resources and weaponry needed to accomplish this feat. The U-boat fleet now numbered four hundred;[8] Hitler had enthusiastically approved a substantial increase in production.

His fleet was not only expanding but acquiring new ways to destroy. A new torpedo detonator combining contact and magnetic capabilities had just become available. Soon to follow would be a torpedo that looped or zigzagged within a convoy formation. Beyond that were acoustic torpedoes capable of homing in on the sound of a ship's propellors—ideal for countering attacking escorts.[9]

Despite such advances, however, Dönitz knew his U-boat mainstays, the five-hundred-ton Type VIIs and 740-ton Type IXs, were becoming obsolete. Their replacements, devised by a brilliant engineer named Helmuth Walter, would be blindingly fast, closed-cycle-propulsion submarines fueled by hydrogen peroxide. The first prototype had achieved a submerged speed of twenty-eight knots. Based on improved designs, contracts had been let for two dozen more prototypes of what was to be designated the Type XXVI.[10]

Recent operational results, meanwhile, offered equal measures of hope, pride, and disappointment. Using Dönitz's preferred measure—sinkings per boat per day at sea—October's 172 tons soared to 220 tons in November, only to dip to 96 tons in December. Sinkings went down, but so did U-boat losses: twelve boats in October, six in November, and just five in December.[11]

Once horrid North Atlantic weather relented, *Rudeltaktik* would resume full force. As spring 1943 approached, Dönitz sensed forthcoming victory.[12]

"The days go by so fast & here we are at the end," Gully Brown wrote in a January 31 letter to Mike's parents and grandmother. "Needless to say, I'm pretty low at the thought of leaving my hubby but I do feel that we'll all be together before long."

Mike took over from there: "I really feel that it won't be long before I'll be home again—change of duty. We now have 14 officers assigned to the ship, so I think that some of us are due for a change shortly."[13]

Todd-Johnson Dry Docks was indeed wrapping up work on *Borie*. Seen from a distance the old four-stacker appeared little changed, but from Bob Maher's vantage, upgrades were substantial: "Six twenty-millimeter machine guns, surface to air radar and six K guns* were installed. Fire-control equipment was overhauled and new receivers, a range finder and fire-control gyro were all installed."

When *Borie* finally got under way, the crew naturally assumed they were returning to Panama. Instead, their destination was Port of Spain, Convoy TM-1's departure point scarcely a month before.[14]

*K-guns were successors to Great War–era "Y-guns," so called because their twin projectors branched from a vertical stand. K-guns instead used a single projector, angled outboard. A short, side-mounted "stump" at the base of pedestal (used both as a breech mechanism and expansion chamber to vent explosive gasses) explained the K-gun moniker. ("K-Gun—Depth Charge Projector," Destroyer Escort Historical Museum, n.d., http://www.ussslater.org/tour/weapons/k-gun/k-gun.html [accessed June 14, 2020])

23 | BETWEEN THE MOON AND OURSELVES

IN HIS NAVAL ACADEMY football days, Jonas H. Ingram had been called the "One-Armed Admiral." Whenever the score was close, the two-way standout ("thrashing fullback" on offense, "fierce linebacker" on defense) told teammates: "I'd give my right arm to win this ball game." Ingram went on to coach Middie elevens for two seasons.

A quarter-century later, according to tabloid gossip columnist and radio news commentator Walter Winchell, who visited the vice admiral in Rio de Janeiro, "Jonas Ingram . . . talks the way a football coach talks. He punches everything he says."[1] Just now, however, his team was being outscored.

During November and December 1942, as commander of the U.S. Navy's South Atlantic Force, Ingram watched from the sidelines as U-boats sank twenty merchant vessels. Now, in late January 1943, intelligence sources claimed the Germans were sending waves of U-boats to South Atlantic shipping lanes, determined to cut off supplies and reinforcements to Allied forces in North Africa. Ingram was equally determined that it not happen.[2]

"Rio Parley Shapes Drive on U-boats" read the headline of the January 30 special cable to the *New York Times*. "Plans for intensifying the war against enemy submarines in the South Atlantic were considered today by United States and Brazilian officers and officials."[3]

The parley was the by-product of a January 28 meeting between Franklin Roosevelt and Brazil's president Getulio Vargas on board an American destroyer anchored in the Potengi River at Natal, a Brazilian coastal city described as "the easternmost stronghold of the hemisphere."[4]

FDR was retracing his steps to Washington after Symbol, this time adding fifteen hundred air miles, first by detouring to Monrovia, Liberia, and then touching down in Natal to visit American military bases while conferring with Vargas. During their time together, the two leaders agreed that "counter-offensive action against U-boat raids on shipping must be redoubled."

The operational details of this public pronouncement would be worked out in Rio de Janeiro. After this Rio confab, Ingram stated his intentions. "We are now bent on cleaning up the submarine pest in South American waters."

Later, speaking from his Recife headquarters, Ingram insisted commitments to the Southwest Atlantic offensive were paying off. "But the submarine menace," he added, "remains very serious and . . . [is] likely to get worse before it gets better." Ingram ended with a halftime flourish: "The motto of this fleet is ruthlessness. I don't want any prisoners. All I want is a Nazi ear and a bottle of alcohol to put it in."[5]

During his flight north from Natal, FDR stopped on Trinidad. After landing at Waller Field and inspecting the military reservation at Fort Reed, the president motorcaded over the Churchill-Roosevelt Highway to the naval base in Port of Spain.

Word of the president's visit had quickly spread. Cheering Trinidadians lined the sidewalks as his entourage passed through Port of Spain. "It was the first time since he left the United States early in January," remarked the *New York Times* correspondent, "that any populace, in either Africa or South America, had been aware that the American Commander-in-Chief was in their very midst."[6]

For many Brazilians, learning that Roosevelt had returned from West Africa meant Vichy-held Dakar no longer posed a threat.[7] For Roosevelt, meanwhile, the raucous reception in Port of Spain was an invigorating reminder of just how much he had enjoyed Symbol: the furtive travel, the high-stakes decision-making, and the basking in temperate climes far from the political gloom of his nation's capital.

Borie's arrival in Port of Spain less than a fortnight after FDR's departure met with no comparable reception. Without trappings or ceremony, *Borie* joined convoy Escort Unit 23.2.4. The unit's other vessels: *Goff* (DD 247), like *Borie* a *Clemson*-class four-stacker; *Courage* and *Tenacity* (PGs 70 and 71), former Royal Navy Flower-class corvettes; and PCs 575 and 592, two freshly built U.S. Navy patrol craft.

Borie's crew went right to work, sailing from Trinidad on February 13 to escort Convoy TB-5. As SOE, Phil Osborn was to shepherd TB-5 as far as Recife and a CHOP with the Brazilian navy. Although the January convoy out of Trinidad had run into trouble, losing four of twelve ships to U-boats off Surinam (Suriname today), subsequent passages, including TB-5's, went without incident.[8]

Following a coastal route, TB/BT convoys got daytime protection from Catalina and Mariner flying boats. Because the convoy was able to steam no faster than the slowest merchant (about eleven knots), however, the two-thousand-mile outbound journey tested *Borie*'s endurance. Add in the almost constant zigzagging, Mike Brown's black gang realized, and the actual distance amounted to a little over four thousand miles.[9]

With no fuel stops between Port of Spain and Recife, *Borie* refueled at sea for the first time. While a challenge to helmsmen, boatswain's mates, and deckhands, the process—to be repeated many times in the months ahead—went without a hitch.

Borie's fresh food supply, however, was exhausted halfway through the twelve-day voyage. Thereafter, the crew consumed a steady diet of canned food, corn bread, and waxy cold cuts (known to the crew as "horse cock"). Rest and reprovisioning in Recife couldn't come soon enough.

To Bob Maher, something of an expert on these matters, "Recife had all the requirements for good liberty—nice restaurants, bars, shows, and high-class brothels." There was also evidence there—and elsewhere in Brazil—of the inflationary impact of U.S. dollars. Before going ashore, Bob received a thick wad of Brazilian cruzeiros, "which I had to carry in my hand because it wouldn't fit in my pockets. . . . We started out treating a Brazilian dollar as a nickel. . . . Suddenly we were all rich."[10]

Such free spending gave Americans a certain allure. According to the governor of the state of Rio Grande do Norte, "American service men are winning the hearts of Brazil's young women with jitterbug music and hamburgers." The governor insisted that since women far outnumbered men in Rio Grande do Norte, this was no problem. "There are many marriages and many, many engagements."[11]

Such arrangements came with complications. Walter Winchell, the gossipy outsider, supplied his perspective: "In civilized sectors of Brazil," Winchell wrote, "if you take a lady out twice her family asks your intentions." But "In other areas, especially where our men are based, hordes of them wait and ambush those on leave or furlough."[12]

⌖

During the opening months of 1943, contrary to Allied intelligence projections, U-boat Control dispatched relatively few Type IXs to the Americas: four in January, three in February, and four in March. And Jonas Ingram made sure they ran up against well-protected convoys and well-organized antisubmarine forces.

First to sail that year was *U-518*, commanded by twenty-six-year-old *Oberleutnant zur See* Friedrich-Wilhelm Wissmann. Having sunk four ships and damaged two more during an inaugural patrol off Canada, Crew 35's Wissmann was a rising star. Off Brazil, however, the young *kommandant* found the hunting disappointing. Few merchants sailed alone. On February 18, after sinking a six-thousand-ton Brazilian vessel, *U-518* experienced a long drought.

Finally, though, on February 28, Wissmann beheld a submariner's dream: a twenty-nine-ship merchant convoy northbound from Bahia, escorted by just three Brazilian warships. Wissmann carefully planned his attack. Choosing several Liberty ships as first targets, he closed in at night on the surface.

What followed, Wissmann conceded, was a travesty. *U-518* launched altogether fifteen torpedoes, each equipped with the new magnetic pistols. Six shots missed. Eight others were either duds or ran too deep. Just one ran straight and sure.[13]

⌖

"We were steaming along," U.S. Naval Reserve lieutenant Neal B. Parsons told a newspaper reporter, "when one seaman reported a torpedo had just missed the bow." Then, however, "another ran up to say that [the torpedo] was just a fish." Parsons weighed his options. "I had a feeling that it was the real thing and doubled my watch."

Parsons, a thirty-one-year-old Nebraskan and former high school athletics coach, commanded the seventeen-man armed guard contingent on board SS *Fitz-John Porter.* Since its completion at a Wilmington, California, shipyard in mid-October, the 10,500-ton, steam-powered, cargo-carrying Liberty ship had sailed from the West Coast to Bombay, where Parsons, along with *Fitz-John Porter*'s master, forty-nine-year-old Herbert G. Gregg, hosted the prince and princess of Bhavnagar State.[14] After a stop at Cape Town, *Fitz-John Porter*'s next destination was Bahia, where it joined convoy BT-6.

Hosting Indian royalty was proof of how Liberty Ships like *Fitz-John Porter* captured global imagination and symbolized America's remarkable wartime output. Based on a British design, *Fitz-John Porter* was assembled by welding together prefabricated sections. Original War Shipping Administration (WSA) contracts allowed an average of 105 days to assemble a single ship. By September 1942, however, the California Shipbuilding Corporation, which produced *Fitz-John Porter*, was delivering new Libertys in less than sixty days.

While FDR described the vessel as "a dreadful looking object" and *Time* magazine called it an "Ugly Duckling," looks weren't the Libertys' only problems. Because they came off the ways at such a frenetic pace, finding capable crewmen for them was tricky. No wonder, considering the primitive living conditions. Crew spaces lacked electricity and running water. Though some compartments (including the galley) were illuminated by oil lamps, the Libertys lacked any fire detection system.

The earliest of these "seagoing boxcars" also suffered structural flaws. Hull and deck cracks (attributable to faulty steel, inexpert welding, overloading, and frigid Atlantic weather) posed significant risks. Indeed, on several occasions—including one at sea—Libertys broke in half without warning.

Once cracking problems were resolved, however, the versatile Liberty fleet (eventually 2,700 strong) laid the foundation for unprecedented growth in Allied sealift.[15] And, as more and more Libertys crowded sea-lanes, they became prime U-boat targets.

"That was a good hunch," Neal Parsons said later of his decision to redouble *Fitz-John Porter*'s lookouts. Even so, he recalled, "the sub had us between the moon and ourselves."

That initial alert—an errant *U-518* torpedo crossing *Fitz-John Porter*'s bow with just feet to spare—was followed by second near miss: a torpedo passing about twenty-five yards astern. Finally, at 3:04 a.m., a third torpedo struck the port side athwart *Fitz-John Porter*'s aftermost (number 5) cargo hold. The explosion blew large holes in both sides at the waterline, demolished the after gun mount, and severed the ship's main propeller shaft.[16]

Warren C. Freihofer, a twenty-year-old U.S. Merchant Marine Academy (USMMA) cadet midshipman from Berkeley, California, had been dozing topside on a cot. As he later wrote—third person—in a report to the WSA: "He saw debris fly into the red light of the explosion. . . . It seemed . . . the entire ship was going to fly apart."

Freihofer reported to the wheelhouse. "Told [by Captain Gregg] to attend to the flares," Freihofer tore opened the taped cans that contained them. Then someone told him not to bother. A bridge-mounted 20-mm gun was already firing tracers to attract attention.

Although freeboard* had scarcely changed, Gregg realized *Fitz-John Porter* was doomed. After helping Gregg carry some valuables—a sextant, a strongbox—to the number 1 lifeboat, Freihofer went aft to look for Louis Acklen, an armed guard last reported sleeping on number 5 hatch cover. "All the hatch boards were blown away; the booms were badly splintered and broken and lying about the deck. The writer looked into No. 5 hold and found the water up to the level of the sea." There was no trace of Acklen.

*Distance from the main deck to the waterline.

Freihofer and Gregg were on board number 1 lifeboat when it was finally lowered. "Pulling some distance away from the ship," Freihofer remembered, "it could be seen well silhouetted against the sea."

As the rest of BT-6 cleared the scene, one of the Brazilian patrol craft (PCs) stopped to retrieve *Fitz-John Porter*'s survivors: eight officers, thirty merchant crew, and sixteen armed guards. "Those who were oil soaked took showers," reported Freihofer. "In a few hours the PC boat caught up with the convoy and survivors were transferred . . . to a merchant ship. Remained aboard that all day, all night, and most of the next day before the ship arrived in a Brazilian port."[17]

Acklen, a twenty-two-year-old married man from Harris, Louisiana, was *Fitz-John Porter*'s lone fatality. His parents had last heard from Louis, one of eight brothers and sisters, by letter from Bombay.[18]

24 | AIN'T THIS THE NUTS?

BOB MAHER STOOD midwatch when the first explosions rocked Convoy BT-6. *Clang! Clang! Clang!* "GENERAL QUARTERS! GENERAL QUARTERS! GENERAL QUARTERS! ALL HANDS MAN YOUR BATTLE STATIONS!"

Bob waited for his relief before going to his own GQ post. Within moments, Domingo Concha materialized in the darkness. "Mingo," a twenty-four-year-old shipfitter from North Arlington, New Jersey, about a mile north of Kearny, was not one to get excited. But now, as he took Maher's watch station, there was no containing him. "Ain't this the nuts?" Mingo repeated excitedly. "Ain't this the nuts?"[1]

⌖

Borie, *Courage*, *Tenacity*, *PC-575*, and *PC-592* had left Recife on March 2 to rendezvous with BT-6. After losing *Fitz-John Porter* between Bahia and Recife, BT-6's merchant masters and crews were on edge. Severin Broadwick, the Norwegian-born master of Liberty ship *Thomas Ruffin*, had already lost two merchants to U-boats, the first in March 1942, the next a month later in the South Atlantic. After that sinking, survivors had drifted eight days in a lifeboat while a U-boat lurked nearby. "When we were finally rescued," Broadwick told reporters, "we told the officer of the rescue ship the sub had been trailing us. He got out of there as fast as he could."[2]

After rounding the bulge of Cape San Roque, BT-6 steered northwest to begin the long coastal leg to Trinidad. It was now widely known to be a dangerous stretch. Ships loading cargo in Argentina for delivery in New York would often detour around Cape Horn and pass through the Panama Canal to avoid U-boats.

Little wonder jitters took hold after dark on March 3. When lookouts on Liberty ship *Jared Ingersoll* reported a submarine, the convoy commodore took matters into his own hands by ordering an emergency turn. To avoid collisions, merchants switched on navigational lights or fired flares. Radar picked up nothing suspicious, but Phil Osborn ordered star shells fired. It took until morning to sort out the mess.

Just after midnight three days later, *Borie* radar picked up a dense surface formation dead ahead. It was Convoy TB-6, BT-6's "opposite number," bound south for Bahia. TB-6 was supposed to pass twenty miles to port of BT-6 and not before daylight. Osborn signaled a precautionary turn to starboard, but only two merchants complied—and those two nearly collided. The convoys passed in the darkness without further incident—but with little room to spare.

BT-6's ill-disciplined journey dragged on. Off the mouths of the Amazon River, the influx of fresh water garbled sonar readings. Meanwhile, human snafus never ceased. Ships strayed, telltale smoke curled up by day, telltale lights pierced the dark, and (for no compelling reason) whistles blew, horns blared, flares popped, and rockets soared. At one point, exasperated, Phil Osborn threatened to open fire on the next blackout violator.[3] The haphazard, every-ship-for-itself voyage invited disaster.

Sure enough, sometime after midnight on March 9, as BT-6 steamed two hundred miles northeast of Paramaribo, Dutch Guiana (Suriname today), attacks began. Accounts vary. Some describe two separate attacks: the first just after 3 a.m., the second just after 6 a.m. But an eyewitness account from a cadet midshipman on board Liberty ship *James Smith* recorded the opening blow at 1:18 a.m.

Smith, flying light, manned by a thirty-two-man crew and fourteen armed guards, was originally scheduled to detach from BT-6 and head for Paramaribo. Instead, *Smith* was ordered to continue to Georgetown, British Guiana (now Guyana), to pick up a load of bauxite.

Donald F. Fennessey, a twenty-two-year-old native of Northampton, Massachusetts, had studied aeronautical engineering in California before transferring to the USMMA. *Smith* (as Midshipman Cadet Fennessey detailed in diary entries and an after-action report to academy authorities) "was struck by a torpedo on the port side of #5 hold." The jolt to *Smith* tossed Fennessey from his bunk (much as, days before, USMMA classmate Freihofer had been thrown from his deck cot on *Fitz-John Porter*).

Fennessey's diary entry: "Terrific crash and shaking of ship. . . . Not the slightest doubt . . . but what we were hit. . . . Tried getting my pants on. . . . steam escaping up the engine casing making a weird noise. Tangled in suspenders—black as hell—confusion everywhere."

On deck, Fennessey "couldn't see a thing[;] . . . strained voice of our gunnery officer giving orders to bewildered gun crew[;] . . . staccato of machine gun bullets from a neighboring ship blasting away at sub which might not even exist."

Soon, though, ravages became evident: "It struck number 5 hold [where] . . . men were sleeping on the hatch . . . blowing 11 of my shipmates—my friends—to hell."

After his own close call ("damn near got mine when hatch cover fell down from awning brace on boat deck"), Fennessey came across a wounded man. "Very deep and serious wounds in his leg and ankle. Dragged him up in the wheelhouse and patched him up as best we could. Lost a terrible amount of blood and very weak. Wheelhouse a mess."

Acting (as Fennessey described it to USMMA authorities) "with the coolness of a veteran and hardly like a man of only 29 years of age," Capt. William Aguillar ordered *Smith*'s engine plant secured and the ship abandoned. Fennessey readied in haste. "I had a small brief case stuffed with papers. Smashed [girlfriend] Rita's picture frame screwed on wall with shoe. Took some things wrapped up in coat and dived into lifeboat."[4]

Prospects for *James Smith* and its crew appeared bleak. But, nearby, for British merchant *Kelvinbank* and many in its crew, fates were already sealed. A twenty-year-old diesel-powered vessel half the size of *James Smith*, *Kelvinbank* was likewise traveling in ballast. It had joined BT-6 after previous stops in Egypt and South Africa. Now, off Dutch Guiana, riddled by a series of deadly explosions, *Kelvinbank* plunged quickly, taking with it a Royal Navy gunner and twenty-eight Indian merchant navy "lascars."*[5]

George G. Meade, the second of seven BT-6 Liberty ships torpedoed that night, had been launched in September 1942 after a breakneck assembly time of thirty-nine days. Doubling as BT-6's designated rescue ship, *Meade*, just slightly damaged and still making headway, slowed to save *Kelvinbank*'s twenty-three survivors.

Fortunately for its crew (and *Kelvinbank*'s survivors), *George G. Meade* had escaped catastrophe. Elsewhere in the stricken formation, however, damage to three more Libertys rivaled *James Smith*'s plight.

A single blow to *James K. Polk* entirely stove in one cargo hold, ruptured another, and demolished engine room pumps and piping. While topside damage was less extensive—a radio antenna carried away, two main-battery guns sprung from their carriages, a lifeboat blown off its davits (crushing Lane Weinberg, a young seaman armed guard from Oregon)—*Polk* was left down by the stern, dead in the water.

For its part, Capt. Severin Broadwick's *Thomas Ruffin* was immobilized too—heeled to starboard, steam lines broken, fuel tanks ruptured. And, while still on an even keel, *Mark Hanna*, abandoned by the crew after its rudder jammed, was dangerously adrift.

Meanwhile, after designating *Tenacity* and *PC-575* to tend to the fractured convoy, Phil Osborn took *Borie*, *Courage*, and *PC-592* off in pursuit of the enemy. In effect, all three ships now entered combat for the first time: chasing down the real thing, determined to interrupt further strikes and exact revenge. But while the U-boat threat was real and the escorts' intent lethal, their counterattacks were woeful. Hours passed, search patterns repeated, sailors bent to their tasks, but the Germans eluded all contact.

*Sailors from the Indian Subcontinent, Southeast Asia, and the Arab world. Thousands of lascars served on board British shipping company vessels during World War II. Under "lascar agreements," shipowners could retain lascars in service for up to three years, transferring them at will between company vessels.

Urgency gave way to frustration. "The *Borie* and the other escorts," by Bob Maher's account, "fired star shells and maneuvered frantically between the ships as the sound operators listened for cavitation noises from the attacker. But with all the noise and chaos around us, it was impossible to detect the enemy and keep any semblance of protective convoy order."

BT-6's best hope lay to the east. Sunrise would bring air cover and force the enemy to lie low; daylight would allow harried merchantmen to assess damage, stanch wounds, count heads, tend to survivors, regroup, and press on towards Port of Spain.

Earlier that morning, just before *James Smith*'s master William Aguillar ordered number 1 and number 2 lifeboats launched, Midn. Cadet Donald Fennessey and the ship's chief engineer left their lifeboat for a last-minute inspection. Though they found number 5 hold fully flooded and number 4 hold filling rapidly, *Smith*'s engine room was still intact.

Men had difficulty lowering *Smith*'s lifeboats. After his lifeboat's painter line got tangled with the falls, Fennessey grabbed a hatchet and cut the painter. Fennessey later noted in his diary:

> Sea running a bit and heaved us about. Tried to make for the forward end of the ship but sea just washed us away. Rowing difficult because of big swells and waves . . . circled ship at least twice. . . . SS MARK HANNA, also damaged, crashed into our ship about 4:00 AM. Tired and sick at heart.
>
> Finally, after night of flares and blackness, we pulled for the ship.

Climbing back on board at 6:30 a.m., Fennessey found *James Smith* "well down by the stern" with "large holes in the deck which made it look like a perforated tin can. Bodies and pieces of bodies were found here and there on the deck."

Fennessey was among those volunteering to attend to the human remains. "Jesus Christ never saw a sight more terrible," he confided to his diary. "[One of] our firemen lying peacefully on his back[,] hands folded on his stomach and his head missing. [Another crewman] on life raft rigging draped like an old rag on a clothesline. [A third] was in three pieces. [Two men] were identifiable. That is about all. . . . Jigsaw puzzle with human bodies.

"Despite a stomach that was tied up in a knot," Fennessey helped others "move cold-blooded men and cover up the remains in canvas . . . the most terrible thing I've ever been through.

"Strangely enough, in contrast[,] . . . this was a beautiful day and as peaceful a one as I ever hope to see."[6]

Later that day, as aircraft circled overhead, a small flotilla of tugs and patrol craft arrived to sort out the pieces of BT-6. Early in the afternoon, most of *James Smith*'s survivors, among them Donald Fennessey, "were transferred to a naval patrol vessel." He described one man from another ship (probably *Kelvinbank*) as "a tickled kid. Blown off gun tub. Sighted P.C. boat and blew his whistle like a steamboat. Had been floating around in life jacket."

As the balance of BT-6 sailed on to reach Port of Spain without further incident, its floating derelicts were tended to one by one. Taken under tow to Trinidad by British sloops, Libertys *Mark Hanna* and *James Smith* were later repaired and returned to service. Meanwhile, though Liberty ship *Thomas Ruffin* also reached Trinidad under tow, it was judged a total loss; in effect, U-boats had claimed Severin Broadwick's third merchant ship.[7]

James K. Polk was likewise declared a total loss, but not before its master and seven volunteers briefly returned to the age of sail. Rerigging the foremast and mizzenmast with tarpaulins, the merchant mariners purportedly "sailed" *Polk* some 360 miles before a British tug took over.

Although BT-6's seagoing ordeal was finally at an end, the wheels of military officialdom were only beginning to turn in reaction. In time, an official postmortem would render harsh judgments on Escort Unit 23.2.4 and its SOE. At no time—before, during, or after two separate, uncontested torpedo attacks—had BT-6 shepherds sunk, deterred, or even detected a U-boat.

To be sure, there were mitigating factors. Although BT-6 was classed as a coastal convoy, for example, the distance between Recife and Trinidad was actually longer than the transatlantic route between Newfoundland and North Ireland. Furthermore, having disregarded convoy protocols, the convoy commodore and his masters bore some responsibility. Nonetheless, concluded the Atlantic Fleet's May 13 report, written by U.S. Navy captain P. R. Heineman, "it is apparent that the passage of BT-6 was not a well-regulated operation."[8]

25 | THE SEA WAR IS ALL ONE

IN LATE JANUARY 1943, a news dispatch from London speculated that Adm. Sir Percy Noble, RN, recently arrived in Washington to head Britain's Naval Mission, "might be appointed supreme commander of the anti-U-boat campaign."[1] "This war," an American commentator opined, "cannot be won quickly without removing the U-boat menace. Unified command . . . is the best method for cleaning it up, and perhaps Sir Percy Noble will be the man for the job."[2]

Ever since Arcadia in January 1942, the British Admiralty had been pressing for a unified Battle of the Atlantic command. Indeed, the candidate the Admiralty once had in mind was Percy Noble, until November 1942 the head of Western Approaches Command. Now, however, Sir Percy had fallen out of favor.

WAC, the Royal Navy component most integral to ASW, had made significant strides under Noble. Above all, Sir Percy had sustained WAC morale when, as he readily admitted, "we never got any great news."[3] Still, dark times bred discontent. Fine qualities aside, Noble might simply not be aggressive enough for the job. Stunning losses to U-boats in the last months of 1942 decided his fate.

About that same time, Winston Churchill convened an Anti-U-boat Committee, a new War Cabinet subdivision charged with closing the Greenland air gap. One participant was Adm. Sir Max Kennedy Horton, the flamboyant commander of Royal Navy submarines.

Sir Max, a high-scoring Great War submarine skipper, had built his own estimable record as a force commander. Churchill believed solutions to ASW deficiencies were close at hand.[4] In Max Horton he saw the man to drive those solutions home.

Horton immediately stamped WAC with his forceful personality. Unlike the trim, elegant, unfailingly courteous Percy Noble, the stocky fifty-seven-year-old Max Horton was brusque, obsessive, and domineering. In Sir Max's favor, however, he had commanded submarines in combat, thereby gaining an essential grasp of submarine warfare's human and technical complexities. Who better to match wits with Karl Dönitz?[5]

That December, with Max Horton installed at Western Approaches, Winston Churchill fielded a recommendation from Sir Stafford Cripps, Leader of the House of Commons. Cripps proposed a supreme ASW commander *within* the Admiralty. Churchill squelched the idea, thinking it unsound.

"The sea war is all one," the Prime Minister insisted. "To try to take out one particular aspect . . . and place it under a separate authority . . . would . . . cause immense friction and confusion."[6]

Despite January's avowal that defeating U-boats "must remain a first charge on the resources of the United Nations," Symbol had done remarkably little to iron out details. Stung by TM-1's devastation, the conferees did establish two new Middle Atlantic oil convoys, one to deliver fuel to Gibraltar for Torch, the other to Britain for replenishing home reserves.[7]

Symbol also gave its blessing to hunter-killer support groups, the sort of seagoing "cavalry division" that Churchill had once vigorously espoused. Support groups would ultimately patrol convoy routes. As a first step, however, groups cobbled together by Max Horton would team up with very-long-range B-24s to comb the Bay of Biscay for U-boats going to and from French bases. To muster needed resources, Sir Max stripped warships from close escort groups. "It is a gamble," he acknowledged. Weakening close escorts "without gaining a dividend would be a fatal blunder."

The strategic decisions made at Casablanca—the invasion of Sicily; the commitment to a cross-channel invasion in 1944; the insistence on unconditional surrender—had transformed an alliance of convenience into a single-minded effort to secure final victory. But such giant schemes depended on gaining full mastery of the Atlantic.

Franklin Roosevelt had afforded Ernest King ample time and resources to revamp the U.S. Navy. Now, according to biographer Nigel Hamilton, FDR pressed COMINCH to curb his truculence, resolve arguments (with the AAF and the Admiralty), and turn the tide in the Battle of the Atlantic—or face dismissal.

On March 1, King addressed dozens of American, British, and Canadian flag and staff officers gathered in the District of Columbia for the Atlantic Convoy Conference. In opening remarks, wittingly or unwittingly, King echoed the sentiments Winston Churchill expressed to Stafford Cripps back in December: "You cannot consider antisubmarine warfare as divorced from the rest of the war effort."

Even with his job on the line, King adhered to the primacy of convoys. King knew conferees would generate bold schemes to find and kill U-boats, but getting convoys safely to their destinations came first. In short: "A ship saved is worth two built."[8]

On March 9, as convoy conferees in Washington continued deliberations, a transmission from *Korvettenkapitän* Karl Neitzel's *U-510* electrified U-boat Control in Kerneval. Overnight, off the coast of Dutch Guiana, *U-510* had, virtually uncontested, sunk three merchants and damaged five more.

For Crew 23's Neitzel (now forty-two but heretofore credited with just two sinkings), mauling convoy BT-6 was career redeeming.[9] Meanwhile, for Karl Dönitz, Hitler's newly anointed *Oberbefehlshaber der Kriegsmarine* in Berlin, Neitzel's victory was a flicker of promise in what thus far had been a lackluster 1943.

Aside from the destruction of Allied oil convoy TM-1, January results were slim. And, while February 1943 produced a significant uptick in merchant sinkings, it likewise produced an unsustainable uptick in U-boat losses. Perhaps Neitzel's South Atlantic feat signaled better days ahead.

In fact, what proved to be halcyon days in the North and Central Atlantic had already begun. In late February, B-Dienst detected the sailing of SC-121, a slow eastbound convoy. At first, SC-121 eluded interception by some two dozen U-boats. But finally, on March 6, *Korvettenkapitän* Rolf-Heinrich Hopmann, the thirty-six-year-old (Crew 26) *kommandant* of *U-405*, a Type VIIC recently transferred from Arctic waters, found it.[10] Weather was horrid and worsening, but a half-dozen U-boats, among them *U-405*, clung to SC-121's floundering herd of three-score merchants and an overmatched quartet of U.S. Navy escorts.

Next, B-Dienst decrypts revealed that HX-228, a fast eastbound convoy, was being rerouted north. This steered HX-228 clear of SC-121's predicament, pointing it instead towards another U-boat patrol line. Interception looked certain. Sure enough, on March 10, came a sighting signal from *Kapitänleutnant* Hans Hunger in *U-336*.[11]

Hunger (Crew 35) had indeed located HX-228, but he had also encountered trouble. As *U-336* took advantage of bad weather to surface and recharge batteries, a single-engine aircraft swept in out of the rain. In two low-level runs, the pilot somehow failed to drop bombs, affording Hunger time to crash-dive. In escaping, however, *U-336* lost sight of the convoy. Fortunately, *U-444* picked up the scent and continued to stalk.

Just as the Allied response to SC-121's plight led to the discovery of HX-228, so it exposed the positions and courses of two more eastbound convoys: slow SC-122 and fast HX-229. Four Allied convoys, all eastbound and heavily laden, were simultaneously in play.

"It was of primary importance," Dönitz wrote later, "to close . . . as quickly possible." On March 15, *U-91*, a Type VII on its third patrol, stumbled across a convoy in the air gap southeast of Greenland: "Over sixty ships course northeast nine knots." (Thought to be SC-122, it later proved to be HX-229.) Sensing a "common objective," Dönitz ordered two additional groups to "proceed with maximum speed" to designated sectors.[12] In response, upwards of three dozen U-boats converged. From Berlin, Dönitz closely monitored the developing action. Excitement would climb and pride swell as *kommandanten* "hurled themselves like wolves."[13]

⊕

Leutnant zur See Herbert Werner, twenty-two, first watch officer (XO equivalent) on board *U-230*, then already months at sea, described the pursuit of

SC-121 in his journal. "We calculated we could reach the enemy in 12 to 14 hours and raced with . . . vigor toward the new targets. . . . [T]he crew's morale was at its peak."

At 2:40 a.m. on March 7, a *U-230* lookout (to Crew 39's* Werner he was "our man with the magic eyes") spotted the quarry: "Shadows on port, distance 6,500. It's the whole herd."

Though shaken by towering seas, *U-230*, a Type VIIC, moved inexorably into firing position. SC-121's masts, as seen through the lenses of *U-230*'s bridge aiming device, "stuck up along the horizon like a heavy picket fence."[14]

"One by one [the shadows] wandered through" Werner's field of vision. He "aimed carefully at the fattest targets" even as the convoy's destroyers bore down from astern. As soon as Werner "pulled the [firing] lever five times," *U-230* sped for "the tail of the convoy," smashing "through the giant waves, a feat the escorts could not duplicate." Finally, "we heard the terrific rumble of three hard explosions. Blinding flashes revealed innumerable cargo ships, destroyers, and trawlers. Three of the vessels careened out of file, floating torches."[15]

Now "barren of torpedoes," Werner recorded, *U-230* "retreated from the battlefield." Though Werner was sure that "two of the stricken vessels" he targeted "broke apart in the heavy sea," *U-230* had actually sunk just one: a three-thousand-ton British freighter.

Still, *U-230*'s strike had been exemplary. With merchants, escorts, and U-boats alike battling near-hurricane-force winds, SC-121 lost just one other vessel that first night. Over the next two days, however, as storms abated, U-boats claimed six more ships, including the convoy commodore's vessel, a five-thousand-ton Norwegian motor ship, sunk by *U-405*'s Rolf-Heinrich Hopmann.[16]

On March 10, with the assault on SC-121 winding down, elsewhere a different pack of wolves set upon Convoy HX-228. Faced with a closing window of opportunity—HX-228 would soon escape the Greenland air gap—U-boats

---

*More accurately Crew XII/39. Indicative of U-boat expansion, XII/39's 1,080 cadets needed only two years and four months to reach the first officer rank.

opened attacks amidst blowing snow squalls. The cataclysmic explosions of two victims, merchants loaded with ammunition, hurled "hundreds of steel plates . . . through the air like sheets of paper." After two more nighttime successes, however, daylight exacted reverses. First, a U-boat was spotted, rammed, and fatally damaged by a British destroyer. Then, as a nearby U-boat sank the destroyer, it too fell to fatal attacks, by corvette depth charges and surface gunfire.

With equal reason to be exhilarated by success against SC-121 and dismayed by setbacks against HX-228, Dönitz eyed oncoming assaults on SC-122 and HX-229. Both herds—the faster HX-229, it turned out, gradually overtaking the slower SC-122—were deep in the air gap and thinly escorted. After days of navigating thick fog, the two convoys ran into fierce gales and monstrous seas.

British historian Richard Woodman describes conditions on March 16–17: "The night . . . was almost ideal for exploiting . . . *Rudeltaktik*. . . . Although a heavy sea and swell were still running and a strong wind had got up again, the visibility was clear, with a moon near the full." By Dönitz's account, "the U-boats took full advantage."[17]

The night's most telling blows struck HX-229: eight U-boats combined to sink eight ships and damage six others. But SC-122 also suffered, thanks to the efforts of *Kapitänleutnant* Manfred Kinzel, the twenty-seven-year-old *kommandant* of *U-338*.

Though just three weeks into his first command patrol, Kinzel (like Hans Hunger, a member of Crew 35) displayed the audacity and tactical mastery of a wily veteran. After penetrating SC-122's outer defenses, he nimbly evaded an attacking destroyer then steered *U-338* through the merchants' center ranks, firing both bow and stern tubes. Four of Kinzel's five shots connected, sinking three freighters and damaging a fourth.[18]

Sunrise on March 17 brought moderating winds and temporary respite for the beleaguered convoys as snow squalls occasionally obscured the sea's surface. Back in Berlin, meanwhile, Dönitz exhorted *kommandanten* to press on. After all, this "combined mass of ships" still had half an ocean to cross.

As the day progressed, two Liberator bombers appeared—one over each convoy. The bombers harassed U-boats and deterred attacks, but not for long. Once their venturesome pilots turned back, Dönitz's U-boats again closed in.

More than a dozen U-boats harried SC-122's flanks as darkness fell on March 17–18. Night began well. Just after 8 p.m., torpedoes launched by *U-305*'s *Kapitänleutnant* Rudolf Bahr (yet another Crew 35 member) sank an 8,200-ton refrigerator ship and a 4,300-ton steamer. Then, adept as he'd been the night before, Manfred Kinzel sank a 4,100-ton freighter. Once *U-305* dispatched the ship Kinzel had damaged the night before, SC-122, its ranks thinned by seven vessels, seemed poised for utter destruction. But then a storm of "near hurricane" fury descended, compelling U-boats and convoy vessels alike to batten down.

Residual snow squalls and northerly gusts made for a bleak dawn on March 18. During the day, many more VLR B-24s intruded, driving the U-boats under. Still thirsting for SC-122's elimination, however, Dönitz pressed his boats to ignore the aircraft, maintain contact at all costs, and haul ahead to maneuver for night attacks.

Dönitz's whip-cracking wasn't totally in vain. Before the day was out, SC-122's losses totaled nine ships for 93,000 tons. But, by the 19th the wolves had had to be called off. Surface escorts for both convoys had been substantially reinforced. and HX-229, after losing thirteen ships for 93,500 tons, was now protected by the largest VLR air umbrella ever afforded a North Atlantic convoy.

Afterwards, Berlin propagandists embellished actual achievements for public—and enemy—consumption: "In all 32 vessels of 186,000 tons and one destroyer were sunk and hits scored on nine other ships."[19]

For his part, Dönitz didn't downplay losses. In addition to three U-boats destroyed (one by ramming, a second by depth charges and gunfire, a third from the air), "nearly all the . . . boats suffered from depth charges or bombs"—two severely.

Still, his message to U-boats was heartfelt: "Appreciation and recognition for the greatest success yet achieved."

Meanwhile, as a "rusty, dilapidated" *U-230* crawled east towards France, Herbert Werner and his mates felt that "everything seemed to be right with the world."[20]

26 | SOMETHING APPROACHING HORROR

ON MARCH 10, Ens. Alexander C. "Goose" McAuslan, a twenty-three-year-old Avenger pilot from carrier *Bogue*, was patrolling near Convoy HX-228 when he spotted a surfaced U-boat just two miles away. McAuslan "poured on the coal" and positioned his big, bulky Grumman for a bombing run.

Moving at 180 knots, camouflaged by a squall just fifty feet off the wavetops, Goose pressed the bomb release—just as practiced. But nothing happened. Both depth bombs (aerial depth charges) clung to the belly racks. McAuslan banked back towards the sub, but it was already crash-diving and soon would be gone.

Bogue and the nine Avengers and twelve Wildcats of Composite Squadron Nine (formerly VGS-9, now VC-9) were on loan to the Royal Navy until its own jeep carriers were ready. Screened by *Belknap* and *George E. Badger*—*Clemson* four-stackers until recently used as seaplane tenders—*Bogue* had sailed from Argentia on March 5, rendezvousing with HX-228 the following day.

The ensuing days of foul weather demonstrated just how difficult it was for escorts like *Bogue* and the four-stackers to operate in North Atlantic winter. "Her captain," wrote a journalist on board, "sometimes referred to [*Bogue*] as a guinea pig[:] . . . the first to be tested in the harsh, gale-born laboratory of the Atlantic." VC-9's aircraft, the journalist noted, "too often had been held prisoner in their lashings by the fogs and gales, the freezing rain and sleet and spray."

Bogue couldn't stay with HX-228 very long. Low on fuel and pestered by equipment failures, the guinea-pig flotilla steamed back to Argentia just hours after McAuslan's bombing mishap.[1] "No man could say with confidence," concluded the journalist, "that her presence in a convoy had been the deciding factor."[2]

Bogue's abortive North Atlantic trial run was just one piece of discouraging news interrupting the Washington Convoy Conference proceedings. On March 9, First Sea Lord Dudley Pound had received an advisory from OIC. "The foreseen has come to pass," it began. "The Tracking Room will be 'blinded' in regard to U-boat movements, for some considerable period, perhaps extending to months."

In relaying this "severe setback" to Percy Noble in Washington, Pound tried to add a glimmer of optimism: "After 2 to 3 months the situation should improve considerably." Cold comfort that, as reports detailing attacks on Convoys SC-121, SC-122, HX-228, and HX-299 came in. Whenever Ultra blackouts occurred, Allied U-boat trackers were severely hampered.

Thanks to heroic efforts by Bletchley code breakers, the blackout was short-lived; Kriegsmarine Enigma decrypts resumed before month's end. Nonetheless, U-boat sinkings soared to eighty-four vessels in March. Worse, two-thirds of those losses occurred in convoys.

These facts, coupled with projections that Germany would amass more than six hundred U-boats by year's end, portended a "crisis of crises." British military and political leaders feared losing the Battle of Atlantic. "The enemy never came so near to disrupting communications between the New World and the Old," ventured an Admiralty report.[3] Subsequent historical analysis were to prove such fears overblown.[4] Still, wrote Royal Navy historian Stephen Roskill, no one would "look back on [March] without something approaching horror."[5]

Despite assurances from Franklin Roosevelt that Lend-Lease shipping could offset cargo-carrying shortfalls, Churchill contemplated dangerously shrunken stockpiles of fuel and other vitals. Speaking bluntly before the Anti-U-boat Warfare Committee, meanwhile, Dudley Pound warned that the Atlantic was so "saturated" with U-boats that "we shall have to fight the convoys through them."[6]

"Fighting through" seemed dire. But the direr alternative was abandoning the entire convoy system (what Roskill called the "lynch pin of our maritime strategy)." Indeed, as an Admiralty official confided to Max Horton, "Their Lordships were secretly of the opinion that the convoy system should be abandoned."

Despite the politicians' malaise, the Washington convoy conferees resolved to stick with convoying. Of equal consequence, they forged agreement on reconfiguring the Atlantic battles pace. Counter to newspaper speculation, there would be no "supreme commander of the anti-U-boat campaign." Instead, effective in early April, Commonwealth navies would take sole responsibility for escorting convoys across the North Atlantic, while the U.S. Navy would take sole responsibility for convoy routes in the Central and South Atlantic.

Subdividing Atlantic routes allowed each nation unfettered control of its anti-U-boat forces. As important, it avoided the confusion of teaming together warships from multiple navies, each with different procedures, tactics, signals, weaponry, logistics—even rules about or prohibitions on shipboard alcohol consumption. The many disconnects, though individually surmountable, were hard to sort out collectively, particularly under fire. (Indeed, an Allied "Command Procedures Board," established to reconcile these differences, essentially gave up trying.)[7]

The new arrangement suited King.* He was appalled by what he saw as the Admiralty's tradition-bound ways—largely unchanged since the Great War. But homegrown politics also explained King's obstinance. FDR and King both understood the American public would countenance only so much British sway over American airmen, sailors, soldiers, ships, planes, tanks, and so on. Now that the very next Allied thrust would be against Sicily (Operation Husky), the importance of Central Atlantic convoy routes, already major

*The British, however, were "surprised and dismayed" at King's "unilateral action," because it "put pressure on the Canadians." (Dimbleby, *Battle of the Atlantic*, 410)

conduits of men and matériel, loomed large. If COMINCH, his future already tenuous, was to be held accountable for passage of American soldiers and supplies on these routes, it should fall within his domain.

And there was also an immense practical consideration. Even before the Washington Convoy Conference convened, King was far from satisfied with his own navy's performance. Now, having demarcated battle-space boundaries with the British and Canadians, King was determined to shake up his own realm—and thereby save his job.

March's Enigma blackout, though short-lived, pointed out the fragility of a singular Allied advantage in the Battle of the Atlantic. Bletchley's swift breakthrough had taken luck and virtually all the working time of its three-rotor Bombes. This amounted, however, to just a temporary reprieve. Until OP-20-G achieved its own breakthrough, Bletchley remained the sole source of Kriegsmarine Enigma decrypts.

The original U.S. Navy contract with National Cash Register had called for the first American-made Bombes to be ready in February 1943. That schedule was unrealistic, but the January approval of revised prototype plans heightened expectations and prompted the Navy to undertake next steps. Accommodations were arranged in Dayton for the Navy enlisted sailors and WAVES (Women Accepted for Volunteer Emergency Service) who would build the Bombes. Meanwhile, construction got under way at the former Mount Vernon Seminary.

The first Navy sailors reached Dayton in February. Six hundred WAVES were to arrive in April. Yet by March, Desch's NCR team still had not produced "Adam" and "Eve," the two pilot Bombes promised.

Had the U.S. Navy misplaced its trust in Desch's group?

To be sure, Desch and his engineers never lacked for anything from suppliers and subcontractors. For men accustomed to tight budgets, slow deliveries, and manpower shortages, it was like working in a fantasy realm.

The price of such generosity, however, was shouldering conflicting demands. Navy scientists and mathematicians demanded operating speeds dramatically faster than BP's Bombes. Navy cryptologists, meanwhile, pressed for machine reliability and easy maintenance. The dilemma: how to balance the two sets of demands.

Each NCML Bombe was to house sixteen commutators (four-rotor Enigma analogs)—the equivalent of sixteen Enigmas designed to work in reverse. To test hundreds of thousands of possible combinations of Enigma rotor positions, the 104 electrical contact points on each Bombe rotor (wheel) had to align perfectly—a tall order at speeds of two thousand revolutions per minute. The machine's first wheels, made of a formaldehyde-based plastic called Bakelite, often chipped and warped. But the Navy rejected Desch's recommendation to substitute small wheels for the big wheels in one commutator. Replacing the extra wheels between runs would be too time-consuming.

Other problems appeared: how to transmit electrical power evenly through so many motors, shafts, and gears; oil leaks that fouled sensitive brushes. With the Bombe's electrical advances seemingly at war with its machinery, Desch and his team struggled to deliver what was promised.

But such pressures also spurred them—much as they had Joe's wagon-making forebears—to tinker. If, for example, machine runs suffered too many short circuits, then install a circuit tester that checked for shorts before each run. And if oil leakage was a problem, presoak the machine's leather seals in oil before installing them.

As spring approached, Joe Desch's sole refuge from all the inward anger, frustration, and guilt associated with NCML was his small garden plot. There he could seed and tend his plants, all the while whistling snatches of classical music and romantic film scores.[8]

Bogue, with VC-9 embarked, returned to Argentia on March 30 after its second North Atlantic sortie. If weather had been foul on the first sortie, it was somehow much worse on the second. Rough seas prevented *Belknap* and *Badger* from refueling, and most flights were cancelled. On March 23, Ens. Harry Fryatt, the son of a Waukesha, Wisconsin, pharmacist, narrowly averted death when his Avenger bounced over a flight-deck barrier during a landing attempt. The big plane staggered off the bow barely airborne. Somehow

Fryatt managed to ease it along until he regained enough speed to stay aloft. The twenty-two-year-old then made a second approach and landed safely.

Finally, on the afternoon of March 26, *Bogue* and its battered escorts left SC-123 to head back. As the ships arrived in Argentia on March 30, VC-9 aviators beheld USS *Ranger*. The fleet carrier (undersized for its breed) had first joined the Atlantic Fleet (then the Atlantic Squadron) in 1939 as its only carrier.

Ranger had participated in Torch and had just completed transatlantic missions ferrying AAF fighter aircraft to Casablanca. None of this, however, mattered much to VC-9's aviators. All they knew was that *Ranger* sat safe in Argentia while they endured North Atlantic wind and waves.

When several VC-9 officers were barred from Argentia's officers' club, they vented resentment by taking the place apart. After someone took a fire axe to the club's piano, the Shore Patrol stormed in. As the culprits fled (according to Stomp Santee's account), some "bright VC-9 lad had the presence of mind" to cry, "Let's get back to the Ranger[!]" This quick thinking resulted in the *Ranger* aviators' being restricted to the ship for several weeks.[9]

Meanwhile, because of weather damage and a faulty catapult, *Bogue* left Argentia for several weeks of repair at the Boston Navy Yard. Safe to say, *Bogue* and VC-9 had yet to have an impact on closing the Greenland air gap.[10]

27 | GRAY ELEPHANTS

AMERICA'S FEBRUARY 1943 triumph in the Battle for Guadalcanal gave COMINCH the opportunity to recall Francis "Frog" Low to Washington.* Promoted to rear admiral, Low became assistant chief of staff for ASW. King temporarily assigned him control of the U.S. Navy's scattered anti-U-boat resources, but also ordered that he produce an "appreciation of the antisubmarine situation." Time for Frog to follow through on his suggestion (when he left COMINCH to command *Wichita*) for a "completely separate organization to deal with the U-boats."

Before his years with King, Low, much like Britain's Max Horton, had served extensively in submarines. He knew firsthand all the strengths and weaknesses, advantages and disadvantages of undersea warfare. But, unlike Horton, Frog shunned the spotlight.

Low, according to COMINCH colleague Ladislas Farago, was a catalyst who could "think his way" into King's mind and "concentrate" his chief's ideas. Over the next weeks, culling the mountains of Anglo-American ASW

**Wichita*, with Low in command, was flagship of a flotilla of cruisers and destroyers that engaged Japanese aircraft during the January 29–30 Battle of Rennell Island. The fateful decision of the flotilla commander, Rear Adm. Robert C. "Ike" Giffen, to forgo aerial cover from jeep carriers *Chenango* and *Suwannee*—Giffen considered their slow speed a "ball and chain"—ultimately contributed to the sinking of cruiser *Chicago*. (John Wukovits, "Battle of Rennell Island: Setback in the Solomons," *World War II* [March 2000])

action reports and studies, Low methodically cobbled his way towards a revamped strategy.

"The prosaic answer to the problem," he finally wrote King on April 20, "is *enough* escorts *and* aircraft, recognition of fundamentals, and pressure to make them work." King coupled Low's thinking with an organizational framework he favored. What was needed, King insisted, was a "a fleet organization for antisubmarine warfare." Believing he'd caught the boss's drift, Frog assumed that ASW resources would shift to the Atlantic Fleet commander in chief, Adm. Royal Ingersoll. King, however, had something quite different in mind.

King instructed Low to draft necessary documents, including a preliminary statement for America's Joint Chiefs—a sort of trial balloon. "It is arranged," began that statement, sent on May 1, "to set up immediately in the Navy Department an antisubmarine command to be known as the Tenth Fleet."[1]

King's next move was to announce the concept at Trident, the mid-May Anglo-American summit convened in Washington.

Trident's primary agenda was to determine next steps after Husky, scheduled for July. Winston Churchill and Britain's Field Marshal Alan Brooke, true to form, favored invading Italy. Ultimately, they got their way, but not before Churchill formally acceded to a spring 1944 Anglo-American invasion of northern France.[2]

The stooped and hawk-faced Brooke dismissed Ernest King as still "determined to press Pacific at the expense of all fronts." But the Brits supported King's May 18 announcement of a centralized command to coordinate all U-boat information and direct all American naval countermeasures. As heralded in a classified dispatch two days later, the Tenth Fleet would "exercise [under COMINCH authority] unity of control over U.S. antisubmarine operations in that part of the Atlantic under U.S. Strategic control."*

---

*The dispatch omitted the fact the USAAF still controlled land-based ASW aircraft. Not until July 9, after years of sometimes fractious dispute, did Ernest King and George Marshall reach agreement that the U.S. Navy take over these forces. The transition was completed in November.

Though this new "fleet in being" was approved at the highest level, King understood Tenth Fleet was ripe to be misunderstood, misconstrued, and fiercely resisted. Tenth Fleet conveyed an air of mystery. Indeed, beyond King's inner circle, few people understood how this "paper fleet" would actually work—not least, U.S. Navy commanders actually fighting U-boats.

One reason that the concept found favor with the secrecy-obsessed British was that Tenth Fleet would be the sole and direct recipient of all Ultra intelligence. Rodger Winn (now back at the tabletop in Lenin's Tomb) could collaborate securely and exclusively with COMINCH's Kenneth Knowles.

Tenth Fleet came into being just as Knowles' tracking room unit, part of COMINCH's Combat Intelligence Division, was expanding. A dozen WAVES—a mix of officers and enlisted—joined as watch officers, responsible for compiling and correlating raw intelligence, plotting U-boats paths, and estimating enemy intentions.

Much of the incoming intelligence was based on radio direction finding and radar data, particularly when BP cryptographers "lost" Enigma. Even so, the better to secure Ultra, Knowles carved out an interior "secret room," accessible only to him, two junior officers, and an enlisted yeoman.[3]

The frequency and candor of Winn's and Knowles' exchanges often made them better informed about U-boat operations than those on the scene. Winn compiled, edited, annotated, and dispatched "Ultra serials" to Knowles. Radioed to Washington, then secured in double-sealed pouches, hand-carried to Knowles' secret room each morning. Though Knowles reciprocated by producing secret-room "serials" for Winn, their contents could not compete with what the Brits delivered. Unless or until OP-20-G and Naval Computing Machinery Laboratory (NCML) produced workable U.S. Navy Bombes, Ultra traveled west on a one-way track.

After lunch on May 28, Phil Bochicchio, a twenty-year-old Navy machinist's mate from New Jersey, entered a secured inner room on the second "deck" of NCR's Building 26 and prepared to fire up "Adam" for a scheduled run. Bochicchio had transferred from Boston to Dayton two months before, carrying orders to report to the U.S. NCML. The orders lacked a street address so, when he alighted at Union Station, Phil checked a local phone book. Finding no listing, he wandered downtown Dayton, asking at police and fire stations and even the Navy recruiting station. No one had ever heard of NCML.

Finally, someone from Dayton's chamber of commerce drove Phil out to NCR. "I don't know what to do with you," admitted an NCR Navy liaison officer after looking over the youngster's orders. Insisting that he somehow be put to work, Phil was assigned to NCR building maintenance.

Several days later, Phil received a letter urging him to call home. "What kind of trouble are you in, boy?" was his dad's first question. "The FBI has been here. Naval Intelligence has been here. All the neighbors are wondering."

Bochicchio's time in limbo may well have been due to his still-pending background check. But it may also have owed to unresolved disputes between NCML and Washington over Bombe design and manufacture.

For one thing, recommendations made by Alan Turing during his Dayton visit had required changes in Bombe prototypes. For another, Joe Desch and Howard Engstrom still argued about the Bombe's first wheel (commutator). Desch was equipping both prototypes with small-wheel sets, insisting they were the needed solution. But Engstrom balked. By his calculation, using small-wheel sets in the one hundred four-rotor Bombes already on order would increase the wheels needed to more than 40,000. Maintenance would be a pain. And, whenever the Germans tweaked Enigma, rewiring could prove daunting.

Resolving these matters likely stalled putting Navy technicians like Phil to work. Complicating matters further were the arrivals of the Bombe operations workforce. The Navy had refused OP-G-20's request for a large contingent of sailors in favor of personnel from the service's new women's branch. The WAVES were mostly in their twenties, fresh out of boot camp, and sworn to utmost secrecy.* Even their assigned rate, Specialist Q, was cloaked in mystery.

Ordered to travel "out west" by train with no idea of their ultimate destination, the women were housed at Camp Sugar, a rustic thirty-one-acre reserve built as an NCR sales-force retreat. Their jobs would be to wire, solder, and assemble parts for Bombe production. Based on mid-twentieth-century gender

*If quizzed by outsiders, WAVES were to say they were receiving adding-machine training.

norms, it was reasoned that women would be less likely to go out on the town, get drunk, and spill secrets. "And we did keep our mouths shut," said Evelyn Hodges Vogel, a WAVE veteran and Missouri native interviewed half a century later. "We were so proud to be . . . doing something that women had never done before." The WAVES' availability, waiting in Camp Sugar to be put to work, increased the pressure to flip the switch on Bombe production.[4]

NCML's first two Bombe prototypes, meanwhile, had been set up in Building 26. Though dubbed "Adam" and "Eve" (subsequent prototypes were named "Cain" and "Abel"), the two-ton machines (each a collection of components, motors, and wire spread across sawhorses and mounted in cabinets) were more familiarly known as the "gray elephants."

Each gray elephant consisted of nearly four hundred vacuum tubes, sixty-four individually wired Bakelite rotors, and countless feet of wire. They were, according to historian Collin A. Burke, wheezy, prone to oil leaks and short circuits, and capable of running just minutes, not hours. Likely so, but, by Engstrom's postwar reckoning, they were also "immediately successful" and were promptly employed running decryption trials on a backlog of Enigma messages.[5]

As a Bombe project floor manager, Phil Bochicchio's job was to conduct test runs and correct glitches. Prevent sparks and short circuits from crashing the runs. Keep sensing brushes oil free. Ensure power flowed evenly through the prototypes' motors, shafts, and clutches.

For Adam's May 28 afternoon test run, Phil followed an assigned menu to set the prototype's dials and rotors. Once he flipped a starting switch, Adam's rows of black Bakelite rotors began spinning through the twenty-six positions on each wheel. The gray elephant emitted its usual cacophony of rapid clicks until, unexpectedly, the machine slowed, stopped, slowly reversed, then stopped again. After printing out some numbers, Adam returned briefly to its forward motion. Finally, after twenty minutes, the gray elephant came to a complete stop.

Bochicchio didn't know what to make of these printed numbers. He ran the settings again, just to double-check. Adam repeated its actions, printing out the same numbers. Bochicchio called over a radioman buddy, showing him the printout. The radioman didn't know what to make of it either but suggested resetting Eve's dials and rotors to match Adam's.

In the midst of Eve's run, the very same things happened: the same slowing and stopping, the same slow reverse and second stop, a printout of the same numbers, the same brief return to forward motion, the same complete stop after twenty minutes.

Bochicchio took the printouts to Ralph Meader. He didn't know the meaning either but told Phil to pass on Adam's results to Howard Engstrom, now back in Washington.[6]

28 | PATTERN OF THE ACTION

"F— THE STAR-SPANGLED BANNER; I wish I was in the German Navy. I'd draw a bead on the 215. I'd sink every son of a bitch on it." These allegedly "seditious words," shouted "at or about 10:30 p.m., April 10, 1943, in the presence of various persons on board U.S.S. *Borie*," plunged Fireman 2/c Charles J. Reamer into trouble.

"Under the influence of intoxicating liquor," Reamer also purportedly assaulted Fireman 1/c George H. Sturla "with . . . a stiletto." Then, when Water Tender 2/c Richard B. Branch, duty master-at-arms, intervened, Reamer sealed his fate. "Go f— yourself," he screamed at Branch.[1]

Altogether, Reamer earned disciplinary charges warranting a general court-martial, the highest military tribunal. If convicted on all counts, the hotheaded nineteen-year-old faced dishonorable discharge or worse.

Fortunately for the accused, being drunk was the only charge that stuck. Though Reamer was promptly transferred, his outburst was a sign of a restive crew. Except for rare interludes, *Borie* had spent virtually all the war far from home waters—and the main action. While Reamer had taken the disorderly path out of purgatory, a more honorable escape beckoned others.

Smaller than destroyers but bigger and better equipped than British corvettes, brand-new destroyer escorts (DEs), first built for the British, were proving ideal escorts and sub fighters. The building of landing craft temporarily stalled DE construction but, by December, more than two hundred were in commission, creating tremendous opportunities for junior officers and petty officers.[2] Opportunities not only for promotion to a sleek, new frontline ship but also for stateside training, maybe even home leave.

"DE fever" gripped *Borie*'s wardroom. "Possibly yours truly may be an Exec on a D.E.," Mike Brown crowed to his dad in April. Certainly, Mike was angling for "something getting me back to the states."

Mike's frustration at not getting one of the plum transfers certainly showed in a mid-May letter to Gully. Two wardroom mates had "finally shoved off for Norfolk to be execs on the new DE's," he groused. One was "even handing out the story that he was going to be Capt. of a DE. . . . [W]hat a lot of damn dope that guy hands out."[3]

Disappointment and envy aside, there was also begrudging pride in those moving on. One day, *Borie* XO Charles Hutchins spotted a flag hanging conspicuously on the ship's office bulkhead. "That's a service flag," the office yeoman explained. "We thought it would be kinda nice to put a star on it for every man transferred from the *Borie*. To show he's finally gone to war."[4]

One other key transferee was skipper Phil Osborn. "He is going to the Naval Academy for duty," Mike Brown wrote his dad on May 23. "The present exec. [Hutchins] is taking over the command. We all feel that he'll make a darn good skipper."

Since taking command, the "Hollywood Skipper" had championed crew morale. Now, in a predeparture recommendation to Commander Fourth Fleet, Adm. Jonas Ingram, Osborn pled *Borie*'s case one last time. Since *Borie* had "been stationed out of the United States for three years," perhaps it was time to "shift whole groups to other areas."

It's impossible now to determine whether Ingram seriously considered Osborn's recommendation. Nonetheless, near the end of May, Bob Maher recalled, "we found ourselves heading east, instead of south[;] . . . we headed east and east and then we headed east."*

*Bob Maher, an Osborn admirer who came across the May 9, 1943, letter decades later, assumed it was sent, received, and acted on favorably. (Maher and Wise, *Sailors' Journey into War*, 79–81)

Bogue, after its stay in Boston to repair faulty catapult gear, returned to work in late April, this time farther south in the Atlantic. Flying conditions here were much improved, but Bill Drane's aviators still fumbled. On April 28, for instance, Stomp Santee attacked a surfaced U-boat, only to have his depth bombs ricochet off the surface before exploding. The sub escaped undamaged.

Fortunately, the earnest but often misguided improvisations of many ASW combatants were now being scrutinized by a mustachioed, bushy-browed, violin-playing MIT physics professor named Philip McCord Morse. Morse, now thirty-nine, was born in Shreveport, Louisiana, and raised in Cleveland, Ohio, where his father was a telephone engineer. Like Dayton, Ohio's Joe Desch (who was four years younger), Phil Morse developed a passion for radio technology. While attending Case School of Applied Sciences (Case Western Reserve University today), Morse and several friends built, demonstrated, sold, and installed custom radios.

In 1929, three years after graduating from Case, Morse earned a Princeton physics doctorate, a PhD. In 1931, after two years abroad, Morse snagged a Depression-era MIT professorship. A decade later, Morse led a U.S. Navy project to develop shipboard countermeasures against acoustic mines. Next, in March 1942, Morse was tapped to lead civilian experts engaged in operations research, a new scientific discipline pioneered by Britain's Patrick Blackett—a former Morse colleague. (In addition to championing use of bombers against U-boats, Blackett had advised the RAF on Battle of Britain tactics.)

Morse's eclectic team included physicists, mathematicians, geneticists, even insurance actuaries. "Some of us," recalled Morse in his autobiography, believed "we could . . . assist in deciding what equipment should be used and how it should be used [but] I personally wanted to get closer to the operational decisions."

Initially headquartered in Boston, Morse's ASW unit relocated to Washington in June. Folded into Tenth Fleet the following spring, the ASW Unit was rechristened the Anti-Submarine Warfare Operations Research Group

(ASWORG.)* Morse's men served, like fellow civilians Tizard, Turing, Welchman, Blackett, and Desch, on the front lines of the Wizard War.

ASWORG's remit was to "help the fighting Navy improve its antisubmarine technique." "We were . . . innocent . . . academics," Morse recalled, dropped into "a life-or-death task."

Shown a "room full reports of all actions by or against enemy submarines, real or imagined," Morse's team refused to "studiously digest all the reports, and . . . deliver some oracular pronouncement." Instead, after "a one-week huddle," they worked out "a simplified but quantitative pattern of the [antisubmarine] action."

U-boats spent much time on the surface, where, as Morse put it, "they could see and breathe" but aircraft could find them by sight or air-search radar. But how far away could a surfaced submarine be seen? Were they always seen? How often—and why—were they missed?

With precise answers to these and other questions, ASWORG could determine efficient aerial search patterns. Unfortunately, the reports answered few of ASWORG's questions. In the end, wrote Morse, "We believed our theory. We didn't believe the reports." Wanting "technical data . . . collected by technical men," Morse lobbied to send ASWORG scientists into the field. It was a hard sell, but by the end of summer 1942 "field reps" were operating out of New York, Miami, Trinidad, and Argentia. Occasional patrol flights enabled reps to generate numbers that dramatically enhanced the "pattern of the action." Troubleshooting radar performance defects led to corrective tweaks. New search plans for planes and ships dramatically increased U-boat sightings.

Digging into aerial attack details, field men also learned that depth bombs were routinely set to explode at seventy-five feet. This might be okay for destroyers attacking *submerged* U-boats. Aircraft, however, attacked *surfaced* U-boats; blasts seventy-five feet down rarely damaged them. Better to set depth charges at twenty-five feet and only attack U-boats caught by surprise.[5]

In the bigger picture, ASWORG also came to understand that *keeping* U-boats submerged was nearly as effective as sinking them outright.[6] So,

*Morse detested the ungainly acronym but, according to Francis Low, never came up with an alternative. (Low, "Personal Narrative," 34)

by extension, was limiting the number of days a U-boat could remain at sea and on station.

In spring 1943, one response to the "crisis of crises" that gained favor was eating up U-boats' precious sea time (and the boats themselves). The skies over the Bay of Biscay, the 300-by-120-mile bottleneck U-boats traversed going to and from French bases, were being saturated by land-based aircraft equipped with microwave radar and high-powered searchlights.

After reaching Belfast at the end of April, *Bogue* and VC-9 spent two weeks in intense training: VC-9 airmen at the RAF's Fleet Air Arm Anti-Submarine School in Ballykelly, Scotland; officers from *Bogue* and its flush-decker escorts at Liverpool's Western Approaches Tactical Unit. Meanwhile, *Bogue* received new gear: portable high-frequency direction-finding (HF/DF, or "Huff-Duff") equipment, along with a British expert to facilitate its use.

Shipboard Huff-Duff supplemented the radio-direction-finding bearings supplied by shore-based stations ringing the Atlantic.[7] Huff-Duff plots prepared by network centers in America, Britain, Iceland, Africa, and Brazil reached Kenneth Knowles, who, aided by combat intelligence Huff-Duff specialists, massaged and refined these plots for operational use.[8]

On May 19, when *Bogue* (designated flagship of American Support Group 6) joined westbound Convoy ON-84, the cumulative impact of schooling at Ballykelly and Liverpool was poised for testing—if conditions permitted. "What we would like to do," Capt. Giles Ezra Short, *Bogue*'s short, pug-faced forty-seven-year-old skipper, told a reporter, "would be to hunt the subs and sink them. But we've got to be able to fly. When we can't we're just another target for the U-boats."

Bad weather curtailed flight operations until finally, on the afternoon of May 21, with ON-84 five hundred miles southwest of Greenland's Cape Farewell, sun-drenched skies gave Bill Drane's aviators a chance to show their stuff.

Bill Drane saw action first. Near twilight, sixty miles ahead of the convoy, he spotted something break the surface, change bearing, and then lengthen into a streak of silver with a black splinter at its center: a U-boat. Drane glided in astern, the splinter now a long dark shape, a hull tapering away to bow and stern, a conning tower amidships. He released depth bombs before the U-boat even started to dive. Banking after a steep climb, Drane and his crew saw towers of spray but no sign of the U-boat. After dropping a smoke marker and bird-dogging a flush-decker to the scene, Drane flew back to *Bogue*.

That the "Skipper's Sub" had vanished so quickly without a trace of oil, debris, or bodies was a mystery—one that still baffled as VC-9's dawn patrol pilots prepared for launch. At 4:30 a.m., planes lifted off into a heavy, broken overcast. Over the next hour personnel in air plot, a low-ceilinged compartment below the flight deck, could only wait. Some were dozing when the ship/plane loudspeaker squawked to life at 5:45 a.m. "Sub sighted, just surfacing. Am attacking."

At the other end was Lt. (jg) Roger C. "Bud" Kuhn, a Hoosier from Plymouth, Indiana, patrolling fifty-five miles southeast of *Bogue*. "Well, I'll be damned!" Kuhn exclaimed for all to hear. "They're shooting at us!"

Kuhn fired back: he punched through low clouds, steepened his dive, and released depth bombs. From a steep climbing turn, the airmen saw the U-boat wallow, pivot slowly, and trail a sheet of oil. "Sub still afloat," Kuhn radioed at 5:57 a.m. "Stern definitely damaged. Send help." Unfortunately, Kuhn misjudged his position; help, though on the way, found neither Kuhn nor his adversary.

It was nearly four hours before air plot's ship/plane loudspeaker again trembled with urgency. "Sub sighted! I got the son of bitch!"

The excitable voice belonged to Ens. Stewart E. "Burrhead" Doty, the son of a California citrus grower and VC-9's newest and youngest TBF pilot. "He's straight up and down!" Burrhead exclaimed as he saw the sub's bow point skyward, hang there momentarily, then slide down.

A big patch of diesel persuaded Burrhead this U-boat was a goner, but a radio signal captured by Huff-Duff soon after showed otherwise. Then, tracking along the Huff-Duff bearing, Avenger pilot Lt. Robert L. "Bob" Stearns spotted a slender black hull. After dropping bombs low and watching all explode close along the bow, Stearns, a twenty-two-year-old Californian, saw the sub lose headway and settle by the bow. Stearns returned with dramatic photos but, like Drane, Kuhn, and Doty before him, no solid evidence of destruction.

May 22's swings between anticipation and anticlimax continued until 5:05 p.m., when the air plot loudspeaker issued one last plea. "Send help!" it insisted, this time with the voice of Avenger pilot Lt. (jg) William F. "Champ" Chamberlain. Chasing down a 4:23 p.m. Huff-Duff bearing twenty miles from *Bogue*, Champ, a twenty-seven-year-old veteran from Aberdeen, Washington, had surprised a surfaced U-boat and straddled it with four depth bombs.

"It's down by the bow and trailing smoke. . . . Send help immediately."

An Avenger piloted by Lt. H. S. "Stinky" Roberts shot off the deck. Once Roberts arrived, Chamberlain headed back. He was preparing to land when his radioman overheard Roberts's transmission: "The sub has surfaced, am attacking."

Chamberlain sped back.

Roberts, meanwhile, with the U-boat rising directly below, had scored bomb blasts that pushed the sub back down, rolling like barrel. Finally it lay full length on the surface, listing to starboard.

Chamberlain was back now. As he and Roberts circled, their rear gunners blazing away, German sailors spilled from the conning tower onto the tilting deck. Seeing a white sheet, pilots ordered their gunners to cease fire. U-boat sailors jumped into the sea, their heads rising and falling with the swells. Then, racked by explosions, the U-boat went under.

By the time the captain of *U-569* and twenty-four of his crew were rescued by a Canadian destroyer, Champ, Stinky, and their crews were back on *Bogue*'s flight deck amidst a raucous celebration.[9]

Bogue and VC-9's success added new credence to the idea of targeting U-tankers. What had once been a herd of seven milk cows had expanded to nineteen. Milk cows had refueled as many as four hundred U-boats, mostly north and west of the Azores. The routine process went virtually unchallenged.

Targeting them had intrigued Kenneth Knowles. Scouring logs of U-Boat Control transmissions, he identified traffic used to arrange milk-cow rendezvous. Bearings on these so-called movement messages pointed to reprovisioning locales, most in the heart of the mid-Atlantic air gap.[10]

What more impactful use for Enigma decrypts than ambushing milk-cow rendezvous—provided resources could reach the scene?

One possible option was a squadron of Scotland-based U.S. Navy submarines. When Ernest King cabled Dudley Pound in April suggesting their clandestine dispatch, Britain's First Sea Lord vigorously objected. "We should not risk what is so valuable to us [referring to Enigma, not the submarines]." Shipping losses would, he insisted, soar "from 50 to 100 per cent."

King cabled back; while equally concerned about Enigma security, "we are not deriving fullest value from it." Depriving "the enemy refuelers would . . . decrease the effectiveness . . . of the entire U-Boat deployment." Moreover, "with careful preparations . . . destruction might be accomplished without a trace."

When Pound stood firm, King arranged to have the submarines return to America. To forewarn Allied convoys of their westbound transit, an alert was transmitted using Anglo-American Cypher Number 3. Although Cypher 3 was widely used for Allied convoy operations, intelligence analysts had long worried it might be compromised. Indeed, Enigma decrypts revealed the Germans knew about the returning American subs, and fears were confirmed.

Ironically then, King's aborted scheme contributed to closing a key security breach. Switching codes saved convoys ships, but didn't sink milk cows. Now, however, with jeep carriers about to join King's arsenal and with the Central Atlantic as a U.S. Navy preserve, a new means to eliminate them came into focus.[11]

29 | HARD AND UNEXPECTED

THE MAY 22 sinking of *U-569* was just the latest in a weeks-long litany of U-boat losses. As that month opened, Dönitz balanced the Allies' average monthly U-boat "kill rate"—fifteen and climbing—against his determination to rebound from April's dramatic dip in merchant sinkings. Still confident in his *kommandanten*, he dispatched five dozen U-boats to four patrol lines athwart North Atlantic convoy routes through the air gap. "You are better placed than ever before," he insisted on May 2. "Don't overestimate your enemy but strike him dead."

But on May 4, amidst a concentrated attack on westbound convoy ONS-5, disaster (as revealed in desperate radio transmissions) unfolded:

> May 5: DESTROYER. ATTACKED. SINKING. U-368.
> May 5: ATTACKED BY DESTROYERS. DEPTH CHARGES. LEAVE BOAT. U-531.
> May 6: ATTACKED BY CORVETTE. SINKING. U-438.
> May 7: AIR ATTACK. SINKING . . . U-663.[1]

Herbert Werner, *U-230*'s first watch officer, who in March had thought everything right with world, now sensed a "naval disaster . . . in the making."

When *U-230* surfaced at 9:15 a.m. on May 12, Werner beheld a panorama of mastheads and funnels edging to the northeast. It was Convoy HX-237, bound for Liverpool. "Once we are close to that wall of ships," *Kapitänleutnant*

Paul Siegmann, *U-230*'s twenty-nine-year-old (Crew 35) *kommandant*, assured Werner, "Our torpedoes can't miss."

U-230 "forged through the sea," recalled Werner, "to reach a forward position before dark." Suddenly, at 9:55 a.m.: "A startled cry at my back, '*Flugzeug*!'" Seeing a plane "dropping out of the sun . . . [w]e plunged head over heels into the conning tower. The boat . . . shot below the surface."

This began a nearly two-day-long ordeal. "Condemned to sit it out in the crushing depths," *U-230*'s crew counted over two hundred close-by detonations that "deafened us and took our breath away." It was 4:30 a.m. on May 14 before *U-230*, surfacing, finally "broke through to air and life."

Werner knew "a convoy with its own air defense smashed our basic concept of U-boat warfare."[2]

Dönitz did too. That same day he sent a message to all U-boats. Conceding that advances in enemy radar had robbed them of "invisibility," he vowed "to do everything in my power . . . to change the situation as soon as possible." For the present, however, "I expect you continue your determined struggle with enemy by pitting your ingenuity, ability and hard will against his ruses and technical developments yet to finish him off."[3]

Surely his rallying cry rang hollow. Over the preceding days, the efforts of forty U-boats against eastbound convoys HX-237 and SC-129 had yielded only five sinkings. For each merchant sent to the bottom, a U-boat had gone down too. Such tit-for-tat could not possibly continue.

On May 18, personal loss compounded Dönitz's distress. *U-954*, one of twenty-five U-boats stationed on the fringes of the air gap, was lost with all hands. One of the crew was Dönitz's twenty-one-year-old son Peter, a watch officer embarked on his first war cruise.

The Oberbefehlshaber der Kriegsmarine concealed his grief but not his consternation.[4] Dispatching a U-boat pack towards yet another convoy, he sent what amounted to an ultimatum: "Now if there is anyone who thinks that fighting convoys . . . is no longer possible, he is a weakling and no true submarine captain. . . . Be . . . clear you must answer for your actions. Be hard and attack."[5]

Despite this stinging exhortation, hard reality cornered Dönitz. "By May 22," he wrote later, "we had already lost thirty-one U-boats since the first of the month . . . a hard and unexpected blow."[6] U-boats would have to shift to areas where Allied airpower was believed less threatening. On May 24, he assured *kommandanten* that withdrawal from the North Atlantic was merely as a temporary defensive measure.[7]

While discouraged, the Lion was no less determined to fight. As a measure of that resolve, he ordered sixteen U-boats to form a patrol line along the forty-third meridian, naming it Gruppe Trutz (Group Defiance).

All through the spring, Adam and Eve, NCML's gray elephants, had continued to sputter and break down, their Bakelite rotors overheating, losing their shape, and creating faulty electrical signals. Quick fixes just seemed to generate more oil leaks, raising fears that with its current design the NCML Bombe might never reach production. For Howard Engstrom, now back in Washington, Dayton's technical glitches topped an accumulation of project setbacks.

In return for carte-blanche funding and access to resources, Navy bean counters were demanding more accountability. On their side of the ledger, NCR management balked at Navy interference in plant operations and complained about opportunities being lost to "nonprofit" work.

Meanwhile, personality and personnel headaches abounded. Joe Desch increasingly resented Ralph Meader's continued intrusion in his domestic life. NCR's civilian engineers griped about overtime.

Even WAVES made waves. One had hidden her pregnancy, a breach of enlistment preconditions.* Weddings—breaches as well—were also in the offing. And, whenever a WAVE "cracked" under pressure, other less stressful project work had to be found for her.[8]

As he wrestled with Dayton's problems, Engstrom was also squeezed by OP-20-G's outsized expectations. Craving redemption after the Pearl Harbor and *Paukenschlag* debacles, OP-20-G hoped to outmatch the British Bombe. Now came news that functional models of BP's four-rotor Bombes were nearing completion.

*She was discharged unpunished but sworn to secrecy.

Beyond this were demands to support Tenth Fleet's anti-U-boat campaign. May was shaping up as a British show: American U-boat kills were just a small fraction of the total. If Tenth Fleet was to succeed, timely and reliable intelligence was essential. Absent its own Enigma-cracking capability, OP-20-G was beholden to BP and shackled to Admiralty constraints on exploiting Ultra.

Not least, Howard Engstrom's own reputation was at stake. NCR's failure would be his failure too. He believed Joe Desch would produce a code-breaking game changer, but only tangible evidence would make the case.

Joe Bochicchio's May 28 test run may well have delivered enough such evidence. The rotor settings produced by Adam (and confirmed by Eve) apparently enabled Washington code breakers to unscramble a series of critical German "movement" messages. Several days later, Ralph Meader passed on some exciting news from Washington: the May 24 hit alone "had paid for the entire cost of the project."[9]

NCML's May 28 "machine-generated" breakthrough may have indeed been timely, but it was also part of an even more consequential train of events. In a comparable "human-generated" breakthrough, GC&CS code breakers managed to decipher Dönitz's May 24 transmission establishing Gruppe Trutz—and do so just hours after its transmission.

By all accounts, it was a remarkable stroke of good fortune: so tenuous was BP's hold on Kriegsmarine Enigma that had Dönitz's message been sent a few days earlier, it might not have been cracked for weeks. That said, the decrypt posed a problem for Rodger Winn and Kenneth Knowles.

Dönitz had sent his Group Defiance U-boats to an area west of a geographic point coded *TT*. Winn, the acknowledged expert in these matters, interpreted *TT* as an area two hundred miles east of Nova Scotia. But Knowles, despite much less experience, strenuously disagreed. In his judgment, *TT* instead represented an area "about six hundred [miles] southwest of the Azores"—a difference of about a thousand miles.

Knowles' reasoning was bold but savvy. Dönitz had every incentive to move his U-boats as far as possible from land-based ASW aircraft. Moving them southwest of the Azores would put them in position to attack U.S.–Gibraltar convoys (UG/GU).[10] With Winn still holding to his original estimate, Knowles' divergent view was about to be put to the test.

⌖

On May 30, *Bogue*, flagship of Capt. Giles Short's Support Group 6, departed Argentia with orders to protect U.S.–Gibraltar convoys while simultaneously wreaking havoc on U-boats. Kenneth Knowles' analysis had pointed to the boundaries of *Trutz*'s hunting ground. Now it was up to Short (aided by Huff-Duff, radar, sonar, and sharp-eyed lookouts) to narrow the search. Once U-boats were flushed, VC-9's job was to kill them.

Action kicked off on June 4, "a fine day with just a few puffy clouds." In an afternoon replete with opportunity and peril, five Avenger pilots—Harry Fryatt, Edmund W. "Ned" Biros, Edward R. Hodgson, Bill Drane, and Wilma S. "Monk" Fowler—pounced on three different U-boats in three separate engagements.[11]

Although each boat spotted was fully surfaced and apparently unsuspecting, none proved easy pickings. Even as Avenger depth bombs rained down, stalwart U-boat gun crews retaliated with flak. During the afternoon's closing engagement, tracer rounds zipped by either side of Drane's cockpit while Lt. (jg) Fowler, a twenty-two-year-old Texan, took hits to his engine. All pilots and crews returned safely to *Bogue*—crestfallen at not making kills, yet grateful to be alive.

June 4's experience argued for rethinking VC-9 aerial tactics. To *Bogue*'s Giles Short, meanwhile, the three sightings proved that Support Group 6 was in the right place. After recovering aircraft at dusk and steaming west overnight, Short doubled back east prior to launch at dawn.

That very morning, Short's tactical savvy rewarded Wildcat pilot Lt. Richard S. Rogers and Avenger pilot Goose McAuslan. At 6:50 a.m., while on dawn patrol, the pair spotted a surfaced U-boat and capitalized on June 4's lessons.

Rogers, twenty-six, an Annapolis graduate and son of a much-decorated Great War artilleryman, silenced *U-217*'s flak with his .50-caliber wing guns.[12] Rogers' tracers also set the sub's conning tower ablaze, leaving McAuslan unchallenged as he swooped in with depth bombs. After Goose's charges exploded and Rogers delivered a valedictory strafing, *U-217*'s bow reared straight up then slid into the depths, leaving behind patches of oil and debris.[13]

If June 5's deft dispatch of *U-217*, a Type VIID minelayer, served to dispel June 4's wariness over U-boat flak, however, June 8's experience tempered the swagger.

Just after 3 p.m. that day, twenty-two-year-old James H. Finch, the radioman on board Letson S. "Sam" Balliett's Avenger, spotted a fast-moving U-boat.[14] Even as Lt. (jg) Balliett, a twenty-six-year-old Nevadan, circled to attack, flak barrages from multiple guns pocked the sky. Balliett's depth bomb explosions hoisted the sub's stern, but the flak scarcely let up.[15]

Calls for help brought Wilma Fowler's Avenger to the scene. But as Monk approached, flak holed his wing and tail section and filled his cockpit with acrid smoke.

"Wojcik's hit!" cried rear gunner Harold Buchholtz over the intercom. Radioman Clement Wojcik, shrapnel in his foot, was bleeding heavily.

After opening the hatch to reduce smoke, Monk toggled his bombs.

"All bombs away?" he asked Buchholtz, who had gone to Wojcik's aid. "Negative!" the gunner replied. "You have one left!"

Having no luck with his emergency bomb release, Monk radioed air plot: "I'm hit—my radioman wounded—plane smoking badly—cannot drop last bomb."

"Can you bail out? (Not with Wojcik's foot.) Can you ditch?" (Not with the bomb on board.) "Negative. Will try to make it aboard, get ship into wind for return."

Even as Fowler limped towards *Bogue*, two more VC-9 aircraft arrived. Lt. (jg) Frank Fogde's Avenger stayed clear of flak as twenty-one-year-old Lt. (jg) Phil Perabo's Wildcat made three strafing passes. Finally, as Fogde began his bombing run, the U-boat—guns silenced, conning tower and decks cleared—submerged.

Not until his wheels hit *Bogue*'s deck did Monk Fowler learn that flak had shredded a tire. Fortunately—for Buchholtz, Wojcik, Monk, and *Bogue*—an arresting cable caught the Avenger and the depth bomb didn't blow. As medics rushed Wojcik to sick bay, Monk and Buchholtz, surveying damage, found a German projectile, probably a dud, impaled just inches from the bomb.[16]

⊕

Kapitänleutnant Helmut Manseck, *U-758*'s twenty-eight-year-old *kommandant*, a hero of the assault on Convoy HX-229, had been bound for Trinidad when Sam Balliett ambushed his vessel. *U-758*, a Type VII, carried additional armor plate and a quadruple mount of 20-mm machine guns—prototypes of the "new and stronger weapons" Dönitz promised. Manseck's orders, should he encounter enemy aircraft, were to "fight back."

Just as instructed, when Balliett's Avenger dove at *U-758*, Manseck's gunners sprinted for the weapon "bandstand" aft of the bridge. Depth bombs rocked *U-758*, but Manseck's crew kept guns firing until he called them back and "pulled the plug."

"Eight carrier planes warded off," Crew 34's Manseck boasted to U-boat command, "one shot down, four damaged." Command's response: "Well done. Long live your quadruple."[17]

Manseck's chest-thumping downplayed the heavy price: eleven crew wounded, many crucial fittings damaged, and *U-758*'s diesel compartment so flooded that he feared sinking.

U-118, a German Type XB minelayer doubling as a milk cow, was soon on its way but didn't reach *U-758* until the next afternoon. *U-460*, a conventional milk cow, joined up the next day. As *U-118*'s doctor tended *U-758*'s wounded (transferring some to *U-118*), spare parts were shipped across and emergency repairs made. On June 11, after *U-118* took on forty tons of diesel oil no longer needed by Manseck, *U-758*, accompanied by *U-460*, limped back towards France.[18]

If *Korvettenkapitän* Werner Czygan, *U-118*'s thirty-eight-year-old *kommandant* took caution after Manseck's experience, it wasn't evident. Midday on June 12 found *U-118* idling on the surface under a cloudless sky at a different refueling rendezvous. Just before noon, as several sunbathers ambled belowdecks for a meal, a bridge lookout screamed *"Flieger! Flieger!"*

The strafing fighter raked *U-118*'s deck from stern to bow. Lacking *U-758*'s firepower, Czygan (Crew 25) immediately ordered a crash dive even as three bloodied watch standers dragged themselves into the conning tower, shutting the hatch behind them.

The conning tower's peak was still cutting the surface when four depth bombs exploded close amidships. Interior lights blinked off. Seawater poured in through exhaust valves. *U-118*'s chief engineer ordered men forward to restore the boat's trim. Then more depth charge blasts wrenched *U-118*'s rudder and knocked out steering.

U-118's tag-team assailants were Wildcat pilot Lt. (jg) Robert J. Johnson and Avenger partner Bob Stearns. After spotting *U-118* twenty miles astern of *Bogue*, Johnson had approached first, strafing from three thousand feet down to mast level. Stearns came in close behind, dropping wheels to decelerate, then retracting them again before dropping depth bombs.

Their tactics—Johnson's machine-gun pummeling; Stearns's power glide, artful deceleration, and precision bomb drop—were, at this moment, picture-perfect.

U-118 had been diving when Stearns's bomb blasts bracketed its hull. Now, as Monk Fowler's Avenger and Lt. (jg) Raymond J. Tennant's Wildcat flashed overhead, Czygan's boat, clearly in distress, poked back up. Tennant strafed twice, chasing men back and forth across the deck, desperate for cover. When Fowler dropped bombs, one exploded close to the boat's stern.

His ammunition expended, Johnson returned to *Bogue*, but aircraft flown by Harry Fryatt, Champ Chamberlain, and others joined the melee. Two of Champ's depth bombs exploded right under *U-118*'s conning tower, sending metal, debris, and globs of oil skyward. With so many planes now circling, Fryatt found he couldn't get anywhere close to the sub.

U-118's survivors were now virtually helpless. A few diehards still tried to reach the deck guns, but most were jumping. Life-jacketed men—some alive, most dead—soon bobbed in the vortex left by the sinking sub. When Fryatt flew over low to drop his life raft, several Germans clasped their hands over their heads, others waved.

Altogether, fourteen depth bombs had been dropped and more than five thousand machine-gun rounds fired. All of *U-118*'s officers had been killed. Wounded crew transferred from *U-758* were among the seventeen survivors retrieved by one of *Bogue*'s destroyers.[19]

Support Group 6's next sweep of *Trutz* found nothing. Enigma and Huff-Duff revealed why: *Trutz* remnants had been ordered east, where, reinforced by sixteen more U-boats, they were to target new convoys westbound from Gibraltar.

Low on fuel now and again hampered by an overworked, balky catapult, *Bogue* was ordered west with its screen to Hampton Roads. However, *Bogue*'s departure wouldn't mean additional peril for UG/GU convoys. Three more Tenth Fleet carrier support groups were assembling, each built around a jeep carrier. One of them, *Card*, which had ferried aircraft over to Morocco, had left Casablanca on June 9. Outside the harbor, three four-stackers, *Card*'s destroyer screen, joined up.

For Bob Maher and his *Borie* shipmates who'd been marking time in Casablanca, returning to sea and rendezvousing with carrier *Card* was a "hot damn!" moment. "We were thrilled. . . . We didn't know what the new duty would be," but it was bound to be "more like the navy."[20]

30 | A GOOD TEAM

ASSIGNING "fragile and short-legged" destroyers like *Borie* to carrier support groups was a short-term expedient. However, "because of their speed and their veteran crews," reasoned historian Samuel Eliot Morison, "pending the arrival of the much-desired destroyer escorts (DEs), they made a fair screen."[1]

Steaming back from Casablanca, *Borie*'s, *Barry*'s, and *Goff*'s veteran crews learned to operate with *Card*. Screening a warship was more agreeable than herding merchants, but plane guarding—trailing in *Card*'s wake should aircraft ditch during launch or recovery—was new. An emergency might happen at any moment.

Finally detaching from *Card* off Hampton Roads on July 5, *Borie* sailed to Brooklyn for refit and upkeep. During their stay, in Morison's telling, *Borie*'s officers were as stoked as the enlisteds about teaming with *Card*: "A naval constructor . . . found members of the wardroom practicing marksmanship by throwing Bowie knives at the bulletin board." After seeing "merchant ships torpedoed [without catching] one U-boat," they had "blood in the eye."[2]

Time at Brooklyn Navy Yard brought three-quarters of the crew within reach of home. And, as in Panama, St. Petersburg, and Philadelphia, Mike and Gully Brown managed to reunite. Afterwards, though, both agreed it was "too darned hard . . . the waiting & not knowing when or where."[3]

Card's layover in Norfolk, meanwhile, gave Seaman 1/c Joseph H. "Henry" Babson his first chance for home leave. Babson, twenty, a Maine native, had been working at the Quincy, Massachusetts, Fore River Shipyard when war broke out. Though his younger brother was a Pearl Harbor survivor, Henry waited until October 1942 to enlist. He became a *Card* deckhand in December. A former Sea Scout with a nautical sibling, Henry already knew some things about naval life; what's more, he never got seasick.

Back in Massachusetts on leave, Henry "got kind of bawled out" by his girlfriend for not writing every day. Because mail was censored, he explained, there often wasn't much to tell. Still, he promised to make notes and write more often. Keeping diaries was forbidden. "I could see myself being caught and ending up in Portsmouth Prison [a New Hampshire military detention facility], but love won me over."[4]

⌖

With ships docked and sailors scattered, forty-three-year-old Capt. Arnold J. "Buster" Isbell geared up for the *Card* group's next crossing. Isbell, a pilot and ordnance expert with tours on board carriers *Lexington*, *Ranger*, and *Saratoga*, had taken command on April 24, just weeks before *Card* set off for North Africa ferrying troops and aircraft. That round trip dovetailed with the formation of Tenth Fleet but also overlapped changes—long overdue—in the composition of convoys.

The changes were owing in part to queries from Churchill's Anti-U-boat Committee: Just how many escorts were needed for a convoy of a given size? Indeed, what was the ideal size for a convoy?

Patrick Blackett's operational research "boffins" (British military shorthand for civilian experts) pored over years of data and came up with answers that challenged stubbornly held misconceptions. Smaller convoys, for instance, were *not* safer convoys. Losses in sixty-ship convoys were (on average) almost identical to those in twenty-ship convoys. Nor did convoy size impact the likelihood of being spotted and torpedoed; about 0.9 ships (again, on average) were torpedoed per convoy, *no matter its size.*

As to escort requirements: enlarging convoys needn't require proportionate increases in escorts. The chances of U-boats penetrating a screen depended on the linear spacing of escorts around the convoy's perimeter. Since perimeter length increased very slowly as convoys expanded, bigger convoys needed more escorts, but not many more. Bottom line: surface escorts were best employed protecting the biggest convoys practicable. Incredibly, in theory anyway, increasing convoy size by 50 percent could cut merchant sinkings in half![5]

Military authorities like Dudley Pound—he thought forty-ship convoys optimal—vehemently disagreed. But a separate argument prevailed: fewer, bigger convoys also optimized air cover. By late spring and summer 1943, eighty-ship convoys were common. USG-8A, the convoy *Card* accompanied east that May, sailed with seventy-eight ships. As it approached Gibraltar, USG-8A encompassed 129 merchants and nineteen escorts (besides *Card* and its screen), covering seventy square miles of ocean.[6]

Tenth Fleet's Frog Low proved more receptive than Pound to tactical and operational advice from ASWORG experts. Low likewise relied on Ken Knowles, Tenth Fleet's intelligence chief. The sinkings of *U-217* and *U-118* made Ken a trusted resource. He was welcomed at presailing briefings. "He was a soothsayer," enthused one escort group commander, "absolutely uncanny in his predictions."[7]

Low, meanwhile, excelled as Tenth Fleet maestro, an authoritative yet diplomatic intermediary between COMINCH, CINCLANT, and task group commanders. At first, Frog found himself conducting a very confused orchestra: not until July 29 did a more widely disseminated Navy announcement precisely describe Tenth Fleet's functions and the units (including ASWORG and Convoy Routing) being shifted to its control.* Efforts to tread lightly on command prerogatives underlay the cordiality of his Tenth Fleet "advisories": "Suggest that you . . . "; "It is recommended that you . . . "; "Would it be possible for you . . . "; "Would you concur in . . . ?"

Low largely left it to Royal Ingersoll to execute these advisories. It helped that Ingersoll bought into Tenth Fleet's dual purpose—simultaneously defend convoys and hunt U-boats. When Isbell prepared to depart Casablanca on June 9, for example, he'd received CINCLANT instructions that it wouldn't be necessary to keep a continuous umbrella over the convoy. Instead, he could operate independently against any U-boat in striking distance.

*Tenth Fleet's existence was not acknowledged publicly until the end of September.

⊕

June's U-boat sinkings—seventeen in all—portrayed a shifting battle space. Seven claimed in the North Atlantic, four in the Bay of Biscay (down from seven in May), a pair (*U-217* and *U-118*) in the Central Atlantic, another pair in the Mediterranean. Aircraft—Avengers, B-17s, B-24s, Catalinas, Hudsons, and Sunderlands—accounted for eleven. But, just as in May, British forces still dominated the score in June: eleven sinkings (six by air, four by surface ship, one by submarine) compared to five American.

With three confirmed kills,* Johnny Walker's surface hunter-killers—teams of destroyers, corvettes, and sloops that relentlessly stalked, pinned down, and attacked U-boats—again stood out. The group's June 24 assault on *U-119*, a milk cow, especially so. After depth charges forced *119* to surface, Walker's sloop *Starling* rammed and capsized it.[8]

This Walker tactic was not unprecedented; a dozen or more British war vessels had tried ramming, either as opening gambit or coup de grace—often with success. *Starling* incurred substantial (but not fatal) damage: its bow bent thirty degrees, its sonar dome destroyed. But, afterwards, "locker doors and other floating wreckage marked in German" confirmed Walker's kill.

July began as another British month: Eight U-boat sinkings claimed through July 13, five by air,† three by surface ship. Action increased in the Bay of Biscay (five sinkings); AAF B-24s claimed two sinkings off Morocco. The Central Atlantic, however, appeared a zone of confusion on the German side. Scattered U-boats, some wandering towards the Brazilian coast (where a U.S. Navy Catalina sank one on July 9), other lone wolves with no perceptible destination or intention.[9]

It was July 13 before Tenth and Atlantic Fleet collaboration produced more results. Monitoring radio transmissions, Knowles' tracking room identified a refueling site northwest of Cape Verde (Republic of Cabo Verde today).

---

*One victim was *U-202*, the Type VII that had landed George Dasch's sabotage team on Long Island on June 12, 1942. (Blair, *The Hunted*, 340)

†Hans-Jürgen Auffermann's *U-514*, which first sighted Convoy TM-1, was destroyed (with no survivors) by a British B-24 on July 8. (Blair, *The Hunted*, 399)

Launched to investigate, two aircraft from escort carrier* *Core*'s Composite Squadron 13 (VC-13) spotted *U-487*, a milk cow, lolling on the surface, some crewmen sunbathing, others retrieving a drifting bale of cotton. Avengers and Wildcats dispatched *U-487*, but not before a Wildcat was shot down and its pilot killed.†[10]

VC-13's costly battle with *U-487* contrasted with next day's surgical dispatch of *U-160*. An Avenger/Wildcat team from *Santee*'s Composite Squadron 29 (VC-29) sighted the milk cow south of the Azores. The Avenger carried a Fido, one of the Wizard War's most lethal devices. A seven-foot-long hydrophone-equipped torpedo, Fido could "sniff out" propellers and "home in" for the kill.[11]

The VC-29 Wildcat led with a strafing run that forced *U-487* to crash-dive, and the Avenger followed with depth charges and a Fido. The combination worked to perfection, sinking *U-487* with all hands. Fido performed equally well the next day when a VC-29 Avenger destroyed *U-509*, a Type VII, west of Casablanca.

U-boat sinkings by U.S. forces now outpaced Commonwealth tallies. By July 27, when Isbell's *Card* group set forth from Hampton Roads, the Americans claimed sixteen U-boat kills, six attributable to *Core*, *Santee*, and *Bogue* support groups.

Henry Babson, now training as a helmsman, split his four-hour watches between *Card*'s pilothouse and the steering-engine room aft. While on the helm, he got the scoop on *Card*'s plans. Yet without seclusion in after steering, "I don't know how I could have written what I have."

On August 2, after *Barry*, *Borie*, and *Goff* topped off from a convoy tanker, Isbell's group headed for the Azores. "We may be seeing some excitement," Babson recorded, "maybe pretty soon."

---

*First classified "aircraft escort vessels" (AVG), then "auxiliary aircraft carriers" (ACV), all officially became "escort carriers" (CVE).

†Lt. (jg) Earl H. Steiger, twenty-four, had survived the Pacific Ocean sinking of fleet carrier *Wasp*. ("Navy Flier Left Quarters before Torpedo Struck," *Dunkirk* [NY] *Evening Observer*, October 27, 1942)

Babson knew the destination but not the rationale. Privy to "good" (i.e., promising) Enigma decrypts, Tenth Fleet clued Isbell into an upcoming refueling rendezvous between *U-66*, a Type IXC, and *U-117*, a Type XB minelayer. The next day, a Composite Squadron 1 (VC-1) Avenger/Wildcat team caught *U-66* by surprise. *U-66* escaped but not before being strafed and damaged. Babson was topside when the Wildcat pilot touched down: "He had strafed some of the [*U-66*] crew. He was white as a ghost and had to be taken down to sick bay."

Burdened with casualties, *U-66* reset its rendezvous with *U-117*. On August 6, wrote Babson, "our radiomen picked up another radio transmission about three hundred miles from here. We are now on our way. Tomorrow will tell."

Tomorrow did. "Around one o'clock this afternoon, one of our planes dropped depth charges on a sub and it sank. In the meantime, another sub fired anti-aircraft and [the *Card* pilot] needed help. The Captain [Isbell] had four more planes launched."[12]

The sighting plane was an Avenger whose pilot, defying the odds, attacked alone, targeting *U-66* with a Fido despite *U-117*'s flak fire. *U-66* escaped once more, but the Isbell-dispatched reinforcements made quick work of *U-117*, strafing it "unmercifully," then destroying it with depth bombs and Fidos.[13]

Afterwards, Babson's recorded: "The Captain is pleased by . . . the crew, the air department and . . . the three destroyers. 'A good team,' he said."[14]

⌖

"Today," Babson journaled on August 8, "a turn of events. We lost two men and two planes. The planes were on regular patrol. All but two returned. After two hours of searching, two men were spotted in a life raft, the captain told the [destroyer] Barry to pick them up.

"This is the sad part of war," reflected Babson, "when someone you know, even very slightly[,] is killed." The deaths* indeed dampened spirits on board *Card*. But it also spurred Isbell to revise tactics. To improve the odds against "fight back" U-boats, air teams would comprise one Wildcat and two

---

*Ens. John F. Sprague, twenty-one, from Washington State and Radioman James D. Downes from Long Island.

Avengers—one Avenger equipped with 500-pound bombs, the other with depth bombs and a FIDO.

For his part, Babson sensed omens. "We are in the middle of something, and I am wondering about the tomorrows."

Next afternoon, the first of those tomorrows, "one of the planes caught two subs on the surface together, about fifty miles from the ship. Two more planes joined in."

First to spot *U-664* was a Wildcat pilot flying in company with two Avengers—one Avenger carrying a bomb, the other depth charges. After the Wildcat strafed, one Avenger dropped its 500-pound bomb, the other its depth charges. *U-664* tried to dive, but the combined blasts promptly blew the sub back to the surface.

A dozen Germans leapt from the conning tower under continued Wildcat strafing. Confusion reigned. Leaving its defenseless sailors behind, *U-664* submerged again, but not for long. When it reemerged, the rest of the crew jumped overboard.[15]

"The planes reported German survivors in the water," Babson recorded. "The Captain sent the *Borie* to pick up as many as she could."

⌖

U-664's shipwrecked crew tossed in rough seas. *Borie*, already pitching and rolling, heaved about even more as it slowed and stopped near life rafts. The Germans, some badly wounded, appeared fearful. Was this rescue or death?

Chief Gunner's Mate Dick Wenz and Chief Boatswain's Mate Walt Kurz, perhaps *Borie*'s two strongest sailors, climbed down the port sea ladder—iron rungs welded on either side near the stern—ready to pull in survivors. It was risky; the rungs dipped and rose in the turbulence. Neither knew what to expect of the Germans.

Wenz and Kurz grabbed them one by one. For most, American or German, it was their first time confronting a living enemy. The Germans turned out to be frightened young men; the young *Borie* sailors, some armed with .45-caliber pistols, were less apprehensive but equally awestruck.

Boatswain's Mate 1/c Bill Schmalberger, a twenty-four-year-old from Union, New Jersey, took charge of processing the forty-three survivors. A born leader,

Bill exuded compassion and authority. Seeing one German bleeding heavily, Bill opened the POW's shirt to expose a huge shoulder wound.[16]

The boy was hustled to the wardroom, where *Borie*'s medical officer, Lt. Walter F. Merscher, had set up an impromptu surgery. Merscher, twenty-eight, a Delaware physician, had just joined *Borie* in July. Backing him up was twenty-year-old Pharmacist's Mate 1/c Walter J. Cituk, product of a Baltimore orphanage.[17]

The sailor with the shoulder wound was by no means the most challenging casualty. The two *Borie* medicos (aided by Larry Quinn, who in civilian days had seen his share of gruesome sports injuries) had already amputated one man's foot.[18]

U-664's only able-bodied troublemaker, it turned out, was its tall, skinny, bespectacled *kommandant*. Though not yet summoned by Schmalberger, *Kapitänleutnant* Adolf Graef (Crew 36) stepped forward, demanding to see *Borie*'s CO. "Get your ass out of here!" Schmalberger snapped.

Seaman Selig Sirota, a draftee in his late thirties new to the ship, stood guard over Graef and two other officers. It may have been an insensitive lark to assign one of *Borie*'s few Jewish sailors to the job. But Sirota was uncomplaining and even used his smattering of German to decipher what was said.

Next day, the POWs were high-lined to *Card*—the wounded by stretcher, the rest in canvas mail sacks. Some POWs seemed apprehensive, and later interrogation revealed why: *U-664* had been stalking *Card*, a priority target, for two days; in fact, a spread of *U-664* torpedoes had just missed the carrier the night of August 8.[19]

31 | UNFORTUNATE ROGUES

EVEN ELITE U-BOAT *kommandanten* now questioned the Lion's judgment. How, two of them argued, could *Tonnagekrieg*'s "immense losses" be justified with no "prospect of success?" Dönitz, meanwhile, described himself as torn—"faced with the most difficult decision of the war." Persevering meant "certain and deliberate self-sacrifice by U-boat crews," yet "we had no option but to fight on."[1] Hitler agreed. "There can be no talk of a let-up in submarine warfare," he insisted. Fighting a defensive battle in the Atlantic "is better than defending myself on the coasts of Europe."[2]

But even a defensive battle required more resources. The exchange rate (U-boat losses compared with merchant tonnage sunk), previously at one U-boat lost for 100,000 tons of Allied shipping, was now one boat for ten thousand tons. It would take many more boats just to hold on. On March 31, with Hitler's endorsement, Albert Speer's Ministry for Arms and Munitions committed to building forty U-boats per month, a pace well ahead of previous targets. U-boat veterans like *U-230*'s Herbert Werner, however, knew that without "dramatic countermeasures, all our proud new U-boats would be turned into a surplus of iron coffins."[3]

New weapons and technologies were emerging, but the most effective countermeasure would be replacing obsolescent Type VIIs and IXs with boats capable of higher speeds and longer submersion. The goal of a "one-hundred-per-cent under-water vessel" was epitomized in the XXVI, the so-called

Walter boat. But, owing to technical obstacles and competing production priorities, Dönitz's hopes for the Walter faded. More realistic was the prospect of a 1,600-ton hybrid that packed additional batteries and advanced electronics into the Walter's streamlined hull. The Type XXI (and the Type XIII, a three-hundred-ton shallow-water version) would be powered by conventional diesel engines and electric motors. But, equipped with *Schnorkel* (snorkel, a tube extending above the surface to take in air and simultaneously expel diesel gasses), these "electro-boats" would travel farther and faster and stay submerged longer than submarines ever had before.

Standing in the way of Speer's ambitious 1943 fleet building program, however, were German shipyards' archaic, dilatory methods. Fed up with the waste and slow pace, Speer called on forty-two-year-old mechanical engineer Otto Merker to reorganize construction. Merker proposed that U-boat sections be prefabricated at industrial plants for final assembly at the yards.[4] Having settled final program details with Speer in late July, Dönitz focused on compelling Allies to keep convoying, thereby tying down ships and aircraft.

Dönitz had lost thirty-seven U-boats in July. The sinking of twelve in the Bay of Biscay forced a change in tactics. In June, he had ordered boats to transit on the surface in groups, using flak to ward off attackers. With "fight back" tactics faltering, inbound and outbound boats were now to transit singly and furtively, submerged all day and surfacing only at night.

Elsewhere, the loss of U-tankers—four in July, two more in early August—portended dire consequences. After the August 7 sinking of *U-117*, Dönitz ordered some boats to curtail patrols. Henceforth, U-boats sailing into the Atlantic from Germany would stop first in Norwegian ports to refuel.

Already in early June, to enhance refueling security, Dönitz had forbidden the transmission of rendezvous signals until boats involved had sought each other for at least two days. Now additional precautions took effect: wireless silence within four hundred miles of a rendezvous, and no attacks on enemy ships within three hundred miles of it.

U-boat losses slowed at summer's end. But so did U-boat operations—a hiatus that Dönitz could ill afford. Determined to regain initiative, he commanded U-boat Control to prepare a North Atlantic onslaught.

Gruppe Leuthen (reference to a Prussian eighteenth-century land victory) would comprise twenty-one Type VIIs supported by *U-460*, a Type XIV

U-tanker. The vessels would sail secretly beginning August 23. Equipped with improved radar detectors and heavy flak batteries, the VIIs would "fight back" if surprised. More important, each boat would carry two T-5 *Zaunkönig* (Wren) acoustic homing torpedoes, designed to detect the telltale pitch of convoy warships.[5] Leuthen *kommandanten* would use them to assault escort screens *before* sinking merchants.

⌖

By late summer, four "Bombe, Model 530s" (NCR's first production four-rotor Bombe) had been shipped from Dayton to Washington. Each weighed five thousand pounds and measured seven feet tall, eight feet long, and two feet wide. Meanwhile, Navy technicians and WAVE operators transferred from Dayton to Washington to set up shop in what was now called the Naval Communications Annex.

The 530s generated terrific heat and noise. Despite air conditioning, WAVE operators sweltered as ever more 530s came online. Many also developed ear problems—and a few even dodged flying parts. Machine setup was painstaking and physically demanding. In time, the 530s would prove faster and more reliable than their BP counterparts.* But while machines represented OP-20-G's path to decryption self-reliance, for now its hands were full installing gear and training people to use it.

As the annex labored to get up to speed, the Allies' overall decryption endeavors were just emerging from what cryptology historian Collin Burke describes as "frightening blackout months":[6] in part because fewer U-boat transmissions meant fewer decryption opportunities. Despite this latest blackout, however, the Allies continued to rack up stunning successes. The U.S. Navy claimed forty-one U-boat kills (twenty-five in July); the British recorded thirty-nine.

These accomplishments, according to World War II naval intelligence authority Ralph Erskine, were owed to a "devastating combination of centimetric radar, shipborne high frequency direction finding (HF/DF), very long-range aircraft, new weaponry, and above all, the efforts of Allied seamen

---

*To Desch's satisfaction, the 530s' digital tracking and braking system, dismissed by Alan Turing, amazed Navy experts.

and airmen." But, as Erskine also found, British and American anti-U-boat operations showed "a significant difference of approach in the way . . . naval authorities employed Ultra."[7]

The Brits continued to use Enigma decrypts with utmost discretion. Meanwhile, Tenth Fleet used whatever tactical advantages were at hand to pounce on refueling operations. Low and Ingersoll were simply more willing to take calculated risks with Enigma decrypts—a source of friction between the Allies generally but also between Winn and Knowles. At one point, Winn sardonically quipped that Knowles' use of Enigma decrypts was simply "too true to be good."

Following a July–August cruise on board *Bogue* during which it had sunk two U-boats, VC-9 had "cross-decked" (transferred) to carrier *Card*. To complicate matters, on September 25, when Buster Isbell's support group sailed from Hampton Roads, VC-9 had new leadership.

Officially credited with four U-boat kills between May and July, VC-9 had built an estimable reputation, but it had yet to operate with *Card*. Moreover, thirty-four-year-old Lt. Cdr. Howard M. Avery, VC-9's new skipper, had yet to see ASW action.

Meanwhile Buster Isbell, who had considered VC-1 a critical component of a "good team,"* carried high expectations. Credited with sinking three U-tankers (*U-117*, *525*, and *847*), Isbell aimed for more. Could an Avery-led VC-9 deliver?

If measured by the first week at sea, it seemed questionable.

On September 29, Henry Babson recorded that when Wildcat pilot M. C. "Buddy" Jones's attempted to land, "he . . . headed for the bridge and just missed it by inches. . . . All I heard was the roar of the engine and went sailing on the deck like everybody else."

Managing to get airborne, Jones circled for another approach, this time coming in too fast. On catching a wire, his tailhook and tail assembly broke off, hurtling the Wildcat into the catwalk. Jones emerged unhurt, but, according to Babson, "the captain was mad and called the pilot to his quarters."

*After sinking *U-117* and *U-664*, VC-1 had upped its contribution by sinking *U-525* and *U-847*.

Worse followed next day, when Lt. Arnold C. Harwood, VC-9's new XO, tried to land his Wildcat. The twenty-five-year-old Harwood, though a qualified flight instructor, had scant experience in carrier landings. His approach looked good until he dropped the plane's nose too hard. Deck personnel scattered and splinters flew as the Wildcat's undercarriage collapsed, its nose skidded, and its prop chewed into flight deck planking. "What a mess he made out of his wheels, propeller and . . . flight deck," Babson remarked.

"Ground that pilot!"[8] Buster Isbell screamed on the ship's loudspeaker. Afterwards, there was a sense that Isbell despaired of the entire squadron. Went one VC-9 lament,

> I'm just a poor luckless pilot, an unfortunate rogue.
> Take me off this abortion, put me back on the *Bogue*.[9]

A September 30 advisory from Tenth Fleet likely increased the pressure on VC-9's "unfortunate rogues." Babson made note: "From what we hear, there is [*sic*] supposed to be five or six [U-boats] together. We changed course to 064 degrees true. Now about eight hundred miles away."

On October 1: "We are getting closer to where the captain wants to go. The tin cans are sniffing along. All the planes were out."

Card continued northeast. Flores, the westernmost island in the Azores (a rough demarcation between the North and South Atlantic) hove into sight October. "We are in the area where the subs are supposed to be. With a little luck we may run into them."

Then, at 11:04 a.m. on October 4: "Old lady luck was with us."[10]

While on routine patrol, Avenger pilot Bob Stearns interrupted a refueling operation. As he described it afterwards: "The Fueler and 740-tonner were only about 50 feet apart on parallel courses. . . . One of the flanking U/Bs [U-boats] was about 500 feet off the Fueler's starboard side. . . . The other was about 200 feet ahead of the Fueler and about 100 feet to port."

After his radioman Frank Dittner sent a contact report, Stearns climbed and circled. Now the U-boats were "widening their formation, with the two flanking U/Bs pulling out to the sides . . . [all] throwing up intense AA fire."

Stearns' Avenger carried a Fido, but this wasn't the time to use it. The sub wasn't diving, making "it impossible to get . . . anywhere near [my Fido] release point before being shot down."

Instead, anxious to do something, Stearns decided to use his five-hundred-pound bomb. Surveying the formation, he "pushed over and dove, increasing speed to 300 K [knots]. . . . AA bursts were . . . behind but . . . drawing steadily closer."

Dittner's transmission to *Card* turned out to be garbled. Unaware of how many U-boats had been spotted, Isbell dispatched just three aircraft—two Wildcats and an Avenger armed with depth charges. Launched first at 11:15 a.m., Lt. (jg) Donald E. Weigle's Avenger reached the scene a quarter-hour later.

While Weigle circled, awaiting fighter support, his radioman J. H. Sullivan updated *Card*. Soon, every available plane—altogether five more Avengers and two more Wildcats—was en route.

Bob Stearns, meanwhile, had dropped his five-hundred-pounder at 1,700 feet. While doing no "material damage," the blast prompted the U-boats' *kommandanten* to close ranks again and begin "weaving about."

Two Wildcats, one piloted by Elbert S. "Stu" Heim Jr., the other by David O. "Son" Puckett, both twenty-three-year-old lieutenants (jg), next reached the scene. Weigle recalled the subs had now changed tactics—"circling . . . to cover the other's dive." Pulling out of formation, the sub being refueled dove first.

After exchanging signals with Stearns and Weigle, Heim then Puckett pushed over "to attack the U/B on the port flank of the formation." They entered "a solid curtain of fire filled with black and white puffs." Heim, a Louisianan, strafed down low before "pulling out straight up." Puckett, a Mississippian, encountered AA fire that was "not cut down [had not been suppressed] at all." Shrapnel hit his port wing, disabling one wing gun. During Heim's second run, though, just one German gun returned fire.

When this U-boat—surely damaged but still operational—also slipped out of sight, Don Weigle, Stu Heim, and Son Puckett turned their attention to the U-tanker. Once AA fire was suppressed, Weigle began his depth-charge run, attacking up the tanker's stern. Intended to strafe first, he mistakenly pressed the bomb-release button. All four depth charges dropped, exploding well astern.

Stearns, meanwhile, had set out after the fourth U-boat—erroneously believing *it* to be the "Fueler." But, when this target vanished, Stearns aborted and turned back towards Weigle, Heim, and Puckett.

After Weigle's miscue, Heim and Puckett continued strafing. By the time they'd finished, Bob Stearns was back poised to drop his Fido on the U-tanker's starboard side. Just then that sub pulled the plug and turned hard to port. Anticipating the tactic, Stearns (already credited for his roles in sinking *U-118* and *U-527*) flattened his approach, turning hard to port and dropped his Fido on the sub's starboard quarter.

After a twenty-five-second delay, the Fido exploded, causing a "well-defined shock wave." Forty-five seconds later, "heavy oil and debris of all kinds rose to the surface."

"If the U-boat dives," Stearns commented later, "that is just what the [Fido-equipped] pilot wants."[11]

⌖

Four hours later, and just a few miles from the midday action, Avenger pilot Lt. (jg) Stewart B. Holt also got just what he wanted. After he and Wildcat pilot Ens. Joseph D. Horn spotted a surfaced U-boat, Holt positioned his bomber astern while Horn strafed the German's bow. "The conning tower disappeared as I came up his stern," said Holt. "My aim was ahead of the swirl and slightly to starboard."

Climbing away, Holt couldn't see what happened next, but Horn did. "The [Fido] entered the water . . . then . . . headed directly for the U/B. The . . . explosion occurred midway between the stern and the conning tower[;] . . . oil and debris started coming to the surface."[12]

The day's two U-boat sinkings* brought satisfaction all around. "Although I would much rather be home," Babson reflected, "I'm glad that I am on this ship . . . it is one big happy ship."[13]

Meanwhile, back in Washington, Frog Low took to the airways to convey the U.S. Navy's official satisfaction. According to a newspaper account:

---

*As with all U-boat sinking claims, these reported results underwent intense, seemingly endless scrutiny before being confirmed—a sore point with ASW aviators and seamen.

"Rear-Admiral Francis Low, director of the Navy's war against the submarine menace . . . said in a radio interview today . . . the Germans have 'failed once and for all to break our lifelines across the Atlantic. At the present rate of sinkings the U-boat fleet is undergoing an attrition rate it cannot stand.'"

Low then "revealed American warships assigned to the anti-U-boat campaign have been designated the 10th U.S. Fleet and said the unit, constituted last May, is largely responsible for curbing the menace. He indicated escort carriers are probably [its] most potent weapon."[14]

32 | ONE GUNG-HO GUY

"**WE HAVE BEEN HEADING** northwest for a concentration of subs," Henry Babson wrote on October 7. "I imagine that we will be getting much colder weather."[1] To be sure, not just cold but windy and fogbound. To Bob Maher on board *Borie*, it seemed incredible that *Card* aircraft, especially the heavy Avengers, continued to takeoff, patrol, and land.

Aircraft were usually recovered by sunset. But as darkness fell that day, four Avengers were still aloft. Three landed successfully. But the fourth, piloted by Ens. Charles H. Goodchild, tried to land with visibility at its worst. Waved off, Goodchild went around for another try but crashed, hitting the water quite close to *Borie*. "We could see the pilot in the canopy," Maher recalled. "Only one crew member got out, so we assumed it was the pilot."[2]

A logical enough assumption. Ditched Avengers sank like stones. The pilots needed only open the canopy, but escape was difficult for the crew.

Grim tidings reached *Card*. "They are still looking for the other two," Babson noted. "It's pitch black out there now. One of the plane crew, who is a gunner, has a brother on the ship. I can imagine how he must feel." Though no further update came over the ship's loudspeakers, Babson was scheduled to stand the midwatch and figured "I'll know for sure later on."

To Babson's surprise, "I found out that the man picked up was not the pilot, but the gunner's mate." Good news for his brother. As to the other airmen:

"The pilot and radioman are presumed lost. . . . A tough break for them and their families."

However, there was scant time to mourn Goodchild and his radioman.* Prompted by Tenth Fleet, *Card* turned directly north on October 9. "There must be more subs out there somewhere," Babson speculated. If so, "the captain is determined to get as many as he can. He is one gung-ho guy."[3]

"The Führer is watching every phase of your struggle. Attack! Follow up! Sink!"[4]

Dönitz's exhortation reached Gruppe Leuthen's *kommandanten* as they entered the Greenland air gap. Their objective: attack empty westbound convoys moving away from Iceland's air bases.

U-270's September 19 sighting of a heavily defended convoy triggered a race to the contact position. Meanwhile, with Control's permission, Paul-Friedrich Otto, *U-270*'s twenty-six-year-old (Crew 37) *kommandant*, successfully launched a T-5 homing torpedo at a British frigate. The crippling of the frigate† marked the first success of the Wren—as much a boost for U-boat morale as a blow to the Allies.

The following night, as a dozen Leuthen U-boats converged, eight more fired "antidestroyer" torpedoes, claiming the sinking or probable sinking of ten Allied warships. Much pleased, U-boat Command dutifully logged these "destroyer" totals along with the destruction of three freighters.

Seven U-boats struck the next night, September 21–22, claiming one destroyer sunk and another damaged, plus hits on a five-thousand-ton freighter. But not without cost: *U-270* was depth-charged so intensely that the hull cracked, forcing Paul-Friedrich Otto homewards. Meanwhile, after *Oberleutnant zur See* Gerhard Kluth, twenty-five (also Crew 37), *U-377*'s *kommandant*, was wounded by aircraft fire, his boat pulled out too. But the night's severest blow came when British destroyer *Keppel* rammed, depth-charged, and sank *U-229*, killing all on board.

---

*Thaddeus E. Bartoszek, an aviation radioman third class from New Jersey.

†HMS *Lagan* lost thirty crewmen. The wreck was towed to port but never repaired.

There was also a very close call on the 23rd when *U-422*, a new boat with a fledgling *kommandant*, was spotted by a British aircraft. *U-422* sustained damage, and two of its crew were wounded seriously. When *Oberleutnant zur See* Wolfgang Poeschel (Crew 38) requested medical assistance, U-boat Control arranged a rendezvous with *U-460*, Leuthen's tanker.

Despite gaps in their ranks, Leuthen's wolves, commanded by Dönitz to deliver *der Hauptschlag* (the big blow), stuck to the beleaguered convoy. When heavy fog grounded Allied aircraft, U-boats indeed hit hard. Three *kommandanten* laid claim to two sunk destroyers and five freighters.

With fuel supplies dwindling, most torpedoes spent, and the convoy approaching Newfoundland airspace, U-boat Control finally called a halt. In a detailed, self-congratulatory report, Control boasted sinking fifteen surface escorts with casualties twenty to one in favor of the Kriegsmarine.

"This convoy operation, the first in months, brought a complete success," Dönitz gloated. "The new weapons proved their worth in every respect." Effusive in his praise, Dönitz wrote that "special recognition is due to all U-boats that took part. . . . Their readiness . . . has pointed the way . . . to the crown of the U-boat career, the convoy battle."

The report cited a few incidental flaws but promised imminent remedies. There were also two admonitions. First, to avoid misjudgments on "fight-back" tactics, only U-boat Control could authorize "A/A defense" should boats come under surprise aerial attack. Second, reprising an all-too-familiar warning, idle U-boat radio chatter must be eliminated. Above all, "do not afflict the morale of others with tales of terror."[5]

Blinkered by what he himself considered Leuthen's accomplishments, Dönitz directed U-boat Control to keep up pressure in the North Atlantic. Using a dozen Leuthen U-boats as foundation and dispatching nine more Type VIIs from ports in France and Germany, Control established Gruppe Rossbach (a reference to another Prussian eighteenth-century victory) in the closing days of September.

Having rendezvoused with Wolfgang Poeschel's *U-422* to repair damage and treat wounded, *U-460*, Rossbach's designated refueler, was then far to the south. *U-460* and *U-422*, as well as *U-455* and *U-264* (Type VIIs that had tried but failed to enter the Mediterranean), were all dispatched north to support Rossbach.

If Leuthen's vaunted achievements briefly spurred hopes for the resurgence of *Tonnagekrieg*, Rossbach's October 4 reverses could well have dampened them. Off Iceland that day, three Rossbach U-boats separately succumbed—all hands lost—to multiengine Iceland-based aircraft.

But October 4's even more consequential reversal struck *U-460* and its three cohorts. Spotted in the process of refueling *U-264* while *U-422* and *U-455* idled on the surface nearby, *Kapitänleutnant* Ebe Schnoor (Crew 15) contravened Control edicts—and common sense—by opting to fight back instead of crash-diving. Swarmed by waves of carrier-based fighters and bombers (*Card*'s), *U-460* and its crew paid the ultimate price for their forty-eight-year-old *kommandant*'s rash heroics.

Making matters only worse, *U-422* and *U-264* inexplicably resurfaced that afternoon—seeming to forget the attack on *U-460*. *Kapitänleutnant* Hartwig Looks, *U-264*'s thirty-six-year-old *kommandant* (Crew 36), managed to escape but not before his boat sustained such heavy damage that it had to abort. Wolfgang Poeschel's *U-422*, meanwhile, was never heard from again.

The loss of *U-460* threatened to cripple Rossbach. Two Rossbach U-boats, dangerously low on fuel, headed home. With no other alternative, U-boat Control ordered *U-488*, its last available Type XIV tanker, to head for a refueling rendezvous with *U-402* and *U-584* north of Flores Island.

Despite all the setbacks to Rossbach—it now consisted of just six combat-ready U-boats—Dönitz remained undaunted. With the addition of eight other boats (*U-455* plus seven boats from France and Germany), Rossbach's remnants became Gruppe Schlieffen (named for a World War I German field marshal), tasked with attacking westbound convoys.

Borie sailors realized they were basking in the reflected glory of VC-9 airmen and *Card* sailors. Still, because they were integral to a fighting outfit, they believed that every tin-can sailor contributed.

"What a satisfying cruise . . . so different from our convoy duty!"[6] Bob Maher had raved back on September 10 when *Borie* docked in Norfolk after completing a third Atlantic crossing (and second westbound) with *Card* and four-stackers *Barry* and *Goff*—all part of Task Group (TG) 21.14. A prestigious personal "well done" had come from none other than COMINCH, Ernest J. King. And now that another "rite of passage"—a ferocious Atlantic storm—had been weathered, Maher's enthusiasm could even encompass the potentially catastrophic.

Seas had kicked up near Bermuda on September 6. At first, nothing that couldn't be handled. But then winds intensified, and seas mounted. Waves, some forty feet high, lashed everything topside. Winds gusted to seventy knots, making work on deck impossible.

Bob Maher split bridge watches between the ship's helm and standing lookout in a "bucket" mounted outside the pilothouse. Both jobs were exhausting. *Borie*'s big wheel was about as old as the ship. Turning it pulled cables attached to a steering engine aft; it was the steering engine that actually moved the rudder. *Borie*'s propeller shaft, screws, and rudder often got exposed at the crest of the biggest waves. Afterwards, the helmsman struggled to get it back on course.

Bob was at the helm one night when steering jammed entirely. Stan Hull, Bob's watchmate, was sent aft to man emergency steering. After a perilous trip—this backup helm sat atop the midships galley deckhouse—Stan had to be lashed to nearby stanchions to keep his footing.

Things worsened the next afternoon, when the steering engine compartment flooded and the steering engine itself had to be shut down. Bob and Stan spent their watch hip deep in water, one facing forward, the other aft, each turning a huge wheel connected directly to the rudder.

Not until September 9 did the storm finally abate. Somehow, all that time, Bob's faith in *Borie* never wavered. Even on the verge of swamping or capsizing, the ship seemed to be saying "Don't worry, Maher," and regained its footing. Still, Bob hoped, it was as close as the "B" would ever get to sinking.

During much of the layover in Norfolk, everyone kept busy repairing storm damage. For the fire-control gang, the work involved refurbishing the main-battery electrical and optical instruments.

Bob Maher was now married, but his wife Doris remained with her parents in Newark, New Jersey. With all the work to be done and home leave impossible, he and Jim Allegri used what spare time they had just going ashore for a decent meal. For Mike and Gully Brown, however, two weeks in Norfolk and the relative proximity of western North Carolina's hills presented opportunities too precious to forego.

Their September rendezvous centered on a stay at "Brown's Hill Billy Cabin." "Can't even begin to tell you how we enjoyed ourselves with you up at Waynesville," Mike wrote in a V-mail* dated September 26, the day after TG 21.14 set sail from Norfolk. "We certainly were a sorry pair driving back. . . . I wanted to turn the car around + head *back*, but duty calls, I guess."[7]

In October, with Ultra's summer blackouts easing, BP's and OP-20-G's collaborative code breaking renewed prospects for tracking—and tracking down—U-boats. Not only were more daily Enigma settings being uncovered but also, according to historian Burke, a higher *percentage* of settings was being found in five days or less.

Joseph Desch and Ralph Meader in Dayton and Howard Engstrom and Joseph Wenger in Washington could well take pride in the Model 530s, more than a dozen of which were up and running at the Naval Communications Annex. Meanwhile, BP's new Bombes were plagued with reliability issues.

The emergence of these behemoths made clear that technology was displacing "human-scale" code breaking. Less clear was just how much the four-rotor Bombes directly impacted the Battle of the Atlantic. OP-20-G's meticulous records, says Burke, belie later claims that 70 percent of America's U-boat "kills" in the Atlantic were owing to "communications intelligence."†[8] That said, in October and November 1943, when U-boat Control was transmitting many location-movement messages, both the Americans and the British used Enigma decrypts in connection with nearly half their respective kills.

*V-mail—Victory Mail—was a hybrid mail process for correspondence between service personnel overseas and stateside civilians. A one-sheet V-mail letter would be censored, copied to film, and printed back to paper on reaching its destination. (After departing Hampton Roads, TG 21.14 stopped first at Bermuda. Mike Brown's V-mail was presumably written and sent from there.)

†From May through August 1943, for example, the U.S. Navy destroyed roughly one-third of the U-boats it claimed during the entire war—all before the production 530s went to work.

As important, the Bombes constituted a formidable strategic capability, in many ways comparable to powerful radar, escort carriers, merchant-ship prefabrication, Fidos, OR, and other advances in the Wizard War. At this point of inflection in the Battle of the Atlantic, the wizards at OP-20-G and NCML were indeed "earning their keep."

"We are heading north again," Henry Babson recorded on October 11. "There was a report [of] some subs about three or four hundred miles from here. We are going after them."

Clued by Enigma decrypts about Gruppe Schlieffen and *U-488*'s refueling rendezvous, Tenth Fleet was "advising" Buster Isbell to pounce. Time and fuel were tight, but Isbell was not easily deterred, even by poor weather. "We can see only a few hundred yards around us as the fog is very thick," wrote Babson.[9] But the very next day produced multiple sightings of and repeated attacks on two different U-boats.

First, at about 11 a.m., Sam Balliett's Avenger set upon a large surfaced U-boat—what *had* to be the fueler *U-488*. Once again, it was James H. Finch, Sam Balliett's sharp-eyed radioman, who first spotted *U-488* breaking the surface. Heavy seas, however, made it hard to discern the sub's actions.

Not until *U-488* was indisputably submerged again did Balliett finally roar in from astern with his Fido. Witnessing no explosion, Balliett assumed turbulence had led Fido astray. Monk Fowler, attacking *U-488* several hours later, experienced similar confusion and disappointment.

That same afternoon—about fifty miles from *Card*, and with seas still rough—Avenger pilot Burrhead Doty spotted a different, smaller U-boat. Doty strafed, trying to force his target down. Instead, the sub picked up speed and headed for a nearby squall. Stewart Holt's Avenger tried to head it off, coming in dead ahead with a bomb that exploded well astern. Finally, the U-boat began firing back, forcing Avenger pilot Ens. Edward R. Hodgson to dodge flak during a depth-charge attack. After the U-boat disappeared, Doty, Holt, and Hodgson assumed—wrongly—that they'd bagged their prey.[10]

"The captain knows there are more subs around," Babson noted afterwards, "and wants to try his luck for tomorrow." As many on board *Card* acknowledged of Buster Isbell, "He is certainly out there looking for blood." Accordingly, "most of us are wearing life belts all the time. As much as I hate to think about it, who knows what is going to happen?"[11]

The next day brought more rough seas and an early-morning sub sighting by Avenger pilot Wilma Fowler. When flak came his way, Monk alerted *Card*, then lined up a bomb attack. His bomb failed to release and the U-boat pulled the plug, leaving Monk to launch his Fido much too late.

By the time Avengers flown by VC-9 skipper Howard Avery and Ens. Barton C. Sheela arrived to lend a hand, Monk's sub was gone, his ordnance expended, and his Avenger low on fuel. Monk returned to *Card*, leaving Avery and Sheela, a twenty-two-year-old Californian, to comb the scene. At about 11 a.m., as reward for their tenacity, a U-boat—perhaps the same sub, perhaps another—surfaced about a dozen miles from Monk's earlier attack.

As before, rough seas made it hard to judge the sub's disposition. Avery thought better of dropping a bomb. Instead, after a desultory strafing pass, VC-9's skipper pulled back to wait. Sheela went in next, strafing and dropping depth charges. They exploded well wide of the mark but convinced the U-boat *kommandant* to crash-dive.

It was a moment Avery must have relished. A chance to prove his mettle. Narrowing the distance, then chopping throttle and lowering landing gear, the skipper steadied his Avenger and dropped his Fido. It splashed twenty-five seconds after *U-402*'s conning tower disappeared. Fido "sniffed," turned left, and seconds later exploded, generating a massive, debris-filled slick.[12]

Chronicled Henry Babson: "The pilot who got him was the Squadron Cmdr. by the name of Avery, and I know that he must feel good as it his first one."[13]

33 | WON'T BE LONG NOW

DÖNITZ'S NORTH ATLANTIC OBJECTIVE—holding Hitler's "first line of defense"—faced steep odds. Not least, losses to aircraft (as Dönitz later conceded) all but precluded warfare on the surface for U-boats. Still, Kriegsmarine prospects in the North Atlantic outweighed prospects elsewhere.

In mid-March, for example, with Arctic daylight lengthening, Britain suspended North Russia convoys. The "Murmansk Runs" would resume, but in the meantime, nearly two dozen U-boats (plus remnants of the Kriegsmarine's once-vaunted surface fleet) idled about in Norwegian waters.

To the south, the Kriegsmarine's impact off Northwest Africa and in the Mediterranean, never decisive, had steadily eroded. In July, a flotilla of German and Italian submarines scored some success against Husky shipping but were savaged in the process. U-boat reinforcements were dispatched, but seven were sunk trying to wiggle through Gibraltar's Strait. Others turned back. Then in September, scarcely a month after securing Sicily, Allied forces gained footholds on the Italian mainland. In short order, Benito Mussolini was deposed, Italy capitulated to the Allies, and Italy's fleet sailed for internment in North African ports.[1]

Thus, despite Rossbach's and Schlieffen's early October disappointments and the ongoing perils for U-boats crossing the Bay of Biscay, Dönitz dared not relent in the North Atlantic. On October 24, to replace a depleted Gruppe

Schlieffen, U-boat Control organized Gruppe Siegfried (named for a mythological Germanic hero).

The U-boat force had reached peak strength in May;[2] however, veteran boats with seasoned crews and experienced *kommandanten* were harder to come by. In fact, of Siegfried's eighteen U-boats, eleven were skippered by first-time commanders.[3]

The riskiest combinations were new boats (and crews) under fledglings. *U-282*, a recently commissioned Type VIIC, was in the hands of twenty-six-year-old *Oberleutnant zur See* Rudolf Müller. The same was true of *U-274* (another Type VIIC) and its *kommandant*, twenty-four-year-old *Oberleutnant zur See* Günther Jordan. (Both were from Crew 37.)

One of Siegfried's rare combinations of experienced boat, crew, and *kommandant* was Type VIIC *U-405*. Thirty-seven-year-old *Fregattenkapitän* Rolf-Heinrich Hopmann had commanded *U-405* ever since its 1941 commissioning. With little to show after five Arctic patrols, *U-405*'s transfer to the Atlantic revived Hopmann's career. The month after sinking American Liberty ship *Wade Hampton* in late February, *U-405* sank one of Convoy SC-121's merchants.

Meanwhile, the loss of *U-460* (the seventh Type XIV sunk since mid-May) limited Siegfried to attacking eastbound convoys only. If necessary, outbound U-boats could top off Siegfried U-boats—though not without exposure to Allied aircraft.

To further ease the burden on *U-488* (the only surviving XIV *milchkühe*), Control dispatched a pair of XB minelayers, *U-219* and *U-220*, to act as refueling backups. Fuelers of any sort needed special protection, a task assigned to *Kapitänleutnant* Wilhelm Brauel's *U-256* and *Kapitänleutnant* Curt Barleben's *U-271*. Their Type VIICs had recently been refitted as heavily armed "U-flak boats."[4]

When *Borie* docked in Casablanca on October 18, gunner's mates, boatswain's mates, and fire controlmen had their work cut out. After exposure to weeks of cold weather and rough seas, the 4-inch bow gun had seized up. The stopover in Casablanca would be brief—just thirty-six hours—so, whatever the problem, it had to be resolved straightaway.

Forgetting liberty, regular meals, even sleep, the ablest hands pitched in. While Bob Maher and Jim Allegri disconnected the gun's remote wiring, Gunner's Mates Dick Wenz, George Murphy, Carmen Driver, Oliver Pederson, Ken Reynolds (bow gun captain), and Eddie Johnson wrangled the hardware. For their parts, Boatswain's Mates Walt Kurz, Oakley Hamilton, and Bill Schmalberger handled lines and, assisted by a dockside crane, aided in heavy lifting.

Altogether, it took more than thirty hours to isolate and fix the problem: a faulty grease fitting. Those involved finished just a few hours ahead of TG 21.14's October 20 morning departure.[5]

Few, including Bob Maher, were sorry to leave Casablanca behind. In a region still rife with Axis sympathizers, local toughs often tried to drop boulders on the heads of unsuspecting strangers. Writing to his parents on August 17, during *Borie*'s first Casablanca stopover, Mike Brown had given his own take on the city's drawbacks (without revealing its name): "Every port we pull into . . . get[s] worse. . . . Wish I could tell you about this 'hole'!"

Disastrous mail service was a real concern. "It probably takes at least ten days for a letter to get anywhere near the U.S.," Mike cautioned. So, "until I do get back to the states don't expect to hear from me."

Mike's next letter from Casablanca, sent on October 18, was circumspect about *Borie*'s exploits: "The trip this time has been as successful as the last. Hope we have good luck on the return."

"Will say goodbye now," he closed, "until I call you from somewhere. Won't be long now."[6]

America's industrial juggernaut had taken time to gather momentum, but now the Arsenal of Democracy ran full throttle. Of course, resources, particularly shipping, were finite. But by autumn 1943, new-ship construction outpaced shipping losses.

Evidence of America's ascendency was global. In the Pacific, for example, Japanese advances had been turned back in the frigid Aleutians and the sweltering Solomons. But, while plans were afoot to oust Japan from the Southwest and Central Pacific, "Germany First" held firm as the Allied priority.

Success now seemed certain. Still, the exact timetable was not. Allied forces had pierced Axis peripheries. The next big—inevitable and unavoidable—step was to breach Hitler's Atlantic coast defenses. More than ever, achieving "Germany First" required supremacy in the Battle of the Atlantic.

Splitting responsibilities, it turned out, was a big step towards gaining that supremacy. The British Admiralty and the U.S. Navy had devised separate command structures each preferred: WAC under Max Horton, Tenth Fleet under Ernest King and Francis Low. Moreover, "carving up" the Atlantic battle space horizontally rather than vertically left each Ally freer to employ respective strengths.

For the Admiralty it was capitalizing on the audacity of such support group commanders as Johnny Walker, and Walker's acolyte Peter Gretton. Most recently, between July 28 and August 2, Walker's Support Group B-2 had collaborated with Coastal Command and USAAF B-24s in the "big Bay slaughter": the sinking of nine U-boats transiting the Bay of Biscay.

As the Admiralty's Bay of Biscay operations severed the "trunk" of the U-boat menace, Tenth Fleet refueling ambushes choked its "blood supply." Both navies had hit their strides. Operations were simultaneously expanding and becoming nimbler.

And deadlier. In May 1942, for example, the Axis lost just four U-boats while sinking 120 Allied merchants. In August 1943, for only the second time since the war began, more German U-boats (twenty-six) were sunk than Allied merchant ships (just four). Ship losses, Winston Churchill announced in a September 21 broadcast, "were the lowest we have ever had since the United States entered the war."[7]

Under these tide-turning circumstances, as Karl Dönitz formed new battle lines in the North Atlantic, the Allies initiated a concerted assault on Siegfried.

"We have been heading northwest all day," Henry Babson wrote on October 28. "And I guess we will be hunting subs again. On the Captain's sub chart, I counted twenty-three pins, all possible subs. . . . We won't be alone, as there are supposed to be three other carriers like us in and around there."[8]

Once more acting on timely Enigma decrypts, both Allied navies set decoys and traps for Siegfried. Inbound HX and SC convoys were diverted south out of harm's way. Meanwhile, Convoy Outbound North 207, its fifty-two ships "flying light," was offered as "bait"—albeit afforded considerable protection: a Canadian escort group augmented by British jeep carrier *Biter,* two British support groups (one of them Johnny Walker's 2nd with carrier *Tracker* attached, the other Peter Gretton's 7th), and as many Coastal Command aircraft as could be mustered.

The first clash came on October 21, when aircraft from jeep carrier *Core,* assisted by land-based Catalinas, attacked *U-271* as it sought to join up with *U-488.* Curt Barleben's U-flak boat survived the skirmish but was so badly damaged that it aborted to France.[9]

On the 23rd, Hedgehog and depth-charge attacks by destroyers *Duncan* and *Vidette,* part of Gretton's Support Group B-7, produced "gruesome evidence" of the demise of *U-274,* Günther Jordan, and his forty-seven-man crew. Then, six days later, *Duncan* and *Vidette* replicated the feat. This time evidence "even more gruesome and numerous" confirmed the destruction of *U-282* and the abrupt end of Rudolf Müller's first and only U-boat command.[10]

Meanwhile, the job for carriers *Card* and *Block Island* (which relieved *Core*) was to sink U-tankers *U-488, U-219,* and *U-220. Block Island* had left Norfolk on October 15 on its first operational cruise. The jeep carrier was new to Atlantic ASW, but its VC-1 airmen, freshly outfitted with the latest Wildcat and Avenger models, were not.

On the night of October 25–26 Huff-Duff pointed *Block Island* towards a refueling rendezvous. Two of its four-stackers managed to find and harass *U-488* but neither sank nor damaged it. At 9:05 a.m. on October 28, however, a VC-1 Avenger pilot spotted two dark shapes ahead on the water. Steering a reciprocal course to the Avenger's, steaming side by side about two hundred yards apart, were provisional tanker *U-220* and its flak bodyguard *U-256.*

After alerting *Block Island,* the Avenger pilot signaled his Wildcat companion to strafe *U-220,* the nearer of the two. Sweeping under the bomber, the fighter banked into a single strafing run on *U-220*'s starboard beam.

Then, swooping in on *U-220*'s starboard bow, the Avenger released two depth bombs that bracketed the sub's conning tower. As plumes and spray subsided, *U-220* skidded into a tight starboard turn, lost headway, and listed heavily. "Then suddenly," as the Avenger pilot described it in his action report, "the stern appeared in the air, screws showing, and after hanging there briefly, the U-boat disappeared . . . at an angle of 45° or more."

Both subs had been taken by surprise. *U-256* opened fire but, according to the Avenger pilot, the German gunners "seemed to be poor deflection shots." Both VC-1 aircraft moved out of range until *U-256* crash-dived—the cue for the Avenger to launch Fido. Dropped from an approach on *U-256*'s port beam, Fido landed just ahead of the *U-256*'s submersion swirl, then turned to port.

Though air crews "looked for an explosion or a shock wave[;] . . . neither . . . was observed."[11]

⌖

Since leaving from Casablanca, the *Card* group had been protecting eastbound Convoy GUS-18. But once its merchants and close escorts cleared the Azores, the group had doubled back around Santa Maria Island, then turned northwest towards what Tenth Fleet advised would be a refueling concentration north of Flores Island.

October 30 found *Card*, *Barry*, *Borie*, and *Goff* nearly equidistant from Newfoundland and Flores. "We woke up to heavy rains and rough seas," recalled *Borie*'s Bob Maher.[12] *Card*'s Henry Babson's notes concurred: "It has been cold all day, raining most of the time, also getting rougher. . . . The word was passed to rig the ship for heavy weather, so we may be in for something."[13]

Unknown to Buster Isbell, *U-220*'s demise had upended Siegfried logistics. Under orders from U-boat Control, *U-488* and *U-219* had fled south to safer waters. But U-boats still trolled about—among them *U-91* and *U-584*.

⌖

Since the trials and executions of the saboteurs it had landed near Jacksonville in summer 1942, *Kapitänleutnant* Joachim Deecke's *U-584* had completed three patrols, joined more than a dozen wolf pack groups, and, in the process, sunk three merchants.

Deecke's boat had last left France on September 2. Now homebound, with nothing to show for its role in Leuthen or Rossbach, *U-584* was nearing sixty days at sea. Its rendezvous with *U-488* preempted, Crew 33's Deecke desperately needed fuel.

Fortunately, *U-584* linked up with *U-91*, another homebound Type VIIC, with fuel to spare. Deecke's *U-91* counterpart, twenty-six-year-old *Kapitänleutnant* Heinz Hungershausen, was on his first patrol as *kommandant*. Though Deecke, now thirty-one, was a veteran and Crew 36's Hungershausen a neophyte, commanding U-boats was something of a family tradition for both. Deecke's older brother Jürgen (Crew 31) had commanded a North Sea "duck" lost with all hands in 1940. Meanwhile, Hungershausen's younger brother Walter (Crew 38) was the commissioning *kommandant* for *U-280*, a new Type VIIC.

Since leaving France in September 21 to join Rossbach, Schlieffen, and now Siegfried, Hungershausen had had few chances to display his mettle. On one occasion, after sighting a destroyer, he'd launched a T-5 torpedo, but it failed to hit. On another, his gunners repelled an aerial attack. Now, however, *U-91*'s 20-mm barrels were badly bent and utterly useless.[14]

It was Russell I. Goering, Monk Fowler's twenty-six-year-old radioman, who first "spotted" *U-584* and *U-91*, a little after 4 p.m. on October 31 about 650 miles north of Flores. This time by oscillations on the screen display of his ASB radar—rudimentary but effective gear now installed in VC-9's TBFs. After sending a contact report, Monk descended to five hundred feet, confirmed the sub visually, then circled, awaiting help.

Once Fowler's TBF appeared overhead, Deecke's gunners promptly "put up a heavy . . . curtain of antiaircraft fire." Hungershausen, however, pulled the plug, escaping and leaving Deecke to fight on.

But not for long. The first sight of Monk's reinforcements, TBFs piloted by Goose McAuslan and Letson Balliett, promptly changed Deecke's mind. Too late. *U-584*'s conning tower was still visible as McAuslan's and Balliett's Fidos hit the water on either side. Seconds later, plumes of water broke the surface, precursors of a spreading oil slick replete with debris.[15]

VC-9 had dispatched *U-584* less than twenty miles from *Card*. But a kill considered certain to please Buster Isbell instead sparked his discontent. Fowler had clearly encountered a refueling rendezvous. But if McAuslan and Balliett had destroyed a Type VII then the other, "the larger of the two escaping,"* *must* be a U-tanker. Either *U-488* or *U-219*, but, at any rate, the real prize.

Halloween darkness approached. TBFs might take off, fly—even land—at night but not track down U-boats. A better bet—in terms of radar, weaponry, and endurance—was sending one of his tin cans. Given the proximity of the suspected U-tanker, a destroyer could easily overtake it.

But there were drawbacks, too, one of them expressly recorded in *Card*'s war diary: "Scene of action approximately center and touching several reported heavy submarine concentrations." The destroyer would be out there alone and, while gone, leave Isbell's surface screen weakened.

Arnold Isbell's orders to *Borie*'s Hutch arrived shortly after sunset. "U-boat dived thirteen miles away bearing 180 when we turned to pick up our planes. Conduct night search, destroying enemies encountered, rendezvous with this group after dawn tomorrow."[16]

Borie's immediate destination: latitude 49° 03′ N, longitude 31° 55′ W.

Hutch confirmed Isbell's orders, informed the crew by loudspeaker, then went below to finish dinner and don heavy clothing.

Hutch's announcement to the crew, recalled Bob Maher, was that "we had 'volunteered' to search for the escaping U-boat."

Cheers erupted through the ship. In Maher's words: "We young bucks, dumb and happy, were really excited. We were the hunters, not the hunted, and it was an exhilarating feeling for all of us."[17]

Borie turned into a blackening night. Fair visibility, but with neither moon nor stars. Waves sent spray and spindrift over the bow. At full speed, it took *Borie* roughly an hour to reach the designated search area. The ship then went to General Quarters to search with radar and sound.

Atop the flying bridge, Bob Maher overheard the steady *ping . . . ping . . . ping* of the outbound sound pulses. Sailors around and below were shadowy figures, cloaked in waterproof jackets and lidded with steel helmets.

---

*It was not uncommon for aircrews (and ships' lookouts) to misjudge U-boat type and size. When a VC-1 pilot engaged *U-220* and *U-256*, for example, he reported *U-220* (a Type XB roughly three times the size of *U-256*, a Type VIIC) as the "smaller submarine."

"Radar contact, bearing 095° True, range 6,500 yards."

It was just after 8 p.m., *Borie* heading due east.

Radar detected a vessel on the surface, tracking on a nearly reciprocal course, speed about fifteen knots.

Hutch ordered flank speed and a course to intercept.[18]

34 | SCRATCH ONE PIGBOAT

AS IF SOMEHOW afforded multiple lives, *U-256* appeared to use all of them during its inaugural patrol. Under *Kapitänleutnant* Odo Loewe, a twenty-seven-year-old first-time *kommandant*, the Type VIIC had been caught and shelled by a convoy escort, escaping only to be hobbled by depth charges. On August 31, 1942, while crawling home through the Bay of Biscay, the boat was bombed and strafed by two British aircraft. Fortunately, another U-boat radioed for help and took on board thirty men, leaving behind Loewe and a salvage party to save the floundering vessel.

Luftwaffe aircraft and Kriegsmarine motor torpedo boats finally escorted *U-256* to safety but in such bad shape that it was slated to be scrapped.* Only the need to defend U-boats in the Bay of Biscay saved it. *U-256* was overhauled and resurrected under the alias *U-Flak 2*, now equipped with two shielded, quadruple 20-mm cannons on "bandstands" forward and aft of the conning tower; a rapid-fire 37-mm on a second, lower bandstand farther aft; and multiple smaller-caliber machine guns on the bridge. Armed with just five torpedoes for self-defense, her stern tube was used to store ammunition.

The boat's new *kommandant*, twenty-seven-year-old Wilhelm Brauel, had been a jobless teenage bricklayer when he first enlisted in 1932. He'd aspired

*After temporarily filling in for an ill U-boat *kommandant*, Crew 34's Odo Loewe went on to command *U-954*, lost with all hands (including Karl Dönitz's twenty-one-year-old son Peter) on May 18, 1943. See chapter 23.

to a career in construction, "but the economy was dead." A decade later, after early stints in minelayers, selection for Crew 37, and seasoning on various U-boats, the *Oberleutnant zur See* earned his first submarine command.

U-Flak 2's baptism of fire came before dawn on October 8, when an RAF four-engine bomber spotlit and straddled the boat with a half-dozen depth charges. Caught off guard with no chance to mount a defense, Brauel pulled the plug and escaped. Surprised again on October 28, *U-256*'s gunners gamely fought back—though not soon or accurately enough to prevent *Card* aircraft from destroying tanker *U-220*.

Then, at 10:30 p.m. on October 31, the closest call—a destroyer bearing down fast. Caught in the glare of enemy flares, Brauel once more crash-dived. *U-256* was nosing steeply through 110 meters when a barrage of depth charges exploded to starboard. Brauel ordered silent speed, all auxiliary engines shut down.

Once the boat leveled out at 170 meters, the crew waited in communal terror, breath shallow, pulse racing. The menacing spin of destroyer propellers faded briefly then returned, this time to port. More depth charges tumbled towards them, exploding extremely close. As *U-256*'s log told it: "Taking water at the bow room, boat falls through to 220 meters. Only by blowing diving tank #3 able to hold boat."

After eight hours submerged, batteries low and water still spilling into the forward compartment, Brauel finally chose to surface. "We couldn't hear or see anything," Brauel recalled. *U-256*'s periscope was broken, its sound equipment inoperative.

Though escaping imminent danger, *U-256* was blinded and deafened. Circumstances left Brauel little choice but to abort. After seventeen days in transit, surfacing only to recharge batteries, *U-256* finally reached Brest. "Every time we came to the surface," Brauel ruefully recalled, "we had to put our ears to the walls of the sub to listen for the enemy."[1]

"Dispatch from BORIE: 'Scratch one pig boat eleven miles south of your contact. Am searching for more. Estimated position 49-03 N, 31-55 W.'"[2]

Breaking radio silence at midnight on Halloween, Charles Hutchins had declared, in so many words, "mission accomplished." But, while his dispatch evinced conviction, it was premature.

The initial radar contact ("good, sharp, metallic, closing, moving rapid left"), called out by Sonarman 2/c Earl J. Potter, had put everyone on their toes. Those having a vantage stared to starboard. "We couldn't see anything that far away in the dark," Bob Maher admitted. "But we all looked anyway."[3]

With the distance between *Borie* and the radar contact closing to 1,700 yards, Hutch ordered Walter Dietz to fire star shells and GQ helmsman Jim Aikenhead (the diminutive signalman from the old Baltimore Battalion) to steer thirty degrees to starboard. The skipper's objective (as he wrote in his official account): "to expose battery and permit ramming from broad on the bow."[4]

Even as the sky above *Borie* "came alive with bright flares," Bob Maher heard, "Radar contact lost."[5]

As Hutchins later told *Life* correspondent Ray Mackland, "He had disappeared," but "he didn't get away."

The *ping-ping-ping* of outbound sound pulses, in Maher's telling, abruptly gave way to "*ping-boing, ping-boing,* the sound of returning echoes." Sonarman 2/c Lerten V. "Les" Kent, a nineteen-year-old Coloradan, called out "Sound contact!"[6]

"Changed course left and slowed to 15 knots to conduct depth charge attack," continued Hutch's official account. "Sub tracked on 306 T [true], speed 4 knots. Held contact in to 150 yards."[7]

Then equipment glitches intervened: both bridge-mounted firing mechanisms—electric for the K-guns, hydraulic for the stern racks—failed. Following voice commands, Chief Torpedoman's Mate Frank J. Cronin's crew manually fired K-guns and rolled ashcans (all set shallow), their launch location marked by float light.

Almost at once, as he described it to Mackland: "*BORIE* was shaken by an underwater blast so strong it knocked . . . brickwork out of one of our boilers and blew several fuses. . . . Out went our lights. . . . We were certain we'd got him, but we cursed the blackness."

Not for long. Sonarman 2/c Robert E. Manning and Radio Technician 1/c Frank J. Duke (nee Dutkowiak), a thirty-five-year-old mustachioed Chicagoan, found and replaced the fuses—cutting short *U-256*'s respite.[8]

Once Les Kent reacquired sonar contact ("1,600 yards, sharp to mushy"), *Borie* approached the light marker and launched more ashcans into waters "heavy" with the "odor of diesel oil."

These deeper blasts (four hundred to five hundred feet) spared *Borie*'s hull plates and interior spaces—but (according to Brauel's log) severely jolted *U-256*. Then, as some *Borie* sailors attested and Hutchins subsequently reported, "a U-boat shot to the surface, balanced an instant, his bow very high in the air, then slid quietly back into the dark waves."

This death rattle (had it happened) would have confirmed *U-256*'s demise. More likely it was an apparition: what *Borie*'s witnesses *expected* to rise from the deep. ("No one on the flying bridge saw it," confessed Bob Maher, who had a better view than most.)[9]

Still, whether imaginary or real, it convinced Hutchins that *Borie* had "scratched" the quarry. "We . . . got back in a hurry and let him have another very large barrage." But these charges—all set for medium depth—were just "insurance."

⌖

With Hutchins' dispatch in Buster Isbell's hands, Halloween gave way to November 1. "Shadowy figures" (as Mackland portrayed the scene topside) made "a ghostly crew, garbed . . . against both winter and foul weather."

Indeed, it was winterlike: dark, overcast, and cold. Still, winds remained light and seas moderate. *Borie* was not very far from TG 21.14 (though in frigid waters nearly two miles deep and many hundreds of miles from nearest landfall). Fuel bunkers were full; all seemed in good order. Craving more kills, Isbell left his instructions unchanged. Off leash until dawn, Hutchins resumed the hunt.

At 1:53 a.m., with *Borie* steering due south at seventeen knots (now roughly thirty miles east of its last reported position) Hutchins got his chance. Hearing Frank Duke call out a new radar contact, OOD Phil Brown punched the intercom: "Captain to the bridge."[10] And, in the words of John Hersey (also writing for *Life*):* "A kind of electric shock hit . . . the blacked-out bridge."[11]

Men who'd long been at General Quarters relied on bridge "talkers" (sailors connected to *Borie*'s sound-powered battle telephone circuits) to keep them updated. Hearing the latest, Gunner's Mate 1/c Kenneth J. Reynolds, captain of gun one, alerted his crew, as did Chief Boatswain's Mate Walter Kurz who captained guns two and three atop the galley house. Tom Morris, a cherubic-faced twenty-year-old electrician's mate third class from Baltimore, gripped the controls of the powerful twenty-four-inch searchlight affixed to a small pedestal just above the flying bridge.

When Hutchins reached the pilothouse, *Borie*'s new contact bore 170 degrees true (slightly east of south), eight thousand yards. He instructed Aikenhead to ease left, then ordered "Flank speed!"

The order, relayed by engine order telegraph, reached chief engineer Mike Brown at his forward engine room battle station. The space, just aft of number 4 stack, was the nerve center for a power plant that occupied a substantial part of *Borie*'s bowels. The plant's interconnected compartments (in sequence forward to aft: number 1 fireroom, number 2 fireroom, forward engine room, and aft engine room) were warrens of burners, boilers, steam drums, turbines, condensers, and evaporators (plus intervening gears, pumps, pipes, valves, bearings, gauges, and controls).

Not surprisingly, Mike's black gang performed duties that mystified sailors stationed elsewhere. After all, his enlisted engineer ratings and strikers bunked, ate, and usually socialized (and caroused) separately from deck, weapons, and technical ratings and strikers.

Despite *Borie*'s age and wear, there were good reasons to extol the vessel's high-pressure steam-driven turbines. Protectively encasing them was crucial to *Borie*'s propulsion resilience. Even more crucial: *Borie*'s overall plant, like those of more modern destroyers, was split into two, self-contained systems.

One plant comprised number 1 fireroom and the forward engine room. The other comprised number 2 fireroom and the aft engine room. The two

---

*A war correspondent widely traveled in Europe and the Pacific, Hersey would cover the aftermath of the atomic bombing of Hiroshima and win a Pulitzer Prize for *A Bell for Adano*, a wartime novel set in Sicily.

systems could be "cross-connected" so that any boiler—or combination of boilers—could drive either engine. But maximum reliability, especially in enemy waters, usually meant operating "split-plant."

Complexities aside, each plant's workings were fundamentally straightforward. Fireroom oil-burning furnaces and water-tube boilers generated high-pressure, superheated steam. Engine room machinery throttled that steam through turbines, releasing energy to spin propeller shafts.* Engine-room condensers then converted steam back to feed water for fire-room boilers.

"They were wonderful plants," claimed Norman "Tony" Algiers, four years a machinist's mate on board a four-stacker. Simply put, they "could get up and move."

Getting up and moving demanded maximum heat and air pressure in the firerooms ("the faster you went," explained Algiers, "the more air was needed to atomize the oil") and, above all, pure, mineral-free feed water coursing through boiler tubes. According to Algiers: "Some steam leaked, so we had to make up feed water." But, he emphasized, "The boiler water had to be perfect—you could drink a taste of salt, but boiler tubes scaled if you got *any* salt to them."[12]

Mike Brown's GQ team included four Garden Staters: Chief Machinist's Mate Walter J. "Bill" Green from Jersey City; bridge talker Ben Hugo, a machinist's mate from Rutherford; Bill Howard, a twenty-four-year-old machinist's mate from Verona; and Mario J. Pagnotta, a twenty-six-year-old motor machinist's mate from Hoboken.[13]

Though "deck apes" might misunderstand, ignore, or dismiss what Mike's "snipes" accomplished, the lives of everyone on board would soon depend on how long they could keep *Borie*'s "teakettles" humming.

---

*Forward engine-room turbines drove the port propeller, the aft engine-room turbines the starboard propeller.

35 | STAND BY FOR A RAM!

FRANK DUKE lost the surface radar contact at 2,800 yards, but, as before, Les Kent quickly picked up a clear and solid echo. “Sound contact, one nine oh.” With the target submerging, *Borie* again slowed and approached to drop depth charges. When, at five hundred yards, the contact suddenly slewed hard right, *Borie* followed.

Charges were set shallow. But to avoid jarring the ship, fewer* would be dropped. As was customary, though, Cronin set rack controls for automatic release, and when Phil Brown ordered “Lay out a pattern of ashcans,” Cronin let them go.

“One . . . two . . . three . . . ,” Hutchins recalled counting as the first charges dropped. Then, suddenly, a distressed Cronin came on-circuit shouting: “Release is defective! We can’t check ’em—they’re *all* going over, goddamn it!” Then, a moment later, in resignation: “They’re all gone.”[1]

Cronin’s runaway barrage erupted with enough force to lift *Borie*’s stern and shove it forward.

There followed—as in the earlier duel with *U-256*—a dramatic sight. “There it is!” Bob Maher cried, “about forty feet to the right of [the ashcan drop marking] the flare.”[2] Though Maher’s lookout protocol was faulty, he had spotted something undeniably real.

---

*Official records and available accounts are unclear on just how many.

Hutch ordered the ship's big searchlight switched on, and baby-faced Tom Morris swung the beam to the port quarter. As water cascaded off the decks of the spotlit sub, *Borie* crewmen saw a milky-gray conning tower emblazoned with the image of a white polar bear. Though numerical markings were indiscernible, it was Rolf-Heinrich Hopmann's *U-405*.

The sub had risen where only *Borie*'s gun four (the 4-incher atop the aft deckhouse) could bear. Its crew got off a shot but missed.[3] The sub—apparently unable to submerge—was fleeing on the surface. To pursue while bringing more guns to bear, Hutch called for twenty-five knots and ordered Aikenhead to put the wheel hard right.

The swing to starboard freed *U-405* from *Borie*'s searchlight until, coaxed by radar bearings, Morris swung it back on target. *U-405* tracked north-northeast, speed twelve knots. For now, the range was opening: a thousand yards . . . twelve hundred yards . . . fourteen hundred yards.

As *Borie* accelerated out of its turn, 4-inch and 20-mm guns able to bear began shooting in local control. "Hit 'em away on a lazy day—*fi-yuh!*" Ken Reynolds bellowed to his gun crew. Then silently (but with burning resolve): "If I can only sink the U-boat myself!"[4]

After crossing its own wake, *Borie* gained on *U-405* even as it too accelerated to maximum speed. Hutchins's objective: "expose battery" on *U-405*'s starboard beam. But he also had to beware of torpedoes—and other subs. Everyone—topside lookouts, sonar and radar operators—looked sharp.

A few *U-405* German sailors could now be seen—spotlit flickers of arms, legs, and torsos, like inmates staging a prison break. With forward decks awash, the sub's big deck gun could not be manned, but not so its 20-mm cannons.

"Duck!" someone shouted as rounds whistled in.[5] Several pierced *Borie*'s forward engine room. Shrapnel splintered bridge window glass. "Bend up their guns," gun captains exhorted their crews. "Get those goddam guns bent up!"[6]

"I was scared," recalled Tom Morris, "the gun concussions jarred the light[;] . . . *Borie* kept bouncing around." Tom's eyes watered from the combination of light, gunsmoke, and salt spray. His apparatus was an obvious target, but "the captain kept telling me to keep the light on the sub."[7]

Borie's return fire was swift and severe. "In a matter of seconds," Hutchins reported later, "*BORIE*'s 20MM battery had wiped out every exposed member of the sub's crew topside." To Bob Maher the impact was equally "horrifying and fascinating." Darting tracer rounds added streaks of color to the searchlight's broad white beam. "For some reason," despite the murderous strafing, "Germans came out of a forward hatch, about five at a time, and made an impossible dash of about thirty feet to get to their guns. None of them made it[;] . . . [t]hey were knocked bodily over the side, arms and legs flying."[8]

Once the port main battery (gun one on the bow, gun two portside on the galley deck, and gun four on the aft deckhouse) could bear, control "shifted from local to centralized control, pointer fire."[9] The three guns, aimed from the flying bridge by Bob Maher and Jim Allegri, would shoot as one.

Ken Reynolds no longer felt it was up to him. "Then [we] really began to throw steel."[10] As Hutchins described it to Ray Mackland: "We could watch three shells fly from the main battery, could see them converge and then flash upon him in one big burst."[11]

The first casualty of *Borie*'s three-gun salvos was *U-405*'s unmanned deck gun. According to Hutchins: "On the second or third full salvo—the gunnery officer swears it was the first—the three shells fell together at the base of his deck gun[;] . . . [s]everal men reported they saw it go over the side, and sure enough, when the mass of smoke and flame cleared away, there was no gun there."[12]

Though outgunned, *U-405* was far from being outmaneuvered or defeated. *Borie* had pulled nearly abreast when Hopmann swung *U-405* to port, presumably aiming its stern torpedo tube. Intent on staying broadside, Hutchins told Aikenhead to come left as well. *Borie* turned gently at first, but when Hopmann matched this maneuver, Hutchins ordered hard left rudder—as if he planned to cut across *U-405*'s stern and come inside its turning radius.

The two vessels were so close now that main-battery fire reverted to local control. Rendered a bystander, Bob Maher watched the two vessels jockey. "I was sure we were going to collide." Then "the U-boat appeared to turn on all of its power, picking up enough speed to pass us. Looking down, I could see clearly the German faces still on the bridge."[13] Several heads trailed long matted hair, while others sported bandanas in green, yellow, and red.

After Hutchins' feint to port and Hopmann's countermove, the two vessels temporarily resumed parallel courses, now steering roughly southwest. Uncounted rounds from *Borie*'s 20-mm cannons had mowed down virtually every exposed German sailor. Meanwhile, dozens of explosive 4-inch projectiles, having blown away *U-405*'s deck gun, hammered its conning tower. Like many other *Borie* sailors, Bob Maher wondered "how long they could endure."

The answer seemed at hand when *U-405* slowed and, in Maher's recollection, "a man appeared on the bridge . . . waving his arms in crossing movement."

"Cease fire!" Hutchins ordered. All except gun two complied. (Earlier, finding himself encumbered by it, Walt Kurz had removed his headset.)

Below him, Maher saw the skipper dash from the pilothouse, shouting, "Cease fire! Cease fire!" But Kurz still couldn't hear him, and gun two kept shooting.

Maher looked back to the man on *U-405*'s bridge: "His body stood there momentarily, arms extended over his head, then his head just disappeared."[14]

No one knew the reason for the flares or why the German had ventured out to wave his arms.

At any rate, the moment was lost.

Borie retained the advantage, but the longer the fight lasted the more the balance teetered. Concerned about his power plant, Hutch checked in with Mike Brown.

"How much am I getting? Are your men alright?"

"You're getting 29.5 [knots]," Mike reported. "We're bloody [a few shrapnel wounds] but alive," However: "We're taking water."[15]

Bilge pumps could handle that for now, but how long could burners, boilers, engines, and generators sustain this pace? How much more damage could *Borie*'s gun batteries inflict without jamming or faltering? Only a handful of *Borie* casualties so far, but what if losses mounted? How much longer would Hutchins have the upper hand?

Though outmatched in speed, size, and gun power, *U-405* could turn more nimbly. If its engineer figured out how to submerge, *U-405* might shake loose and disappear. Worse, *U-405*—or another sub coming to its rescue—might torpedo *Borie*.

"A few days before," Hutchins told Ray Mackland, "I had painted a rude sight, a couple of rings and a bull's eye with lined up crosswires on the forward port[hole]."* He'd joked of it as "*Borie*'s ramming sight." But now Hutch's "rude" circles symbolized a real possibility.

Despite advances in weaponry and tactics, antisubmarine doctrine still allowed ramming when circumstances permitted. Indeed, it was an aggressive tactic relished by the likes of Britain's Johnny Walker. During four years of war, at least a dozen warships, mostly British, had purposely knifed, bow first, into surfaced U-boats. As recently as September 22, *Keppel*, a British destroyer (a bit longer, heavier, and younger than *Borie*), had spotted, shot at, and rammed *U-229*, a Type VIIC. Once the two vessels separated, Cdr. Martin Evans, RN, *Keppel*'s thirty-nine-year-old skipper, rolled ten shallow-set depth charges that upended and sank *U-229*.[16]

Keppel's feat occurred roughly eight hundred miles northwest of *Borie*'s current position. Evans, a more seasoned skipper, had pulled it off as daylight neared, not in the dead of night. In September's seas, winds, and temperatures, not November's. Even so, *Keppel* suffered a mangled bow and barely made it safely to Greenland, a thousand miles farther north.

Hutchins faced a command decision—his alone to make, his burden alone to shoulder. A choice of perils: continue the chase or dash in to ram. There'd be no consulting Buster Isbell, no conferring with *Borie*'s officers or polling of the crew. Based on his judgment and instincts, *Borie* would succeed or fail—perhaps even perish. Hutchins, the thirty-year-old reservist, the erstwhile packaging salesman from Terre Haute, Indiana, courted fame—or ignominy.

With *Borie* at flank speed, now on *U-405*'s starboard quarter and poised to pull ahead, Hutchins made up his mind. He alerted bridge personnel. Then, bowing his head and raising his right arm—an idiosyncratic command posture—he dropped the arm like a tollgate, fingers pointing to the makeshift bullseye.[17]

---

* In other accounts, Hutchins credited XO Phil Brown with drawing the bullseye.

"All right, Aikenhead, get this on the sub."

"Aye sir," Aikenhead replied—then, moments later: "I got her on."

"All stations stand by for a ram!" Hutch announced. Bridge talkers duly parroted the skipper's alert—simultaneously reaching to grab something sturdy.[18]

36 | AT CLOSE QUARTERS

PHONE CIRCUIT CHATTER stopped once Bob Maher alerted gunnery stations to Hutchins' command. Peering out over the flying bridge's splinter shield, Maher envisioned himself "sailing right over, down on the forecastle."[1] Finally bracing himself against the range finder, he looked towards the bow gun. Though positioned nearest the point of expected impact, its crew kept firing.

Indeed, despite wet deck, bucking bow—fourth loader Ernest Gardner, a steward's mate second class from Baltimore, twice saved others from washing overboard—and the prospect of collision, Reynolds's crew "was clicking perfectly," their gun "throwing shells like an automatic."

Until, without warning, the electric firing circuit and foot-pedal backup failed.

Reynolds repeatedly "shoved on the trigger button, but nothing happened." After a moment of panic ("Don't let this happen! Not to me!"), Reynolds impulsively yanked the breech latch. This released the firing pin and the gun barked, but its swift recoil also slammed his arm, nearly toppling him.

Reynolds thought to rig a lanyard, but none was at hand. So, as *Borie*'s bow swung towards *U-405*, Reynolds' loaders kept loading, Reynolds kept yanking the latch, gun one kept barking—and its recoil kept punishing Reynolds' arm. Not until the very last moment did Reynolds "guess what was coming."[2]

Meanwhile, decision made and commands given, Charles Hutchins stepped to the port bridge wing and braced himself against its splinter shield. Back in the wheelhouse, James Aikenhead gripped the helm. "I couldn't see the sub all the time," he confessed later. "I was trying to ram it, but it was pretty elusive. I kept wheeling to the left, then to the right, trying to hit with the point of the bow."[3]

Borie lay (in Hutchins' telling) "Only seconds away from our expected kill" when "the sub dodged left. Our bow deflected and rode up over his bow. We stopped the engines and pinned him there."[4]

Breathless anticipation, recalled Bob Maher, gave way to "stunned lull." Implausibly, *Borie*, a high-seas surface creature, sat astride *U-405*, a denizen of the deep. Both were designed, built, equipped, and accustomed to stalk—even fight—by stealth. Often invisibly or at a distance. But here both were stranded, locked keel atop deck at close quarters.

Their crews, heretofore trading shots at midrange, now stood practically face to face. Destined, perhaps, to fight hand to hand.

At first, some *Borie* sailors could only gawk. Ken Reynolds, for one, left his gun, stepped to the port rail and stood, transfixed, peering at the Germans below. In the searchlight beam they looked haggard and filthy. Some wore sweaters and dungarees, others (perhaps rousted from sleep) little more than skivvies. Signalman Ed Malaney, Bob Maher's liberty companion, stood at the port bridge wing, exclaiming, "My God, what is that?"[5]

For his part, meanwhile, Dick Wenz hardly paused. Instead, the burly chief gunner's mate went to the small arms locker. Lacking a key but wielding a fire ax, Wenz broke the lock, wrenched open the steel door, and began dispensing *Borie*'s small arsenal of tommy guns, rifles, shotguns, and pistols.

"Fire! Fire! Open fire!" Hutch's order snapped the spell, igniting a melee dominated by the murderous, point-blank hammering of *Borie*'s 20-mm cannons.*

*Accounts disagree on the use of *Borie*'s 4-inchers. "During this part of the action," Hutchins wrote in his official account, "main battery guns #2 and #4 kept up a continual fire." In Kenneth Reynolds' telling, however, "Neither my gun, nor any of the destroyer's [main-battery] guns could be brought to bear." And while Reynolds recalled that #2 and #4 finally *did* fire at close quarters, in Bob Maher's memory "all firing came from the twenty-millimeter guns and small arms."

From Hutchins' oral history account: "Machine gun number six, located on the main deck aft, port side, [swept] the submarine decks continuously." Meanwhile, gunners for "machine guns three and four in the raised platform aft amidships depressed the guns and fired right through metal [shielding] around that platform."[6]

Ed "Meat" Johnson, Jim Allegri's pal and workmate from Allegri Ice and Coal, was first to try that. Maher saw Meat's "first shots explode through the wind screen"—pelting and wounding *Borie* crewmen nearby with shards of sheet metal.[7] Hearing a "terrific racket from the AA stations," Ken Reynolds witnessed *Borie*'s platform gunners (their field of fire forcibly cleared) "pouring steel down as if they were putting out a fire with hoses."[8]

At the same time, standing on the port bridge wing, XO Phil Brown, and C. L. "Mousey" Moultrop, a twenty-two-year-old signalman from Providence, Rhode Island, shouldered tommy guns—weapons "hardly ever used except to shoot sharks."[9] Brown, reported *Life*'s John Hersey, "wait[ed] coolly until a German torso lifted itself on deck across the way, then pull[ed] the trigger." Tommy gun slugs pinged off the sub's deck and conning tower "like hail on a tin roof."[10] To keep these weapons loaded, Moultrop had retrieved extra magazines he'd secretly stashed in the signal-flag bags. "It was," Hutchins told *Life*'s Mackland, "like shooting ducks in a millpond."[11]

Other *Borie* sailors, meanwhile, employed objects at hand. On the bow, for example, Ken Reynolds, seeing a German sailor right below him, "grabbed an empty [4-inch] shell casing and slammed it down." Staggered by the ten pounds of hollow brass, the German "folded in two, then rolled off the sub's deck into the water."[12]

Signalman Ed Malaney, unable to get a conventional firearm, instead used a Very pistol—a device certainly capable of blinding or maiming at short range. Indeed, Bob Maher beheld "a bright ball of fire [a flare fired by Malaney] arc across into a man's chest." The German victim fell and rolled over, "his chest still burning."[13]

Farther aft, standing on the galley deckhouse—mere feet from *U-405*'s conning tower—Walter Kurz, emulating Reynolds, heaved brass shell casings at Germans climbing from the conning tower. Hutchins "saw one hit a man squarely on the head and send him spinning into the water."[14]

David F. Southwick, stationed at one of the depth-charge projectors, unsheathed his utility knife and threw it at a would-be German gunner. Southwick, a fireman first class from Somerville, Massachusetts, was shocked when the five-inch blade lodged in the German's abdomen. The German doubled over, stumbled, and fell overboard.

Much else of what happened during these minutes is difficult to verify fully. Multiple accounts (from official reports, oral histories, magazines, newspapers, journals, and personal correspondence) sometimes corroborate events but other times inflate or contradict them. Decades later, Maher conceded that "accounts of 'hand-to-hand combat' were exaggerated." Still, he insisted, "there was firing at close range more akin to infantry warfare than battle at sea."[15]

Desperation on both sides is undisputed. A "them or us" imperative—intensified by darkness, cold, and the prospect of not just being wounded or killed but lost irretrievably at sea—held sway. Savagery revealed itself in actions but also in wishes and words. "Only one thought gripped my mind," insisted Ken Reynolds. "Don't let them board; keep them off; kill every last one."[16] Recalled Robert Jefferis, a twenty-two-year-old ensign from Kansas City, stationed on the galley deck: "The enemy's faces appeared almost close-up, contorted, yelling." *Borie*'s men, meanwhile, were "screaming directions. "Get that ——! Kill that —— over there!"[17]

Even weaponless (and usually mild-mannered) Carl Banks, the range-finder operator, stomped back and forth across the flying bridge, screaming "Kill the bastards! Kill 'em! Kill 'em! Kill! Kill! Kill!"[18]

⌖

Hutchins guessed nearly half the crew was either "firing guns or throwing things." The air was "full of lead and steel," virtually all of it raining *down* on *U-405*'s overmatched crew. Altogether, Hutch and others estimated, two dozen or more dead and wounded Germans had disappeared overboard. Perhaps a score more still huddled in *U-405*'s interior. *Borie*'s propellers had stopped spinning but not *U-405*'s. Though besieged, with half his crew overboard, Rolf-Heinrich Hopmann (or whoever now commanded *U-405*) intended to break free.

So too did Hutchins. Time and again he screamed "Hard left!" into the wheelhouse, not ten feet away. "Captain!" Aikenhead would scream back. "I *am* hard left!" Soon, though, Aikenhead confessed, "I was so tired I could hardly wheel her."[19] As Phil Brown put it, "Aikenhead flopped down against the port bulkhead," as "another swabbie grabbed the wheel."[20]

Seas—heavier now and rolling—punished both vessels. "We'd bring a gun to bear," said Hutchins, "the ship would pitch, and the gun would be pointing to the sky."[21]

Gunnery's Walt Dietz was keen to lead a boarding party over the side, but Hutchins rejected the idea. "I didn't know how long we would stay together and wanted no one on the sub."[22]

"We will not board. Repeat, we will not board," admonished phone talkers.

Below decks, some *Borie* crew remained unaware of the commotion topside. "What the hell is going on up there?" the fire-control switchboard operator asked Bob Maher. Surprisingly to Bob, "He didn't even know that we had rammed the U-boat."[23]

Their senses already overloaded by heat, vibration, and noise, *Borie*'s black gang scarcely registered *Borie*'s oblique swipe at *U-405*. But ever since, as much of *Borie*'s hull pounded, twisted, and scraped against the sub, their efforts to control damage had turned all-consuming. And, though Hutch reveled in how well the fighting topside was going, he nonetheless assumed the hull's pounding, twisting, and scraping "was doing us no good."[24]

To be sure, *U-405*'s steel-alloy shell, built to withstand tremendous underwater pressures and explosions, fared better than *Borie*'s rolled-steel hull plates. Within minutes, much of *Borie*'s port side was crushed and holed below the waterline. The main deck was broken across just aft of number-two stack. But the worst damage—gaping holes and widely opened seams—was in the forward engine room.

"Taking water from big holes," reported Mike Brown.[25]

Flooding was, in fact, near-catastrophic. With the forward engine-room bilge pump unable to keep up, lead machinist's mate Mario Pagnotta worked injection valves and applied the main circulating pump to the bilges. This increased suction—but not enough. Only a cross-connection to the after-engine-room bilge pump staved off a deluge.

37 | VICIOUS CIRCLE

ALL AT ONCE, Ken Reynolds "felt our ship lurch and drop by the bow. I thought maybe the sub had gone down under us, but I was wrong. In a few seconds I saw her floating clear."[1]

Indeed, *U-405* was again off *Borie*'s port side, running parallel. And, with its diesels all the while engaged, edging ahead into the darkness. As Hutchins recounted to Mackland, "the choppy seas finally threw us apart."[2]

Remarkably, *Borie* 4-inch guns one, two, and four roared back into action. Gun one's Reynolds, though still "taking a wallop" from each recoil, resolutely kept "lamming shells."[3]

On the galley deckhouse, meanwhile, when other loaders went to retrieve ammunition and a muzzle flash blinded gun two's pointer, Christopher C. Sheppard, commissaryman first class from Norfolk, instinctively took over.[4] Sheppard loaded a round, closed the breech, climbed into the pointer seat, aimed, and fired. For a time, Sheppard became—as Ensign Jefferis afterward told Hutchins—"a one-man gun crew."[5]

Thanks to gunners like Reynolds, Sheppard, and Johnson, *Borie*'s 4-inchers and 20 mms scarcely let up. "Even over the roar of the explosions," Ken Reynolds recounted, "I could hear the shells plopping into [*U-405*'s] sides. There were no [Germans] swarming on her deck." In fact, "nothing could have lived on that deck."[6]

But, as *U-405* suffered this relentless exterior drubbing, *Borie* suffered an equal interior drubbing. Said Hutchins to Mackland: "We slowed [*U-405*] down with the most telling blows, but we were badly crippled."[7]

At this stage, *Borie*'s engineer order telegraph was inoperative, restricting communication to sound-powered telephone. "Keep the teakettles spinning as long as you can," Hutch urged Mike in one exchange.[8]

Carpenter's Mate 1/c Ed "Eggs" Robertson (Bob Maher's Shore Patrol partner in St. Petersburg) led one of *Borie*'s damage control parties.[9] Stationed topside during the first stages of the battle, Robertson, joined by Machinist's Mates Ed Shockley, Irving Saum, and Edward Trenz, rushed below to stem flooding. The three carried mattresses (for use as patches) but also a sense of foreboding. "They [the Germans] got us," Eggs recalled, "in the one compartment that would render us helpless."[10]

The damage control team tried desperately to plug holes. "Shockley and Pagnotta," wrote Hersey, "crawled in behind some live steam pipes dragging mattresses behind them."[11] After bracing the mattress patches with four-by-six-inch shoring beams, Robertson's team turned to fortifying the bulkhead between the two firerooms.

Flooding temporarily slowed, but *Borie*'s rolling and pitching now stirred interior waves that lapped against bulkheads and hull plates. Floating debris—rags, paper, cigarette butts, coffee cups—topped the dross. But heavier items—floor plates, tools, empty fuel drums—stirred below the surface, banging bulkheads, machinery, and piping.[12]

When Robert Jefferis first arrived to help with damage control, he "found the water around my knees." But later, when ordered out, "the onrushing water pressure had simply removed the plates and there was nothing under my feet." Luckily, "I managed to grasp a rail as I fell and McKay [twenty-year-old Fireman 2/c Daniel G. McKay] caught my arm and helped pull me to firm footing."[13]

For the moment, *Borie*'s steamtight, watertight turbines spun apace. But flooding deepened the ship's draft, reduced buoyancy and speed, and hampered maneuvering. Even in the best of circumstances, *Borie*'s turning radius—a four-stacker design flaw—was far bigger than *U-405*'s. Taking advantage, *U-405*'s *kommandant* began steering his vessel counterclockwise.

The disparity seemed insuperable. "Bring her left, dammit!" Hutchins kept imploring the new helmsman. "Bring her left!"

"But Captain, I *am* left," he pleaded (just as Aikenhead had before).[14] Sure enough, a glance at the bridge compass needle confirmed *Borie* was turning.

The U-boat clung to a narrow lead on what resembled a floating merry-go-round—its stern (and after torpedo tube) aimed menacingly at *Borie*. Deeming it worth trying, Hutch ordered Larry Quinn (*Borie*'s torpedo and depth charge officer) to have port torpedo tubes cranked out.

Stationed at the mount's pointer station, Tom Neary, a torpedoman's mate from Jersey City, aimed its three tubes by matching pointers with torpedo director readings. Then, when Larry pushed the firing button, a powerful "woosh" expelled a "fish." The torpedo promptly sped off but, buffeted by seas, went wildly astray.

Occasionally, out of the corner of his eye, Hutch spotted the float light dropped when *Borie* first depth-charged *U-405*. Mindful of *Borie*'s upcoming rendezvous with TG 21.14, the sight brought some comfort. Despite roiling this patch of ocean, neither *Borie* (the carousel "hound") nor *U-405* (the carousel "hare") had strayed far from their first point of contact.

Still, the concentric chase, Hutchins groused to XO Brown, was "like ring around the rosy [*sic*]." "To my dying day," Hutch explained afterwards to Mackland, "the sub's movements [would] always be the vicious circle."[15]

Finally fed up, Hutchins decided to be cagey.

When Hutchins ordered "out light!" Tom Morris promptly doused the beacon. Sea and sky went black, transforming the duel into a high-seas guessing game.

Hutch "was certain he [*U-405*] would flee, gambling that we [*Borie*] couldn't pick him up again in our searchlight."[16] But, merely by prolonging the match, Hutch was gambling too.

With everyone else ordered out of the forward engine room, Mike Brown, Bill Green, and Mario Pagnotta now stood chest deep in water. Abandoning the space would mean losing its turbines and generators. Bottom line, all the essentials for *Borie*'s motive power (electricity, watertight integrity, clean-burning fuel, and pristine feed water) hung in the balance.

It was a godsend, then, that *U-405*'s beleaguered *kommandant* jumped at the bait. Radar plot clearly showed *Borie*'s quarry straightening for a run northeast. Range four hundred yards.

"On light!"

Tom Morris' beam, slicing through the mist, locked on *U-405*'s cratered conning tower and barren decks.

Another (penultimate) burst of speed brought *Borie* neck and neck with the U-boat, this time broadside to starboard, range two hundred yards.

"Commence firing!"

"We had stood by," said Oakley Hamilton, number four's gun captain, "hoping he would call us again."[17]

Indeed, Hamilton's, Reynolds', and Kurz's 4-inchers might well have dealt the final blows, but, in John Hersey's estimation, "sinking the enemy by crashing into him was still an obsession on board *Borie*." Sure enough, "Lieut. Hutchins ordered a collision course."[18]

But so, by all accounts, did Hopmann (or his successor.)

As "we swerved right to ram," Hutchins told Mackland, *U-405*'s "precipitous swing left changed my mind."[19]

Flashing what John Hersey called "instantaneous combat genius," Hutchins reacted immediately: "Port engine back full, starboard engine stop, hard left rudder!"

Borie's stern swung right, skidding "to a stop only 50 yards away and a little ahead of the U-boat."

"Okay Larry," Hutch ordered Quinn, "give 'em the starboard battery."[20]

Quinn flicked three switches and three K-gun charges—one each from the forward, center, and after gun*—arched into the sky. "Quicker than it can be told," Hutch told Mackland, "the barrage completely straddled the conning tower."[21]

---

*"These had been set," Hutchins specified in his subsequent oral history, "at 30-foot depth with 50-yard [range] impulse charges in the forward and after [K] guns and 75-yard impulse in the center gun."

To Ken Reynolds, the "flock of depth charges" looked to be a "knockout punch."[22]

"All exploded at thirty feet [deep]," recalled Bob Maher. "Almost knocked *us* over."[23]

"The submarine," in Hersey's telling, "lurched out of the water like a hurt mammal and came to a stop very close to *Borie*'s flank."[24]

Knocked out. Stopped dead. Yet somehow, marveled Bob Maher, *U-405* "just would not give up. They turned toward our stern and tried to get away."[25]

Hutch's flash of combat genius, meanwhile, had nearly knocked out *Borie* as well. Under severe strain, patches in the forward engine room gave way. With water reaching neck level, Mike Brown ordered Green and Pagnotta out. Mike stayed behind. But for how long?

"The officers on the bridge," wrote Hersey, "have a very hazy memory of what happened next." Said Hutchins: "The ensuing chase lasted several more minutes. One fish was fired which missed the submarine's bow out [by] ten feet." After this, "we continued to close, scoring a very, very effective hit in his starboard diesel exhaust."[26]

U-405 slowed "almost to a stop." Two Very pistol flares shot out of the conning tower. About fifteen men went over the side, five of them, obviously injured, lowered in yellow rafts. Shouts of "*kamarad*" convinced Hutchins to call cease-fire, but not before Ken Reynolds' bow gun fired parting shots. "A direct hit caught his conning tower," Hutchins recalled. "We watched the bridge structure, with several men on it, fly completely off."[27]

Water continued pouring into *U-405*, steadily lifting its bow. Finally, at 2:57 a.m., one hour and four minutes into the duel, *U-405* slid down stern first, exploding just below the surface. "One second the U-boat was there, wallowing in heavy sea," Reynolds recalled. "Then there was only oil and wreckage."[28]

The reaction on board *Borie* was immediate. "A yell went up from all hands," recalled Hutchins. "Men clasping each other and patting each other on the back." Ship's doctor Walt Merscher recalled being "pretty fagged." But, having treated just four shrapnel wounds, none of them serious, Merscher soon got swept up in the "feeling of great celebration."[29]

Meanwhile, battle's end afforded gun one's Ken Reynolds his "first chance to think over what had happened." With it came an epiphany—likely shared by others: "Even without considering the rips and holes that scarred the ship, *Borie* wasn't the same. Men you'd nodded to before and said hello and then thought nothing more about seemed different."

As *Borie* changed to course 240° true, *U-405* survivors, still illuminated by Tommy Morris' searchlight, bobbed just off the destroyer's port bow. "For a few seconds," Reynolds recalled, "our lights stayed on them. I could see the men straining, splashing toward us."[30]

"With the hope of picking up a few of them," Hutchins maneuvered closer. That is, until he saw a flare on the horizon and heard a warning from Sonarman Earl Potter: "Torpedoes, bearing 220."

Hutchins wasted no time. "Lights out! Hard to port! Heading 220, all available speed."[31]

The sudden turn carried *Borie*'s bow straight through the cluster of yellow rafts. Directly below him, Bob Maher saw "the face of one young boy. His eyes were wide and his mouth open as he extended both arms, hoping we would pick him up."[32]

Soon, said Reynolds, "There was only blackness again." He turned fatalistic. "Out there were men who'd be alive only a few minutes. They had lost, so they must die."[33]

38 | ON BORROWED TIME

***BORIE* WAS AFLOAT**, under way—and on borrowed time.

Hutchins considered damage "exceedingly serious. The forward engine room was completely out of commission. Speed on the one remaining engine was fluctuating and not determined very accurately."

Flooding had knocked out main generators. Except for gasoline-fueled auxiliaries, emergency battle lanterns, and flashlights, *Borie* was without electrical power. "This handicapped our damage control."

Uncertain speed reduced *Borie*'s prospects for rendezvousing with *Card*, as did radio and radar constraints. "The only means of operating radio was by cutting in the auxiliary generator. We also had this piped into the SL [surface search] radar. We kept these two pieces of equipment going while we had fuel. Since gasoline had been used first in the handy billy pumps to control the level of water, we had only a little available for radio purposes."

Mindful of this—and reluctant to break radio silence—Hutchins sent just two messages to *Card*. The first at 3:05 a.m., the second at 4:52 a.m.

Fuel status concerned him: "Seep samples showed our oil badly contaminated." As bad, "trailing behind us was a tremendous slick which any U-boat could follow."

Still, "feed water was our biggest problem." Competing demands—chasing down *U-405* while battling engine room flooding—had overtaxed plant capacity to circulate steam and simultaneously expel seawater. Having to exhaust steam to the atmosphere "used up most of our feed water."

Mike Brown secured boilers three and four. But even with steam pressure halved in one and two, all usable feed water would soon be expended and "salt water carried across to the turbines."[1]

Damage control personnel gave their all to ward off calamity. Amidst fears its breach might trigger boiler explosions, Eggs Robertson, Shipfitter Mingo Concha, and Paul Brabant, a twenty-year-old carpenter's mate from Minneapolis, went below to reinforce the sagging bulkhead between the forward engine room and number two fireroom.

Leading the way, Robertson skirted boilers and piping to find solid backstops, then called up shoring-beam measurements to Concha and Brabant. Once beams were cut to size, lowered, and positioned, the three men wedged them in place.[2]

An even riskier job called for a volunteer. Earlier, during failed attempts to stem flooding in the forward engine room, a cross-connection had been made to the aft engine room's bilge pump. The drain cutoff valve used to establish the link remained open. To save the aft engine room, it had to be closed.

Machinist's Mate Irving Saum agreed to try. To reach the valve, Saum, stripped to dungarees, plunged into cold, murky water ten feet deep. As Hutchins told *Life*'s Mackland, "We never expected to see him again."

Holding his breath and dodging debris, Saum groped his way to the valve and struggled to close it. The twenty-five-year-old machinist's mate finally succeeded, but only after breaking several bones in his hand. Somehow, Saum kept his composure. Hand swollen and lungs near bursting, he returned to the surface, shivering and "dripping with filth."[3]

Meanwhile, Hutchins ordered lighten ship. "All hands turned to in removing topside weight." Anything "not essential to get the ship back to port was thrown over the side."

This included everything from Electrician's Mate Tommy Morris' searchlight to much of *Borie*'s residual fighting capacity: "The rest of the torpedoes were fired. We threw over all machine guns and saved only enough [4-inch] ammunition to fight any last defensive action—ten rounds per gun."[4]

Depth charge disposal proved fraught. Despite detonators being set to safe, the first two ashcans dropped overboard exploded unexpectedly. Frank Cronin had detonators entirely removed before releasing the rest.

Walter Kurz's deckhands handled some of the most challenging work, deep-sixing heavier pieces of equipment, such as the anchor chains, torpedo tubes, and gun director.

Maher had been specifically admonished by Hutchins not to let the director "come down on my bridge." This posed a real challenge. Not only was the director heavy—Maher guessed as much as a ton—but the navigation bridge extended several feet farther out on both sides than the flying bridge.

Crowding around the director base, Maher, Jim Allegri, and several deckhands used prying bars and wedges to lift and tilt it. Then, as *Borie* heeled heavily to starboard, everybody shoved. To Maher's relief, the director "dropped neatly into the sea."[5]

Letting go of *Borie*'s captain's gig, lifeboat, and anchor chain—symbols of connection to harbor and home—stirred emotions. "We still had our rafts," said Hutchins, but after deckhands "chopped a hole in the lifeboat and gave it to the waves, I watched eyes sober as it sank." And so with the anchor chain, which plunged to the bottom "with a long, rattling roar."[6]

The crew worked without sleep, food, or water all that night and on into a morning wreathed in fog. *Borie* was barely under way; its best hope rested on somehow being discovered by the task group. Radar and radio might well help, but gasoline for the auxiliary generator had been exhausted.

Then Robert H. Lord, a twenty-four-year-old lieutenant (junior grade) from Dorchester, Massachusetts, hit on an idea. Lord, a Holy Cross and V-7 graduate who'd joined the ship's communications department in Casablanca, recalled seeing some lighter fluid on another officer's desk. It might work in the auxiliary generator. "Word was passed," wrote John Hersey, "to send all lighter fluid to the radio shack."[7]

Consolidating small contributions from the crew, two *Borie* radiomen (Pete Clubb and Cameron Gresh, a twenty-two-year-old Pennsylvanian) coaxed the generator back to life long enough for Gresh to tap out *Borie*'s prospects: "Can steam another two hours. Commencing to sink."[8]

Hutchins described the engineering plant's demise: "The starboard turbine continued to function until about nine o'clock, at which time the salt in the system blocked it."[9] The ship went dead in the water.

It was time, Hutchins decided, to play "our last card." Resuscitating the auxiliary generator "with medicinal alcohol from the ship's doctor—mixed with kerosene, to slow down the explosive force—[we were able] "to send our last direction finder signals."[10]

⊕

Card copied only fragments of *Borie*'s predawn dispatches. Fortunately, the 4:52 a.m. intercept revealed *Borie*'s position (49° 08′ N, 31° 26′ W), course (000° T), speed (ten knots), and something of its difficulties ("May have to abandon —— [garble]"). Two hours later, with *Card* steaming on course 210° true roughly sixty miles northeast of *Borie*'s last known (4:52 a.m.) position, two VC-9 Avengers took off in search. Three hours later, bedeviled by bad weather and unable to locate *Borie*, the aircraft returned.

At 10:40 a.m., suspecting that *Borie* might have passed astern, Buster Isbell ordered a countermarch. About twenty minutes later, on course 040° true, *Card*'s Huff-Duff got a bearing on *Borie*'s last transmission.

Help closed in. At 11:10 a.m., sister *Clemson*-class destroyers *Goff* and *Barry* received orders to "light off all boilers and be ready for any emergency." Ten minutes later, two more Avengers catapulted, their pilots directed to "search for *BORIE* along HF/DF bearings varying from 020° T. to 138° T."[11]

The Avenger piloted by Alexander McAuslan was first to spot *Borie*, fourteen miles northeast of *Card*. Then, at 11:48 a.m., as detailed in *Card*'s war diary: "Sighted *BORIE* at 15,000 yards . . . making little headway but reporting no immediate danger of sinking."[12]

"We were in sight of her this morning," *Card*'s Henry Babson jotted in his furtive personal journal, "throwing out steam like a locomotive."[13]

Via signal light, Buster Isbell asked Hutchins how things were going.

"I want to save this bucket if I can," Hutch replied. "Give me a few hours."[14]

Isbell's concurrence touched off valiant but futile efforts which consumed—arguably squandered—precious daylight hours.

Borie's two foremost needs were gasoline and pure feed water. At 2:00 p.m., with Avengers watching overhead and *Barry* screening, *Goff* went alongside

Card. Twenty more minutes ticked off before *Goff*—supplied with lengths of fire hose—set off towards Hutchins' floundering ship.

Huge waves made it impossible for *Goff* to go alongside *Borie*. It took until 3 p.m. for *Goff* to maneuver bow to bow—no small feat. Then more precious time to get a line across and transfer gasoline. By now, prospects of transferring feed water must have seemed dim. At 3:53 p.m., *Goff* edged away from *Borie*, leaving Charles Hutchins to confront reality.

Darkness was at hand, seas were mounting, and weather worsening. Phil Brown had just returned from inspecting ship's compartments. The prognosis looked hopeless.

"The *Borie* was nothing but torpedo bait," Hutchins concluded. "If the U-boats didn't get us at dusk, we would slowly founder. In either event, all aboard might be lost."[15]

He signaled Isbell: "I don't believe we can make it."[16]

Hutchins' responsibilities encompassed one ship and 157 men, Buster Isbell's four ships, two dozen aircraft, and more than 1,200 officers, sailors, and airmen. What's more, as Isbell later told reporters, "We were quite sure there were submarines in the area." Under such a threat, "a carrier is pretty helpless thing left alone with the two destroyers picking up survivors."[17]

As recorded in *Goff*'s war diary at 4:30 p.m.: "USS *BORIE* preparing to abandon ship. *GOFF* standing by to pick up survivors, *BARRY* approaching to aid in rescue."[18]

⊕

"After we had done what we could," Phil Brown later wrote Gully Brown, "Mike and I were sitting on the bridge. We talked over old times. He wasn't the least bit worried about going over the side."[19]

When Bob Maher heard the abandon-ship order, part of him felt miffed. "I was wearing a brand-new red Kearny High School warmup coat my brother had given me. Everyone, including the captain, had admired it."[20] Resignedly, Bob shed the coat, inflated his life belt—a rubber tube under his arms—and went to his abandon-ship station.

Farther aft, shipmates roused Machinist Mate Bill Howard from a deep sleep—his first minutes of respite in twenty-four hours. "Come on, Howard," they shouted, "We have to go!" Bill, still groggy, donned a thick foul-weather jacket. "An old tar," he explained decades later, "once told me it would help keep a layer of warmer water between my body and the sea. I think the jacket saved me."[21]

At 4:44 p.m., according to *Goff*'s war diary: "*BORIE* commenced launching life rafts."[22]

Each of *Borie*'s rafts—rectangular "donuts" fabricated from thick balsa swathed in canvas—accommodated, depending on its size, anywhere from ten to twenty-five men. Once in the water, occupants stood on a latticed wood floor suspended by rope netting, the clothes they wore and the heat of adjacent bodies the only protection from the elements. Men unable to fit inside dangled from handholds along the outer rim.

"Because of the high winds and waves," said Bob Maher, "rafts on the starboard side would not move."[23] Seven usable life rafts somehow had to accommodate *Borie*'s 157 souls.

There was no disorder at first—*Borie* was being abandoned, not scuttled. "We threw rafts over the port side, attached to ropes," Eggs Robertson recalled. "The crew then slid down the ropes to the rafts. While going over the side we could see our sister ship [*Goff*], only a stone's throw away."[24]

It wasn't long, though, before conditions—not least the temperature—induced apprehension and confusion.

"Cold?" marveled Water Tender Kenneth L. O'Kelly, then an eight-year Navy veteran. "It was 48 degrees—but that doesn't describe just how cold it was."[25]

Borie was heeling to starboard as Bob Maher, rappelling down its hull, crossed over a bead of armor six inches thick. He was past the obstruction when the ship rolled back. "The beading hit me on the top of the head and drove me deep into the water."[26]

Such mishaps gave others second thoughts. Bill Howard, already in a raft, watched as one young sailor started down a knotted rope. "He put his foot in to test the water and then started back up, but the bosun cut the rope and in he went."[27]

Ken O'Kelly ignored the ropes entirely. Instead: "It was a question of jumping whenever you got the nerve up." Once in, "men tried to catch the rafts that swirled by."[28]

As Robertson put it, "Rafts drifted apart, and it was quite a job to corral the men in the water."[29]

With so many survivors splashing about, rafts endangered as well as sheltered. When Bob Maher came to the surface, he spotted two rafts close by. "One was overflowing, so I swam to the other, which was almost empty. I had just reached it when I found myself crushed between the two."[30] Had seas not pulled the donuts apart, Maher might have been squeezed to death. As it was, his life belt deflated.

39 | STILL OUT THERE

***BORIE*'S SENIOR OFFICERS** went off last. As Phil Brown's letter explained to Gully Brown, "Mike and Curly [Dietz] went over just ahead of me. We all were to go to different rafts. Mike started out to swim it alone."[1]

Hutchins, the very last in the water, carried *Borie*'s battle flag with him. "The operation," he told *Life*'s Mackland, "hadn't looked too forbidding aboard *Borie*. The rescue ships drifting towards us, broadside to the gale, seemed very close. But in the water, they were far away."[2]

Eventually, the seven rafts set off in two groups, one towards *Goff*, the other towards *Barry*. Almost immediately, though, one raft capsized, spilling its occupants.

"I wound up on three rafts lashed together," said Robertson. "Our skipper was with us, but he stayed in the water hanging on a paddle."[3]

Hutchins "looked at my men huddling against the cold. Eyes were beginning to glaze. I could see morale drop."[4]

Indeed, in Ken O'Kelly's mind, "it became tempting to let go and forget the whole thing."[5]

Bob Maher's raft, part of the second group, was so full its occupants held on to each other "like a bunch of grapes." Still, "we began to take the situation in stride." A few hearty souls even sang, though not for long. "Every time you opened your mouth you got it full of water."[6]

As early as 5:15 p.m., according to its war diary, *Goff* began pulling in survivors.[7] "To get the men aboard," said Robertson, "our sister ship would pull up close by and allow the waves to wash the men up to the side of the ship where they would grab ropes and climb up."[8]

Easier said than done. "By the time rescuers threw out lines," said O'Kelly, "some men were so stiff they couldn't hold on."[9]

For more than a few, *Goff*'s propeller guards—the skeletal appendages jutting to either side of the fantail—seemed to offer an easier exit from the sea. Seeing his chance, Robertson "worked my way to the stern, where the screw guards came down to the water. I got on when the guards were underwater and climbed up on the deck."

Some unfortunates, however, misjudged—and paid a high price. Robertson "saw men lose their lives when the screw guard came down on their heads."[10]

Mike Brown was one of these. As Phil Brown described it to Gully: "He got over to the *Goff*, I know. Several of the men saw Mike trying to get on board over the propeller guard and that he was hit in the head by it."[11] Mike's swimming prowess may have undone him. In O'Kelly's account: "Swimming in the rough sea was impossible. The chief engineer tried it. By the time he had reached the *Goff* he was exhausted."[12]

The limits of exertion also claimed Ensign St. John, the former Texas high school football coach. As Bob Jefferis, his closest friend, recalled, "St. John was halfway up the side of [*Goff*] when he saw a group of men too far gone to help themselves aboard. Exhausted as he must have been, he dropped back into the sea with them."[13] According to the U.S. Navy's official postmortem: "After helping to lift all but four or five to safety, Ens. St. John and the men [still] on the raft were swept under the stern of the ship and to their deaths."[14]

Even reaching *Goff*'s deck didn't save eighteen-year-old Jimmy Winn, a seaman first class from Danville, Virginia. "James became unconscious from the cold," Charles Hutchins later wrote Winn's parents, "and I had taken him under one arm. With another boy under my other arm, I thought we were all set." Later, after all three were pulled on board, Hutch "went looking for Winn and Isenberg,* the other boy, only to find that, somehow, James had fallen back into the sea."[15]

*Harold J. Isenberg, a twenty-three-year-old coxswain from Brooklyn, New York.

"As I write this," Henry Babson confided to his journal, "they are still out there looking for the survivors. It got real dark shortly after they abandoned the *Borie*, and to make matters worse, it is raining out and a fog is setting in. For a little while, our lookouts were reporting lights in the water. Some flares were being shot off by the guys in water."[16]

Goff's war diary entries portray an operation of fits and starts. At 6:19 p.m., for example, *Goff* "ceased rescue operations, having taken aboard 104 survivors." But then, three hours later: "Came alongside, picked up three men."[17]

In the darkness, rescuers lost track of survivors—and survivors of rescuers. Bob Maher recalled a fatal brush with *Barry*: "She was going to hit us with her bow, dead center." Only the beam of a raft occupant's flashlight averted total disaster. Nevertheless, *Barry*'s crushing sideswipe drowned many. "After the pass, we remained alone in the darkness again. About a dozen men were still on, or holding on to, the raft, and we were all very wary."[18]

At 10:25 p.m., per *Goff*'s war diary: "*BARRY* reported sighting life raft and proceeding to pick up survivors."[19]

"The ship hit us again," said Maher, who may well have been on the raft in question. But this time, "A mad scramble ensued as we all tried to climb aboard."

At first, Bob held back to assist an officer alongside him (it might have been Robert Lord). "I hit him on the shoulder to alert him, but he didn't respond." Then, seeing the propeller guard within reach, Maher "knew this was my best chance and I had to go." Standing to grab the guard as *Barry* rolled away, Maher again got slammed on the head as the ship lurched back.

"I was conscious long enough to see the guard crush the officer's head against the raft. Then I was out cold."[20]

Though suspended temporarily at 4 a.m. to investigate suspected U-boat contacts, the search for survivors continued through the night. As dawn approached the tally of the *Borie*'s missing—and presumed lost—was twenty-seven. Meanwhile, the 130 survivors—108 on board *Goff*, 22 on board *Barry**—were grateful just to be alive.

A fortunate few were pulled on board cold but little worse for wear. One, Ken O'Kelly, rescued by *Goff* at about 6 p.m., considered himself lucky to be rescued so soon. Said another, Robert Jefferis, "I was in the water four hours and twenty minutes, and I guess I'm not giving anything away to say that the water was definitely cold. Worst reaction was from leg cramps. . . . *Goff* and her officers were mostly friends of mine—and it was really nice to see them."[21]

For most survivors, however, revival—and thanksgiving—took more time. Many, in Hutchins' estimation, "suffered badly from shock and cold." Indeed, the skipper himself "was so frozen I couldn't walk" and "in a hot shower, continued to shiver."[22]

After he was finally dragged, semiconscious, on board *Barry*, Bob Maher was "as stiff as a board and totally helpless. I could not move a muscle, so my rescuers dragged me by the neck across the deck." It was some hours before a medic tended to him, cleaned him up, and "fed me a large shot of brandy." Though it was belated, "no time could have been better."[23]

Some later reflected on the interventions—internal, spiritual—that somehow pulled them through.

Curly Dietz, for example, decided, after being hit and submerged by *Goff*'s propeller guard, "I must get away from this and wait." But then, when he tried to paddle back, Dietz's arms hardly moved. Still, his mind refused to admit defeat. "They will come after me," he assured himself. Sure enough, minutes later, hands pulled him on board.

Presbyterian Phil Brown, dangling upside down from *Barry*'s propeller guard, "looking at the propeller slowly turning in the heavy seas," prayed,

---

*Those rescued by *Goff* included Jim Aikenhead, Jim Allegri, Carl Banks, Richard Branch, James Clubb, Ernest Gardner, Cameron Gresh, Oakley Hamilton, Bill Howard, Charles Hutchins, Harold Isenberg, Robert Jefferis, Lerten Kent, Walt Kurz, Ed Malaney, Robert Manning, Daniel McKay, Walter Merscher, Tommy Morris, George Murphy, Ken O'Kelly, Mario Pagnotta, Oliver Pederson, Earl Potter, Larry Quinn, Ken Reynolds, Ed Robertson, Irving Saum, Bill Schmalberger, Edd Shockley, David Southwick, George Sturla, and Edward Trenz. By *Barry*: Paul Brabant, Phil Brown, Walter Dietz, Carmen Driver, Bill Green, Ben Hugo, Ed Johnson, Bob Maher, Lester Moultrop, Tom Neary, Christopher Sheppard, Selig Sirota, and Dick Wenz.

"Lord if you have anything for me to do in this life here on earth, you are going to have to help me get aboard this ship." In the end, "I managed to hang on there until I was hoisted aboard."[24]

Meanwhile, the rescue of Carl Bomgardner, a fireman third class from Lebanon, Pennsylvania, had something of the cosmic about it. Bomgardner's personal savior, *Goff*'s Leon Bowmaster, a fireman first class, had hoisted Bomgardner on his shoulders and carried him below to the aft crew compartment. Bowmaster first gave Bomgardner a vigorous rubdown then dressed him in warm, heavy underwear and a pair of Bowmaster's own dungarees. Only then, as Bomgardner began to revive, did the two realize that they were hometown buddies. "My God. Leon!" Bomgardner exclaimed.[25]

At sunrise, *Goff* made a final sweep of the rescue area. At 7:25 a.m., as recorded in its war diary: "Passed four bodies floating on the surface." And five minutes later: "Passed life raft with body in it."[26]

Noted *Card*'s Henry Babson: "About a mile away, we began to see the bodies of the sailors in the water, some on their backs and [others] floating face down. They were all dead of course. It was just awful to see those fellows like that."[27]

For Bill Howard, standing at *Goff*'s rail with other *Borie* survivors, it was heartrending "looking down at my shipmates floating in their life jackets or lying on the rafts as if they were sleeping." Heartrending, too, to leave them there. But, as Howard understood, "It would have been dangerous. And besides, they would just have to be put in the sea again."[28]

For his part, having recovered enough to be up and about, Charles Hutchins stood vigil on *Goff*'s bridge. During the night *Borie* had drifted some twenty miles from where it was abandoned. It lay down by the stern, wallowing in heavy seas—a clear hazard to navigation.

Still, the old four-stacker—proven fighter and pride of its battle-scarred crew—was defiantly afloat. And would not go easily. Beginning at 9:05 a.m. *Barry* fired guns and torpedoes at *Borie*. But at 9:40 a.m., after three fish ran astray and projectiles inflicted little damage, Buster Isbell ordered TBFs to finish the job with depth bombs.

Then, as portrayed by *Life*'s Hersey: "Lieut. Hutchins stood on a strange bridge and watched his ship as a Grumman Avenger attacked with a heavy bomb and missed. A second plane hit her amidships. A third holed her again, badly. The *Borie*, her back broken, lifted her protesting bow and settled fast."[29]

EPILOGUE

TRUE HEROES

PERSISTENT BAD WEATHER delayed highlining *Borie* survivors to *Card*. "Guess they are glad to be here," Henry Babson noted on November 5. "They are all a bunch of average guys, laughing and joking."[1]

On November 7, Sheridan Bell, *Card*'s thirty-four-year-old Methodist chaplain, conducted a memorial service for the twenty-seven missing.*[2] "Only then," recalled Bob Maher, "did the true impact of our loss sink in."[3]

Card's November 9 arrival in Norfolk generated headlines coast to coast. In the *New York Times*: "Destroyer Sits Astride U-boat as Crew Battles Nazis to Death." In the *Chicago Tribune*: "U.S. Tars Fight a U-boat with Pistols, Knives." And in the *Los Angeles Times*: "Destroyer Crew in Epic Death Battle."

Newspapers big and small published stories of local interest, most inspirational or celebratory. In Baltimore's *Evening Sun*: "Maryland Men Fight in Wild Sub Battle." In the *Montclair* (New Jersey) *Times*: "Bridegroom Is a

---

*S2/c Opal Alford, S2/c Max Blane, SC2/c Warren Blouch, S2/c Charles Bonfiglio, Lt. Morrison R. Brown, PH1/c Frank Cituk, SF2/c Domingo Concha, CWT Harold DeMaio, RT1/c Frank Duke, F1/c James Fields, S2/c Lawrence Francis, WT2/c Joseph Kiszka, F1/c Joseph Lombardi, CCSTD Ralph Long, Lt. Robert Lord, Y2/c Francis McKervey, F1/c William Medved, SC2/c William Mulligan, F2/c Daniel Pouzar, COX Aguinaldo Pruneda, CQM William Shakerly, Ens. Richard St. John, F2/c Frank Swan, S2/c Richard Tull, S2/c D. L. Tyree, F1/c Andrew Wallace, S1/c James Winn.

Survivor of Destroyer *Borie*."* And in Minneapolis' *Star Tribune*: "Survivor of *Borie* Sinking Visits City, Tells of Battle with Three Nazi Subs." Others, though, conveyed tragedy. In the *Austin* (Texas) *American*: "Kilgore High Coach Killed on Destroyer." And in the *Boston Globe:* "Missing Navy Officer Wed Dorchester Girl before Going Overseas."

The plight of families still awaiting word on loved ones stirred sentiment. In covering Walter Dietz's rescue, for example, the *Boston Globe* mentioned a former Bay Stater still among the missing: "While gratified at the escape of Lieut. Dietz, concern was expressed by relatives and friends in Swampscott tonight over the safety of Lieut. Morrison R. Brown of whom no official word had been received."[4]

Residing now with her mother in Miami Beach as she awaited birth of the couple's child, Gully Brown received personal condolences. Uncle David R. Castleman, for example, wrote: "My Dear Little Gully: We all love you so much and pray that you will find comfort in your beautiful memories of this heroic man."†[5]

The Navy soon bestowed individual medals on select *Borie* crew: Navy Crosses for Charles Hutchins, Morrison R. Brown (posthumously), and Irving Saum;[6] Silver Stars for Bill Green and Mario Pagnotta; and a Legion of Merit for Phil Brown.‡

---

*On November 18, 1943, in Verona, New Jersey, with shipmates in attendance, *Borie* Boatswain's Mate Oakley Hamilton married Dorothea Reynolds. Dorothea's brother, Torpedoman's Mate Walter Reynolds, gave away the bride while another brother, Gunner's Mate Kenneth Reynolds, was best man. Torpedoman's Mate Thomas Neary and Boatswain's Mate William Schmalberger ushered. ("Dorothea Reynolds Is Wed in Verona," *Montclair* (NJ) *Times*, November 18, 1943.)

†Mike and Gully's daughter, Morrison "Sunny" Ropes Brown, was born in June 1944.

‡Separately, as announced by the Navy in March 1944, nearly two dozen VC-9 airmen were decorated for October actions. Awards included Navy Crosses for Elbert Heim, David Puckett, and Robert Stearns (his second); Distinguished Flying Crosses for Howard Avery, Wilma Fowler (his second), Stewart Holt, and Joseph Horn; a Silver Star for Phil Perabo; Air Medals for Barton Sheela, Claude Falwell (Sheela's turret gunner), and Henry Shirley (Sheela's radioman). ("22 Members of Aircraft Squadron Win Decorations for Sinking Nazi Subs" [AP], *Evening Star–News* [Culver City, CA], March 24, 1944)

Collective recognition, a Presidential Unit Citation (PUC), was awarded to all of TG 21.14 (*Card*, *Barry*, *Borie*, *Goff*, VC-1, and VC-9). The citation detailed how TG 21.14 "pressed home a vigorous offensive which was largely responsible for the complete withdrawal of hostile U-boats from . . . the United States–North Africa convoy route."

"The Suicidal Sea Campaign" headlined a Reuters dispatch dated April 24, 1944. "Rear-Admiral Francis Low, Chief of Staff of the U.S. Tenth Fleet, revealed today that 'The German U-boat today is sinking considerably less than one half of one per cent of the ships being convoyed across the Atlantic. How long Hitler can keep up this suicidal type of . . . warfare only Hitler seems to know.'"[7]

With his U-boats sinking just sixty-seven merchants during the first six months of 1944, Karl Dönitz understood *Tonnagekrieg*'s dismal prognosis as well as Hitler. Nothing could prevent the Allied invasion of France.

While Allied surface escorts still acted as deterrents, for many crews the excitement and drama of merchant convoy crossings gave way to routine, even monotony. In December 1943, when *Borie* survivors returned to Norfolk following home leave, most learned they'd been assigned to *J. Fred Talbot* (DD 156), a *Wickes*-class four-stacker being overhauled for Atlantic convoy duty. The survivors had envisioned joining a newly constructed *Borie* (DD 704). DD 704, however, wouldn't be commissioned until September 1944.*

On February 13, 1944, after shakedown, *Talbot*, skippered by Lt. Cdr. Charles Hutchins, sailed for Casablanca on convoy escort duty. "The days passed without incident," recalled Bob Maher of the round trip. "Dull, dull, dull."[8]

In late summer, *Talbot*'s home port shifted to Port Everglades, Florida. With Phil Brown in command,† *Talbot* served as a target ship for torpedo bombers.

*DD 704 joined the Pacific fleet in January 1945. On August 9, a Japanese suicide plane crashed into the ship, killing forty-eight men and wounding sixty-six.

†Commander Hutchins (1913–92) went on to command destroyer *Doran* in the Pacific. At war's end, he returned to Terre Haute, Indiana, to resume his career in paper manufacturing. ("Charles Hutchins '36," *Shipmate*, November 1992). Phil Brown (1915–2002) returned to Dillon, South Carolina, where he purchased a radio station. ("Philip Bosché Brown," *Florence Obituaries*, September 5, 2022, https://www.legacy.com/obituaries/florencenews/obituary.aspx?n=philip-bosch-brown&pid=349502)

While many *Borie* veterans had long since departed,* those remaining welcomed a return to the war's backwaters. Jim Allegri, for example, writing to his fiancée Florence Garone, described the new routines. "Tomorrow ought to be a good day. Most of the crew is going over to play baseball and have a beer party. I don't think I'll go until late in the afternoon. You see Eggs Robertson and I are going over to play a little golf."[9]

⌖

"It was a beautiful day, and it is the same way tonight," *Card*'s Henry Babson wrote in his journal on October 30, 1944, near the end of yet another uneventful U-boat-hunting voyage. "The way it looks, it hardly seems there is a war going on."[10]

Since the previous October, *Card*, now escorted by new destroyer escorts (DEs), had deployed on six more Atlantic cruises, two of them to ferry USAAF fighter aircraft to Europe.

On March 9, 1944, during a stopover for repairs in Norfolk, Arnold Isbell transferred off *Card*. "It was a surprise to all of us," Babson wrote, "but that's what happens to good captains, they advance to better things."†[11]

Card's new composite air squadron, VC-55, experienced aerial and flight-deck mishaps, but except for one serious injury and one fatality (an officer on temporary duty to assist with aircraft radar), its pilots and crews (though not all its aircraft) emerged from the voyages largely unscathed.

Not so, tragically, for a quartet of former VC-9 aviators. Two pilots went to Atlantic Ocean graves: one-time squadron XO Lt. Arnold Harwood, killed in a 1944 midair collision off Quonset, Rhode Island;[12] and two-time Navy Cross recipient Lt. Robert Stearns, killed in 1945 when his plane crashed into the North Atlantic.[13]

---

* In April, Robert Maher transferred off *Borie* to begin advanced fire-control training in Washington, DC. (Maher and Wise, *Sailors' Journey into War*, 183)

† In February 1945, after shore duty with Tenth Fleet, Isbell received orders to the Pacific to take command of fleet carrier *Yorktown* (CV 10). On March 19, while embarked as a passenger on board fleet carrier *Franklin* (CV 13), Isbell perished when Japanese bombs touched off a ship-wide conflagration. ("Capt. Arnold Isbell Dies aboard Carrier Franklin," *Pensacola* (FL) *News Journal*, May 27, 1945)

Meanwhile, for a squadron that originally aspired "to sink the Rising Sun," it was fitting though tragic that two ex-VC-9 pilots met their fates in the Pacific: Lt. Stewart E. Doty during a bombing mission over Tokyo;[14] and Navy Cross recipient Lt. Elbert Heim Jr. during an air strike against the Ryukyu Islands.[15]

At the September 1944 Allied conference in Quebec, with the Battle of the Atlantic well in hand, Winston Churchill offered to deploy a British battle fleet to the Pacific. Roosevelt accepted the offer in principle, but Ernest King vigorously opposed it. In the end he relented, although, according to Adm. Andrew Cunningham, Dudley Pound's successor as First Sea Lord,* "with very bad grace."[16]

The British took King's opposition as final proof of his Anglophobia. Perhaps so, but the British had their own ignoble motives. By lending a hand in the Pacific, Churchill aspired to reassert colonial claims—something FDR opposed.

In COMINCH's defense, he was being, as always, "tartly practical."[17] The Royal Navy's intervention entailed the same operational and logistical hurdles that had plagued Allied cooperation in the Atlantic. Meanwhile, Ernest King continued to ramrod a formidable five-ocean Navy to victory.†

Until war's end, Karl Dönitz threw U-boats into the "suicidal sea campaign." From D-Day until war's end, two hundred U-boats were lost. Upon Hitler's demise, Dönitz briefly served as Head of State (as the Führer had designated him before his own suicide). Charged with war crimes, he faced the death penalty for having waged "unrestricted submarine warfare." But after his attorney argued that the U.S. Navy had—as Adm. Chester Nimitz acknowledged—done the same in the Pacific, the Lion was instead sentenced to ten years' imprisonment.‡

---

*Stricken with brain cancer, Pound had stepped down in August and died in October.

†On December 15, 1945, Fleet Adm. Chester Nimitz relieved King as Chief of Naval Operations. (The COMINCH title had been abolished on September 29, 1945.) As a five-star admiral, King officially remained on the Navy's active list until his death on June 25, 1956.

‡Released in 1956, Dönitz died in 1980.

By December 1943, with 120 NCML Bombes installed and operating round the clock in Washington, DC, the average time required to decrypt a Kriegsmarine Enigma message had been slashed from six hundred hours to eighteen. The NCML machines ran 30 percent faster than the British four-rotor versions. As a result, most Atlantic deciphering operations were handed over to the Americans.

The Navy's and NCR's success exacted a heavy cost on Joe Desch, the man deserving the most credit. One day in November 1944, in part fed up with the wartime carnage attributable—directly or indirectly—to his invention, Desch left Building 26, vowing never to return. Six weeks later, after much coaxing, he returned, but NCML duties passed to a subordinate.

After the war, Joe Desch (1907–87) continued his NCR research while also serving as a consultant to the National Research Council on submarine warfare. In 1947, at a private ceremony at the Navy Department, Desch received the Congressional Medal for Merit. Another five decades would pass before NCML's achievements would be revealed.

Philip M. Morse (1903–85) received his Medal for Merit in 1946, the same year he became the first director of what would become Brookhaven National Laboratory, a nuclear research facility. Morse was involved in weapons research for much of the remainder of his career.

After being sidelined by Winston Churchill, Sir Henry Tizard (1885–1959) returned to Oxford University. Frederick Lindemann, Tizard's de facto successor, was deemed largely responsible for the decision to embark on strategic bombing of Germany, a decision opposed by both Tizard and Patrick Blackett (1897–1974). Researchers would find that Lindemann had wildly overestimated the campaign's projected impact. Much of the aviation strength devoted to it might well have been more effectively used in curbing the U-boat menace.

Writing in a 1946 top-secret postmortem, Francis Low (1894–1964) assessed that the "Battle of the Atlantic was . . . a battle of wits in which intelligence played a major role. Unfortunately, this fact is fully understood by a relatively small group of officers because of the highly classified nature of the subject."[18]

In reciprocal recognition of their partnership, both Kenneth Knowles and Rodger Winn received (U.S.) Legions of Merit and Orders of the British

Empire. Winn (1903–72) resumed his barrister career and in 1959 was elevated to knighthood.

During an interview late in life, retired Navy captain Knowles (1904–86) commented on the pair's distinct vantages: "Rodger had the feel of the British, of protecting ULTRA at all costs. Whereas . . . we were using ULTRA more aggressively. Winn, later on, indicated that . . . we really saved the game because we utilized ULTRA to the utmost."[19]

"Nine years ago, fresh off the St. Lawrence University campus," reported the November 9, 1950, edition of the Rochester, New York, *Democrat and Chronicle*, "Lawrence Sullivan (Larry) Quinn walked onto the practice field at East Rochester High School to take over . . . as assistant football coach.

"In '46 Quinn returned to East Rochester—this time as head coach. Quinn grins about that season. 'We . . . lost eight straight games.'

"For the next three years Quinn's kids finished second. This time, they tell you in East Rochester, it's going to be different. The Bombers have won seven in a row."[20]

For *Borie* veterans such as Larry Quinn (1920–99), wartime service postponed but didn't curtail dreams and vocations. With untimely exceptions,* most would live full and purposeful lives.

Meanwhile, their duel with *U-405* settled into the background.† Yet over the years, some *Borie* veterans periodically reconvened to reminisce, even with former enemies. A September 1988 conference in Baltimore, for example, brought *Borie* sailors and *Card* aviators together with German U-boat officers.

*James Aikenhead, just thirty-two, died of an injury suffered diving into shallow water during a picnic. ("Helmsman in Sub Battle Dies," *Evening Sun* [Baltimore, MD], August 22, 1951)

†In time, there were more enduring memorials to *Borie*'s fallen heroes. In October 1947, in Kilgore, Texas, the Kilgore Athletic Stadium was renamed R. E. St. John Memorial Stadium; ("Athletic Field Named in Memorial to Hero," *Kilgore* (TX) *News*, August 17, 1958). More recently, on June 15, 2015, as part of a ribbon-cutting ceremony and twentieth-anniversary celebration for Commander, Naval Surface Force, U.S. Pacific Fleet (ComNavSurfPac) Headquarters in San Diego, ComNavSurfPac's Building 11 was dedicated as Lt. Morrison R. Brown Hall.

"Boy, was I glad to see you!" exclaimed Alex McAuslan (1919–2013), the VC-9 pilot who found the *Borie* on November 1, 1943. Said Jim Allegri (1920–2012) of the rescue effort: "What stays vivid is the moment someone helped saved your life." Others, including William Schmalberger (1919–2006) and Edgar T. "Eggs" Robertson nodded agreement.[21]

In 1992, Robert Maher (1919–2013), at the invitation of former *kommandant* Wilhelm Brauel (1914–2002), flew to Germany to attend a *U-256* crew reunion. "How many men," he remarked before setting off, "come face to face with the enemy in friendship?"[22]

As far as can be determined, all the sailors and airmen mentioned here have passed away. What remains, however, is an indelible bond earned by those who served on, below, or above the sea. The bond extends to those who never returned.

Perhaps Donald F. Fennessey's obituary best describes its essence. In March 1943, Fennessey, a twenty-two-year-old cadet midshipman, survived the U-boat sinking of Liberty ship *James Smith* in the South Atlantic. His October 2020 death marked the final voyage of an accomplished and "boundlessly proud" centenarian.

Fennessey, said his obituary, "served on tankers and Liberty ships, sailing around the world. Always quick to deflect praise for his wartime service, he would say that the true heroes could be found at the bottom of the sea."[23]

GLOSSARY OF TERMS AND ACRONYMS

ALLIED COMMAND ACRONYMS

ASWORG	Anti-Submarine Warfare Operations Research Group
CIGS	Chiefs of the (British) Imperial General Staff
CINCLANT	Commander in Chief Atlantic Fleet
CINCPAC	Commander in Chief Pacific Fleet
CinCUS (later COMINCH)	Commander in Chief United States Fleet
CNO	Chief of Naval Operations
COIC	(U.S. Navy) Combined Operations and Intelligence Center
ComAirLant	Commander Naval Air Force U.S. Atlantic Fleet
ComNavSurfPac	Commander Naval Surface Force U.S. Pacific Fleet
ComPaSeaFron	Commander Panama Sea Frontier
ComSoLant	Commander South Atlantic Force
DNI	(British) Director of Naval Intelligence
IGS	(British) Imperial General Staff
JCS	(U.S.) Joint Chiefs of Staff
NID	(Royal) Naval Intelligence Division
OIC	(British Admiralty) Operational Intelligence Centre
ONI	(U.S.) Office of Naval Intelligence
ONC	(U.S.) Office of Naval Communications
OP-20-G	Office of the Chief of Naval Operations, branch 20, communications subsection G
RAF	Royal Air Force
RCN	Royal Canadian Navy
RDF	radio direction finding
RFC	Royal Flying Corps
RN	Royal Navy

USAAF (or AAF)	U.S. Army Air Forces
USAT	U.S. Army Transport
USN	U.S. Navy
USNR	U.S. Naval Reserve
WAC	(RN) Western Approaches Command
WATU	Western Approaches Tactical Unit

Code Names for Allied Operations and Conferences

ABC-1	American British Conversations; March 1941 agreement defining Anglo-American prewar roles
Arcadia	Code name for the First Anglo-American Washington Conference in January 1942
Bolero	The buildup of Allied forces in the British Isles for Operation Roundup
Gymnast	Original designation for proposed 1942 Allied invasion of Northwest Africa
Husky	July 1943 Allied invasion of Sicily
Riviera	August 1941 Anglo-American Conference off Argentia, Newfoundland
Roundup	Proposed 1943 Allied invasion of Northern Europe
Sledgehammer	Proposed 1942 invasion of Occupied France
Symbol	January 1943 Anglo-American conference in Casablanca, Morocco
Torch	Ultimate designation for November 1942 Anglo-American invasion of North Africa
WPL-51	Western Hemisphere Defence Plan Number 4

Allied Merchant Convoy Designations

HX	Halifax →
ON	Outbound north (Liverpool → Halifax)
SC	Sydney Cape Breton →
SL	Sierra Leone → Liverpool
TB/BT	Trinidad ←→ Bahia
TM	Trinidad → Mediterranean
UG/GU	U.S. ←→ Gibraltar

Other Acronyms

ACV	auxiliary aircraft carriers
AP	Associated Press

ASDIC	Anti-Submarine Division–related activities
ASV	Air Surface Vessel (radar)
ASW	antisubmarine warfare
AVG	aircraft escort vessel
BOAC	British Overseas Airways Corporation
BP	Bletchley Park
BTM	British Tabulating Machine Company
CAMS	(British) catapult aircraft merchant ships
CAP	combat air patrol
CH	Chain Home
CHOP	change of operational control
CO	commanding officer
CVE	escort carrier
DE	destroyer escort
D/F	direction finding
DEMS	(British) defensively equipped merchant ships
DesRon	destroyer squadron
EASTOMP	East Ocean Meeting Point
EOT	engine order telegraph
GC&CS	(British) Government Code and Cypher School
GQ	General Quarters
HF/DF	high-frequency direction finding (or Huff-Duff)
IBM	International Business Machines Company
INS	International News Service
LR	long-range (aircraft)
LSO	landing signal officer
MAC	(British) merchant aircraft carrier
MIT	Massachusetts Institute of Technology
MOEF	Mid-Ocean Escort Force
MOMP	Mid-Ocean Meeting Point
MP	Military Police
NAAFI	Navy, Army and Air Force Institutes
NCR	National Cash Register Company
NCML	(U.S.) Naval Computing Machine Laboratory
OOD	officer of the deck
OR	operations research

PC	patrol craft
PhD	doctorate degree
POW	prisoner of war
PPI	plan position indicator
PUC	Presidential Unit Citation
RADAR	radio direction and ranging (radar after first mention)
SIGINT	signals intelligence
SL	surface-search microwave radar
SOE	senior officer escorts
sonar	sound navigation and ranging
SP	Shore Patrol
TG	task group
TU	task unit
UA	unauthorized absence
UP	United Press
USMMA	U.S. Merchant Marine Academy
USO	United Service Organizations
VLR	very-long-range
WAVES	(U.S.) Women Accepted for Volunteer Emergency Service
WOMP	West Ocean Meeting Point
WRENS	Women's Royal Naval Service
WSA	War Shipping Administration
XO	executive officer

German-Language Terms and Titles

Beobachtungsdienst (B-Dienst)	(Kriegsmarine) Signal Intelligence Service
Befehlshaber der Unterseeboote (BdU)	commander of Kriegsmarine submarines
Federapparat Torpedo	spring-operated torpedo
Fregattenkapitän	commander (officer rank)
Gruppe Leuthen	U-boat group
Gruppe Rossbach	U-boat group
Gruppe Schlieffen	U-boat group
Gruppe Siegfried	U-boat group
Gruppe Trutz	(U-boat) Group Defiance

glückliche Zeit	"The Happy Time"
Hauptschlag	big blow
Heer	army
Kapitänleutnant	lieutenant (officer rank)
Kommandant	commanding officer
Korvettenkapitän	lieutenant commander (officer rank)
Kriegsmarine	erman navy (1935–45, literally War Navy)
Leutnant zur See	ensign (officer rank)
Löwe	lion
Luftwaffe	German air force
Milchkühe	milk cow
Nordsee Enten	North Sea ducks
Oberleutnant zur See	lieutenant-senior (officer rank)
Oberbefehlshaber der Kriegsmarine	supreme commander of the Kriegsmarine
Paukenschlag	roll of the Drums
Reichsmarine	German navy (1918–35)
Rudeltaktik	(U-boat) pack tactics
Schnorkel	snorkel
Seekühe	sea cow
Shutzstaffel (SS)	Protection Squadron (paramilitary)
Tonnagekrieg	tonnage war
Wehrmacht	German armed forces (1933–45)
Zaunkönig	Wren (acoustic torpedo)

U-BOAT TYPES

Type II	Small, prewar U-boat; *Nordsee Enten*
Type VII	Midsize, medium-range
Type VIIC	Later version of type VII
Type IX	Large, long-range; *Seekühe*
Type IXC	Larger, long-range; *Seekühe*
Type XB	U-tanker converted from minelayer
Type XIII	shallow-water version of Type XXI
Type XIV	U-tanker; *Milchkühe*
Type XXI	Replacement for Type VII and Type IX; electro-boat
Type XXVI	Walter boat

NOTES

INTRODUCTION

1. Robert A. Maher and Capt. James E. Wise Jr., *Sailors' Journey into War* (Kent, OH: Kent State University Press, 1998), 20.
2. Patrick Abbazia, *Mr. Roosevelt's Navy: The Private War of the U.S. Atlantic Fleet, 1939–1942* (Annapolis, MD: Naval Institute Press, 1975), 75, 76.
3. "U-Boat Warfare, Volume 351: debated on Tuesday 26 September 1939," *House of Commons Hansard,* https://hansard.parliament.uk/Commons/1939-09-26/debates/b9258fd9-1c2a-4b5c-8e5b-9b64c8407585/U-BoatWarfare (accessed on March 12, 2022).
4. Winston S. Churchill, *The Second World War,* volume V, *Closing the Ring* (Boston: Houghton Mifflin, 1979), 6.
5. Jonathan Dimbleby, *The Battle of the Atlantic: How the Allies Won the War* (New York: Oxford University Press, 2016), xxvi.

CHAPTER 1. SHOVE OFF

1. "N.J. Shipyards Reap Harvest" (AP), *Morning Call* (Paterson, NJ), July 3, 1940.
2. Maher and Wise, *Sailors' Journey into War,* 3–14.
3. Whitten Morse, "Virginia Becomes an Armed Camp," *Richmond* (VA) *Times Dispatch,* December 8, 1940; "Virginia Reaps Billion-Dollar Harvest from War Abroad and Defense at Home," *Richmond* (VA) *Times Dispatch,* December 27, 1940.
4. Maher and Wise, *Sailors' Journey into War,* 19–22.

CHAPTER 2. FOUR-STACKERS

1. Hanson W. Baldwin, "Our Five New Destroyers," *Baltimore Sun,* December 4, 1932.
2. "Those 'Overage' Destroyers," *St. Louis Post-Dispatch,* September 8, 1940.

3. Capt. S. W. Roskill, DSC, RN, *The War at Sea 1939–1945*, vol. I, *The Defensive* (London: Her Majesty's Stationery Office, 1954), 134.
4. Craig L. Symonds, *World War II at Sea: A Global History* (New York: Oxford University Press, 2018), 109.
5. Roskill, *War at Sea*, I:348.
6. Abbazia, *Mr. Roosevelt's Navy*, 94.
7. Midn. Brian F. Hussey Jr., *The U.S. Navy, the Neutrality Patrol, and Atlantic Fleet Escort Operations, 1939–1941*, Trident Scholar Report (Annapolis, MD: U.S. Naval Academy, 1991), 47.
8. The Ambassador in the United Kingdom (Kennedy) to the Secretary of State, London, August 15, 1940, in *Foreign Relations of the United States Diplomatic Papers, 1940, the British Commonwealth, the Soviet Union, the Near East and Africa, Volume III*, [U.S. State Department] *Office of the Historian*, https://history.state.gov/historicaldocuments/frus1940v03/d59 (accessed February 13, 2022).
9. "Out to Sea under White Ensign on Former U.S. Navy Destroyer," *Ottawa* (ON, Canada) *Citizen*, October 29, 1940.
10. Abbazia, *Mr. Roosevelt's Navy*, 94.
11. "Those 'Overage' Destroyers."
12. Murney Mintzer (McClure Newspaper Syndicate), "Overbuilding of Types Is Bane of Navy," *Sandusky* (OH) *Register*, February 23, 1938.
13. Capt. Donald I. Thomas, USN (Ret.), "The Texas Navy: 1940," *Shipmate*, January/February 1993.
14. Maher and Wise, *Sailors' Journey into War*, 26–27.

Chapter 3. Wizard War

1. "British Airliner *Clare* Arrives on Second of Transocean Trips," (Montreal, Canada) *Gazette*, August 16, 1940.
2. "Sir Henry Tizard Dead at 74; British Scientist," *Berkshire Eagle* (Pittsfield, MA), October 13, 1959.
3. Hussey, *U.S. Navy, the Neutrality Patrol, and Atlantic Fleet Escort Operations*, 31–32.
4. "Sir Henry Tizard, British Scientist," *New York Times*, October 10, 1959.
5. Hussey, *U.S. Navy, the Neutrality Patrol, and Atlantic Fleet Escort Operations*, 40.
6. "Profile: Sir Henry Tizard," *Observer* (London, England), February 2, 1947.
7. Anthony Tucker, "Angels and Bandits," *Guardian* (London, England), July 31, 1996.

8. Donald E. Richmond, "The Crucial Area where Science and Politics Meet," *Berkshire Eagle* (Pittsfield, MA), April 8, 1961.
9. Winston S. Churchill, *The Second World War,* vol. I, *The Gathering Storm* (Boston: Houghton Mifflin, 1976), 141.
10. Clay Blair, *Hitler's U-Boat War: The Hunters, 1939–1942* (New York: Random House, 1996), 189.
11. For the quote, Dr. E. G. Bowen, "The Tizard Mission to the USA and Canada," *Radar World*, http://www.radarworld.org/tizard.html (accessed July 3, 2020).
12. Bowen.
13. Blair, *Hunters*, 129.
14. William Stevenson, "Secret Report Scuttled Joseph Kennedy" (excerpted from *A Man Called Intrepid*), *Vancouver* (BC) *Sun*, March 13, 1976.
15. Winston S. Churchill, *The Second World War,* vol. II, *Their Finest Hour* (Boston: Houghton Mifflin, 1976), 337.
16. Richmond, "Crucial Area."

Chapter 4. Rites of Passage

1. Abbazia, *Mr. Roosevelt's Navy*, 293
2. Maher and Wise, *Sailors' Journey into War,* 27–28.
3. Maher and Wise, 22.
4. Maher and Wise, 31–32.
5. Maher and Wise, 33–34.
6. "Navy Reserves Entrain for N.Y. on First Lap of Trip to Panama," (Baltimore, MD) *Evening Sun*, October 18, 1940.
7. "Port Huron Sailor Is Survivor of Destroyer Fight," (Port Huron, MI) *Times Herald*, November 13, 1943.
8. Louise Lux, "*Borie* Survivor Tells of Hazardous Transfer in the Atlantic's Freezing Cold," (Cedar Rapids, IA) *Gazette*, November 14, 1943.
9. Maher and Wise, *Sailors' Journey into War,* 22–24.
10. Maher and Wise, 34–35.
11. Maher and Wise, 41–43.

Chapter 5. Shot from the Bushes

1. Abbazia, *Mr. Roosevelt's Navy,* 215.
2. Samuel Eliot Morison, *History of United States Naval Operations in World War II,* vol. I, *The Battle of the Atlantic, September 1939–May 1943* (Annapolis, MD: Naval Institute Press, 2010), 64–65.

3. Hussey, *U.S. Navy, the Neutrality Patrol, and Atlantic Fleet Escort Operations*, 75.
4. Robert E. Sherwood, *Roosevelt and Hopkins: An Intimate History* (New York: Harper & Brothers, 1950), 242–44.
5. Hussey, *U.S. Navy, the Neutrality Patrol, and Atlantic Fleet Escort Operations*, 91.
6. Roskill, *War at Sea*, I:472.
7. Hussey, *U.S. Navy, the Neutrality Patrol, and Atlantic Fleet Escort Operations*, 120.
8. Hussey, 112.
9. Hussey, 124–26.
10. Lyle C. Wilson (United Press Washington Manager), "Destroyer Fired on Deliberately, F.D.R. Indicates," *Cincinnati Post*, September 5, 1941.
11. "Wife Not Surprised by Attack on U.S.S. *Greer*," International New Service [hereafter INS], (Scranton, PA) *Times-Tribune*, September 8, 1941.
12. "Proud of *Greer* Chief," *Los Angeles Times*, September 6, 1941.
13. Morison, *United States Naval Operations in World War II*, I:87.

Chapter 6. Brownie and Gully

1. "Mrs. Brown to Join Husband in Latin America," *Miami Herald*, October 21, 1941.
2. Nash Witten, "Schofield Officer Tells of 1918 Indian Uprising," *Honolulu Star Bulletin*, August 4, 1934.
3. "Heroism on USS *Borie* Told by Newton Officer," *Boston Globe*, November 12, 1943; Alexander "Sandy" Creighton (Morrison R. Brown's nephew), telephone interview, August 14, 2020; Mary "Marnie" Creighton Felder (Morrison R. Brown's niece), telephone interviews, August 27 and September 4, 2020.
4. Morrison R. "Sunny" Brown (Morrison R. Brown's daughter), telephone interview, March 13, 2020.
5. "Silver Hearts Reveal Engagement of Miss Gullion and Ensign Brown," *Miami News*, July 19, 1941.
6. "441 Commissioned by Naval School" (AP), (Rochester, NY) *Democrat and Chronicle*, March 1, 1941; "Midshipmen Graduation," (New York) *Daily News*, March 1, 1941.
7. "406 Are Graduated by Naval Reserve" (AP), *Central New Jersey Home News*, June 6, 1941.

8. "Admiral Instructs Midshipman Grads," *Brooklyn Daily Eagle*, June 6, 1941.
9. Morrison R. Brown to his parents, June 22, 1941.
10. Morrison R. Brown to his parents, August 30, 1941.
11. Virginia Eason, "Parties, Guests Arriving Keep Bride-Elect Busy," *Miami News*, September 3, 1941.
12. "Army Officer Slated for Post Here Dies," *Charlotte* (NC) *News*, April 20, 1940.
13. "Gold Braid of Both Army and Navy Add Glamor to Weddings," *Miami Herald*, September 7, 1941.
14. (Danville, KY) *Advocate-Messenger*, August 1, 1941.
15. Morrison R. Brown to his parents, September 24, 1941.
16. Morrison R. Brown to his parents, September 25, 1941.
17. Morrison R. Brown to his parents, October 24, 1941.

Chapter 7. The Shooting Has Started

1. Blair, *Hunters*, 182.
2. Blair, 368.
3. Timothy P. Mulligan, *Neither Sharks nor Wolves: The Men of Nazi Germany's U-boat Arm* (Annapolis, MD: Naval Institute Press, 1999), 63–64.
4. For the quoted phrase, Dimbleby, *Battle of the Atlantic*, 16.
5. Grand Admiral Karl Dönitz, *Memoirs: Ten Years and Twenty Days* (Annapolis, MD: Naval Institute Press, 2012), 4.
6. Jennifer Wilcox, *Solving the Enigma: History of the Cryptanalytic Bombe* (Washington, DC: National Security Agency, Center for Cryptologic History, rev. 2006), 1–2.
7. Max Hastings, *The Secret War: Spies, Ciphers, and Guerillas* (New York: HarperCollins, 2016), 94.
8. Hussey, *U.S. Navy, the Neutrality Patrol, and Atlantic Fleet Escort Operations,* 227.
9. Mulligan, *Neither Sharks nor Wolves*, 11, 114.
10. Samuel Eliot Morison, *History of United States Naval Operations in World War II*, vol. X, *The Atlantic Battle Won* (Annapolis, MD: Naval Institute Press, 2011), 58; Mulligan, 1, 45.
11. Mulligan, 91.
12. Mulligan.
13. Mulligan, 95.
14. Blair, *Hunters*, 369.

15. Abbazia, *Mr. Roosevelt's Navy*, 265–66.
16. "*Kearny* Skipper Aerial Expert," *Miami News*, October 17, 1941; "Chief Officers' Wives Get News," *New York Times*, October 18, 1941.
17. Abbazia, *Mr. Roosevelt's Navy*, 268.
18. Abbazia.
19. Drew Middleton, "Climax of One of Most Heroic Episodes in History of U.S. Navy Is Reached" (AP), *Sioux City* (IA) *Journal*, November 4, 1941.
20. Abbazia, *Mr. Roosevelt's Navy*, 273; Blair, *Hunters*, 93, 369–70; Hussey, *U.S. Navy, the Neutrality Patrol, and Atlantic Fleet Escort Operations*, 243; Symonds, *World War II at Sea*, 189–90.
21. Walter Kiernan, "Impossible to Mistake *Kearny* as Enemy Vessel" (INS), *Miami News*, October 17, 1941.
22. "*Kearny* Was Hit Chasing a U-Boat," *New York Times*, October 29, 1941.
23. Abbazia, *Mr. Roosevelt's Navy*, 265–80, 300.
24. "The *Kearny*," *Chattanooga Daily Times*, October 21, 1941.
25. "Shooting Begun, President Says in Navy Day Talk" (AP), *Chicago Tribune*, October 28, 1941.

Chapter 8. House, Tomb, and School

1. "British Name Leader for War in Atlantic," *St. Louis Post-Dispatch*, March 15, 1941; "Obituary, Admiral Sir Percy Noble," *Guardian* (London, England), July 27, 1955.
2. Dimbleby, *Battle of the Atlantic*, 193–94.
3. "New Director of Naval Intelligence," *Guardian* (London, England), December 16, 1938.
4. Blair, *Hunters*, 245.
5. Hastings, *Secret War*, 212.
6. Hastings, 69.
7. David Kohnen, *Commanders Winn and Knowles: Winning the U-Boat War with Intelligence, 1939–1945* (Krakow: University of Krakow; Enigma, 1999), 14–15.
8. Blair, *Hunters*, 245–46.
9. Wilcox, *Solving the Enigma*, 8.
10. Hastings, *Secret War*, 12.
11. Hastings, 79.
12. Hastings, 80; Wilcox, *Solving the Enigma*, 8–11; "The Turing-Welchman Bombe," *The National Museum of Computing*, https://www.tnmoc.org/bombe (accessed February 16, 2022).

13. Hastings; Wilcox; "Turing-Welchman Bombe."
14. Wilcox, 14–15.
15. Hastings, *Secret War*, 100.

Chapter 9. What Were Their Names?

1. Hussey, *U.S. Navy, the Neutrality Patrol, and Atlantic Fleet Escort Operations*, 168.
2. For North Sea ducks, Mulligan, *Neither Sharks nor Wolves*, 63.
3. Abbazia, *Mr. Roosevelt's Navy*, 293.
4. "U.S. Destroyer Goes Aground" (AP), *Lancaster* (PA) *New Era*, November 30, 1939; "U.S.S. *Reuben James* Was Lightly Armored," *Brooklyn* (NY) *Daily Eagle*, October 31, 1941.
5. Robert J. Cressman, "Have You Heard of a Ship Called the Good *Reuben James*?" *The Sextant*, October 31, 2016, https://usnhistory.navylive.dodlive.mil/Recent/Article-View/Article/2686185/have-you-heard-of-a-ship-called-the-good-reuben-james/ (accessed July 25, 2020).
6. Abbazia, *Mr. Roosevelt's Navy*, 300.
7. "Men Describe Loss of *Reuben James*," *New York Times*, November 25, 1941; "Survivor Describes *Reuben James*' Loss" (AP), *Pittsburgh Post-Gazette*, November 25, 1941.
8. "U.S.S. *Reuben James* Survivor Reaches His Home Here for Visit," *New Castle* (PA) *News*, December 6, 1941.
9. "Ohio Sailor Tells about Ship's Loss" (United Press [hereafter UP]), *Journal Herald* (Dayton, OH), November 30, 1941; "*Reuben James* Survivor, Home in City, Seeks Solace of Swing," *Detroit Free Press*, November 29, 1941.
10. "Galeton Sailor Saved from the *Reuben James*: Whole Town Celebrates," *Star-Gazette* (Elmira, NY), November 4, 1941.
11. James Spotswood, "Jackson Survivor of Destroyer *Reuben James* Gives Brief but Vivid Account of Sinking, Ordeal in Icy Waters of North Atlantic," *Clarion Ledger* (Jackson, MS), December 1, 1941.
12. Dave Garrison, "'Good to Be Alive,' Ship Survivors Say," *Knoxville* (TN) *Journal*, November 29, 1941.
13. "Utahn, Survivor of *Reuben James* Sinking, Is Home," *Daily Herald* (Provo, UT), December 2, 1941.
14. Abbazia, *Mr. Roosevelt's Navy*, 301.
15. Robert Sinclair Parkin, *Blood on the Sea: American Destroyers Lost in World War II* (New York: Sarpedon, 1995), 4–5.

16. Abbazia, *Mr. Roosevelt's Navy*, 301.
17. Abbazia, 302–3.
18. Ted Thackery Jr., "New *Reuben James* Stirs Tales of the Old," *Los Angeles Times*, March 23, 1986.
19. "*Reuben James*' Bombs Exploded under Men," *New York Times*, November 27, 1941.
20. "The *Reuben James*," *New York Times*, November 2, 1941.
21. "He Should Have Fired 1st Torpedo, Mother of a *James* Sailor Declares," *Daily News* (New York, NY), November 1, 1941.
22. "Hot Time," *Austin* (TX) *American-Statesman*, October 31, 1941.
23. "Utah Sailor Tells of Escape from Torpedoed Warship," *Salt Lake Tribune*, December 1, 1941.

Chapter 10. We Knew about You

1. Maher and Wise, *Sailors' Journey into War*, 48–49.
2. Maher and Wise, 51–52.
3. "Gully" Brown to Morrison R. Brown's parents, February 17, 1942.
4. John Dietz, telephone interviews, March 30 and June 19, 2020.
5. "Admiral Leahy Warns Graduates That Grave Emergency Lies Ahead," *Times-Herald*, June 1, 1939; W. A. MacDonald, "Navy Class Is Told to Cherish Liberty," *New York Times*, June 2, 1939.
6. "Charlotte Midshipman and Other Carolinians at Annapolis to Report June 24," *Charlotte* (NC) *Observer*, June 4, 1939.
7. Dr. Michael Nathaniel Brown, MD (Philip Brown's son), telephone interview, October 2, 2020.
8. William E. Howard to Mary C. Felder, December 12, 1998.
9. Maher and Wise, *Sailors' Journey into War*, 46, 52–54.

Chapter 11. Target America

1. Blair, *Hunters*, 431–32, 435.
2. Dimbleby, *Battle of the Atlantic*, 245.
3. Blair, *Hunters*, 437.
4. Mulligan, *Neither Sharks nor Wolves*, 65.
5. Blair, *Hunters*, 440.
6. Mulligan, *Neither Sharks nor Wolves*, 76.
7. Abbazia, *Mr. Roosevelt's Navy*, 296.
8. Blair, *Hunters*, 452–53.

9. Symonds, *World War II at Sea*, 253.
10. Dimbleby, *Battle of the Atlantic*, 260.
11. Morison, *United States Naval Operations in World War II*, I:130.
12. Blair, *Hunters*, 448.
13. Thomas B. Buell, *Master of Seapower: A Biography of Fleet Admiral Ernest J. King* (Annapolis, MD: Naval Institute Press, 2012), 166.
14. Blair, *Hunters*, 445–46.
15. Blair, 446.
16. Blair.
17. Blair, 447.
18. Blair, 458.
19. Blair, 458–59.

Chapter 12. Roots of Evil

1. Blair, *Hunters*, 444.
2. Adm. Francis S. Low, U.S. Navy (Ret.), "A Personal Narrative of My Associations with Fleet Admiral Ernest J. King, U.S. Navy" (unpublished manuscript, April 1961), 25–26.
3. Ladislas Farago, *The Tenth Fleet* (New York: I. Obolensky, 1962), 177; Craig Nelson, *The First Heroes: The Extraordinary Story of the Doolittle Raid—America's First World War II Victory* (New York: Penguin Books, 2003), 107–12.
4. Dönitz, *Memoirs*, 228.
5. "Only 11 Saved on Destroyer," *Boston Globe*, March 4, 1942.
6. "Only 11 Saved on Destroyer."
7. "Only 11 Saved on Destroyer."
8. Dimbleby, *Battle of the Atlantic*, 252.
9. Symonds, *World War II at Sea*, 255–57.
10. Winston S. Churchill, *The Second World War*, vol. IV, *The Hinge of Fate* (Boston: Houghton Mifflin, 1950), 102–4.
11. For the quotation, Nigel Hamilton, *FDR at War: The Mantle of Command* (New York: Houghton Mifflin, 2020), 296.
12. Blair, *Hunters*, 520.
13. Mark St. John Erickson, "Buried under Cover of Night," *Daily Press* (Newport News, VA), April 17, 2017.
14. Liam Nolan and John E. Nolan, *Torpedoed: Was Convoy T. M. 1. Sacrificed?* (Victoria, BC: Bellevue/Trafford, 2007), 85–86.

15. "Hamilton W. Howe Oral History Interview," *Eastern North Carolina Digital Collections*, June 21, 1978, https://digital.lib.ecu.edu/.
16. Blair, *Hunters*, 542.

Chapter 13. Safe Duty Area

1. Morrison R. Brown to Mr. and Mrs. Carroll R. Brown, April 14, 1942.
2. Maher and Wise, *Sailors' Journey into War*, 54.
3. "War Department and Navy Orders," (Newport News, VA) *Daily Press*, April 18, 1936; "Naval Orders," *Los Angeles Times*, January 22, 1938; "Navy Orders," *Pensacola* (FL) *News Journal*, May 14, 1938; "Navy Orders," *San Francisco Examiner*, September 28, 1939; "Naval Orders," (San Pedro, CA) *News-Pilot*, November 13, 1940.
4. "Lyndhurst Man Tells Graphic Story of *Borie*'s Last Hours," (Passaic, NJ) *Herald-News*, November 12, 1943.
5. Maher and Wise, *Sailors' Journey into War*, 55–57.
6. Symonds, *World War II at Sea*, 258.
7. Blair, *Hunters*, 237, 297, 301, 304, 382–83, 405.
8. Blair, 410–17.
9. Blair, 499, 502, 582; "Ships Hit by *U-107*," n.d., uboat.net, https://uboat.net/boats/successes/u107.html (accessed March 23, 2022).
10. See David Sears, "Murmansk or Die," *Military History Quarterly* (Winter 2015).
11. "Charlotteans Join Reserve," *Charlotte* (NC) *Observer*, July 13, 1941; "Charlotte Families," *Charlotte* (NC) *Observer*, April 12, 1942.
12. "Navy Reports Tampa Vet, 43, as Missing," *Tampa Tribune*, July 14, 1942.
13. "13 Chicagoland Sailors Cited for War Valor," *Chicago Tribune*, November 10, 1942.
14. "Alert Caribbean Patrol Routs Axis Submarines," *Newark* (NJ) *Advocate*, October 26, 1942.
15. Morrison R. Brown to Mrs. Archibald Morrison, June 23, 1942.
16. Maher and Wise, *Sailors' Journey into War*, 59–61.
17. Maher and Wise, 50.

Chapter 14. Out of Focus

1. Kohnen, *Commanders Winn and Knowles*, 8–10.
2. Kohnen, 64.
3. Blair, *Hunters*, 493–95.

4. Blair, 496–97.
5. Blair, *Hunters*, 557; Craig Blair, *Hitler's U-Boat War: The Hunted, 1942–1945* (New York: Random House, 1998), 12–13, 13n,
6. Kohnen, *Commanders Winn and Knowles*, 49, 75–76.
7. Kohnen, 76.
8. Kohnen, 77–78.
9. Kohnen, 80–81; Kenneth A. Knowles Jr., telephone interview, August 24, 2020; David Kohnen, telephone interview, September 4, 2020.
10. Morison, *United States Naval Operations in World War II*, I:116.
11. Low, "Personal Narrative," 27.

Chapter 15. Stuck in Limbo

1. Maher and Wise, *Sailors' Journey into War*, 62.
2. Morrison R. Brown to Carroll R. Brown, August 10, 1942.
3. Maher and Wise, *Sailors' Journey into War*, 62.
4. "U.S. Radar: Operational Characteristics: Shipborne Search Sets," n.d., *HyperWar*, http://www.ibiblio.org/hyperwar/USN/ref/Radar/Radar-1.html (accessed July 13, 2020).
5. "Navy Orders," *Oakland* (CA) *Tribune*, April 25, 1936; "Navy Orders," *News-Pilot* (San Pedro, CA), October 21, 1938; "Wabash Fibre Box Company, One of City's Leading Industries, Celebrates Its Thirtieth Anniversary," *Terre Haute* (IN) *Tribune*, September 12, 1954; "Charles Harris Hutchins '36," *Shipmate*, November 1992.

Chapter 16. Carte Blanche

1. Roskill, *War at Sea*, I:91, 200.
2. Kohnen, *Commanders Winn and Knowles*, 81–90.
3. Kohnen, 68–71; Hastings, *Secret War*, 102.
4. Blair, *Hunters*, 243–44.
5. "34 Dayton Youths in Training at Camp Knox, Ky., Are Commissioned Second Lieutenants in the Infantry and Cavalry," *Dayton* (OH) *Daily News*, July 28, 1926; "Radio Expert Has Set Record," *Dayton* (OH) *Daily News*, September 7, 1928; "Reply to a Bishop," *Dayton* (OH) *Daily News*, June 3, 1940; "13 Dayton Reserves Are Ordered to Duty," *Dayton* (OH) *Herald*, June 20, 1940; Jim Debrosse, "How Joe Desch, Working in Secret in Dayton, Beat the Nazi Code and Helped Win the War," *Dayton* (OH) *Daily News*, February 25, 2001; Jim Debrosse, "A

Complex Man Chosen for a Complex and Urgent Mission," *Dayton* (OH) *Daily News*, February 26, 2001; Jim Debrosse, "Intense Scrutiny, Feelings of Guilt Were Heavy Burdens for Desch," *Dayton* (OH) *Daily News*, February 27, 2001; Jim Debrosse, "Enemy Codes Crack, But Not Joe Desch's Staff," *Dayton* (OH) *Daily News*, March 1, 2001; Ronald H. Bailey, "Secret Doings in Dayton," *World War II* (January/February 2016).

6. Blair, *The Hunted*, 603–5; Lewis Wood, "Spy Court Session Viewed by Press," *New York Times*, July 12, 1942; "Nazi Spies Caught within Two Weeks," *New York Times*, August 9, 1942.

Chapter 17. Grim Imbalance

1. Blair, *The Hunted*, 69–70.
2. Dimbleby, *Battle of the Atlantic*, 338.
3. Symonds, *World War II at Sea*, 373.
4. Dimbleby, *Battle of the Atlantic*, 340–41.
5. Blair, *Hunters*, 159–60, 694.
6. Blair, *The Hunted*, 117.
7. Samuel Eliot Morison, *The Two-Ocean War: A Short History of the United States Navy in the Second World War* (Annapolis, MD: Naval Institute Press, 2007), 221, 224.
8. Symonds, *World War II at Sea*, 361.
9. Dimbleby, *Battle of the Atlantic*, 340.
10. Blair, *The Hunted*, 143–44.
11. "Battered Cruiser and Heroic Crew Home from Solomons with 5 on Bridge," *Sentinel* (Carlisle, PA), November 20, 1942; "Cruiser Heroes Whoop It Up as Phila. Grins," *Pittsburgh Sun-Telegram*, November 20, 1942; "Seamen off Boise Acclaimed by City," *Philadelphia Inquirer*, November 20, 1942.
12. Mr. and Mrs. Morrison R. Brown to Mr. and Mrs. Carroll R. Brown, November 20, 1942.
13. Maher and Wise, *Sailors' Journey into War*, 66–67.

Chapter 18. Land of Improvisation

1. William T. Y'Blood, *Hunter-Killer, U.S. Escort Carriers in the Battle of the Atlantic*, (Annapolis, MD: Naval Institute Press, 1983), 34.
2. "Dies in Crash at Sea," *Kansas City* (MO) *Star*, December 7, 1942.

3. M. J. Spear, ed., "Wildcats and Avengers: The History of Composite Squadron Nine" (unpublished manuscript, n.d.), 1–3.
4. Mulligan, *Neither Sharks nor Wolves*, 61–62.
5. Dimbleby, *Battle of the Atlantic*, 385.
6. See David Sears, "'Flying Death' over the Atlantic," *Aviation History* (January 2016).
7. Dimbleby, *Battle of the Atlantic*, 373–74.
8. For Churchill's involvement, Winston S. Churchill, *The Second World War*, vol. III, *The Grand Alliance* (Boston: Houghton Mifflin, 1985), 107.
9. Churchill, III:11.
10. Y'Blood, *Hunter-Killer*, 3–4.
11. Blair, *Hunters*, 229.
12. Blair, 390.
13. Dimbleby, *Battle of the Atlantic*, 238–39.
14. Dimbleby, 239.
15. Dimbleby, 241.
16. Spear, "Wildcats and Avengers," 3.
17. "Navy Pilot Dies at Sea," *Daily Press* (Newport News, VA), February 7, 1942; "Pasadena Naval Man Killed When Struck by Plane on Carrier," *Pasadena* (CA) *Post*, February 8, 1943.

Chapter 19. Season of Joy and Peril

1. Morrison R. Brown to Mrs. Carroll R. Brown, December 13, 1942.
2. "St. John Succeeds FBI Hale as Coach of Kilgore High," *Longview* (TX) *News-Journal*, January 23, 1941; "Neal Appointed Coach for Kilgore School Grid Team," *Times* (Shreveport, LA), August 2, 1942; "Kilgoround," *Kilgore* (TX) *News Herald*, October 28,1942; Mary Meador, "St. John Plaque Presented to School," *Kilgore* (TX) *News Herald*, December 11, 1987; Bruce Stanton, "Men Who Played for Heroic St. John Will Light the Stars," *Kilgore* (TX) *News Herald*, November 15, 2006.
3. George Beahon, "Quinn's Kids Say It'll Be Different," *Democrat and Chronicle* (Rochester, NY), November 9, 1950.
4. Maher and Wise, *Sailors' Journey into War*, 69.
5. Abbazia, *Mr. Roosevelt's Navy*, 343–44.
6. Morison, *United States Naval Operations in World War II*, I:376–86.
7. Blair, *The Hunted*, 16.

8. Debrosse, "Intense Scrutiny"; Bailey, "Secret Doings in Dayton."
9. Hastings, *Secret War*, 89.
10. Blair, *The Hunted*, 83–87; Hastings, 89–90.
11. Dale C. Rielage, "Indirectly in Operational Signals," *Naval History* 16, no. 6 (December 2002).
12. Blair, *The Hunted*, 87.
13. Nolan and Nolan, *Torpedoed*, 150, 214, 218–35.

Chapter 20. He Who Sees First

1. Nolan and Nolan, *Torpedoed*, 95–96, 175.
2. Blair, *Hunters*, 689, 691.
3. Nolan and Nolan, *Torpedoed*, 98.
4. Nolan and Nolan, 247–48.
5. Nolan and Nolan, 240.
6. Nolan and Nolan, 230.
7. Nolan and Nolan, 155.
8. Nolan and Nolan, 244–45.
9. Nolan and Nolan, 266.
10. Mulligan, *Neither Sharks nor Wolves*, 49.
11. Dönitz, *Memoirs*, 316–18.
12. Dimbleby, *Battle of the Atlantic*, 193.
13. Nolan and Nolan, *Torpedoed*, 267–71.
14. Parkin Simon, "A Nazi U-Boat Tactic Stumped Allied Forces—Until a Retired British Naval Officer Designed a Game to Reveal How It Worked," Time.com (accessed January 31, 2020).
15. Nolan and Nolan, *Torpedoed*, 275.
16. Nolan and Nolan, 271–72.

Chapter 21. Tumult to Avoid

1. Cdr. N. H. Ha, "Turning Point in the Atlantic: The British Harnessed Technological Advances and Adopted an Offensive Operational Doctrine to Reverse the Course of the Battle of the Atlantic," *Naval History* 32, no. 2 (April 2018).
2. Rielage, "Indirectly in Operational Signals."
3. Nolan and Nolan, *Torpedoed*, 276–27.
4. Blair, *The Hunted*, 146–47; Dönitz, 318–20.
5. Blair, *Hunters*, 32.
6. Dimbleby, *Battle of the Atlantic*, 20–21; Symonds, *World War II at Sea*, 21–24.

7. Symonds, 26, 32, 35, 38.
8. Symonds, 39–41, 59.
9. Symonds, 124, 126, 129.
10. Symonds, 131–32, 141, 143–44, 149–50.
11. Blair, *The Hunted*, 155; Dimbleby, *Battle of the Atlantic*, 346; Symonds, 377–78.
12. Nolan and Nolan, *Torpedoed*, 281–84.
13. Nolan and Nolan, 285–92.
14. Churchill, *Second World War*, IV:825–26; Dimbleby, *Battle of the Atlantic*, 351–52.

Chapter 22. Consequential Forces

1. Debrosse, "Intense Scrutiny"; Bailey, "Secret Doings in Dayton."
2. Maher and Wise, *Sailors' Journey into War*, 68–69.
3. "Son and Gully" Brown to Mr. Carroll R. Brown, January 14 and 15, 1943.
4. Blair, *The Hunted*, 161–62.
5. Buell, *Master of Seapower*, 267–80; Churchill, *Second World War*, IV:606–21; Dimbleby, *Battle of the Atlantic*, 353–56; Symonds, *World War II at Sea*, 417–19.
6. Blair, *The Hunted*, 156.
7. Dimbleby, *Battle of the Atlantic*, 348–49.
8. Blair, *The Hunted*, 166.
9. Blair, 166; Mulligan, *Neither Sharks nor Wolves*, 80.
10. Mulligan, 10–11.
11. Dönitz, *Memoirs*, 295.
12. Morison, *United States Naval Operations in World War*, I:315–17.
13. "Son and Gully" Brown to Mr. Carroll R. Brown, January 31, 1943.
14. Maher and Wise, *Sailors' Journey into War*, 70–71.

Chapter 23. Between the Moon and Ourselves

1. "'Viva Brazil!' Walter Winchell . . . in New York," *Cincinnati Enquirer*, January 29, 1943.
2. "Brazilian and U.S. Forces Winning Battle against Nazi U-Boats" (AP), *Gazette and Daily* (York, PA), January 20, 1943.
3. "Rio Parley Shapes Drive on U-Boats," *New York Times*, January 31, 1943.
4. "Roosevelt-Vargas Conference Held on U.S. Destroyer in Natal Harbor," *New York Times*, January 30, 1943.
5. "Axis Raids on Brazil's Coast Held Possible" (INS), *Minneapolis Star*, February 20, 1943.
6. Bertram D. Hulen, "Visits West Indies," *New York Times*, January 31, 1943.

7. "Brazilians Want to Fight Now," *New York Times*, January 28, 1943.
8. Morison, *United States Naval Operations in World War*, I:387.
9. Maher and Wise, *Sailors' Journey into War*, 71.
10. Maher and Wise, 72.
11. "Jitterbugging and Hamburgers Aid Romances of Our Soldiers," *New York Times*, April 20, 1943.
12. "Viva Brazil."
13. Blair, *The Hunted*, 217.
14. "The Right Kind of Hunch," *Beatrice* (NE) *Daily Sun*, April 12, 1943.
15. Arthur Herman, *Freedom's Forge: How American Business Produced Victory in World War II* (New York: Random House, 2012), 135–36, 138, 178–80.
16. "Fitz-John Porter (American Steam merchant): Ships Hit by German U-Boats during WWII," uboat.net, https://www.uboat.net/allies/merchants/ship/2705.html (accessed May 14, 2020).
17. "Tells How He Acted after Torpedo Hit Ship," *Brooklyn Daily Eagle*, January 16, 1944.
18. "Harris Man Is Missing," *Times* (Shreveport, LA), March 26, 1943.

Chapter 24. Ain't This the Nuts?

1. Maher and Wise, *Sailors' Journey into War*, 76–77.
2. "Two More Ships Sent Down by Submarines" (AP), *Metropolitan Pasadena* (CA) *Star-News*, April 3, 1942.
3. Morison, *United States Naval Operations in World War*, I:387–88.
4. Cadet Midn, 3/c Donald F. Fennessey "Attack!" (diary excerpt); Cadet Midn. 3/c Donald F. Fennessey to Supervisor, U.S. Merchant Marine Cadet Corps, official report, "SS *James Smith*: Torpedoing of," April 17, 1943. Both documents courtesy of Donald B. Fennessey.
5. "*Kelvinbank* (British Motor Merchant): Ships Hit by German U-Boats during WWII," uboat.net, n.d., https://uboat.net/allies/merchants/ship/2740.html (accessed January 7, 2021).
6. Fennessey, "Attack" and "SS *James Smith*."
7. "Broadwick, Captain of 3 Torpedoed Ships," *Baltimore Sun*, June 9, 1973.
8. Morison, *United States Naval Operations in World War*, I:388–89.

Chapter 25. The Sea War Is All One

1. Robert Bunnelle, "Tipped for High Posts as Allied Strategy Is Outlined in London" (AP), *Dayton* (OH) *Daily News*, January 25, 1943.

2. Talbot Lake, "Adm. Noble Has Job of Fighting Nazi U-boats," *Pottsville* (PA) *Republican*, February 11, 1943.
3. "More Escort Ships Seen Reply to Sub," *Gazette* (Montreal), March 17, 1943.
4. Blair, *The Hunted*, 120–22.
5. Dimbleby, *Battle of the Atlantic*, 383–85; "Submarine Command," *Guardian* (London), November 11, 1942.
6. Churchill, *Second World War*, IV:809–10.
7. Blair, *The Hunted*, 162–63, 811.
8. Blair, 241; Buell, *Master of Seapower*, 292–93; Farago, *Tenth Fleet*, 160.
9. Blair, *The Hunted*, 217–18; "Karl Neitzel," uboat.net, https://uboat.net/men/neitzel.html (accessed March 30, 2020).
10. Blair, *The Hunted*, 252.
11. Blair, 255.
12. Dimbleby, *Battle of the Atlantic*, 378.
13. Dönitz, *Memoirs*, 329.
14. For the bridge aiming device, "Torpedo Fire Control System on German U-Boats," *Torpedo Vorhaltrechner Project*, http://www.tvre.org/en/torpedo-fire-control-system-on-german-u-boats (accessed January 1, 2021).
15. Herbert A. Werner, *Iron Coffins: A Personal Account of the German U-Boat Battles of World War II* (New York: Henry Holt, 1969), 99–102; Dimbleby, *Battle of the Atlantic*, 379–80.
16. Blair, *The Hunted*, 253.
17. Richard Woodman, *The Real Cruel Sea: The Merchant Navy in the Battle of the Atlantic, 1939–1943* (London: John Murray, 2004), 242, 556–57, 608, 610–34.
18. Blair, *The Hunted*, 262–65.
19. Dimbleby, *Battle of the Atlantic*, 382.
20. Werner, *Iron Coffins*, 102.

Chapter 26. Something Approaching Horror

1. For the fuel state, Y'Blood, *Hunter-Killer*, 8–9.
2. Jim Bishop, "The U-Boat Meets Its Master," *Saturday Evening Post*, September 18, 1943, 9–10.
3. Morison, *United States Naval Operations in World War II*, I:344.
4. Blair, *The Hunted*, 164–69.
5. Roskill, *War at Sea*, II:368–69.
6. Dimbleby, *Battle of the Atlantic*, 388.
7. Farago, *Tenth Fleet*, 159.

8. John A. N. Lee, Colin Burke, and Deborah Anderson, "The U.S. Bombes, NCR, Joseph Desch and 600 Waves: The First Reunion of the US Naval Computing Machine Laboratory," *IEEE Annals of the History of Computing* 22 (2000), 7–8; Debrosse, "Enemy Codes Crack, But Not Joe Desch's Staff."
9. Spear, "Wildcats and Avengers," 3–4.
10. Blair, *The Hunted*, 269.

Chapter 27. Gray Elephants

1. Farago, *Tenth Fleet*, 158–67; Kohnen, *Commanders Winn and Knowles*, 20, 22; Low, "Personal Narrative," 27; Y'Blood, *Hunter-Killer*, 31–32.
2. Symonds, *World War II at Sea*, 419–20.
3. Kohnen, *Commanders Winn and Knowles*, 92–94.
4. Jim DeBrosse, "WAVES Rolled in to Work on Top-Secret Project," *Dayton* (OH) *Daily News*, March 2, 2001.
5. Blair, *The Hunted*, 324.
6. Jim Debrosse, "A Hit, a Miss, Then a Parade of Successes," *Dayton* (OH) *Daily News*, March 3, 2001; Jennifer Wilcox, "The Secret of Adam and Eve," *National Security Agency/Central Security Service*, https://www.nsa.gov/Portals/70/documents/about/cryptologic-heritage/historical-figures-publications/publications/wwii/secret-adam-eve.pdf.

Chapter 28. Pattern of the Action

1. "Charges and Specifications in the Case of Charles J. Reamer, Fireman Second Class, U.S. Naval Reserve," April 13, 1943. In author's possession, courtesy of Jeff Quinn, son of *Borie* officer Lawrence S. Quinn.
2. Morison, *United States Naval Operations in World War II*, X:32–35.
3. Morrison R. Brown to Carroll R. Brown, April 8, 1943; Morrison R. Brown to Frances "Gully" Brown, May 17, 1943.
4. Lt. Cdr. Charles H. Hutchins, '36, as told to Ray Mackland, "Destroyer Captain," *Shipmate* (December 1943).
5. Philip M. Morse, "The Beginnings of Operations Research in the United States," *Operations Research* 34, no. 1 (January–February 1986); John D. C. Little, "Philip M. Morse and the Beginnings," *Operations Research* 50, no. 1 (January–February 2002).
6. Stephen Budiansky, "Dead in the Water," *World War II* (September/October 2010).

7. Blair, *The Hunted*, 336; Morison, *United States Naval Operations in World War II*, X:53–54; Y'Blood, *Hunter-Killer*, 40–44
8. Farago, *Tenth Fleet*, 226–27.
9. Morison, *United States Naval Operations in World War II*, X:80–81; Spear, "Wildcats and Avengers," 5–8; "Navy 'Ugly Ducklings' Destroy Two U-Boats," *Philadelphia Inquirer*, September 9, 1943; Bishop, "U-Boat Meets Its Master"; "Aberdeen Flyer Sinks a U-Boat," *Spokane* (WA) *Chronicle*, November 22, 1943.
10. Farago, *Tenth Fleet*, 219–20.
11. Blair, *The Hunted*, 310–11.

Chapter 29. Hard and Unexpected

1. Dimbleby, *Battle of the Atlantic*, 402.
2. Werner, *Iron Coffins*, 117–26.
3. Dimbleby, *Battle of the Atlantic*, 417.
4. Dimbleby, 418.
5. Dimbleby, 421.
6. Dönitz, *Memoirs*, 340.
7. Blair, *The Hunted*, 339.
8. Colin Burke, "Raising the Intelligence Bar Far, Far Too High: The Bombes and the U-Boat War," available at https://userpages.umbc.edu/~burke/raisinglong1-2011.pdf (accessed October 7, 2022).
9. Debrosse, "A Hit, a Miss, Then a Parade of Successes."
10. Ralph Erskine, "Ultra and Some U.S. Navy Carrier Operations," *Cryptologia* 19, no. 1 (1995).
11. For Ned Biros, "Edmund William Biros, LCDR," *Together We Served*, https://navy.togetherweserved.com/usn/servlet/tws.webapp.WebApp?cmd=ShadowBoxProfile&type=Person&ID=453132 (accessed March 28, 2021).
12. "Berkeley Flier Wins High Honor," *Oakland* (CA) *Tribune*, October 28, 1943.
13. Blair, *The Hunted*, 342.
14. For Finch, "Navy Gets 13 Men and Army Nine in Day's Recruiting," *Tampa* (FL) *Tribune*, July 28, 1942.
15. For Balliett, "Letson Samuel Balliett (1917–1978)," *Find a Grave*, https://www.findagrave.com/memorial/3769159/letson-samuel-balliett (accessed December 9, 2018).
16. Spear, "Wildcats and Avengers," 11–12.
17. Spear, 12.

18. Blair, *The Hunted*, 342–43.
19. Spear, "Wildcats and Avengers," 13–14.
20. Maher and Wise, *Sailors' Journey into War*, 91.

Chapter 30. A Good Team

1. Morison, *United States Naval Operations in World War II*, X:122.
2. Morison.
3. Morrison R. Brown to Carroll R. Brown, July 26, 1943.
4. Henry H. Babson, "My Nine Cruises Aboard the U.S.S. *Card*" (unpublished manuscript, 1988), 15–16.
5. Stephen Budiansky, *Blackett's War: The Men Who Defeated the Nazi U-Boats and Brought Science to the Art of* Warfare (New York: Knopf, 2013), 221–26.
6. Morison, *United States Naval Operations in World War II*, X:109.
7. David Kohnen, "Tombstone of Victory: Tracking the *U-505* from German Commerce Raider to American War Memorial 1944–1954," *Journal of America's Military Past* (Winter 2007), 13.
8. Blair, *The Hunted*, 357.
9. For the Catalina kill, Blair, 369.
10. Morison, *United States Naval Operations in World War II*, X:117–18; Thomas Wildenberg, "A Sub-Hunting Bloodhound," *Naval History* 31, no. 5 (October 2017); "3 U-Boats Are Sunk by Plane," *Miami* (OK) *News-Record*, September 28, 1943.
11. "Torpedo Mk 24: 'Fido,'" uboat.net, https://uboat.net/allies/technical/fido.htm (accessed May 8, 2021).
12. Babson, "My Nine Cruises," 27, 29, 31–33.
13. Blair, *The Hunted*, 384.
14. Babson, "My Nine Cruises," 37.
15. Blair, *The Hunted*, 384–87.
16. Maher and Wise, *Sailors' Journey into War*, 102–5.
17. "2 Baltimore Men Missing," *Baltimore Sun*, December 2, 1943.
18. "Navy Hitting Nazi Sub Marauders Hard, Tupper Officer Says," *Tupper Lake* (NY) *Free Press*, September 16, 1943.
19. Maher and Wise, *Sailors' Journey into War*, 105–8.

Chapter 31. Unfortunate Rogues

1. Blair, *The Hunted*, 353–44.
2. Dimbleby, *Battle of the Atlantic*, 426.

3. Werner, *Iron Coffins*, 134.
4. Dimbleby, *Battle of the Atlantic*, 430; Dönitz, *Memoirs*, 352–57.
5. Morison, *United States Naval Operations in World War II*, X:138.
6. Burke, "Raising the Intelligence Bar Far, Far Too High."
7. Erskine, "Ultra and Some U. S. Navy Carrier Operations."
8. Spear, "Wildcats and Avengers," 17.
9. Spear, 26.
10. Babson, "My Nine Cruises," 74–77.
11. "Account of the Combined Attacks on Four Submarines by Lieutenants (Junior Grade) R. L. Stearns, D. E. Weigle, D. C. Puckett, and S. E. Heim, 4 October 1943," *U-boat Archive*, http://www.uboatarchive.net/U-422A/U-422VC-9AcountOfAttacks.htm (accessed June 7, 2021); "Report of Antisubmarine Action by Aircraft," *U-boat Archive*, http://www.uboatarchive.net/U-422A/U-422VC-9ASW-6Report.htm (accessed June 7, 2021).
12. "Statement of Ensign J. D. Horn, F4F Pilot on Submarine Attack October 4, 1943," *U-boat Archive*, http://www.uboatarchive.net/U-264A/U-264VC-9ASW-6Report.htm (accessed June 7, 2021); "Statement of Lieutenant (Junior Grade) Stewart B. Holt, A-V(N), USNR, Squadron VC-9, on Submarine Attack October 4, 1943," *U-boat Archive*, http://www.uboatarchive.net/U-264A/U-264VC-9ASW-6Report.htm (accessed June 7, 2021); Report of Antisubmarine Action by Aircraft (Report No. 24; Date: October 1943; Unit: Composite Squadron NINE; Base: U.S.S. *CARD*), *U-boat Archive*, http://www.uboatarchive.net/U-264A/U-264VC-9ASW-6Report.htm (accessed June 7, 2021).
13. Babson, "My Nine Cruises," 78.
14. "German Sub Crews Seen Nearing Demoralization Similar to 1917" (UP), *Camden* (NJ) *Morning Post*, September 29, 1943.

Chapter 32. One Gung-Ho Guy

1. Babson, "My Nine Cruises," 80.
2. Maher and Wise, *Sailors' Journey into War*, 128.
3. Babson, "My Nine Cruises," 82.
4. Blair, *The Hunted*, 421.
5. Blair, *The Hunted*, 425.
6. Maher and Wise, *Sailors' Journey into War*, 121.
7. Morrison R. Brown to Mr. Carroll R. Brown, September 26, 1943.
8. Burke, "Raising the Intelligence Bar."
9. Babson, "My Nine Cruises," 83.

10. Spear, "Wildcats and Avengers," 20.
11. Babson, "My Nine Cruises," 84.
12. Spear, "Wildcats and Avengers," 22–23.
13. Babson, "My Nine Cruises," 84.

Chapter 33. Won't Be Long Now

1. Morison, *United States Naval Operations in World War II,* X:252; Symonds, *World War II at Sea*, 449.
2. Mulligan, *Neither Sharks nor Wolves*, 82.
3. Blair, *The Hunted*, 436.
4. Blair, 435.
5. Maher and Wise, *Sailors' Journey into War,* 132–33.
6. Morrison R. Brown to Mr. Carroll R. Brown, October 18, 1943.
7. Morison, *United States Naval Operations in World War II,* X:132, 135–37.
8. Babson, "My Nine Cruises," 95.
9. Blair, *The Hunted*, 436.
10. Blair, 437.
11. VC-1 ASW-6 report 9–43, *U-boat Archive*, http://www.uboatarchive.net/U-220A/U-220ASW6.htm (accessed April 14, 2022).
12. Maher and Wise, *Sailors' Journey into War,* 137.
13. Babson, "My Nine Cruises," 96.
14. C.B. 04051 (100): U.257, U.91, U.358 & U.744 Interrogation of Survivors, June 1944, *U-boat Archive*, http://www.uboatarchive.net/U-257A/U-257INT.htm (accessed April 14, 2022).
15. Spear, "Wildcats and Avengers," 24–25.
16. War Diary USS *Card* 31 October–2 November 1943, in "The U.S.S. *Borie* in World War II: Documents and Photographs," ed. E. Andrew Wilde Jr. (privately published, 2001). In author's possession.
17. Maher and Wise, *Sailors' Journey into War,* 138.
18. Hutchins, as told to Mackland, "Destroyer Captain."

Chapter 34. Scratch One Pigboat

1. "The Hunt for U-256," *American Legion* (January 1991); Christopher Schwarz, "Enemies Come Together in Friendship" *Greenville* (SC) *News*, October 12, 1990; Konrad A. Mueller to Phil B. Brown, February 29, 1989, with attachment.
2. War Diary, USS *Card* (CVE-11), 1 November 1943, in Wilde, "U.S.S. *Borie* in World War II."

3. Maher and Wise, *Sailors' Journey into War*, 139.
4. "Addendum to Report of Action by U.S.S. *Borie* with Submarine, 31 October 1943," in Wilde, "U.S.S. *Borie* in World War II."
5. Maher and Wise, *Sailors' Journey into War*, 139.
6. John Hersey, "U.S.S. *Borie*'s Last Battle," *Life*, December 13, 1943; "Lester Kent Obituary (2012)," *Colorado Springs* (CO) *Gazette*, https://obits.gazette.com/us/obituaries/gazette/name/lester-kent-obituary?pid=160192231, (retrieved 7/19/21)
7. Wilde, "U.S.S. *Borie* in World War II."
8. "Frank X. Dutkowiak (1907–1943)," FamilySearch, https://ancestors.familysearch.org/en/L67W-DSD/frank-x.-dutkowiak-1907–1943 (accessed August 1, 2021); Maher and Wise, *Sailors' Journey into War*, 139.
9. Maher and Wise, 140.
10. Stan Smith, "Capt. Hutchins and His U-boat Killers," *Men True Adventure* (February 1944).
11. Hersey, "*Borie*'s Last Battle."
12. Norman Algiers, "Four Stacker Comic Book" (unpublished, n.d.), in author's possession, 16–21; *Boilermaker 1 & C*, NAVPERS 10537 (Washington, DC, 1960); *Steam Turbines: The Steam Cycle*, U.S. Navy Training Film, Loucks & Norling Studios, 1950, https://www.youtube.com/watch?v=3LOEDz7crU4 (accessed August 10, 2021).
13. Charles H. Hutchins, as told to Walter J. Bordas, "Tells Story of *Borie*'s Battle with Nazi Subs" (INS), *Dispatch* (Moline, IL), November 11, 1943; "Lyndhurst Man Tells Graphic Story of *Borie*'s Last Hours"; "*Borie* Heroes Back in N.J.," undated, unidentified New Jersey newspaper clipping.

Chapter 35. Stand By for a Ram!

1. Hutchins, as told to Mackland, "Destroyer Captain"; Smith, "Capt. Hutchins and His U-boat Killers."
2. Maher and Wise, *Sailors' Journey into War*, 141.
3. Hersey, "*Borie*'s Last Battle."
4. Gunner's Mate 1/c Kenneth Reynolds, "The *Borie*'s Last Fight," *True*, March 1944; Smith, "Capt. Hutchins and His U-Boat Killers."
5. Hutchins, as told to Mackland, "Destroyer Captain."
6. Hersey, "*Borie*'s Last Battle."
7. "Morris Tells of 'Shooting' with *Borie*'s Searchlight," *Evening Sun* (Baltimore), November 12, 1943.
8. Maher and Wise, *Sailors' Journey into War*, 143–47.

9. "Addendum to Report of Action by U.S.S. *Borie* with Submarine, 31 October 1943," in Wilde, "U.S.S. *Borie* in World War II."
10. Reynolds, "*Borie*'s Last Fight."
11. Reynolds.
12. Hutchins, as told to Mackland, "Destroyer Captain."
13. Maher and Wise, *Sailors' Journey into War*, 143–44.
14. Maher and Wise, 145.
15. Smith, "Capt. Hutchins and His U-Boat Killers."
16. Blair, *The Hunted*, 424.
17. For Hutchins' gesture, Hersey, "*Borie*'s Last Battle."
18. Hersey.

Chapter 36. At Close Quarters

1. Maher and Wise, *Sailors' Journey into War*, 146.
2. Reynolds, "*Borie*'s Last Fight."
3. "Morris Tells of 'Shooting' with *Borie*'s Searchlight."
4. "Narrative by: Lieutenant Commander Hutchins USS *BORIE*," recorded on November 15, 1943 [hereafter Hutchins Oral History].
5. Mackland, *Shipmate*.
6. Hutchins Oral History.
7. Maher and Wise, *Sailors' Journey into War*, 147.
8. Reynolds, "*Borie*'s Last Fight."
9. "C. Moultrop Obituary," *Providence* (RI) *Journal*, March 4, 2009.
10. Hutchins, as told to Mackland, "Destroyer Captain."
11. Hutchins, as told to Mackland.
12. Reynolds, "*Borie*'s Last Fight."
13. Maher and Wise, *Sailors' Journey into War*, 148.
14. Lieut. [*sic*] Charles H. Hutchins, as told to Walter J. Bordas, International News Photographer, "Tells Story of *Borie*'s Battle with Nazi Subs," *Dispatch* (Moline, IL), November 11, 1943.
15. David Michael Ettlin, "U-Boat Officers, U.S. Foes Meet Again, as Friends," *Baltimore Sun*, September 12, 1988.
16. Reynolds, "*Borie*'s Last Fight."
17. Lee Davis, "Knoxvillian Is in Epic Deck-to-Deck Sea Battle," *Knoxville* (TN) *News-Sentinel*, November 12, 1943.
18. Hersey, "*Borie*'s Last Battle."

19. "Baltimorean at Wheel in *Borie* Battle," *Baltimore Sun*, November 12, 1943.
20. Smith, "Capt. Hutchins and His U-Boat Killers."
21. Hutchins, as told to Mackland, "Destroyer Captain."
22. Hutchins, as told to Mackland.
23. Maher and Wise, *Sailors' Journey into War*, 148.
24. Hutchins, as told to Mackland, "Destroyer Captain."
25. Hutchins, as told to Mackland.

Chapter 37. Vicious Circle

1. Reynolds, "*Borie*'s Last Fight."
2. Hutchins, as told to Mackland, "Destroyer Captain."
3. Reynolds, "*Borie*'s Last Fight."
4. "Heroism on USS *Borie* Told by Newton Officer."
5. "Wins High Praise in Battling U-boat," *Pittsburgh Courier*, November 20, 1943.
6. Reynolds, "*Borie*'s Last Fight."
7. Hutchins, as told to Mackland, "Destroyer Captain."
8. Hutchins, as told to Mackland, "Destroyer Captain."
9. "Lyndhurst Man Tells Graphic Story of *Borie*'s Last Hours."
10. "*Borie* Heroes Back."
11. Hersey, "*Borie*'s Last Battle."
12. "Report of Damage Sustained by U.S.S. *Borie* in Action with Enemy Submarine, 1 November 1943," in Wilde, "U.S.S. *Borie* in World War II."
13. Davis, "Knoxvillian Is in Epic Deck-to-Deck Sea Battle."
14. Hersey, "*Borie*'s Last Battle"; Hutchins, as told to Mackland, "Destroyer Captain."
15. Hutchins, as told to Mackland.
16. Hutchins, as told to Mackland.
17. "*Borie* Heroes Back."
18. Hersey, "*Borie*'s Last Battle."
19. Hutchins, as told to Mackland, "Destroyer Captain."
20. Hersey, "*Borie*'s Last Battle."
21. Hutchins, as told to Mackland, "Destroyer Captain."
22. Reynolds, "*Borie*'s Last Fight."
23. Maher and Wise, *Sailors' Journey into War*, 149.
24. Hersey, "*Borie*'s Last Battle."
25. Maher and Wise, *Sailors' Journey into War*, 149.
26. Hersey, "*Borie*'s Last Battle."

27. Hutchins, as told to Mackland, "Destroyer Captain."
28. Reynolds, "*Borie*'s Last Fight."
29. Hutchins Oral History; "Officer of Borie Tells of Epic Fight with Sub," *Morning News* (Wilmington, DE), November 15, 1943.
30. Reynolds, "*Borie*'s Last Fight."
31. Maher and Wise, *Sailors' Journey into War*, 150.
32. Maher and Wise.
33. Reynolds, "*Borie*'s Last Fight."

Chapter 38. On Borrowed Time

1. Hutchins Oral History.
2. Maher and Wise, *Sailors' Journey into War*, 157.
3. Hutchins, as told to Mackland, "Destroyer Captain."
4. Hutchins Oral History.
5. Maher and Wise, *Sailors' Journey into War*, 159.
6. Hutchins, as told to Mackland, "Destroyer Captain."
7. Hersey, "*Borie*'s Last Battle."
8. "Mississippian Tells How Destroyer *Borie* Sank 2 German Subs," *Clarion-Ledger* (Jackson, MS), November 17, 1943; "Lighter Fluid Kept Radio's Motor Running on *Borie*" (AP), *Knoxville* (TN) *Journal*, November 18, 1943.
9. Hersey, "*Borie*'s Last Battle."
10. Hutchins, as told to Mackland, "Destroyer Captain."
11. *Card* War Diary, 31 October 1943 to 5 November 1943, in Wilde, "U.S.S. *Borie* in World War II."
12. *Card* War Diary.
13. Babson, "My Nine Cruises," 98.
14. Hersey, "*Borie*'s Last Battle."
15. Hutchins, as told to Mackland, "Destroyer Captain."
16. Hutchins, as told to Mackland.
17. "U.S. Destroyer Kills U-Boats; Sunk as Wreck," *New York Daily News*, November 11, 1943.
18. Operational Remarks (War Diary) *Goff* (DD247) Monday, 1 November 1943," in Wilde, "U.S.S. *Borie* in World War II."
19. Lt. P. B. [Philip Bosché] Brown to Mrs. Morrison R. Brown, December 18, 1943.
20. Maher and Wise, *Sailors' Journey into War*, 162.
21. "Naval Battle Survivors Recall Unlikeliest of Duels," *Star Ledger* (Newark, NJ), October 20, 1993.

22. *Goff* War Diary.
23. Maher and Wise, *Sailors' Journey into War*, 162.
24. "Lyndhurst Man Tells Graphic Story of *Borie*'s Last Hours."
25. Lux, "*Borie* Survivor Tells of Hazardous Transfer."
26. Maher and Wise, *Sailors' Journey into War*, 162.
27. "Naval Battle Survivors Recall Unlikeliest of Duels."
28. Lux, "Borie Survivor Tells of Hazardous Transfer."
29. "Lyndhurst Man Tells Graphic Story of *Borie*'s Last Hours."
30. Maher and Wise, *Sailors' Journey into War*, 162.

Chapter 39. Still Out There

1. P. B. Brown to Mrs. Brown.
2. Hutchins, as told to Mackland, "Destroyer Captain."
3. "Lyndhurst Man Tells Graphic Story of *Borie*'s Last Hours."
4. Hutchins, as told to Mackland, "Destroyer Captain."
5. Lux, "*Borie* Survivor Tells of Hazardous Transfer."
6. Maher and Wise, *Sailors' Journey into War*, 162.
7. *Goff* War Diary.
8. "Lyndhurst Man Tells Graphic Story of *Borie*'s Last Hours."
9. Lux, "*Borie* Survivor Tells of Hazardous Transfer."
10. "Lyndhurst Man Tells Graphic Story of *Borie*'s Last Hours."
11. P. B. Brown to Mrs. Brown.
12. Lux, "*Borie* Survivor Tells of Hazardous Transfer."
13. "Young Ensign Tells of Sinking Nazi Submarine" (AP), *Sun* (Jackson, TN), November 14, 1943.
14. "Texan Dies under Stern of Rescue Ship in Heroic Battle" (AP), *Austin* (TX) *American*, November 23, 1943.
15. "Jim Winn, Former Newsboy, Rolled Back into Icy Waters after Being Rescued by Destroyer *Goff* Crewmen," *Bee* (Danville, VA), December 4, 1943.
16. Babson, "My Nine Cruises," 98.
17. *Goff* War Diary.
18. Maher and Wise, *Sailors' Journey into War*, 165.
19. *Goff* War Diary.
20. Maher and Wise, *Sailors' Journey into War*, 165.
21. "Young Ensign Tells of Sinking Nazi Submarine."
22. Hutchins, as told to Mackland, "Destroyer Captain."
23. Maher and Wise, *Sailors' Journey into War*, 166–67.

24. Eppie Richbourg, "Decorated Hero Recalls the *Borie*'s Last Battle," unspecified Charleston, SC, newspaper, May 16, 1966; Philip Bosché Brown, undated personal account of *Borie* rescue. Both in author's possession, courtesy of son Dr. Michael N. Brown, MD.
25. "Survivor of *Borie* on Lebanon Visit," *Lancaster* (PA) *New Era*, November 18, 1943; "Leon Bowmaster Aids *Borie* Rescue," *Daily News* (Lebanon, PA), November 20, 1943.
26. *Goff* War Diary.
27. Babson, "My Nine Cruises," 99.
28. "Naval Battle Survivors Recall Unlikeliest of Duels."
29. Hersey, "*Borie*'s Last Battle."

EPILOGUE

1. Babson, "My Nine Cruises," 101.
2. "Chaplain Sheridan Bell Served on Carrier in Cited Task Force," *Express* (Lock Haven, PA), November 27, 1943.
3. Maher and Wise, *Sailors' Journey into War*, 173.
4. "Heroism on USS *Borie* Told by Newton Officer."
5. David R. Castleman to Mrs. Morrie Brown, November 11, 1943.
6. "*Borie* Hero Given Medal at Norfolk," *Bee* (Danville, VA), December 8, 1943.
7. "The Suicidal Sea Campaign," *Evening Standard* (London, England), April 24, 1944.
8. Maher and Wise, *Sailors' Journey into War*, 182.
9. Jim Allegri to Florence Garone, September 5, 1943.
10. Babson, "My Nine Cruises," 243.
11. Babson, 151.
12. "Navy Identifies Lost Pilot" (AP), *Ithaca* (NY) *Journal*, June 19, 1944.
13. "Stearns, Robert Lloyd, LT," *Together We Served*, https://navy.togetherweserved.com/usn/servlet/tws.webapp.WebApp?cmd=ShadowBoxProfile&type=DecorationExt&ID=3362482 (accessed October 28, 2021).
14. "Camarillo Flier Missing in Action" (AP), *Ventura County* (CA) *Star-Free Press*, March 7, 1945; "Lepper, Doty, Rivera Win Bronze Stars," *Ventura County* (CA) *Star-Free Press*, July 30, 1945.
15. "Lieut. E. S. Heim, Jr., Is Presumed Dead," *Shreveport* (LA) *Journal*, April 5, 1946.
16. Dimbleby, *Battle of the Atlantic*, 456.
17. Allan Taylor, "Then and Now: Adm. Ernest J. King, America's Boss Wartime Sailor, Navigates Less Stormy Waters Today," *New York Times*, May 15, 1949.

18. Kohnen, *Commanders Winn and Knowles*, 137.
19. "Hunter-Killers in the Atlantic, 1943–1945," *The Mariners' Museum and Park*, https://www.marinersmuseum.org/sites/micro/battle_of_the_atlantic/photos/g3b.htm (accessed November 7, 2021).
20. "Quinn's Kids Say It'll Be Different," *Democrat and Chronicle* (Rochester, NY), November 9, 1950.
21. Ettlin, "U-Boat Officers, U.S. Foes Meet Again, as Friends."
22. Bill Bond, "Former Enemies Meet as Friends" *Orlando* (FL) *Sentinel*, May 24, 1992.
23. "Donald Fennessey Obituary (1920–2020)," *Newport Daily News*, https://www.legacy.com/guestbooks/newportri/donald-f-fennessey-condolences/197079438 (accessed December 26, 2020).

INDEX

ABOUT THE AUTHOR

DAVID SEARS is a New Jersey–based author whose books include *The Last Epic Naval Battle: Voices from Leyte Gulf*, *At War with the Wind*, *Such Men as These: The Story of the Navy Pilots Who Flew the Deadly Skies over Korea*, and *Pacific Air: How Fearless Flyboys, Peerless Aircraft, and Fast Flattops Conquered the Skies in the War with Japan.* He is a frequent contributor to print publications focused on aviation history, naval history, military history, and veteran affairs. His early career included service as a seagoing U.S. Navy line officer and Vietnam War veteran. His subsequent business career included industrial relations positions with the cities of San Francisco and Portland, Oregon, and human resources executive positions with the *New York Times* Company and Dow Jones & Company.

The Naval Institute Press is the book-publishing arm of the U.S. Naval Institute, a private, nonprofit, membership society for sea service professionals and others who share an interest in naval and maritime affairs. Established in 1873 at the U.S. Naval Academy in Annapolis, Maryland, where its offices remain today, the Naval Institute has members worldwide.

Members of the Naval Institute support the education programs of the society and receive the influential monthly magazine *Proceedings* or the colorful bimonthly magazine *Naval History* and discounts on fine nautical prints and on ship and aircraft photos. They also have access to the transcripts of the Institute's Oral History Program and get discounted admission to any of the Institute-sponsored seminars offered around the country.

The Naval Institute's book-publishing program, begun in 1898 with basic guides to naval practices, has broadened its scope to include books of more general interest. Now the Naval Institute Press publishes about seventy titles each year, ranging from how-to books on boating and navigation to battle histories, biographies, ship and aircraft guides, and novels. Institute members receive significant discounts on the Press' more than eight hundred books in print.

Full-time students are eligible for special half-price membership rates. Life memberships are also available.

For more information about Naval Institute Press books that are currently available, visit www.usni.org/press/books. To learn about joining the U.S. Naval Institute, please write to:

Member Services
U.S. Naval Institute
291 Wood Road
Annapolis, MD 21402-5034
Telephone: (800) 233-8764
Fax: (410) 571-1703
Web address: www.usni.org